CHINA'S ECONOMIC REFORM

CHINA'S ECONOMIC REFORM

A study with documents

*Christopher Howe, Y.Y. Kueh
and Robert Ash*

RoutledgeCurzon
Taylor & Francis Group

LONDON AND NEW YORK

First published 2002
by RoutledgeCurzon
2 Park Square, Milton Park, Abingdon, Oxon, OX14 4RN

Simultaneously published in the USA and Canada
by RoutledgeCurzon
711 Third Avenue, New York, NY 10017, USA

RoutledgeCurzon is an imprint of the Taylor & Francis Group

First issued in paperback 2011

© 2002 Emmanuel Karagiannis

Typeset in Stempel Garamond by LaserScript Ltd, Mitcham, Surrey

British Library Cataloguing in Publication Data
A catalogue record of this book is available from the British Library

Library of Congress Cataloguing in Publication Data
A catalogue record for this book has been requested

ISBN 978-0-700-71355-4 (hbk)
ISBN 978-0-415-51527-6 (pbk)

*This book is dedicated to
our patient wives*

Contents

Contents

Contents

Preface

The purpose of this book is to give readers with no knowledge of the Chinese language insights into the Chinese economic reform of the kind that can only be provided by direct access to significant and interesting Chinese materials. Secondary accounts of the Chinese economy by analysts outside of the People's Republic are essential and often fascinating. They are, however, qualitatively different to the words of the reformers and participants in the Chinese economy themselves.

In some ways, this project has been a continuation of the volume of Chinese economic documents published in 1990 by the late Professor K.R. Walker and myself. It does, however, differ in important respects. The scale of the searching process for documents was much larger involving as it did the collaboration between Professor Y.Y. Kueh in Hong Kong and Professor Robert Ash and myself in London. Also, in selecting material for this volume we focused more on the intrinsic economic interest of articles rather than their long run place in Chinese economic history. With the exception of one document, all the pieces here are from mainland Chinese sources.

This work has been supported by a wide range of people and institutions. We are enormously appreciative of the translators who provided the draft translations. In Hong Kong, Lam and Associates, Kathy Poon and Elspeth Thomson and in Britain, Mark Allison and Caroline Mason did a wonderful job in preparing the core of this work. They did this from primary sources, which were often of a difficult and technical nature. Final responsibility for the translations remains with the authors and we hope that we have done a reasonable job in maintaining balance between accuracy and readability without losing the Chinese flavour of the originals.

Financially, we were supported by grants from the Economic and Social Research Council in Britain and a grant from the Research Grants Council in Hong Kong to Professor Kueh. In addition, the support of our respective institutions, The School of Oriental and African Studies in London University and Lingnan University in Hong Kong, was indispensable. Professor Ash and I both visited Lingnan in Professor Kueh's Department and I am particularly grateful to two Presidents of Lingnan, Dr John Chen and Professor Edward Chen, for enabling me to spend more than a year in Hong Kong. Without this time, the major survey of the Chinese reform literature would not have been possible. I would also like to express my personal appreciation to Nigel French, former Secretary General, and to the other staff of the Hong Kong Research Grants Council who facilitated so many other visits to Hong Kong that proved useful for this project. All of the authors have many debts to librarians and scholars all over the world for their help in locating the material used in this book.

The division of labour in this book was basically as follows. Professor Kueh was responsible for Chapters 3, 4 and 7. I prepared Chapters 1, 2 and 6 and Professor Ash prepared Chapter 5, which contains materials that could have made up two independent chapters but seemed better as one long one. In addition, while working on the introductory overview in Chapter 1, I consulted Professor Ash on a frequent basis and hence had the benefit of his wide knowledge and good judgement throughout. Nonetheless, the principle of the division of labour was that we were each responsible for both the selection of documents and the commentary relating to each topic as outlined above. In bringing our efforts together in the final stages I did not seek to reconcile the differences of nuance and interpretation which were bound to occur where three economists were gathered together, even in cyberspace.

Christopher Howe

1

China's Economic Reform Strategy

Historical Overview

INTRODUCTION

The articles translated in Chapter 2 have been chosen to throw light on the thinking behind the beginnings of the Chinese economic reform in 1978 and its subsequent evolution. This introduction seeks to put these articles in context. The chapter is not a history of the reform or of the economy since 1978, but focuses on the key events and the ideas needed to understand the reforms, staying as closely as possible to texts and Chinese materials to illustrate the argument.[1] The Chronology that follows has been designed to help readers grasp something of both the interdependence and complexity of unfolding events in a reform process that is now over twenty years old.

The evolution of China's economic reform strategy may be followed along three axes. First, is the broad political and ideological thrust of successive reform phases. The second relates to the detailed changes in planning and resource allocation arrangements, and the third, to shifting resource allocation priorities. In thinking about the first axis, the fundamental link between political and ideological factors developments in the economy should never be under estimated. The Chinese Communist Party has a complex history and has always been concerned to preserve continuity and consistency in its thinking about the world and in its historical understanding of itself. The economic interplay with the twists and turns in this process can be enormous. Indeed, the reform itself could not begin while Mao was alive in part at least because Mao refused to recognise the fundamental nature of his errors and excesses and because he and his followers had the political strength to hold critics and potential reformers at bay while he was alive.

1 In writing this chapter all the materials surveyed have been taken into account. Particular use has been made of a number of chronologies that have appeared in recent years and of other materials mentioned in the bibliographical note at the end of this chapter.

If we look at the whole span of Communist China's development from 1949 to 1978 the key turning points were 1953, 1958, 1964 and 1971. These years mark respectively: the First Five Year Plan (1953–1957); the Great Leap Forward and its aftermath; the formulation of the Four Modernisations strategy by Zhou Enlai; and finally, the fall of Lin Piao and the last phase of Zhou's attempts to restore basic order to the Chinese economy. After the deaths of Zhou and Mao in January and September 1976 there was a two year transition before Deng's rise to paramount power and the initiation of his reform strategy in Autumn 1978. Let us now briefly review these earlier phases to secure our understanding of events since 1978.

STRATEGY BEFORE 1978

The establishment of the PRC and the First Five Year Plan

The key to economic strategy in the early 1950s was the policy of 'Leaning to one side' i.e. leaning towards the Soviet Union. The Chinese Communist Party admired Soviet economic achievements and sought to establish a similar system of central planning and to use this to impose priorities for heavy and defence oriented industry development. This predisposition to the Soviets was reinforced by a hostile international environment in which the West, led by the United States, isolated China from 1950 and imposed a strategic goods embargo on its economy. Under these circumstances the Soviet Union was the only credible source of industrial, technological and possible financial assistance.

In spite of leaning to one side, China departed from the Soviet pattern of development immediately in one important respect. It did not attempt agricultural mechanisation or collectivisation in advance of, or even simultaneously with, the beginning of its industrialisation drive in 1953. Mao and the leadership were well aware of what they called 'Stalin's error' (i.e. a hasty and brutal agricultural collectivisation) and they understood that China could not risk a similar debacle in the rural areas. The Party therefore pushed ahead with a strategy in which industrialisation based on imported Soviet plant was to be supported by a gradual, voluntary process of rural socialisation and combined with a system of compulsory State purchase of key grains and agricultural products.

By 1955 this policy seemed to be failing, at least in the sense of failing to deliver growth at the pace demanded by Mao. In July of that year, therefore, Mao launched a High Tide of Socialism that had swept through the Chinese countryside by Spring 1956. The initial impact of this movement seemed good, but by 1957 the economy was faltering again. Zhou Enlai's draft for the Second Five Year Plan (1958–1962) was cautious both in terms of growth rates and of institutional change. Debates about the economy by planners and academics at this time were largely rational discussions about ways to modify Soviet institutions to suit China's relative backwardness and other special circumstances.

2

The Great Leap Forward

In 1958 caution was once again swept aside and the roller coaster of socialisation peaked in the utopian excesses of the People's Communes and the Great Leap Forward during the years 1958–1960.[2]

The Leap was not simply a rural phenomenon. It was an institutional revolution in which Soviet type planning with its calculated balances, administrative techniques, and personal financial incentives, was swept away. In its place was created a society where the population was organised in gigantic urban and rural communes inside of which individual property rights were largely lost and the criteria for institutional excellence were summed up by Mao in his famous description of the Peoples Communes as, 'One big. Two public'.

These departures from Soviet practices coincided closely with the diplomatic break from the Soviet Union and required that in foreign trade and industry, new strategies of self reliance replace the earlier dependence on the Socialist bloc.

The Great Leap experience is central to any understanding of China's later entry into a phase of economic reform. The Leap was the embodiment of a strategy that defied narrow forms of rationality – Soviet or Western – in favour of chaotic, unbalanced modes of progress driven by socialist enthusiasm and political campaigns and supported by an underlying conviction that disequilibrium and political struggle are the keys to rapid economic advance.

For twenty years no open criticism of the Leap was allowed and adherence to its underlying formulae became a touchstone of an individual's political correctness.[3] In spite of this huge impediment to an objective re-evaluation of the events of 1958–1960, elements in the Party leadership did begin to push towards more realistic and empirically based economic strategies, and towards a reconstruction of economic institutions to implement these. This group included Deng Xiaoping, but it was led by Liu Shaoqi and above all by Zhou Enlai. Liu was to be disgraced and die in the Cultural Revolution, but Zhou negotiated and finally survived all attacks to become the man who more than any other held China together for nearly twenty years, a period during which total economic and political collapse at times seemed a real possibility.[4]

2 When I first studied the Chinese economy at Cambridge in the winter of 1960, the Great Leap was still officially in full force with fantastic claims being made for both industrial and agricultural output. These claims were still being accepted by sympathisers in Cambridge. (CH).

3 In October 1965 Chinese cities were still covered in slogans praising the People's Communes and the Great Leap. As a visiting foreigner I had believed the Great Leap to have ended several years before but by this time its symbolism and vocabulary had been absorbed into the discourse of contemporary political struggles. (CH).

4 This view of Zhou's achievement is confirmed by many sources, of which one of the most impressive is that of Bo Yibo, an economist and former Chairman of both the State Construction Commission and the State Planning Commission. See especially his articles in Bo Yibo, *The Selected Works of Bo Yibo*, Beijing, 1992.

3

The first reversion to realism occurred during the early 1960s as China struggled to recover from the famine, population loss, and economic contraction caused by the Leap and its aftermath. During these years China's priorities were determined by two simple imperatives: the provision of basic food and clothing supplies and coping with the industrial costs of the split with the Soviet Union. These domestic problems were set in the context of a turbulent international situation which included border war and tensions with India and the beginnings of the Vietnam War on China's south eastern borders.

In agriculture, The Party responded to the crisis by re-introducing incentives and private plots to improve supply while millions of urban residents were removed from the cities to lessen the demands on procurement. For the longer term, plans were made to establish five hundred million *mou* of High and Stable Yield farmland.[5]

During 1964 work was begun on a Third Five Year Plan to cover 1966–1970. In October of that year China exploded its first nuclear bomb, an event of major technological and political importance and in December 1964, Zhou Enlai was able to sum up China's situation in his *Government Work Report* at the Third National People's Congress, which went on to approve the new economic plan.

Zhou's speech was the first major statement of China's situation to be openly published since 1957 and the speech incorporated a vision of the Four Modernisations that Zhou defined as the country's long term objective. (i.e. the modernisation of agriculture, industry, defence, science and technology).[6] However, in the same year Mao launched his campaign to relocate Chinese industry in the interior provinces, away from the militarily vulnerable coastal provinces. Known as the 'The Third Front' campaign, this proved to be a costly and unnecessary diversion of resources that undermined Zhou's objectives.

The window of opportunity for rational policies that appeared between 1961 and 1965 vanished with the onset of the Great Proletarian Cultural Revolution. During the first phase of the Revolution (1965–1971), leadership increasingly fell under the sway of Marshal Lin Piao who proved in some respects to be even more extreme than Mao. Lin dismissed balanced planning and realistic targets in favour of ever higher and more militarily focused plans. 'Balance is no balance', 'War is balance' and, 'The Plan is what I say it is', are some of the characteristic phrases attributed to him. Institutionally, Lin was associated with the Daqing and Dazhai models of labour organisation in industry and agriculture respectively. Daqing referred to the major oilfield successfully developed by the Chinese after the

5 One *mou* equals 0.1647 acre, or 0.0667 hectare.
6 The theory and practice of 'modernisation' was to be the theme later picked up and exploited to the full by Deng after 1978, although contemporary scholars have noted that Mao first used the term as early as 1960. See particularly, Tao Yongli and Wu Qijie, 'A comparison of 'modernisation' in the thought of Mao Zedong and Deng Xiaoping', *Northern Essays*, 17–20 January 1999.

Soviets technical experts had left, and Dazhai to agricultural practices in an agricultural Brigade in one of the poorest parts of China. In both models work was driven by political enthusiasm and military style discipline. Lin had little time for incentives or private property. 'In the countryside', he is reported as saying, 'each household may have one chicken, one tree, one pig and one rabbit'.

Under these pressures, high economic planning targets for 1969–1971 led to shortages of goods and food and to national fiscal deficits. Targets for the Fourth Five Year Plan (1971–1975) were also high and rose on each Lin inspired revision; while to Mao's 'Big Third Front' policy Lin now added the 'Small Third Front' – a plan to encourage localities to develop small scale enterprises to increase local self sufficiency in every kind of output.

In September 1971 Lin died in a plane crash fleeing to the Soviet Union. Zhou Enlai immediately ordered a sharp downward adjustment of targets and a drive to improve discipline in industrial enterprises.[7] These measures were accompanied by new population policies and by attempts to revive the statistical system since, without data, planning was impossible. Throughout the 1970s, however, statistical work remained weak and statistics officials were described as being 'in fear of their lives' with few were prepared to take responsibility for this kind of work.[8]

In 1972 Zhou also began the process of reopening China to the world economy. There were major agreements with West Germany and Japan to import plant for the Wuhan Steelworks and Zhou proposed a new plan to import US$4.3 billion worth of plant from a variety of western and Japanese sources. This turning to capitalist sources was part of a much wider foreign policy shift. In 1969 China had suffered military incursions by the Soviet Union in Heilongjiang and Xinjiang and by 1971 Mao was prepared to renew relations with The United States and Japan to strengthen his hand against the perceived threat from his former ally. This political shift opened a new range of economic possibilities, but strong domestic opposition combined with administrative and planning chaos made it impossible to achieve the results that might have been hoped for from this reopening of the trade door.

Throughout the 1970s the political battles raged on. In 1974 China suffered major rail strikes and throughout the industrial sector it was reported that the so called 'Three Nothing' enterprises were the norm. The Three Nothings were 'no administration, no management and no regulations'. Institutionally, the Daqing and Dazhai models were still

---

7 The Fourth Five Year Plan (1971–1975) target for industrial growth was reduced from 12.8% to 7.7%, Gu Longsheng, *A History of the Development of the Economic Thought of the Chinese Communist Party*, Taiyuan, 1996, Chap. 7. Full details of the Plan and its tortured political evolution have been published in *Party Documents*, 2000, No. 2.

8 Statistical work had been attacked and discredited in the Great Leap when officials refused to cooperate with publication of false statistics. The disasters of the statistical system between 1958 and 1978 and its subsequent revival are described in Wang Yifu, *An Outline History of Statistics in New China*, Beijing, 1986.

emphasised and in terms of priorities, Mao's supporters pushed on with his unbalanced emphasis on steel, grain, and local self sufficiency at all costs. Secret internal estimates reported output growth as being close to zero in 1974, and even this may well have been an optimistic exaggeration. In 1975 new plans with high targets for 1980 and beyond were adopted and these continued to be the basis of planning after the deaths of Zhao and Mao and the arrest of the Gang of Four, all of which occurred in 1976 – the year described officially as 'China's year of disasters'.[9]

In the two years between these events and the rehabilitation of Deng Xiaoping in 1978, Hua Guofeng pressed on with plans for a huge expansion of heavy industry and for agricultural expansion based more on Dazhai models of inspiration than any return to the use of material incentives. Even in the summer of 1978 these policies remained in full flight with talk of a new Leap Forward being in the making.

But in important respects change was beginning. Hua, for example, renewed the policy of foreign contact and plant imports and he saw also that efficient trade required that politics and economics be reinforced by a wider cultural and intellectual commitment to the outside world. Also, during 1977 and 1978 the ministries responsible for almost every sector and function in the economy held over thirty important Work Conferences. These discussions were the basis on which the Ministries could put their activities into shape after the decade of chaos. Particularly crucial were the conferences dealing with the railway system, coal and finance. Improvements in these three areas was a major factor in the sharp resurgence of the economy during these years, during which industrial output and national budgetary income both jumped by nearly a third. Many important new economic themes were also picked up at the National People's Congress meeting in October 1977. These included the need to focus effort on weak links in the economy, to overhaul planning procedures, to start solving livelihood problems and to begin urgent research into future reform strategies. Thus while many things remained to be tackled and Party attitudes were still in need of drastic transformation, this two year period is reasonably described in the official literature as 'the period of advance in the midst of hesitation.'[10]

THE LOGIC AND PROBLEMS OF THE SOCIALIST ECONOMY

Before turning to the events of reform and their results we need now to review briefly the core logic and dilemmas of the planned socialist economy. This will provide some guidelines to enable us to traverse from an understanding of development under Mao described above, to an evaluation of the very different world of the Chinese economy since

9 An additional disaster in that year was the Tangshan earthquake when nearly 300,000 people were reported killed, making it one of the worst recorded earthquake tragedies of all time.
10 Gu Longsheng, op. cit., Chap. 8.

1978. We start with the Soviet economy as a general type and proceed to the Chinese case, with attention mainly on the non-agricultural sector.

The essence of the Soviet type economy is that decisions which are centralised and made largely in physical terms replace the outcomes that in a market economy are generated by profit seeking firms working in the monetised environment. In a Soviet type system, the planners attempt to control directly not only macroeconomic objectives (i.e. rates of growth, ratios of savings and investment, the degree of openness of the economy etc.), but also detailed industry and sectoral targets. Once determined at the higher levels, planners objectives are broken down into consistent output targets and also into promises of the supplies of labour and other inputs that are needed by enterprises and factories. These input/output control figures are the core of the enterprise's plan and this whole process of calculation hinges critically on the establishment by the planners of thousands of estimated input/output 'norms', converting for example, coal into electricity, raw cotton into yarn, yarn into cloth etc.

In such an economy money is 'passive'. That is to say that while activities written into the plan are automatically financed by the banks, extra-plan activities have no finance available to them, since the banks are instructed not to support them and any surpluses ('profits') made by enterprises are appropriated by the central authorities.

The institutional implications of such arrangements are that in place of the pressures generated by markets and by firm governance systems responsive to shareholders (or other stakeholders), control of the planned system is inescapably a matter for bureaucrats, managers, and above all the Communist Party. For the Party (under its paramount leader) not only sets the economic agenda and main targets, but also monitors and controls the whole vertical chain of command from the Politburo right down to the shop floor. The working and efficiency of the planned economy is therefore fundamentally a bureaucratic and political matter; and congruence (or lack of it) between the bureaucratic, political and economic spheres is bound to be a central factor influencing economic behaviour and performance.

The advantage of this kind of system is its capacity to translate national political, social and strategic objectives *directly* into the economic process. Hence it is, for example, a system with clear benefits in time of war or other national emergency. The problems with it can be thought of as both theoretical and practical. Theoretically, the rationale for selecting which goods to produce and in what quantities beyond the level of obvious imperatives (feeding the population, making guns to fight threatening enemies etc.) is not clear. Also, neither the plan process nor the balance of incentives facing producing units provide a rationale or exert serious pressure within the system to ensure that costs are minimised or that innovation and quality improvement are encouraged.

In practical terms, moreover, the information problems for the planners are so severe that plans are rarely on time and usually highly imperfect and inconsistent. Hence managers, far from engaging in the routine administration of rational, long term plans find that their major task is to keep afloat in a chaotic environment where the promised resources needed for plan fulfilment are rarely available. Insofar as their personal material rewards and political fates depend on plan fulfilment, managers' focus must be correspondingly fixed on these short term difficulties.

One other intractable difficulty with socialist planning is that of work incentives. Unlike inanimate resources, workers cannot be allocated and instructed to perform at the simple *diktat* of planners. For if incentives do not reward immediate effort on the job, provide differentials that compensate for work in poor conditions and, in the longer run, encourage the acquisition of personal and collective skills, then the workforce will shirk, sabotage, and embrace a culture of indifference. The result will be plan failure and, above all, lack of productivity growth. Thus at the heart of the planned economy we might say that there are market forces of a kind that have to be accommodated, but tend always to be in conflict with egalitarian ideals and the whole ethos of planner direction. Worker behaviour may be modified in the short run by 'campaigns' (usually to emulate model workers) or coercive discipline, but these have never been demonstrated to work in the longer term.[11]

To function effectively the Soviet type economy must ensure that its bureaucratic and Party hierarchies are responsive to elite leadership from the top. This is done in three ways. First there is the provision of special, economically valuable privileges. Second there is the impact of periodic campaigns and purges. And, lastly, there is the Party's record of achievement in relation to the goals embodied in current ideology. Positive results in this latter sense encourage compliance because it reinforces confidence in the Party's wisdom, competence and legitimacy. Up to a point, the greater the effect of these instruments on reinforcing the vertical authority needed by planners the greater the economy's capacity to provide even further resources to reinforce these controls. This is a virtuous circle. However, through time, vertical control and hence planners authority and economic performance tend be weakened by the development of horizontal ties as bureaucrats and managers in particular seek to make their lives more comfortable and less vulnerable to the pressures of the vertical command chain. This weakening effect may be reinforced by a growing culture of comfort and security as revolutionary origins in war and conflict become more distant in the social memory.[12]

In addition to this systemic problem, economic performance will also be influenced by the irrationalities of resource allocation and incentives noted

11 Abram Bergson, *The Structure of Soviet Wages*, Cambridge Mass., 1954. Joseph E. Stiglitz, *Whither Socialism?*, Cambridge Mass., 1996, Chap. 5. A detailed practical account of the difficulty of providing incentives to individuals without an overall structure of incentives and effective enterprise government is provided by Janos Kornai, *Overcentralization in Economic Administration. A Critical Analysis based on Experience in Hungarian Light Industry*, Oxford, 1959, especially Part 11.
12 This process of socialist decay has parallels in market economies as described in the writings of Joseph Schumpeter, Mancur Olsen and Daniel Bell.

earlier as well as by changing structural economic factors such as particular resource shortages, demographic developments, and the evolution of the world environment. In spite of all the latter, it remains the case that what is striking about the Soviet system in the Soviet Union is that it did endure for more than sixty years. This stability arose from the basic congruence of the planning and political (Party led) system – both being highly centralised.[13] This ensured that in spite of massive economic losses through planners' errors, incentive failures etc., resources continued to be mobilised and moved in the direction of the State's priorities.

If we turn to the Chinese experience of socialism as it unfolded during 1949–1978, we can now see 1958 as a turning point of exceptional importance. For although in the short run the decentralisation of the Great Leap Forward was part and parcel of a utopian experiment born of Mao's frustrations with China's backwardness, the longer run persistence of heavily decentralised systems over the next twenty years reflected the fact that China, with its huge size, poor communications, low educational levels and hundreds of thousands of small and technically varied enterprises, simply could not be brought within the framework of a 'norm based' Soviet type system without catastrophic losses being incurred.[14] In these circumstances, the Party was forced to combine political and ideological centralisation with substantial economic decentralisation. This was never a comfortable combination. It gave rise to cycles of organisational instability but nonetheless the dominant thrust of the period was in favour of maintaining political centralisation at the expense of economic efficiency. The Great Proletarian Cultural Revolution (1965–1976) might, from this perspective, be regarded as a huge, costly control mechanism that paralleled the equally irrational seeming purges of the late 1930s in the Soviet Union.[15]

By the late 1970s, controls in China were still sufficiently intact to maintain high levels of forced savings and investment, nonetheless the declining productivity of these investments and of the system as a whole was yielding an economic performance unacceptable to every stratum of society. But in spite of the fact that popular discontent and the price of Party and bureaucratic compliance were rising to unsustainable levels, shifting a system whose characteristics had become ingrained over a twenty year period was to prove an extraordinarily difficult task.

---

13 The role of the Party dictatorship was well understood by the older generation of specialists, see, Alexander Gerschenkron, *Continuity in History and other Essays* Cambridge Mass., 1968, especially his essay, 'The stability of Dictatorships', pp. 313–343. The key role of the privileges provided by the *nomenklatura* system are analysed in Jan Winiecki, 'Why economic reforms fail in the Soviet system: a property rights-based approach', in Lee J. Alston, Thrainn Eggertsson and Douglas C. North, *Empirical Studies in Institutional Change,* Cambridge, 1996. A penetrating formal account of the issue is Ronald Wintrobe, *The Political Economy of Dictatorship*, Cambridge, 1998, especially Chaps. 9 and 10.

14 In the Soviet Union the small scale, workshop sector was eliminated by the late 1920s.

15 See Wintrobe's explanation of the Stalinist purges, op. cit. pp. 226–228.

STRATEGY AFTER 1978

The ferment begins, 1978–1984

On the 21st of December 1978 heavy and much needed snow fell over the whole of northern China. In spite of this, on the following day, the Central Committee of the Chinese Communist Party despatched a plane from Beijing to Hefei – a city in Anhui Province, central China. The plane returned carrying a casket inside of which were the ashes of comrade Tao Zhu. Tao had been a prominent Party leader from South China and something of an economic reformer who, during the Cultural Revolution, had been attacked for the heresy of suggesting that Guangdong Province might open a foreign trade office of its own. Tao had been a vigorous opponent of Mao and the Great Leap Forward and he died in disgrace in 1969.

On the 24th of December the historic *Communiqué* of the Third Plenum of the Eleventh Central Committee of the Party was published in *The People's Daily*. The entire back page of the same issue, however, was filled with colourful, adulatory photographs of Chairman Mao.

Finally, on December 25th Tao Zhu's casket together with that of another famous opponent of Mao and critic of the Great Leap Forward, Marshall Peng Dehuai, were draped with flags in the Great Hall of The People. The New China News Agency reported that over 2000 Party leaders met together on that day and, in the spirit of 'seeking truth', made public reparations to the memory of the two men who were now described as model Communists, falsely accused by Lin Biao and the Gang of Four.[16]

The revelation of these extraordinary events through the mass media, virtually as they occurred, had as its purpose the need to convey to the Chinese people and to the Party at large that an absolutely fundamental turning point had been passed. Although the pictures of Mao and the careful wording of the *Communiqué* were designed at the same time to reassure readers that continuity in the Party was being preserved and that their histories, personal and collective, were not being entirely cut from beneath their feet, thereby rendering them vulnerable to new forms of political persecution.

The precise route by which in a matter of a few months China's economic policies underwent such a dramatic transformation remains unknown, although it is clear that many of the early rounds in Deng's campaign of persuasion were undertaken by intellectuals such as Hu Yaobang, a dynamic and original personality who was to play a leading role in the reforms of the 1980s.[17] In terms of our analysis above we may note

16 These events were reported in NCNA and the Beijing Home Radio Service on the evening of 24 December 1978. Other reports are in *The People's Daily* for the relevant days.

17 Valuable contributions by political scientists to this problem are Rick Baum, *Burying Mao. Chinese Politics in the Age of Deng Xiaoping*, Princeton, 1994 and Harry Harding, *China's Second Revolution*, Washington, 1987 especially Chap. 3.

that the dire economic situation in which China found itself was made up in the following way. Systemically, almost the entire system of economic administration and control had fallen into irreparable dysfunction by 1975–1976. For while 'local economies' were functioning at minimalist levels, poor target selection and the loss of central co-ordination by planners led to severe sectoral imbalances and consequent bottlenecks, while the absence of accurate statistics and up dated 'norm' information, made control and direction of the larger scale, technically more modern enterprises impossible. In workplaces of all kinds, the incentive problem had become intractable and the failure to achieve significant productivity gains made even egalitarian (across the board) income improvements impossible. Thus over a twenty year period, living standards for most of the population had been static or falling, in spite of a large increase in the proportion of the population at work.[18]

Central to the lack of productivity gains was loss of contact with external economics since 1965, not only in strictly economic terms, but in the wider sense of cultural, academic and all forms of person to person contact. Such relationships were needed not only to provide a framework for thinking about the direction in which the Chinese economy should be moving, but also specific channels for technology transfer. Without such transfers, China's technological capabilities degenerated and its industries fell one to two decades behind best practice as set by standards in Japan and the western democracies, not to mention the benchmarks now emerging in neighbouring Asian economies, which were experiencing powerful surges of industrial growth and living standards.[19] Finally, although population growth had fallen in the 1970s under the influence of drastic anti-natality measures, an added dimension of concern by 1977–1978 was that the limits of this decline had been reached and that population growth might resume, putting even more pressure on China's poor living standards and its partially modernised agriculture.

We see these issues more clearly in retrospect. At the time, the reasons for this deeply unsatisfactory performance became clear only gradually and in different ways to different groups of people. The ground was, however, ready for revaluations since the failures of Maoist strategies over a twenty year period contributed to both individual and collective learning experience. Within the Party, a search for remedies was allowing a new tolerance of intellectuals and theorists some of whom could now pick up the threads of reform debates that were more than twenty years old.

To many in the leadership, especially the older planners and bureaucrats, the main problem was departure from the disciplined structures and careful

---

18 According to contemporary materials workers and staff wages and rural grain rations in 1976–1977 were both below those of 1956–1957. *Economic Research*, 1981, No. 1.

19 These two considerations were often linked. For example it was claimed that China's electronics industry was on a par with Japan in 1958 but was now 15 years behind. 'Review of 30 years of electronics industry development', Beijing Radio, *Foreign Broadcast Information Service*, 25 January 1980.

overall planning of the Soviet system at its best. Some in this group emphasised the neglect of proper planning procedures. These rejected entirely the Maoist view that 'taut' planning and imbalance were creative devices which promoted chaotic but high growth. They were also critical of excessive investment efforts and of the forced sacrifices of consumption required to finance these.[20] Others focused on the failures to maintain balance between and within economic sectors and in particular the neglect of agriculture, light industry, energy and transportation. There was also criticism of the costs of 'Third Front' policies and of the collapse of investment in human resources. State expenditure on education as proportion of total investment expenditure was reported to have fallen from 7.6% during the First Five Year Plan (1950s) to 3.1% during the Fourth Five Year Plan (1970s) and an estimated one million university graduates and two million Middle and Specialist School graduates had been 'lost' as a result of institutional closures during the Cultural Revolution.[21] To many of the older generation, therefore, the First Five Year Plan and the post Leap Recovery (1962–1965) were now seen as Golden Ages to which they sought to return, with the qualification that an appropriate level of decentralisation be implemented.

There was, however, another strand in the thinking about China's economic problems which raised more complex issues, issues whose resolution was to have far reaching implications as reform unfolded. This was the question of incentives and the 'Law of Value'.[22]

The payment of individual incentives in industry and toleration of market mechanisms for output from peasants' private plots were established practices in the Soviet Union. Stalin had rationalised these practices in his theory of socialism as necessary aspects of the *transition* from the lower to the higher forms of socialism where, eventually, income would indeed be allocated according to need and all resource use planned by public authorities in the wider social interest. In this transitional stage, violation of the Law of Value could be regarded as occurring where parties to economic exchange were subject to coercion of some kind. Thus in China, labour conscripted to work without pay in the Great Leap Forward

20 In the Soviet system 'taut' planning was a by-product of joint target setting by enterprises and ministries in a situation where the latter lacked the information to make informed estimates of the best that the former could do. They therefore set targets arbitrarily above the levels proposed by enterprises – a rational strategy in the circumstances. In the Maoist economy, moreover, high and unrealistic targets came to be regarded as a political challenge to be overcome by socialist incentives, education and campaigns. After many years of such behaviour the gaps between planning and reality (particularly in terms of input/output relationships) rendered meaningful planning impossible. To rectify this situation required an immense amount of detailed administrative and statistical work.

21 Data quoted in Gu Longsheng, op. cit., p. 699.

22 By far the best introduction to subject in English is Cyril Chihren Lin, 'The reinstatement of economics in China today', *The China Quarterly*, No. 85, March 1981. Sadly no one has yet followed up Lin's path breaking research with a study that explores (with comparable insight) subsequent developments.

(or later in the Dazhai type institutions of rural development) were in this position, as indeed were peasants forced to accept low procurement prices or industrial workers oppressed by low, egalitarian wage policies.[23]

By 1978 most agreed that this kind of behaviour destroyed the will to work and that socialist incentives had clearly failed to raise productivity. But while the dysfunctional characteristics of violations of the Law of Value were easily argued and were acceptable to the old 'planners', in the longer run this kind thinking was to lead in revolutionary directions. For while to the planners and Soviet traditionalists the Law of Value could be regarded as a key to effective *planning* (in the sense that plans were to be consistent with and supported by 'rational' prices and incentive systems), to Zhao Ziyang and to radical thinkers, the Law turned out to be the means by which plan and market could first be 'reconciled', and then could ultimately become the basis for supplanting Soviet type plans altogether.[24]

Although the need for reform was so clear and some ways forward so evident to the inner circle, initiating a Party wide, national process of change was extremely difficult. Deng's success in doing this was a testimony to his exceptional political skills but also reflected a structural situation in which so many people at so many levels in Chinese society stood to gain from an advance, if only it could be got under way. The immediate obstacle to be overcome was the suffocating power and influence of Maoism in the China, summed up at the time as the problem of Party members and others who adhered to the principle of the 'Two whatevers'. Expanded, the meaning of this was: 'Whatever Chairman Mao's policies are, we protect them. Whatever Chairman Mao's instructions are, we follow them loyally from start to finish'. Allied to this mentality was the conditioning of leadership at every level to fear that caution or downward plan readjustment of any kind might lead to criticism and potential political disgrace.[25]

Deng's task was to break this monolithic attitude and introduce an element of critical thinking and re-evaluation into the Party's understanding of Mao and the economic past. This process began at an informal and secret level soon after the death of Mao and a crucial role in it was played by Hu Yaobang. Hu was reportedly responsible for leading a major effort among senior Party officials to get them to understand the absolute imperative of re-thinking world economic and technological issues and the

---

23 See, 'The role of the Law of Value in cotton production', *Enlightenment Daily*, 9 December 1978.

24 A planner's view of the Law is given in Li Chengrui and Zhang Fuyuan, 'Concerning some problems of implementing socialist modernisation at high speed', *Economic Research*, 1979, No. 2. Li and Zhang argued that although prices could be used, free markets for major commodities would never be appropriate under socialism. For an early example of Zhao Ziyang's thoughts on the 'assimilation' of plan and market, see 'Zhao Ziyang attends Sichuan forum on economic problems', *Foreign Broadcast Information Service*, 12 March 1979

25 'Emancipate the mind for an overall balance in economic development', *The People's Daily*, 24 February 1979.

need to address the policy revolution needed in China to handle their implications.[26]

In November and December 1978 the Central Committee Work Conference was presented with Deng's case. This was followed by the December Plenum when the debate became much more public although within the Party, Mao, the Great Leap Forward, and the experiences of the Cultural Revolution were all subjected to an ongoing scrutiny. In a sense this process came to an end in August 1981 when the Party issued its *Resolution on Some Historical Questions in the Party's History since the establishment of the People's Republic of China*. Mao and his policies were at the heart of this document which, while maintaining a positive historical role for Mao, criticised him for errors and deviations, particularly those made in the Great Leap Forward and during the latter part of his life.

One of the keys to Deng's rationalisation of the economic reforms was his concept of 'modernisation' and the continuities and discontinuities between Mao and Deng largely centre around their differing and evolving interpretations of this word. A current summing up of the state of play on this debate might run as follows.

Mao made three great contributions to China's development. First, in the 1920s he grasped the importance of going the 'Russian road'. Thus where previous Chinese reformers had grappled with the challenge of Chinese backwardness using slogans that urged a combination of 'Chinese essence with Western practical learning', Mao saw that the Russian Revolution offered radical new possibilities to China based on the adoption of socialist institutions. By 1945 Mao was clear that these institutions offered a route to 'modernisation', now defined primarily as the industrialisation needed to buttress China's political and strategic independence. He saw, also, that to work successfully China's socialism would have to have unique characteristics. Mao's third contribution was his analysis of the link between modernisation and socialism. In Mao's thought socialist institutions and modernisation were both ultimate and *mutually interdependent* goals. Thus public ownership, planning, socialist education and egalitarian distribution policies were all both socially desirable in themselves *and* would serve to liberate productive forces in the economy.

This approach to modernisation appealed to Mao because it solved the problem posed by China's humiliating technological backwardness in relation to the advanced capitalist economies. It did this because although China might be (temporarily) backward if measured by narrow, quantitative economic and technological indicators, by adopting socialism China could leap ahead of capitalism in terms of social quality, and by adopting a unique

---

26 See the approving comments of Zheng Bijian in, 'A speech at the twenty year anniversary conference on theoretical research', *Select Reports*, 1998, No. 5. In this document Zheng reports that Hu was active in this work in 1977 and particularly so at the turn of 1978. The Central Party School (with which Hu had close connections) was crucial in the re-education process.

'Chinese' socialism could even be considered superior to other socialist societies even where these were economically more advanced.

Mao's ideology and policies are still considered to have been entirely appropriate to China's domestic and international situation in the 1950s. However it is now argued that during 1956–1958 Mao's errors began. These occurred because of his determination to press ahead with advanced socialist institutions *irrespective* of whether an equilibrium between the development of these and the state of the economy was being maintained appropriately. In the Great Leap Forward Mao went so far as to combine new utopian institution building with reckless projections of China's capability to overtake Britain economically in 7 years and America in 15 years. (Culturally the target was to overtake Bach, Beethoven and Mozart with equally ambitious targets.) According to Mao's critics it was this growing preference for advanced socialist institutions as ends in themselves and de-linked from economic modernisation, with all the violations of the Law of Value this approach entailed, that led to the appearance of black markets and dysfunctions of all kinds in the economic system of the 1960s and 1970s. By retreating to rational planning and more appropriate, less radical institutions, the Communist traditionalists believed such perverse phenomena could be made to disappear.

In the context of this interpretation of Mao we can now distinguish the essence of Deng's contribution. The crux of Deng's position was that the definition of socialism had to involve a return to its earlier link with modernisation – particularly economic modernisation. Indeed, Deng essentially *defined* socialism as the means to economic development. 'The essential quality of socialism', he wrote, 'is the liberation of production and the elimination of exploitation and dualism, leading ultimately to a common prosperity'.[27] On this view, markets, planning, technologies and modern organisational devices were all essentially neutral – applicable everywhere but needing to be adapted according to the particular historical circumstances in any case.[28] What distinguished socialism in this view of the world was the use of many such mechanisms, a use always subject to three safeguards: viz. the Party led state, substantial public ownership, and the elimination of exploitation and achievement of a 'common prosperity'. The emphasis on public ownership and the role of the Party implied that reform had significant political implications, as did Deng's particular emphasis on the importance of science and technology and his realisation

27 Deng Xiaoping, *Collected Works*, (Beijing), vol. 3. See also The Economics Department of the Party School, *Deng Xiaoping. Concept and Practice of the Market Economy* (Beijing, 1994).

28 Deng's 'cat theory' and general philosophy echoed the opinions of Liu Chien-hsün, a Party official condemned in the Cultural Revolution for ridiculing Chairman Mao's thought and propagating the theory that 'Food is Marxism-Leninism'. In the course of a 29 page indictment Liu was reported to have said: 'Who is a Marxist Leninist? He who produces grain is a Marxist-Leninist. A good cat catches mice whether it is black or white'. *Facts about Liu Chien-hsün's Crimes*, Honan, 12 March 1967 (English translation).

that this would require non-Party 'intellectuals' to be rehabilitated and given a central role in Chinese society.[29]

The other radical element in Deng's thought was the role to be played by the Open Door. Deng observed that, historically, China's periods of weakness and retrogression had been precisely those associated with the 'Closed Door' (notably the later Qing dynasty) a period that could be contrasted with the Open Door phases of the Tang and Ming dynasties. He also argued that the economic failures of the Soviet Union were an important lesson in the consequences of autarchy and the closed door mentality.

This historical perspective apart, Deng viewed the world situation at the turn the 1980s as greatly favourable to China. He saw world trade growing rapidly and foreign capital and technology circulating with increasing freedom. He also sensed a generally benign international political situation, all of which China could take advantage of to hasten its economic progress. Critics asked Deng whether the Open Door would not lead to the import of capitalism, but again Deng emphasised that the safeguards of the Chinese socialist system would prevent this happening.[30]

Deng's advance on Mao is seen in summary therefore as involving four major changes: a shift from class struggle to economic development as the main goal of the Party; a shift from Mao's emphasis on 'big and public' institutions to a system that retained public as the main form of ownership, but encouraged private and collective forms; a shift from detailed micro planning to macro economic control; and, finally, a shift from a closed to an open door mentality. In this last respect, analysts noted that while Deng's thought was a contrast to Mao's it was actually a reversion to the radical tradition established by Sun Yat-Sen.[31]

First steps in the reform, 1978–1984

During the first three years of the reform Deng's primary task was to persuade the Party to begin the process of realistic thinking, first about the past and then about the future. At this stage his own thinking was partial and his notions about the detail of reform seem scarcely to have been formed at all. In the Plenum *Communiqué* the emphasis was on three things: political rethinking, the international situation, and the need to revive agriculture. The latter was to be done by re-asserting the proper

29 Meng Qingse, 'A comparison of Chinese society's development form [in the thought of] Mao Zedong and Deng Xiaoping', *Liaoning University Journal* (Shenyang), 1998, No. 6; Tao Yongli and Wu Qijie, op. cit.

30 Chen Qian, 'Deng Xiaoping's theory of opening [the economy] and the road to common prosperity', *Nankai University Journal*, 1998, No. 6; Zhang Zhufan, 'A discussion of the special characteristics of Deng Xiaoping's theory of the world economy', *Social Science Battle Front* (Changchun), 1998, No. 6.

31 Wang Dong, 'The four new creative [elements] in Deng Xiaoping's theory and the reform of China's economic system', *The China Government and Party Cadres Forum* (Beijing), 1988, No. 10; Yan Qinghua, 'The three creative milestones in Chinese economic theory in the past hundred years', *Economic Review*, 1998, No. 3.

working of the three level Commune system, while for industry, the main thrust of change was emphasis on the need for decentralisation of powers, a reform issue fully worked over in the 1950s.

Nonetheless, whatever Deng's caution, views were developing. The traditional planners, for example, had a clear conception of past and future. An illustration of this can be seen in an extraordinary document by the veteran planner Bo Yibo. In January 1980, Bo addressed comrades at the Central Party School in a talk entitled, 'Reflections on thirty years of economic construction'. In this he reviewed the history of the Chinese economy since 1949, critically evaluated Mao, argued for the rehabilitation of Liu Shaoqi and Peng Dehuai, and took the blame for many past errors on himself.

His view of the past was that from 1949–1957 both policy and performance had been good. He praised Mao, Liu Shaoqi, Zhou Enlai and Chen Yun. He even praised Stalin, thanking him for the 156 major industrial projects that constituted the First Five Year Plan. He noted with approval Mao's fiscal conservatism during 1949–1952 and he attributed the success of the First Five Year Plan to the careful preservation of balance and overall good arrangements (*an pai*). Bo noted that errors began to creep in during the High Tide of Socialism in 1956 and argued that the Great Leap Forward descended into catastrophe because the political situation refused to allow any Party admission of error or any scaling back of the Leap's targets until it was too late.

For the future, Bo advocated five key policies based on his study of past mistakes. First, economic construction was to be put at the heart of the Party's agenda. Second, plans were to be realistic, balanced, and 'in accordance with economic laws'. In particular, Bo argued that the investment rate of the economy should not exceed 25% of National Income – otherwise consumption would be depressed and projects would become chaotic in formulation and implementation. Finally, he argued for a new balance in the degree of centralisation, suggesting that the First Five Year Plan had been too centralised, but that the decentralisation of the late 1960s had gone too far the other way.[32] In all of this there was no suggestion of a significant shift away from planning in the direction of radical market oriented reform and open door policies.

The world of academics and economists had much in common with Bo Yibo's outlook. A revelation of this world is provided to us by the famous economist Xue Muqiao who addressed the State Economic Commission in October 1978 (i.e. *before* the December Plenum), and again in March 1979.[33]

32 In 1965 the central ministries controlled 10,533 enterprises which were responsible for 46% of industrial output. In 1970 the figures were 142 enterprises responsible for 8% of output. Gu Longsheng, op. cit., p. 727.

33 Xue Muqiao,'Economic work must grasp the laws of economic development', *Report to the State Economic Commission's Research Conference on Enterprise Management* (Mimeo) 14 March 1979.

Xue is more theoretical than Bo Yibo and dealt much more in terms of the Law of Value problem. In his review of the past, Xue declared that Mao's agricultural collectivisation had been 'an error more serious than that of the Soviet Union'. He was also scathing about the Great Leap, which he described as 'a force twelve gale of exaggeration and telling lies'. Nonetheless, Xue's conclusions for the future were similar to those of Bo Yibo. He advocated balance, caution, correct proportions, a 25% investment ceiling and a State Plan to implement all of this. In this scenario, existing (i.e. black) markets would disappear once the supply of consumer goods matched workforce needs, although in the longer run (harking back to debates in the 1950s) Xue did foresee a minor role for allocation of goods through the market.

In spite of these limited and cautious intellectual underpinnings, the reform began to move. The most pressing issues were the need to correct the unbalanced planning trajectory set up in 1976–1978, abandon the unrealistic 60 mmt steel output target, and to encourage agriculture by affirming the rights of all levels within the three tier Commune system and by offering higher official purchase prices.[34] On a small scale, and in the poorer agricultural areas, 'contracting to the household' also began.

In 1980 two outstanding figures in the reform came to power. These were Zhao Ziyang and Hu Yaobang. With their support, Deng pressed on with the Party re-education programme and more detailed reform measures. By 1982 industrial enterprises had been given new powers and incentives, agriculture had revived, and the One Child Family policy adopted. But by 1983 numerous new problems had appeared, many created by the partial liberalisation that had taken place. These problems included misallocation of agricultural land, chaotic price structures in industry, and a wave of corruption and 'economic crime' to which the authorities reacted with a ferocious campaign involving between 8,000 to 10,00 executions in a year.[35]

The dynamic of economic reform in these early years was strongly driven by the Open Door aspects of the new policies. China's share of world trade had fallen to less than 1% in the late 1970s. But with a huge reserve of cheap, reasonably skilled labour and adequate infrastructure in the southern and coastal areas, China's potential for labour intensive exporting, particularly in conjunction with foreign capital, was clearly enormous. Reforms admitting foreign capital, establishing Special Economic Zones and liberalising foreign trade were implemented very quickly and the results were rapid. In 1983 a raft of new measures was adopted to speed the process further.

---

34 It was symptomatic of the times, that the 60 mmt target was widely considered credible outside of China and that many unfortunate businessmen lost money by making contracts on the basis of the optimism generated by it.
35 This was the estimate of contemporary diplomatic sources.

Reform deepening and the Tiananmen crisis, 1984–1991

In 1984 Deng visited the Special Economic Zones (SEZs) in a public show of support. This was followed by further measures to increase the market and foreign orientation of the economy. These included extension of the SEZ privileges to fourteen inland cities; establishment of the Township Enterprise system; and further enlargement of the autonomy of State Owned Enterprises.

This important reform burst was driven by two factors: one was the thrusting leadership of Zhao Ziyang and the other was Deng's political problems in Hong Kong. In Hong Kong, Deng had to show that the 'two systems one country' approach would not be too great a strain because the Chinese economy was rapidly increasing its market orientation and hence was on a course for significant convergence with Hong Kong.

By the end of 1984 the reform had entered a level that was changing the fundamentals in every sector. In agriculture, 'contracting' arrangements were becoming general and permanent. In industry, within the framework of a unitary tax system, state macroeconomic controls and substantial public ownership, the market was set to become the main factor in resource allocation. While in the external sector, long term commitment to the open door with a special and growing role for Hong Kong promised huge expansion of foreign interdependence. Theoretically, this advance of the reform was known as implementation of the Socialist Planned Commodity Economy. This proved to be a concept about which there was considerable disagreement before it was replaced in 1992 by the concept of the Socialist Market Economy.[36]

The optimism of this phase was reflected in growth and new plans. In December 1985 the Sixth Five Year Plan was completed with growth of 9.7% being achieved and a new plan projecting growth of 10% was confirmed in January 1986. Compared to Chen Yun's cautious target of 4% in 1982, these were indeed stunning figures.

During 1987 and 1988 the cycle of 'reform, destabilisation and retrenchment' reasserted itself. The political situation was also becoming complex. In January 1987 Hu Yaobang was purged, while Deng and Zhao Ziyang pressed on with further liberalisation of trade and foreign investment. During the summer of 1988, however, incomes and the price level began to move out of control as enterprises used their new found freedoms to distribute worker and staff benefits and profit from dubious transactions made possible by the mixed system of planned and market prices.

These macroeconomic difficulties continued on into 1989 and the martial law period (May 1989-January 1990). The crushing of the Democracy Movement in 1989 had important economic implications

---

36 See the crucial article by Liu Guoguang, 'Some issues relating to the theory of the Socialist Market Economy', *Economic Research*, 1992, No. 10. In this, Liu runs through the history of the theory of the socialist economy from the pre-reform period up to the 1992 formulation. (Document 2.4).

because it strengthened the hands of the planners in their use of administrative means to control inflation and expenditure.

It was in these circumstances that a second fundamental round of debate about the reform took place during 1989–1992. In this debate, no doubt the temperamentally conservative and reformist mind sets played their instinctive antagonistic roles. However in strict economic terms, the debate was about how to evaluate the 1984–1988 boom and how to clarify the ambiguities of the 1984 formulation of the Socialist Planned Commodity Economy. The political reaction from Tiananmen undoubtedly pushed the balance in the theoretical debate away from market and back towards planning while behind the public debates, important 'internal' critiques of market oriented reform ideas are known to have been circulated.[37]

The conservatives could argue that the inflation, corruption and economic inequalities that had developed in the 1980s were the inevitable result of the reform process, and that such phenomena would grow and ultimately undermine the socialist core of Chinese society if reform continued. They could also argue that the financial sanctions imposed by the international community after Tiananmen illustrated the dangers of Open Door strategies. For conservatives (such as Chen Yun) the answer was reversion to a solid core of planning and public ownership which would continue to guarantee stable, equitable growth and the maintenance of socialism.

The conservatives certainly had a case and perhaps even a chance of winning. For during the 1980s Deng Xiaoping, Hu Yaobang and Zhao Ziyang had indeed taken the reform far beyond tentative thoughts of re-balancing the planning system and modifying incentive arrangements on lines similar to those tried in Eastern Europe. But by 1990 Hu had been purged and died, Zhao disgraced for his role in the Democracy Movement and Deng was clearly ageing.[38] No major initiatives were taken during 1989 and most of 1990 while arguments undoubtedly raged.[39] Then, in December 1990, the Party approved the Eighth Five Year Plan with a growth rate of 11.8% and one month later the respected reform theorist Xue Muqiao pressed forward the intellectual agenda by insisting that as long as public ownership was retained, marketisation could not be said to

37 Liu Guoguang, op. cit.
38 In spite of his loss of office and early death, Hu remains a potent figure in Chinese politics. According to the Hong Kong press 300,000 to 400,000 people a year visit his memorial in Jiangxi Province – a fact not reported internally. Copies of his works and writings by others about his efforts to rehabilitate disgraced officials still sell in large numbers. Jiang Zemin was reported to have visited Hu's widow on 18 February 1996 (the eve of the Lunar New Year) in order to shore up his support among Party liberals still faithful to Hu's name and ideas.
39 See Wang Dong, op. cit. See also the important comments dated January 1993 under the heading 'Ten great debates' included by Ling Zhijun in his informal memoir, *Ups and Downs. A Memo-book of the Chinese Economic Reform (1989–1997)*, Shanghai, 1998, pp. 270–274. According to Ling, ten debates dealing with issues including the nature of markets, the role of agricultural contracting, the power relations between management and Party in industrial enterprises etc. were all resolved during 1988–1992.

lead to capitalism. This push reflected the demands of a grave situation and the urgent need to grow out of the fiscal deficits and rising unemployment created in the post Tiananmen recession. The reformers probably won the argument on the grounds that only further reform and open policies could deliver the dynamism needed to meet these targets.

There was one other important factor in Deng's thinking at this time and this was technology. China's technological weaknesses had been a major element in the original reform thinking and in 1985 Deng personally launched the campaign for a radical reform of China's R and D sector. The Gulf War of January 1990 reminded the leadership of both the importance of technology in the defence context and also of how little had been achieved in terms of domestic capabilities by that time. But reform of R and D could only proceed within the framework of a wider, market oriented development of industry and strong policies to encourage renewed and much enlarged inflows of foreign capital and technology.[40]

The 'Southern Journey' and its aftermath

To mobilise the Party in this direction, in Spring 1992 Deng made his famous Southern Journey to the SEZs where local interests stood to benefit strongly by continued reform. On his journey he again praised reform, implicitly endorsed Xue Muqiao's argument concerning the neutrality of capitalist devices and technologies and generally ignited a further effort. Back in Beijing the economists polished the theoretical links between reform and growth and doubters (reported to have included Li Peng and Jiang Zemin) were won over.[41] In October the Fourteenth Party Congress endorsed the new concept of the Socialist Market Economy in which centralised mandatory planning was (in theory) finally put to rest. With this episode Deng left the scene, dying in February 1997, four months before the Hong Kong transition. Power then passed to Jiang Zemin and the Shanghai group who continue to grapple with his legacy.

Once reform and open policies were again politically acceptable, the combination of decentralised reform and fierce, self interested local competition for foreign capital fused in a mechanism that produced a dramatic upswing in the economy. This upswing was to last through to 1996 and 1997 in a boom prolonged partly to ensure the smooth transition of Hong Kong's reversion to China.[42]

40 See materials in Charles Feinstein and Christopher Howe, (Eds.) *Technology Transfer in China in the 1990s*, Cheltenham, 1996.

41 The economic arguments were made for example in the symposium, 'Grasp the favourable opportunity; accelerate the progress of reform', by Ma Jiantang and others, *Economic Research*, 1992, No. 5.

42 Two accounts of this mechanism are Dali Yang, 'Economic crisis and market transition' in Edwin A. Winckler, *Transition from Communism; Institutional and Comparative Analyses*, Boulder, 1999 and David Zweig, 'Distortions in the Opening. 'Segmented Deregulation' and weak property rights as explanations for China's 'Zone Fever' of 1992–1993', Hong Kong Institute of Asia-Pacific Studies, Hong Kong.

During this phase growth rates rose again to 10% per annum which, even allowing for methodological questions marks, was a remarkable achievement for such a large economy. This boom would not have been possible without a massive response by foreign capital, much of it direct investment. Between 1992 and 1996 total inflows of FDI to developing countries were $450 billions of which China was the most notable single recipient.[43] These inflows further accelerated China's integration into the world economy, since the share of exports estimated to come from foreign related enterprises is estimated to have risen to the range of 50%–60% by 1998. The character of this development had important structural implications not for only for China, but also for Hong Kong, Taiwan and Japan.[44]

By mid-decade macro economic problems were again serious. Inflation, which had been brought under control in 1989–1990, rose again to double digit levels and grappling with the problem of securing a 'soft landing' (i.e. inflation reduction without growth and employment collapse), became a major issue in the latter half of the 1990s. The soft landing was almost achieved but by the end of the decade new trends of price deflation and consumer uncertainty began to make the minimum growth of 7% per annum needed to reconcile continued reform with social stability looked increasingly difficult.

Economic stabilisation, the Asian and Hong Kong crises, and political problems including heightened tension in the Taiwan Straits appear to have almost totally preoccupied the leadership in recent years. The reform agenda is still there, but has probably not ranked as highly as it had done during the 1980s. This is partly because although Premier Zhu Rongji appears to have remained supportive, no *group* has ever emerged to equal the formidable intellectual, political and other skills that were combined in Deng, Zhao Ziyang and Hu Yaobang.[45]

A distinguishing mark of the Jiang Zemin years has been the abandonment of any 'dash for reform' in favour of new emphasis on 'stability'. Stability has been reflected in emphasis on the Party, on ideology and on suppression of dissent.[46] Under Jiang these continue to be the guarantees of stability under reform.

Another element in Jiang's approach has been renewed nationalistic notes reflected in the policy to nominate 'Pillar Industries' and to control

43 Bank for International Settlements, *68th Annual Report*, Basle, 1998, Chap. 2.
44 Christopher Howe, *Japan and China's Changing Economic Environment: with particular Reference to Foreign Direct Investment and Industrial Restructuring*, Centre for Financial and Management Studies, School of Oriental and African Studies, October 1999.
45 A favourable assessment of Zhu Rongji based on his record in Beijing since 1991 is provided by Ling Zhijun, op. cit., pp. 540–547.
46 See for example, Bai Gang et. al., 'Correctly handle the relations between development and stability', *The People's Daily Internal Reading Materials*, 6 October 1999. In August 1999 *The People's Daily* for the first time ranked Jiang with Mao and Deng as a Communist ideologist.

and guide foreign investment to support this industrial policy. In the past, FDI is seen as having been too much a one sided bargain in which foreign investors took advantage of China's labour and other resources while ignoring China's need for structural transformation.

A further strand in this redirection of FDI have been attempts to interest foreigners in the inland regions, especially the far west and north western provinces and this in turn relates to another other prominent plank in Jiang's economic agenda, his emphasis on the problem of poverty. Jiang has spent much publicised time in the poorer regions and while arguing that reform has indeed reduced the numbers in 'absolute' poverty, it is recognised that much poverty is regionally concentrated and that its alleviation must involve economic development as well as redistribution through budgetary and other direct means. Regional problems are also compounded by the growing incidence of natural disasters and localised environmental degradation.

A summing up: some views from the inside

As we enter a new millennium, how can we balance the record of reforms and judge where the process is going?

Let us start with our documents and the views of mainland Chinese analysts and in this context it worth remembering that Chinese economists are now better informed and have a firmer grasp of the issues than at any time since 1949. They analyse the world in terms of globalisation, the knowledge economy, the 'new American paradigm' and the importance of small firms. By and large they see world trends as an unanswerable case for further Chinese reforms, both economic and legal, although of the many who discuss these issues few probably have a serious influence on policy.[47]

An exception to this and the author of an authoritative starting point for our discussion, is Wang Chuenzhong, who offered his balanced analysis of the reform to date in a recent lecture at the Central Party School. As Wang's audience consisted of high level cadres there would be little point in his mixing judgement with propaganda.[48] In his lecture Wang notes the following points to be placed on the positive side of the balance sheet: improved growth, control of inflation, higher consumption levels of key goods and large foreign exchange reserves. These quantitative indicators of improvement are supplemented on the systemic side by China's success in limiting the impact of the Asian crisis. In the balance against these points,

47 See for example, Li Ping, 'The use and necessity of the private economy in the age of the knowledge economy', *Study Materials for Economic Workers*, 1998, No. 74 and Wang Jincun, 'Views on the world economy at the century's end', *Inside Information on Economic Reform*, 1999, No. 1 and He Weiwen, 'From globalism to the borderless economy', *Foreign Trade Research*, 1998, No. 13.

48 Wang Chuenzhong, 'Concerning the present economic situation', *Select Reports*, 1998, No. 5. Wang is Deputy Chief of the State Development and Planning Commission and typical of the high quality of speaker brought to address the School.

Wang discusses agricultural and industrial weaknesses, continued population expansion, severe national fiscal problems, and the unemployment crisis.

In the agricultural sector Wang refers not only to China's well known shortage of arable land, but also emphasises the water problem, citing statistics to the effect that the availability of water per head in China is only 25% of the world average, while in the north western provinces it is only 4% of the world average. Against this background of resource shortage, the population to be fed is still growing at 14 to 15 million per annum.

In industry, Wang focuses on qualitative shortcomings. He reports a 1996 survey by the State Statistical Bureau that found only 26% of capital equipment in enterprises was up to developed country standards, and that virtually all of that had been imported. In other words China's domestic machine making capabilities remain low. Wang's broad brush portrait of China's industrial backwardness is reinforced by the steel analyst, Jin Lin, in a recent examination of trends in that industry. Metallurgy has been a priority sector in China for fifty years and China is now is now the world's largest market for rolled steel. Total steel output is above 120 million tons. The problem is that the industry is nowhere near world levels in terms of price/quality competitiveness, even in standard products. Lin also reported that 26 major steel enterprises were loss makers and he pointed to the scale of the technical challenge facing the industry. The latter may be judged from the fact that under current plans, by the year 2010 *output* is to increase by 50% while *labour input* is to be reduced by 90%. Even if achieved, Jin noted that this would leave the Chinese industry with output per man at only half the levels attained by Japanese firms in the early 1980s.[49]

Poor equipment will be one factor in the weak financial state of Chinese industry, with Wang indicating over 50% of all SOEs make losses. These losses have two effects: they explain the exceptionally low tax take of the Chinese central budget authorities while on the other hand, covering these losses and the social costs of eliminating them through reform has become a liability on the State budget's and on the banking system. The current proposal is to solve this conundrum by a huge 'debt for equity' swop with special institutions taking on the losses, but it is far too early to judge whether this will work.

The labour problems mentioned by Wang are another constant theme of current Chinese economic literature The figures vary, but all agree that there will be a net over supply of labour in the urban areas of tens of millions for several years to come. These estimates are based on numbers being culled from further reform of State Owned Enterprises, the bureaucracy, the educational system and even from small scale enterprises. Estimates of the numbers of surplus rural workers starts at 120 millions and

49 Jin Lin, 'Some problems in the development of our country's iron and steel industry', *Study Materials for Economic Research*, 1998, No. 74. An exception to this state of affairs is the Baoshan plant in Shanghai.

rises as high as 250 millions.[50] The other labour related problems are those of inequality and poverty. Contemporary writers emphasise that inequality has increased whether measured in terms of inequalities between regions, between and within sectors, between occupations, between industries, and even between employed and retired workers. To take the inter-regional case as one example. In 1981 the largest regional income gap was that between the Shanghai Region and Shanxi Province where the ratio of the difference was 1.62:1. In 1997 the biggest gap was that between Guangdong and Gansu Provinces, where the difference was estimated to be 2.38:1.[51] The poverty problem is reported to have eased overall in the sense that the absolute numbers in extreme poverty have declined, but the urban problem, especially under conditions of high inflation during the mid 1990s, is undoubtedly very serious.[52] One measure of how poverty has gone up on the national agenda is the fact that a Central Work Conference on the subject in June 1999 was attended by all of the top seven of China's political hierarchy.[53]

Another topic of contemporary commentary is China's endemic corruption. This issue relates closely to the inner dynamics of reform since local cadres have played a central role as 'entrepreneurs' in the growth of export oriented small scale enterprises. The problem is that this double role creates serious conflicts of interests and corruption opportunities for cadres. The scale of the problem is suggested by one local survey that reported that over half of all recently appointed Party Secretaries were also acting chiefs of local enterprises.[54]

One last group of problems that links agriculture, declining State fiscal power and corruption is that of environmental catastrophe and degradation. Particularly serious here has been the impact of major floods. Between the 1950s and the 1990s the area affected by flood has doubled, with one third of the crop area now typically affected to some degree. Three out of the seven major flood catastrophes of the last 50 years have occurred in the 1990s and these have involved an annual grain loss of 23 million tons between 1990–1997. Overall economic losses are estimated to have been

50 Yang Yiyong and Li Jianwei, 'An estimate of our country's labour demand and supply situation during the next three years', *The People's Daily Internal Reading Materials*, 1999, No. 8.

51 'Our country's income distribution differentials continue to grow', *Inside Information on Economic Reform*, 1999, No. 16.

52 A mainland analyst reports data showing that the numbers of city dwellers with falling per capita income during the three years 1993–1995 were 13%,16% and 22% of the totals respectively. He Qinglian, *China's Pitfall*, Hong Kong, p. 245.

53 The speeches and attendance are reported in the *New China Monthly*, No. 7, 1999. Total numbers in absolute poverty (i.e. below subsistence) are claimed to have fallen from 250 to 42 million. However the pre-reform estimate was 'about 100 million' and the precise meaning of this new statement is not yet clear.

54 The survey is reported in a interview at the Academy Of Social Sciences by Jiang Tiegang, 'Avoid the trap of agricultural reform', *Inside Information on Economic Reform*, 1999, No. 2. A very positive account of the official turned entrepreneur phenomenon is that by Jean Oi, *Rural China Takes Off*, Berkeley, 1999, but the burden of Jiang's argument is that the cost of this in terms of good rural administration is high.

3% to 5% of China's GDP.[55] Part of the problem is that a wealthier China pays a higher price for disasters, but corruption, fiscal weakness and inadequate attention to public works in a more privatised countryside are also reported as serious new factors in the situation.

A summing up: a view from the outside

The Chinese economic reforms started in the late 1970s as a result of the conjunction of three favourable conditions: dissatisfactions from below arising from stagnant living standards; Party awareness of this which, combined with its own concern at lagging Chinese industrial technologies, laid the ground for a break with Maoist ideological hegemony after his death in 1976; and, thirdly, a favourable world environment. The latter enabled the world's major economies to be supportive of Chinese reform aspirations, while developments in Hong Kong and Taiwan were particularly important in enabling China to obtain quick results from open door policies.

Reform has unfolded with considerable geographical and sectoral variations and in strong cyclical patterns. Beginning in agriculture and foreign trade, after 1984 reform moved on to vitalise the urban economy in the course of two powerful cycles. These cycles peaked in 1988/1989 and 1993/1994 respectively. In each cycle, locality-led investment frenzies followed reform initiatives pushed from the centre. In 1999/2000 we are in the trough of the last of these cycles.

The overall results of reform to date include a strong rate of growth, rising average living standards, and an epoch making change in the openness of the economy. In absolute terms, by 1995 China had become the world's largest producer of several agricultural products and also of steel, cement, coal, televisions and cloth. Nonetheless we should remember that the economy as a whole was still little more than a fifth larger than Spain or Canada, only two thirds the size of Britain, and one seventh the size of Japan.

But quantities, however striking, can also be misleading since China's present problems are fundamentally *qualitative* and *institutional*. The technological competence of industrial firms remains relatively backward and the continuing unresponsiveness of China's economic institutions to market needs was strikingly confirmed in March 1999 by Premier Zhu Rongji. In his speech to the National Peoples Congress, Zhu reported that the economy had huge structural excess capacity in several important industries including coal, metallurgy, petro-chemicals, machine building, electronics and textiles.[56] Matters are equally serious in the service sector

55 Hu Angang, 'The impact of inundation disasters and our country's strategy to lessen them', *The People's Daily Internal Reading Materials*, 1998, No. 37.
56 Zhu Rongji, Government Work Report, *Beijing Review*, April 5–11, 1999. A larger more technical study of the problem which examined firm behaviour in 94 important industries is that by Chen Yongjie and Zhang Tai, 'An analysis and some proposals concerning preserving stable growth in the industrial economy', *Study Materials for Economic Research*, 1988, No. 68. See also Marukawa Tomoo, *The Dynamics of Market Emergence. The Transition of the Chinese Economy,* Tokyo, 1999. (In Japanese.)

where the financial system remains in crisis, and throughout the whole economy highly publicised governance failures are legion. In the public sector enterprises are being bankrupted as their best physical assets are effectively stolen by corrupt officials, leaving behind the less competent human assets together with responsibility for all social liabilities.[57] In cases where enterprises are already well down the road of public quotation, *The People's Daily* recently remarked that: 'Big shareholders, by wantonly plundering listed companies' money have seriously violated the fair principles of the stock market and infringed the legal interests of small shareholders'.[58] These abuses and inefficiencies relate directly to income inequality, to anxieties about corruption, and to the sense that the Party is failing to fulfil Deng Xiaoping's promise that reform would lead to a 'common prosperity'.

In the foreign sector, export growth has been enormous. However between 50% and 60% of all exports are produced by foreign invested firms and China's net benefits from this are often small. On the capital account, an extraordinary indicator of China's problems is that fact that in spite of all the well known overseas enthusiasm for investment in China, it has been estimated that China is only a modest net importer of capital and may actually have been a net *exporter* in some years during the 1990s.[59] In other words institutions and individuals inside China are exceedingly anxious to get their capital out. In terms of economic fundamentals this is paradoxical, since the return to capital (especially to insiders) in such a labour abundant economy must be higher than in the more advanced, capital rich ones. The paradox is only resolved if institutional weakness makes it impossible to translate the fundamentals into predictable, assured gains by investors.

If we turn now to thinking about the future, a fundamental point to start with is that China's present state of institutional transformation is part of a very long process. The evolution of western capitalism and its national variants can credibly be traced back to the Dark Ages while the English breakthrough in the eighteenth century arguably requires not only a knowledge of history from the Norman Conquest, but also of geographical, climatic, religious and other special circumstances.[60] China has an even longer recorded economic trajectory, much of it still useful for understanding the pace and relative performance of the Chinese economy since the latter part of the nineteenth century.

57 He Qinglian has a great deal of data on the scale of theft from state enterprises. The key to this has been enrichment through land grabs and she quotes official data suggesting that approximately one fifth of the capital of the SOEs disappeared between 1982 and 1992, and that the scale of this has been growing. He Qinglian, op. cit., p. 126.

58 'State-owned firms "using units as ATMs"', *South China Morning Post*, 16 March 2001.

59 Nicholas R. Lardy, 'The role for foreign trade and investment in China's economic transformation', in Andrew G. Walder, *China's Transitional Economy*, Oxford, 1996.

60 A remarkable synthesis of these issues is, Jean Baechler, *Le Capitalisme* (two vols.), Paris, 1995.

Equally important for our current thinking is the fact that the context for reform in the twenty first century is one in which global economic and technological trends preclude a second retreat to closed door policies such as occurred in the 1960s. For the first time in its history, therefore, the core task for China is to learn how to gain in developmental quality from its international economic relationships. In particular, China must seek to go beyond an expansion of its simple OEM jobbing status ('screwdriver' exporting contracts) and reach the point where adaptation and product and manufacturing process innovation become significant. To do this requires an unprecedented accommodation between the parties. But without this and the gains that would ensue, other economic and social policies will have no firm economic foundation.

What is involved here? Edwin Winckler has summed up the core of socialist transition as a process whereby society moves first from central direction to delegation (in China's case through the route of Party/government decentralisation) and then from delegation to a system in which economic actors have freedom to work within a framework of rules. These rules must embrace well defined property rights as well as healthy legal and administrative systems. Of these transitions it is the second which is most difficult and it is in this stage that China now seems to be stuck.

Moreover Winckler's formulation may still fall short of what is required in the following sense. China's economic organisations now require a great deal of room for flexible experimentation in finding their appropriate structures – finding that is, both internal and external relationship patterns appropriate to China's state of development, to its institutional starting point, and to the environment in which they are having to operate. Within this process, achievement of technical progress in all its dimensions is especially challenging, calling as it does not only for the emergence of new formal systems, but also for the creation of informal networking relationships with domestic and also with foreign partners who are bound to press their own agendas.

In this context, our earlier analysis suggests that the Party and its future itself must remain a central issue. For on the one hand, transition calls for an evolutionary development as the economy establishes rules and institutions that give the predictability needed to make investments worthwhile. It has been argued that this process is successfully under way in the Township and Village Enterprises, in spite of (or perhaps because of) the continuing ambiguities and complexities of the 'ownership' systems. At this level, therefore, abrupt change of the political framework would not help.[61] However, in the large scale capital intensive enterprises the problems remain and here the Party continues to maintain and even expand a monitoring role appropriate to an economic planning system that now belongs to a lost past. This interference – often either arbitrary or in

---

61 Sun Laixiang, *Emergence of Unorthodox Governance Structures in East Asia. An Alternative Transition Path*, Helsinki, 1997; Susan H. Whiting, *Power and Wealth in Rural China. The Political Economy of Institutional Change*, Cambridge, 2000.

open pursuit of old privileges – not only makes the development of law, sound bureaucratic behaviour, and effective corporate governance very difficult, it is also with its totalitarian undertones inimical to 'horizontal' linkages of all kinds, since these seriously and inevitably challenge the Party monopoly of power and old style habits of vertical control.[62]

Thus although Deng left China a brilliant legacy of reform, he left one that was flawed by his insistence on the separation of economics from its wider social, political and human implications. The dilemmas inherent in the present situation are confirmed by the fact that anxieties about China's present predicament are shared from antagonistic viewpoints by important foreign economists such as Katsuji Nakagane, and by influential Marxists inside China, including the formidable conservative, Deng Liqun.[63] To be pessimistic about China's future is to be pessimistic about the human race, but the evidence suggests that in spite of its achievements there are major issues to be resolved before the Chinese economy escapes from the dark wood of underdevelopment. The new dimension to these problems is that in the contemporary world the Chinese economy has ceased to be the exclusive concern and responsibility of the Chinese people. China now concerns us all.

62 In spite of the decline of formal planning numbers of bureaucrats have increased sharply. Total government staff grew from 4.67 millions in 1978 to 10.93 millions in 1996 – rising as a percentage of all state employees from 6.2% to 10%. A similar rate of expansion was seen in bureaucrats at the Township level. The expanding role of the Party in the contemporary economy was underlined by Jiang Zemin in an recent address on the Tenth Five Year Plan. In this, Jiang listed the ten major tasks of the plan and five out of the first six of these related to Party activity and responsibility. See materials in, *The People's Daily*, 29 August 2000.

63 Deng Liqun's views are in Document 2.5. Katsuji Nakagane has provided one of the most penetrating overview's of the Chinese reform process in his article, 'A reconsideration of China's transition policy of gradualism from the perspective of comparison with the old socialist economies', *Economic Research*, October 1999. (In Japanese.)

BIBLIOGRAPHICAL NOTE TO CHAPTER 1

Chronologies have become extremely useful tools for research on the Chinese economy. For a concise summary of the reform, the chronology published in *The People's Daily* on the 14th, 15th and 16th of December 1998, (the reform's twentieth anniversary) is especially recommended. Also valuable are Wei Zhong, (Ed.), *A Big Economic Chronology of the Chinese People's Republic, 1949–1980*, Beijing, 1984; Contemporary Planning Work Office, *A Chronology of The Chinese People's Republic's National Economic and Social Plans, 1949–1985*, Beijing, 1987; Contemporary China Economic Management Editorial Office, *A Big Chronology of Economic Management in the People's Republic of China*, Beijing, 1986. Valuable chronological material and discussion also appear in Zhou Shulian, 'A twenty year review and forward look at China's enterprise reform', *Materials for Economic Workers*, 1998, No.52. A number of histories have been consulted of which the most important is Gu Longsheng, op. cit. Gu is a specialist and writer on Mao's economic thought and because he works at the Party Central Archive his words carry especial weight. Another interesting source has been Ling Zhijun, op. cit. Ling is a senior editor of *The People's Daily* and this unusual work is his personal notebook of unpublished thoughts. While clearly reflecting political sensitivities, it nonetheless contains important insights into the years covered. An unusual study that includes descriptions of the first decade of the reform in twenty five cities and provinces is Su Changchuen et. al., (Eds.) *A Survey of China's Ten Years of Economic Reform*, Beijing, 1989. Many dictionaries have been used during this project, but particularly relevant has been Fan Hengshan, *A Dictionary of the Reform of the Economic System*, Beijing, 1988. Among general monographs published outside of China we would particularly mention Susumu Yabuki, *China's New Political Economy, The Giant Awakes*, Boulder, 1995; Barry Naughton, *Growing out of the Plan, Chinese Economic Reform 1978–1993*, Cambridge, 1996; and Joseph C.H. Chai, *China. Transition to a Market Economy*, Oxford, 1997.

Table 1.1 Main Economic Indicators, 1978–2000 (% per annum growth rates)

	Popu-lation	GDP	Grain output	Coal output	Oil output	Steel output	Exports (US$)	Imports (US$)	Rural income	Urban income
1978–1985	1.37	9.89	3.17	5.04	2.64	5.68	15.88	21.32	15.18	6.98
1985–1990	1.55	5.58	3.31	4.37	2.06	7.24	17.82	4.78	2.96	4.31
1990–2000	1.02	9.93	0.35	−0.79	1.66	6.83	14.91	15.49	4.50	6.83

Table 1.2 Significant indicators of structural/institutional/regional change in the economy, 1978, 1990, 1995 and 2000

	1978	1990	1995	2000
Foreign capital inflows, contracted amounts, billions US$	5.14*	12.09	103.21	52.00
Share of State Owned Enterprisess in total industrial output (%)	77.63	54.60	34.10	23.50
Share of manufactures in total exports (%)	49.40	74.40	85.60	89.80
Output of colour televisions (millions of units)	0.38	4.35	10.53	39.36
Guangdong Province's share of China's exports	10.80	n.a.	38.10	36.90

* is average for 1979–1982.

Table 1.3 Macroeconomic indicators, 1995–2000, (% per annum growth rates)

	1995	1996	1997	1998	1999	2000
GDP	10.5	9.6	8.8	7.8	7.1	8.0
Industrial output (gross value)	20.3	16.6	13.1	10.8	6.1	9.9
Grain output	4.8	8.1	−2.1	3.7	−0.8	−9.1
Fixed capital investment	17.5	14.8	8.8	13.9	5.1	10.3
Retail price index	14.8	6.1	0.8	−2.6	−3.0	−1.5
Contracted FDI	10.4	−19.7	−30.4	2.2	−20.9	51.3
Contracted FDI from Japan	70.7	−32.3	−33.7	−20.7	−4.1	38.0
Export growth	23.0	1.5	21.0	0.5	6.1	27.8
State budget deficit (billions *yuan*)	58.2	53.0	58.2	92.2	174.4	249.1

Sources: China State Statistical Bureau publications and the *Japan-China Economic Co-operation Journal* (Tokyo, in Japanese).

CHRONOLOGY OF MAJOR ECONOMIC DEVELOPMENTS, 1964–2001

	General policy developments	Agriculture	Industry	Other
1964				
15 May–17 Jun	Work meeting of CCP Central Committee (CCPCC) discusses draft 3rd Five Year Plan (1966–1970)			
May		Mao endorses the slogan 'in agriculture, learn from Dazhai' as a model of national farm development		
17 Aug			Mao calls for 'Third Front' policy to relocate industry to western China	
16 Oct	China explodes atomic bomb			
20 Dec	1st Session of 3rd National People's Congress (NPC) approves Zhou Enlai's *Government Work Report* and endorses his call to implement the 'four modernisations' (of agriculture, industry, defence, and science and technology)			
Dec		Annual growth of gross value-output of agriculture (GVAO) = +3.5%	Annual growth of gross value-output of industry (GVIO) = +19.6%	
1966				
May	'Great Proletarian Cultural Revolution starts			
Jun	Revised targets for 3rd Five Year Plan (1966–1970). Growth rate of agricultural and industrial gross value output (GVAIO) raised from 8.1% to 10.7% p.a.			Colleges and universities closed (not reopened for regular study until 1970)
8 Aug	11th Plenum of 8th CCPCC passes 'Sixteen Articles' – the first official document to set out the goals of the Cultural Revolution. Liu Shaoqi and Deng Xiaoping under attack for allegedly capitalist tendencies			

32

	General policy developments	Agriculture	Industry	Other
Dec		Annual growth of GVAO = +8.6%	Annual growth of GVIO = +20%	
1967				
	Red Guard activities cause severe urban economic dislocation, especially in industry and transport. Planning system breaks down			
Jul			All major iron and steel plants at a standstill or compelled to cut production	
Dec		Annual growth of GVAO = +1.6%	Urban coal stocks fall to 11 million tons – 2,5 million tons below previous lowest level (1960). Annual growth of GVIO = −13.8%	
1968				
	Continuing urban economic dislocation; planning chaos; escalating political factionalism and violence			
Summer	On Mao's orders, PLA intervenes to restore order in cities. Red Guards sent to countryside			
Dec		Annual growth of GVAO = −2.5%	Annual growth of GVIO = −5.0%	
1969				
16 Feb	National planning meeting seeks to restore orderly planning and sets out targets for 1969			
1–24 Apr	9th Party Congress brings end to radical phase of Cultural Revolution. Lin Biao formally named as Mao's successor			
				Soviet military incursions threaten Heilongjiang and Xinjiang
Dec		Annual growth of GVAO = +1.1%	Annual growth of GVIO = +34.3%	

	General policy developments	Agriculture	Industry	Other
1970				
Feb			Planned annual growth of GVIO = +17%	
15 Feb– 21 Mar	State Council National Planning Meeting discusses Outline 4th Five Year Plan (1971–1975) – sets unrealistic targets		Plan calls for steel output of 35–40 mmt by 1975	
24 Apr	China launches first earth satellite			
23 Aug– 6 Sep	Open conflict between Mao and Lin Biao at 2nd Plenum of 9th CCPCC			
25 Aug– 5 Oct		Northern Agricultural Conference endorses principles and policies of 'Sixty Articles' (1962). Emphasis on problems of grain deficit regions and use of Dazhai model with minimal incentives		
Dec	Severe macroeconomic imbalances develop	Annual growth of GVAO = +11.5%	Annual growth of GVIO = 30.7%. Centrally planned enterprises mainly handed to local governments	Mao meets Edgar Snow
1971				
Aug				Mao endorses new population policies and targets
13 Sep	Lin Biao killed, as he flees to the Soviet Union			
Nov	Vice Premier Li Xiannian reveals to an Egyptian journalist first statistical data for 13 years			Wages of lower paid workers increased
Dec	Zhou Enlai calls for discipline, re-centralisation and lower targets Reports reveal overheating in 'Mini Great Leap' of 1969–1971	Annual growth of GVAO = +3.1%	Zhou Enlai criticises anarchy in enterprises at a National Planning Conference (December 16 – February 12 (1972)). Annual growth of GVIO = +14.9%	
1972				
21–28 Feb	President Nixon visits China. Signing of *Shanghai Communiqué* signals Sino-US rapprochement			

	General policy developments	Agriculture	Industry	Other
Aug			China signs major contracts with Japan and West Germany for the Wuhan steel plants	
29 Sep	Japan and China resume diplomatic relations			
17 Oct–17 Nov		Food Grain Work Conference warns of depleted grain stocks through excessive urban consumption and neglect of grain farming		
Dec	Reaffirmation of Mao's dictum to 'dig tunnels deep, store grain everywhere, and oppose hegemony'	Annual growth of GVAO = –0.18%	Annual growth of GVIO = +6.6%	
1973				
Jan	Zhou Enlai proposes a $4.3 billion capital goods import plan over 3–5 years	Planned annual growth of GVAO = + 6.1%	Planned annual growth of GVIO = +7.7%	
Feb				Deng Xiaoping returns to Beijing from Jiangxi – his rehabilitation begins (appointed Vice-Premier [April]; Chief of Staff of PLA [December])
5–29 Aug	10th Party Congress. Lin Biao named as Mao's enemy – posthumously expelled from Party. Influence of PLA shows sharp decline			
Dec		Annual growth of GVAO = +8.4%	Annual growth of GVIO = +9.5%	
1974				
	With Mao's support, the Gang of Four launch the *Pi Lin Pi Kung* ('criticise Lin [Biao] and Confucius') movement in order to attack Zhou Enlai			
Apr	National Economic Plan seriously delayed because of political campaigns	Planned annual growth of GVAO = +4.3%	Planned annual growth of GVIO = +8.3%	Wang Hungwen and Gang of Four attack foreign imports of capital goods and exports of oil

	General policy developments	Agriculture	Industry	Other
Oct				Deng Xiaoping appointed as First Vice-Premier
Dec	Economic performance deteriorating because of political campaigns, rail strikes and industrial unrest	Annual growth of GVAO = +4.2%	Political campaigns paralyse factories. Annual growth of GVIO = +0.3%	Trade deficit of US$670 millions
1975				
Jan	Zhou Enlai presents *Government Work Report* to 4th NPC. Ambitious plan targets set for 1980 and 1985			Deng Xiaoping appointed as Vice-Chairman of CCPCC, as Zhou Enlai is hospitalised
10 Feb		Planned annual growth of GVAO = +3%	Planned annual growth of GVIO = c.14%	
Mar–Apr	Gang of Four launches attack on Zhou Enlai and Deng Xiaoping under the slogan: 'empiricism is the main enemy'			
May			Steel conference reveals chaotic situation in industry	
15 Sep–19 Oct		National Conference on Learning from Dazhai in Agriculture: Deng Xiaoping stresses agricultural modernisation as key to 'four modernisations'. Hua Guofeng endorses call for one-third of all counties to be 'Dazhai counties' by 1980		
Dec		Annual growth of GVAO = +4.6%	Annual growth of GVIO = +15.1%	
1976				
	China's 'catastrophic year'			
8 Jan	Zhou Enlai dies			
Feb	Hua Guofeng becomes Acting Premier. Jiang Qing renews attack on Zhou Enlai policy of exporting oil to buy capital goods		Gang of Four say: 'the lower profits are, the better it is'	
28 Mar	*Wenhui Bao* (Shanghai) attacks Zhou Enlai and Deng Xiaoping as 'capitalist roader[s]'			

	General policy developments	Agriculture	Industry	Other
4–5 Apr	Tiananmen Incident (Beijing): force used to disperse popular demonstrations in honour of Zhou Enlai and against Jiang Qing			
6–7 Apr	CCP Politburo holds Deng Xiaoping responsible for 'counter-revolutionary incident' in Tiananmen. Deng stripped of all Party and government posts. Hua Guofeng appointed Premier and First Vice-Chairman of CCP			
9 Sep	Mao dies			
6 Oct	Gang of Four arrested. Hua Guofeng persists with 'left' errors and 'two whatevers' [see text]			
28 Oct	Earthquake in Tangshan kills several hundred thousand people			
10–27 Dec		2nd National Conference on Learning from Dazhai in Agriculture: continuation of 'leftist' policies in agriculture		
Dec	Annual growth of GVAIO 7% – 7.5% below plan	Agriculture fails to fulfil plan. Annual growth of GVAO = +2.5%	Electricity and coal shortages and chaotic management plague industry. Industry fails top fulfil plan. Steel output 21% below plan. Annual growth of GVIO = +1.3%	
1977				
Jan	State Council calls for basic mechanisation of agriculture by 1980			
7 Feb	People's Daily endorses 'two whatevers'			
3–16 Mar	National Planning Conference discusses strategic guidelines	Planned annual growth of GVAO = +4.6%	Planned annual growth of GVIO = +8%	
May	Deng Xiaoping attacks 'two whatevers' faction as anti-Marxist. Calls for cultivation of skills and knowledge to achieve four modernisations		State Council calls for strengthened industrial planning and intensive economic research	

37

	General policy developments	Agriculture	Industry	Other
16–21 Jul	3rd Plenum of 10th CCPCC reinstates Deng Xiaoping as Vice-Chairman of CCPCC and Vice-Premier of State Council			
9 Nov			Targets for steel industry raised to 35 mmt (1980); 60–70 mmt (1985); 100 mmt (1990)	
24 Nov– 11 Dec	National Planning Conference discusses 5th and 6th Five Year Plans. Proposes massive industrial construction programme, involving 120 major projects (completion date: 1985). Calls for completion of four modernisations by 2000	National Planning Conference sets grain output targets: 335 mmt (1980); 400 mmt (1985); 650 mmt (2000)	National Planning Conference sets steel output target of 130–150 mmt by 2000	
Dec		Annual growth of GVAO = +1.7%	Annual growth of GVIO = +14.3%	
1978				
Jan	Academic journal *Economic Research* renews publication			
Feb–Mar	At 1st Session of 5th NPC Hua Guofeng persists with unrealistic targets and planning of 120 major industrial projects, to be completed by 1985. NPC passes Outline 10-Year Plan for National Economic Development (1976–85)	Reports of successful agricultural institutional reforms with strong incentives in Sichuan Province, led by Zhao Ziyang		Chinese Academy of Social Sciences re-established
May	*The People's Daily* calls for payment according to work			
12 Aug				Japan–China Peace and Friendship Treaty signed
5 Sep	State Council convenes National Planning Conference to discuss plans for 1979 and 1980. Urges utilisation of foreign capital and advanced techniques from capitalist countries	Planned annual growth of GVAO for 1979 and 1980 set at 5%–6%	Planned annual growth of GVIO for 1979 and 1980 set at 10%–12%	

	General policy developments	Agriculture	Industry	Other
16 Oct	*The People's Daily* publishes article by economist, Hu Qiaomu 'Do things according to economic laws; accelerate the four modernisations'			
10 Nov– 13 Dec	Central Work Conference lays foundation for economic reform. In his closing speech, Deng Xiaoping affirms that 'practice is the sole criterion of truth'.			Chen Yun appointed a Vice-Chairman of CCPCC
16 Dec				Resumption of Sino-US diplomatic relations announced (effective as of 1 January, 1979)
18–22 Dec	3rd Plenum of 11th CCPCC admits past errors and initiates historic process of economic reform			
Dec		Annual growth of GVAO = +9%	Annual growth of GVIO = +1.5%	
1979				
Jan	Chen Yun calls for realism and for adjustment of proportions in economic planning	Central Committee issues *Decision on Some Questions Concerning the Acceleration of Agricultural Development*: urges use of incentives to promote farm development. Revised version of 1962 'Sixty Articles' issued		Formal announcement of one-child family policy
29 Jan– 5 Feb				Deng Xiaoping visits US
Mar	Chen Yun calls for an economic system with 'the plan as mainstay and the market as subsidiary'	Prices of agricultural output raised to provide incentives	Hua Guofeng's steel target of 60 mmt (1985) abandoned	State Statistical Bureau rehabilitated. Active foreign trade adopted under the slogan 'Use exports to import'
5–28 Apr	Party Central Work Conference calls for 3-year 'readjustment' of economy in order to correct long-standing 'leftist' errors in economic work			
May		Agricultural growth target reduced from 6% to 4%	Industrial growth target reduced from 12% to 8%	

	General policy developments	Agriculture	Industry	Other
Jul			State Council issues 5 sets of regulations relating to industrial enterprises. Call for enlargement of enterprises' managerial and financial powers	Foreign Investment Joint Venture Law enacted. Special Export Zones established. Wages and Prices Conference calls for 40% wage rise and liberalisation of some prices
Aug				State Council regulations on *Some Questions on Developing Foreign Trade and Increasing Foreign Exchange Income*
Nov	Deng Xiaoping affirms that socialism can use markets and that open policies are needed to fulfil Zhou Enlai's Four Modernisations			State Council Decisions on strengthening statistical work
Dec		Annual growth of GVAO = +8.8%	Annual growth of GVIO = +8.5%	
1980				
Jan		Planned annual growth of GVAO for 1980 set at +3.8%	Planned growth of GVIO for 1980 set at +6%	
Feb	Reformer Hu Yaobang appointed Party Secretary			
Apr				Supply system for materials reformed with classification of state, industry and enterprises level powers
May	Deng Xiaoping urges Party political reform to eliminate arbitrary behaviour	Deng Xiaoping affirms need for household contracting system and reform in agriculture		
Jul				Establishment of Special Economic Zones
Aug	Zhao Ziyang replaces Hua Guofeng as Premier			
Sep		Central Committee *Communiqué on Strengthening and Perfecting Agricultural Production Responsibility Systems*	State Council regulations for system of profit retention in enterprises	

40

	General policy developments	Agriculture	Industry	Other
Dec	Party Central Work Conference: Deng Xiaoping and Chen Yun reaffirm policy of readjustment and recall 'leftist errors' of the past	Annual growth of GVAO = +3.9%	6600 State Owned Enterprises (SOEs) chosen for experimental reform. Annual growth of GVIO = +8.7%	
1981				
30 Jan		Planned annual growth of GVAO = +5.6%	Planned annual growth of GVIO = +3%	
Mar				Cancellation of Japanese plant contracts
27–29 Jun	6th Plenum of 11th CCPCC: Hua Guofeng steps down from leadership. Hu Yaobang appointed Party Chairman. Party publishes Resolution *On Some Historical Questions Concerning the Party since Liberation*. Zhao Ziyang calls for the Fifth and Sixth Five Year Plans to be realistic			
Jul				Zhao Ziyang attacks Ministry of Foreign Trade for excessive centralisation
Nov			Enterprises put into four categories according to role of plan and market in their operations	
Dec		Annual growth of GVAO = +5.7%	Annual growth of GVIO = +4.1%	
1982				
Jan	Chen Yun emphasises role of Plan as main force in economy. Overall economic growth target set at low level of 4%	Party calls for acceleration of agricultural reform to achieve modest (*xiaokang*) standard of living by 1980. Planned annual growth of GVAO = +4%	Planned annual growth of GVIO = +4%	China's Third National Census held
Feb				State Council Directive on Family Planning. New population targets adopted
Apr			Expansion of Enterprise Responsibility systems	

	General policy developments	Agriculture	Industry	Other
Jul	Deng Xiaoping also backs planning under the slogan 'the whole country is one chessboard'			
Sep	Hu Yaobang makes key speech re-affirming the reform targets for standard of living to year 2000			Deng Xiaoping meets Mrs Thatcher and tells her that Hong Kong sovereignty is not an issue for discussion
Nov		People's Communes abolished as basic unit of rural government	Regulations on Enterprise Responsibility System	
10 Dec	NPC approves 6th Five Year Plan (1981–85). Calls for 4% annual growth of GNP			
Dec		Annual growth of GVAO = +11%	Annual growth of GVIO = +7.7%	
1983				
Jan	State Planning Commission attempts to strengthen planning processes	Party announces important measures in an attempt to stabilise grain output and retain control of land use. Encouragement of specialised undertakings by farm households	Prices for coal raised in attempts to liberalise the industry, raise output and rationalise consumption	Controlled decentralisation measures for foreign trade and foreign investment announced
Apr			State Council regulations on unification of enterprise tax system	New measures to relate wages and salaries to enterprise performance
May				State Council agrees special incentives for Taiwan investors
Aug	Party pursues 'strike hard' campaign against criminal activity and economic crimes		State Planning Commission announces measures to encourage technical renovation of old enterprises	Plan with incentives for rapid increase in exports from the electrical and electronics sector
Sep				New regulations on the encouragement and use of foreign capital with 'special treatment' for Hong Kong and Taiwan investors
11–12 Oct	2nd Plenum of 12th CCPCC initiates anti-spiritual pollution campaign			

	General policy developments	Agriculture	Industry	Other
Dec		Annual growth of GVAO = +11.1%	Annual growth of GVIO = +7.7%	
1984				
24–29 Jan	Deng Xiaoping visits Shenzhen and Zhuhai Special Economic Zones and supports extension of SEZ policy	Party rules that agricultural land contracting arrangements be extended for 15 years. Calls for contraction of mandatory state purchases of farm commodities		
7–10 Feb	Deng Xiaoping inspects Xiamen SEZ and calls for acceleration of SEZ development			
Mar			Regulations to encourage establishment of township industrial enterprises	CCPCC Secretariat and State Council decision to open 14 coastal cities
May	New era of domestic reform leads to Socialist Planned Commodity Economy		Key new regulations on increasing the self governing and decision making authority of large SOEs	CCPCC measures to stimulate the 14 coastal cities by granting limited rights to accept foreign capital
Jun	Deng Xiaoping announces 'one country, two systems' solution for Hong Kong. Deng also puts forward a new theory of socialism			
Sep	Zhao Ziyang discusses the 7th and 8th Five Year Plans. Stresses need to improve old enterprises; to further develop consumer goods industries; and to rely on foreign capital for the long term		Regulations to implement a reformed uniform tax system for enterprises	China and UK initial agreement on question of Hong Kong
Oct	3rd Plenum of 12th Party Congress passes *Decision of Economic System Reform*. Endorses 'socialist planned commodity economy', further reducing role of compulsory and central plan targets, enlarging that of local planners and enterprises – but keeping public ownership as fundamental			Further measures to encourage foreign capital in the seaboard cities and increase exports of light industry and textile goods
Nov	Zhao Ziyang encourages further efforts to stimulate the open door and develop the 14 coastal cities			

	General policy developments	Agriculture	Industry	Other
Dec	Su Shaozhi stimulates the 'Is Marxism dead?' debate	Annual growth of GVAO = +14.5%	Annual growth of GVIO = +14%	
1985				
Jan	Deng Xiaoping's New Year Message offers guarantee that public ownership will remain in basic industries	CCPCC and State Council publish *Ten Policies for the Further Invigoration of the Rural Economy*. Major reforms of agricultural purchasing system to replace state compulsory purchase with voluntary contracts. Introduction of proportionate pricing. 1985 planned agricultural growth = 6%	State Council promulgates *Decision on Wage Reform in State-Owned Enterprises*. 1985 planned industrial growth = 8%	At National Science and Technology Conference, Deng Xiaoping urges reform of centralised state-supported systems of research and development to serve industry
27 Mar	At 3rd session of 6th NPC, Zhao Ziyang's *Government Work Report* expresses concern about problems of stability, and price and wage increases			
28 Mar	Deng Xiaoping tells Japanese legislators that 'reform is China's second revolution'			
Apr	Deng Xiaoping affirms that reforms will enable targets for year 2000 of US$800 to US$1000 income per head to be met			
Sep	National Party Congress adopts Draft 7th Five Year Plan			Anti-Japanese demonstrations in Beijing
Dec	6th Five Year Plan completed	Annual growth of GVAO = +13%	Annual growth of GVIO = +18%	
1986				
Jan	China launches communications satellite	CCPCC and State Council publish *Strategic Plan for Rural Work in 1986*		New regulations to make Joint Ventures more attractive
Feb	6th Five Year Plan results: average growth of national income = 9.7% p.a. (GVAO = 11.5% p.a; GVIO = +10.8% p.a.)			
23 Mar–12 Apr	4th session of 6th NPC approves draft 7th Five Year Plan: GNP to grow by 7.5% p.a. (agriculture, 6%; industry, 7%)			NPC adopts *Law on Wholly Foreign Owned Enterprises*

	General policy developments	Agriculture	Industry	Other
Jul				Regulations to allow enterprises to hire labour through contracts
Nov				The '863' Programme for high technology research started
Dec		Annual growth of GVAO = +3.5%	Further reform of contracting and management in large and medium sized State Owned Enterprises. CCPCC discusses revised Bankruptcy Law. Annual growth of GVIO = +11.1%	
1987				
Jan	In wake of student protest movement and unfolding of campaign against 'bourgeois liberalisation', Hu Yaobang resigns as Party General Secretary. Premier Zhao Ziyang becomes Acting General Secretary			
Feb	Deng Xiaoping announces that planning is no longer to be the main force in he economy			
Mar		Zhao Ziyang's *Government Work Report* reaffirms central role of agriculture – especially grain – in national economic development		
25 Oct– 1 Nov	At 13th National Party Congress Zhao Ziyang makes major speech on theory of socialism and proposes political reform designed to create a 'socialist political system with a high degree of democracy'. He advocates a 'planned commodity economy based on public ownership' under which planning should accommodate the Law of Value; indicative planning to dominate, with a diminishing role for mandatory planning		Endorsement of key policy slogan: 'let the government regulate the market; let the market guide the enterprises'	
Dec		Annual growth of GVAO = + 4.7%	Annual growth of GVIO = +16.5%	

China's Economic Reform Strategy: Historical Overview

	General policy developments	Agriculture	Industry	Other
1988				
Mar	Acting Premier Li Peng delivers *Government Work Report*: expresses concern about rising inflation			Further enlargement of numbers of seaboard cities to include Shenyang, Nanjing and Hangzhou
Apr				Hainan elevated to provincial status; Hainan Special Economic Zone established
May	Party journal *Red Flag* abolished			
6 Jul				State Council promulgates *Provisions for Encouraging Investment from Taiwan*
Sep	3rd Plenum of 13th CCPCC: Zhao Ziyang announces wage and price reform programme. Refers to efforts to curb inflation and contain demand pressures			Deng Xiaoping announces new push for science and technology as the 'primary productive force'. China launches Feng Yun weather satellite
Nov–Dec	Zhao Ziyang presses for the coastal development strategy. Annual inflation at record high of 18.5%	Annual growth of GVAO = +4%	Annual growth of GVIO = +20.8%	
1989				
Jan	Zhao Ziyang's New Year Message warns against undermining effects of inflation, but reaffirms reform and opening			
15 Apr	Hu Yaobang dies. Pro-Hu democracy movement begins			
May	Pro-democracy and anti-corruption demonstrations begin in Tiananmen. In Beijing, Martial Law imposed	Shortage of funds threatens fulfilment of purchase quotas for summer crops. Farmers receive IOUs instead of cash		Mikhail Gorbachev visits China for talks with Chinese leadership
Jun	Crushing of Democracy Movement Zhao Ziyang purged for 'anti-Party, anti-Socialist activity'. Jiang Zemin appointed General Party Secretary			

	General policy developments	Agriculture	Industry	Other
Sep	Jiang Zemin describes earlier 'turmoil' as evidence of struggle between 'four cardinal principles' and 'bourgeois liberalisation'			
6–9 Nov	At 5th Plenum of 13th CCPCC Jiang Zemin appointed Chairman of the Party Central Military Affairs Commission following retirement of Deng Xiaoping			
	Annual inflation at 17.8%	Annual growth of GVAO = +3.3%	Annual growth of GVIO = +8.3%	
1990				
11 Jan	Martial Law lifted in Beijing			
9–12 Mar	6th Plenum of 13th CCPCC adopts *Decision on Strengthening Relations between Party and Masses*			
20 Mar– 4 Apr	Li Peng's *Government Work Report* reaffirms programme of economic retrenchment ('improving the economic environment and rectifying the economic order')			
1 Jul				4th national census reveals population of 1,136.8 million
Oct	Premier Li Peng criticises Deng Xiaoping and reform policies			
Dec	Annual inflation falls to 2.7%. Party approves 8th Five Year Plan (1991–1995): target growth = 11.6% p.a.; also endorses 10 Year Development Plan (1991–2000)	Annual growth of GVAO = +6.9%	Annual growth of GVIO = +7.6%	
1991				
Jan	Gulf War heightens awareness in China of the significance of advanced technology			
Mar	Li Peng denies stagnation of reform in wake of retrenchment measures			State Council approves expansion of High Technology Districts

	General policy developments	Agriculture	Industry	Other
May				Jiang Zemin calls for intensified efforts in high technology
Jun				State Council reforms social security system to remove burdens from enterprises
Jul	Reprinting of *Selected Works of Mao Zedong* seen as event of 'major political significance'. Jiang Zemin makes strongly neo-Maoist speech			
May–Jul		Flooding in central-eastern China causes heavy damage		
Oct	Party theorist and anti-reformer Deng Liqun emphasises class struggle against liberalism			
25–29 Nov		8th Plenum of 13th CCPCC adopts *Decision on Further Strengthening Agricultural and Rural Work*. Calls for better rural living standards, accelerated rural reform and farm mechanisation. Reaffirms household-based contractual responsibility systems. Calls for 'socialised service system' for peasants. Sets target of 500 mmt of grain by 2000		
Dec	Annual inflation rate = 2.9%	Annual growth of GVAO = +3%	Annual growth of GVIO = +14.2%	
1992				
18 Jan– 22 Feb	Deng Xiaoping undertakes 'Southern journey' and affirms that reform and opening policies must last for 100 years and that the market is not a capitalist institution. Premier Li Peng joins the reform camp			
Mar	CCPCC Politburo meeting discusses reform and development – upholds Deng Xiaoping. At 5th Session of 7th NPC, Li Peng announces end of retrenchment and calls for accelerated development			

	General policy developments	Agriculture	Industry	Other
May	Jiang Zemin joins the reform camp			
Jun				Party decides to speed up the development of services sector
Jul			State Council regulations for transformation of management structures in SOEs	
Jun–Jul				Sixteen further cities opened to outside
24 Aug				China and South Korea establish diplomatic relations
25 Sep		State Council decision on agricultural modernisation and development proposes further farm marketisation, including grain price deregulation		
Oct	14th Party Congress affirms the new 'socialist market economy'. Jiang Zemin endorses Deng's call for intensified reform. Jiang later confirmed as Party General Secretary			
Dec	Annual inflation rate = 5.4%	Annual growth of GVAO = +6.4%	Annual growth of GVIO = +27.5%	
1993				
Mar	1st Session of 8th NPC elects Jiang Zemin as national President. Li Peng reveals State Council upward adjustment of planned growth from 6% to 8–9% p.a. under 8th Five Year Plan			
Jun	Vice-Premier Zhu Rongji introduces 16-point programme to control inflation			
Aug	Jiang Zemin urges the Party to support economic development and attack rising corruption			

	General policy developments	Agriculture	Industry	Other
Oct				Tumen River Development Project meets in Beijing with participation of Mongolia, North Korea, South Korea and Russia
11–14 Nov	3rd Plenum of 14th CCPCC affirms that resources are to be allocated by market under state macroeconomic control and that state enterprises will be converted to modern corporations with clarification of property rights	Collective land ownership to remain, but land contracts under rural responsibility systems extended to 30 years	Regulations for modernisation of SOE management systems	Emphasis on role of science and technology in promoting socialist market economy
Dec	Major reform of the banking system with new independent Central Bank role for People's Bank Annual inflation rises to 13%	Annual growth of GVAO = +7.8%	Annual growth of GVIO = +28%	Annual growth in utilised FDI = 145.9%
1994				
Jan				Abolition of dual foreign exchange rate. Major tariff reduction on imports to liberalise trade
Feb	Jiang Zemin warns that 'corruption is corroding our Party, government and cadre rank'			State Council sets new poverty reduction target for 2000 – elimination of poverty for 80 millions
Jun				Reform of the education system
25–28 Sep	4th Plenum of 14th CCPCC calls for strengthening of Party building. Stresses Deng Xiaoping's theory of 'building socialism with Chinese characteristics'			
Dec	Under impact of wage hikes, rising food prices and money expansion, annual inflation rises to 21.7% (cf. planned figure of 10% or less)	Annual growth of GVAO = + 0.6%	Annual growth if GVIO = +26.1%	
1995				
Jan	Jiang Zemin makes 8-point proposal on cross-Strait relations			Foreign Exchange Certificates cease circulation

	General policy developments	Agriculture	Industry	Other
15 Feb				Total population reaches 1.2 billion – 5 years earlier than planned
5–18 Mar	3rd Session of 8th NPC: Li Peng sets 1995 retail price inflation target of 15% or less		Li Peng stresses integration of SOE reform and improvements in social security system	
Apr	Chen Xitong scandal involving corruption in Beijing erupts			
25–28 Sep	5th Plenum of 14th CCPCC discusses proposals for 9th Five Year Plan (1996–2000) and targets for 2010		Jiang Zemin urges reform of SOEs	
Nov				Completion of new Beijing–Guangzhou railway of 2235 kilometres
Dec	Annual inflation = 14.8%	Annual growth of GVAO = +10.9%	Annual growth of GVIO = +20.3%	
1996				
Mar	4th Session of 8th NPC approves 9th Five Year Plan and 10 Year Development Programme. Year 2000 targets fulfilled 5 years ahead of schedule			
Apr	Party Directives to strengthen drive against criminal elements			
May			Jiang Zemin pushes for reform of SOEs in East China	
Jul	Article by Jiang Zemin in *Seeking Truth* upholds central task of economic construction, but warns against neglect of politics and stresses Party supremacy			With reduced inflationary pressures in first half of 1996, Chinese sources claim achievement of 'soft landing' of economy
7–10 Oct	7th Plenum of 14th CCPCC notes widespread neglect of ideological education and spiritual civilisation; rejects 'Westernisation'			
21–24 Nov	Economic Work Conference affirms inflation control as main task for the next three years			

China's Economic Reform Strategy: Historical Overview

	General policy developments	Agriculture	Industry	Other
Dec	Annual inflation = 6.1%	Annual growth of GVAO = +9.4%	Annual growth of GVIO = +16.6%	
1997				
19 Feb	Deng Xiaoping dies			
Mar	5th Session of 8th NPC: Li Peng's *Government Work Report* affirms reform of State Owned Enterprises as top priority.			Foreign exchange reserves reach US$100 billion
30 Jun	Reversion of Hong Kong to China at midnight			
Sep	15th Party Congress enshrines Deng's 'theory of building socialism with Chinese characteristics. Jiang Zemin ranks Deng's theoretical contribution alongside that of Mao. Three year financial reform and privatisation policy called for		Jiang calls for accelerated enterprise reform and establishment of modern enterprise system within 3 years. Major SOEs to be transformed into joint-stock entities with modern corporate governance	
Oct	Jiang Zemin visits the United States			
Nov		Severe flooding devastates central China		Financial Work Conference sets 3 year target for reform of financial system
Dec		Annual growth of GVAO = +5.1%	Annual growth of GVIO = +13.1%	Foreign exchange reserves total US$140 billion
1998				
Jan	Anti-corruption conference convened in Beijing		Economist Dong Fureng pushes for a wider conception of state ownership	
Mar	1st Session of 9th NPC endorses State Council proposal for major institutional re-structuring of government, including retirement of many officials. Zhu Rongji appointed Premier. Sets economic targets: growth no less than 8%; inflation no more than 3%; no devaluation of *yuan*			White Paper on technology seeks foreign investment in China's technology drive
May–Jun			Textile industry adopts new strategy of reducing capacity	Measures introduced to support livelihood of workers and staff dismissed from enterprises

	General policy developments	Agriculture	Industry	Other
Jun–Aug		Massive floods from Yangzi, Songhua and other rivers cause huge economic losses, estimated at 0.5% of GDP. Southern and north-eastern China worst hit		
12–14 Oct		3 Plenum of 15 CCPCC adopts *Decision on Several Major Issues in Agriculture and Rural Work*. Endorses decision to extend land contracts for further 30 years. More emphasis on two-tier operational system for farming, integrating individual and collective activities. Emphasis on need for reform of grain circulation system		
Dec	Party and State Council Economic Work Conference affirms need to continue with reforms in line with the thought of Deng Xiaoping. Admission that Asian financial crisis and domestic flooding have made 1998 a 'grim and complicated' year. GDP growth (7.8%) falls below planned figure (8%). Conference to celebrate 20 years of reform since 3 Plenum of 11 CCPCC attended by 6000	Annual growth of GVAO = +6%. Grain output at record level of 512.3 mmt	Annual growth of GVIO = +10.8%	Under impact of Asian financial crisis, foreign trade growth falls from 15.3% to 0.3%
1999				
11 and 15 Jan	Jiang Zemin makes important speeches on need for Party and political discipline			
Mar	At 2nd Session of 9th NPC Zhu Rongji's *Government Work Report* stresses need for fiscal stimulation and maintained value of *yuan*			NPC endorses constitutional change to establish status of private and non state sector enterprises
Apr	Hu Jintao makes important speech on maintaining discipline through study of Jiang's 'three stresses'			

	General policy developments	Agriculture	Industry	Other
Jun	Jiang Zemin makes important speech on importance of theoretical study			High profile National Poverty Relief Conference sets new anti-poverty targets and policies
Sep	Hu Jintao promoted as Vice-Chairman of Central Military Commission. Speculation on his role as likely successor to Jiang Zemin		4th Session of 15th CCPCC adopts *Decision on Some Major Issues Concerning the Reform and Development of SOEs*	
Nov	Central economic work conference sets key priorities: to stimulate the economy, and to reform SOEs. NPC bans 'cults'		Plans to transform SOEs with debt for equity swops	Bilateral agreement with US (15 November) prepares way for WTO accession
Dec		Annual growth of GVAO = +4.7%	Annual growth of GVIO = +10.5%	
2000				
Jan	State Development and Planning Commission targets expansion of internal demand as key to growth. State Council Poverty Action Group plan to remove 10 million from poverty in current year			National Environmental Protection Conference in session
Feb	Important newspaper editorials comment on China's right and responsibility to join WTO	Central Party Work Conference reports reduction in the cultivated area of 400,000 hectares in 1999	Zhu Rongji orders tightening of Party leadership and control inside enterprises	
Mar	At 3rd Session of 9th NPC, Zhu Rongji's *Government Work Report* places special emphasis on developing the West of China and improving infrastructure, environment and human resources in these regions			State Council raises 7 major cities including Hefei, Kunming, Chengdu, and Changsha to status of Economic and Technological Development Zones
May	US formally approves trade normalisation with China			Bilateral agreement with EU on WTO accession
Oct	The 5th Plenum of the 15th Central Committee approves an outline of the 10th Five Year Plan and target for 2001–2010. These envisage a growth rate of 7.5% per annum		The 5th Plenum endorses proposals to modernise the enterprise system	

	General policy developments	Agriculture	Industry	Other
Nov				China's 5th National Census day. Preliminary data reveal of total population of 1.295 billion
2001				
Dec	China and Taiwan formally enter WTO			

2

China's Economic Reform Strategy

Document 2.1

'The lessons of history'

Extract from *The National Economy during the Cultural Revolution (1966-76)*, Heilongjiang People's Publishing House, 1986.

LIU SUINIAN AND LIU QUNGAN

The Cultural Revolution brought ruin upon our Party, nation, and every racial group living in China and this has taught us a number of important lessons. The Cultural Revolution repeated the mistakes of the 'Great Leap Forward', namely, promoting an excessively leftist ideology and demanding quick results. In addition, we also have a series of lessons to learn from this period concerning work on the economy.

1. Normal economic development is impossible without political stability and unity

Politics must always adapt to the economy and serve the economic base. Proletarian politics serves the socialist economy by both safeguarding the socialist nature of the economy and guaranteeing stability and unity. It therefore promotes the normal development of the economy. After socialist transformation has basically been achieved and the revolutionary period of large-scale class struggle has come to an end, the essential task of proletarian politics is to energise all the direct and indirect positive factors under the new relations of production and to protect and develop the forces of production. Thus, the focal work of the Party and nation should shift towards socialist construction centred on economic construction. However, the 'Cultural Revolution' upheld the ideology of 'class-struggle as a guiding principle' and waged an 'all-out civil war' on those allegedly attempting to 'seize power by following the capitalist road'. This plunged the whole country into chaos. The counter-revolutionary clique of Lin Biao and the 'Gang of Four' propagated the notion that 'politics overcomes everything' and criticised the so-called 'theory of the unique importance of the productive forces'. The idea that Party officials and the masses should actively develop the socialist forces of production was branded as 'pulling the cart without looking at the road'. The consequence of this was that the economy fell under the influence of ten years of political chaos, ultimately leading to economic stagnation and collapse. This not only wiped out all of the hard-won economic gains achieved through re-adjustment, it also plunged the entire national economy into grave jeopardy.

Our experiences during the 'Cultural Revolution' have taught us that normal economic development is impossible without political stability and unity. After socialist transformation has basically been achieved, the main contradiction is between the growing material and cultural needs of the people and the under-development of our forces of production. The basic task of proletarian politics is therefore to develop the economy. Of course, the tasks of the socialist revolution have still not been completely accomplished and, within certain limits, the development of class struggle is still necessary to safeguard and develop the forces of production. However, if undue emphasis is placed on class struggle and the notion of class struggle within certain limits is stretched to mean widespread class opposition, then the advocacy of any proposal becomes a so-called great political revolution which 'takes class struggle as its guiding principle' and may even promote the notion of 'one class subverting another class'. If this kind of situation is allowed to develop it will both impede the promotion of social progress and cause untold damage to economic development. The only function of 'total anarchy' is to throw a nation into chaos, and if 'politics overcomes everything', its primary target will be the social forces of production and the economic base. Internal political stability and unity is the basic condition for economic development. The focal work of the Party and nation must shift unswervingly towards socialist modernisation centred on economic construction in order to promote the long-term and stable development of the forces of production. We must make major efforts to eliminate any factors which may have a negative impact on stability and unity, and thoroughly expunge the mistakes of 'the Left'. We need to lead the whole nation towards an enthusiastic engagement with the development of production and strive to realise the Four Modernisations.

2. Mistakes in ideology inevitably lead to errors in economic policy

The promotion of socialist construction must be guided by Marxist, Leninist and Mao Zedong thought. The importance of theory is expressed in the words of Lenin himself: 'Without revolutionary theory there can be no revolutionary movement.' However, the universal truths of Marxist-Leninism must be combined with concrete experience and practice in the country concerned. Accurate theory is an encapsulation of revolutionary experience and should undergo testing and development within guiding practice. If we ignore China's specific circumstances and pursue a scientific theory as a matter of doctrine, or allow practice to be guided by distorted 'theory', then this may hold back, restrict or even damage economic development. This was what happened during the ten years of chaos. At that time, right and wrong became twisted in many important aspects of economic theory. For example, mistakes were made concerning the 'bourgeois rights and interests' that Marx proposed in his 'Critique of the Gotha Programme'. The 'bourgeois rights and interests' [concepts] embodied in the principle of equal exchange for equal work under a system of distribution according to work was mistakenly interpreted to mean that a system of distribution according to work itself brings rights of a bourgeois nature. The 'bourgeois rights and interests' that exist within the allocation of consumer goods was mistakenly taken to mean that 'bourgeois rights and interests' exist within almost all economic and social relations. The principle that a Communist society should negate the 'bourgeois rights and interests' manifested in a system of allocation according to work was misinterpreted to mean that this kind of system is improper and should be abolished by a socialist society. Another example [of distortion] is the mechanical adoption of Lenin's theory that: 'Small production steadily and continually produces large-scale capitalism and a bourgeoisie'. This theory was proposed by Lenin not long after his victory in the October Revolution of 1920 when the political power of the workers and peasants that formed the proletarian leadership was very fragile, the small peasant economy had not yet been transformed, and rich peasants were engaged in wild speculation. The principle was then taken and applied to China which had long since accomplished its basic socialist transformation and had reached the stage of socialist construction. The rural economic policies that were drawn up on the basis of these flawed theories inevitably became increasingly 'Leftist' in character and increasingly out of touch with China's real situation. The counter-revolutionary clique formed by Lin Biao and the 'Gang of Four' pushed these flawed theories even further towards the edge. They branded as 'revisionism' the idea that China should maintain its socialist system of ownership, its system of distribution and its person-to-person relations. They brought down those Party officials who kept to the socialist road by labelling them 'Capitalist roaders'. The consequences of this were that within the ten year period, the individual economy was destroyed, the collective economy was stifled, commodity exchange was restricted and many forms of business were choked to death. State Owned Enterprises engaged in production with no regard for costs or losses leading to a large-scale squandering of public wealth. A system of distribution was established based on the principle of egalitarianism. This meant it made no difference whether you worked hard or not since everyone could eat from the same 'big rice bowl' provided by the state. All of this did great damage to our socialist economic system and destroyed incentives for our working population.

Our experience during the 'Cultural Revolution' has taught us once again that we must always be sure that our guiding theories are accurate. We must proceed according to China's concrete situation and use practice as the sole criterion for testing the truth. China's economy is relatively under-developed and the level of our productive forces is low. We must allow the long-term coexistence of various kinds of economic activities and economic forms as long as the socialist system of public ownership has absolute superiority. At the Sixth Plenary Session of the Eighth Party Congress, the CCP Central Committee stated: 'The continued development of commodity production and the maintenance of the principle of distribution according to work are two important principles for the development of a socialist economy'. Therefore, in constructing socialism with Chinese characteristics, we must put into practice the guiding philosophy of seeking truth from facts, uphold the socialist principle of distribution according to work, and adopt a variety of specific methods of distribution according to work. At the same time, we must devote major efforts to developing commodity production as well as a variety of different economic forms and channels of circulation. Under the unified leadership of state planning, we must make flexible use of prices, taxes, interest rates and other economic levers and fully utilise the regulatory functions of commodities, currency and markets. We need to stimulate the domestic market, strengthen enterprises' business accounting, and promote the development of a socialist economy.

3. We must make an accurate appraisal of the international situation and should not be too hasty in attempting to change the distribution of our productive forces

The extent to which the regional distribution of our productive forces is rational has an important bearing on economic development, national security and defence. The distribution of China's forces of production is extremely unbalanced due to historical factors. Modern industry is for the most part concentrated in the Eastern and Coastal regions. While the interior has plentiful resources and vast tracts of land, its economy is relatively under-developed. Imperialism and hegemony form the seeds of war mean that we must ensure that we never drop our guard. In order to develop the abundant resources of China's interior, promote the overall implementation of socialist economic construction and prevent encroachment by foreign powers, we must devote our attention and efforts to the strengthening of industrial construction in the interior, gradually begin to change the irrational regional distribution of our productive forces, and begin to systematically establish a firm strategic rear.

In his speech on the 'Ten Great Relationships', Mao Zedong wrote an accurate account of the relationship between coastal industry and inland industry and the relationship between economic construction and defence construction. However, the international situation in the mid-1960s, and particularly during the early 1970s, led us to over-estimate the risks of war and we therefore placed undue emphasis on preparing for war. We became highly impatient and demanded an acceleration of inland construction. The problems at that time were as follows:

1. We placed great emphasis on strengthening inland construction without giving adequate consideration to developing the coastal economy.
2. We put undue emphasis on building a self-contained economic system in the inland provinces without paying much attention to exploiting each region's own natural advantages.
3. Within inland construction we over-emphasised the importance of defence industries and related heavy industry at the expense of other essentials such as light industry, agricultural and sideline industries, education and health, workers' housing etc.
4. Many construction projects incurred huge losses and waste due to flawed and erroneous planning based on 'local self-sufficiency and decentralisation' and an obsession with 'border surveys, border plans and border construction'.

The results of this were that vast quantities of labour power as well as material and financial resources were directed towards inland construction over the ten year period. Although this led to the constuction of a number of key, backbone enterprises, the economic returns on these ventures were very low. This exacerbated the proportionate imbalance in the national economy and has left us with a number of serious problems. This was a lesson that we learnt at a very high price from economic construction during the Third and Fourth Five Year Plans.

Practical experience shows that we should make a realistic appraisal of the international situation and the threat of war. While we must continue to keep a watchful guard, we must also recognise that the unified struggle of everyone in the world can help to counter and even prevent encroachment by foreign aggressors. We should positively strive to build a peaceful international environment in addition to emphasising the threat of war. At the same time, we must acknowledge the complexities and difficulties involved in changing our regional distribution [of the economy]. We must recognise that our inland regions have a poor economic base and inconvenient transportation links. Conditions for construction and returns on investment are therefore going to be poorer than in our coastal regions. This means that the whole scale transformation of our regional distribution cannot be achieved in the short-term. At the same time as striving to strengthen inland construction, we must also exploit the beneficial conditions for economic development in our coastal regions and give due consideration to the natural advantages that each inland province has to offer. We need to reinforce the links and improve co-operation between relevant regions and industries, integrate our military and civilian industries, work hard to achieve an aggregate balance, and proceed in a step-by-step fashion. Only then will we be able to gradually change China's irrational regional distribution.

4. Scientific systems of management and strict labour discipline are indispensable for large-scale modernised production

The basic features of large-scale modernised production are the widespread use of machinery based on modern science and technology, careful division of labour and close co-operation. In line with these features, we need to create a full set of high-quality, scientific management systems for every sector of the national economy – particularly within enterprises. We must also rely on strict labour discipline to guarantee their implementation and realisation. If this is not achieved, it will be impossible for us to proceed smoothly with large-scale socialised production and our economic activities will inevitably spiral towards anarchy and chaos. We should heed the words of Engels written just after his detailed analysis of large-scale modernised production in his *On Authority*. On the one side there is a certain authority, regardless of how it came into being. On the other side there is a certain subordination. No matter what form social organisation takes, both of these aspects are essential given the material conditions on which the advancement of production and distribution depend.'

The history of the development of large-scale, modernised production in China is comparatively short and the systems of management, rules and regulations and methods that have already been set up are far from perfect. They are beset with a number of flaws and defects and it is important to continue strengthening them and improving them. Nevertheless, these systems did help to promote the regular construction of enterprises and the creation of a socialist economy after 1949. During the ten years of chaos, every economic management system, almost without exception, was attacked and destroyed. Many indispensable systems of regulation were labelled 'material incentives', 'profit-led', 'a dictatorship of convention' etc. and were branded 'the black products of revisionism'. The ideology of the time that 'revolt is justified' created an atmosphere of widespread anarchy. Under these conditions, the existing laws and regulations could be flagrantly flouted and the management of the economy was plunged into extreme chaos for a long period of time. The rhythm of production was disrupted, loopholes appeared at all levels of management, and discipline became slacker and slacker. The outcome was that a number of businesses could not continue with normal production, product quality fell, accidents at work increased, and economic returns were extremely low.

Practical experience shows that management plays an especially important role in large-scale modernised production. It would be impossible to realise the modernisation of the national economy without advanced technology and modern equipment together with the necessary scientific and technical personnel to operate them. In the same way, it would be impossible to achievement our managerial targets without creating advanced systems of management and employing the necessary administrative personnel. In a certain sense, management is also a productive force. Just like equipment, technology and the labour force, the quality of management can have a huge impact on production returns. This means that in its economic development, China should place the utmost importance on studying, and emulating where appropriate, the scientific systems of management that operate in advanced countries as well as attempting to expand production capacity and promote the progress of science and technology. We must improve our management systems and methods, train people to be effective managers, bring about the modernisation of management and look to management for accelerated progress and beneficial results.

5. The training of scientific and technical personnel is a strategic task that has an important bearing on the future of socialist modernisation and construction.

Science and technology plays a key role in China's modernisation and construction. As Zhou Enlai said: It is only by using the most advanced science that we will be able to build a strong national defence and become a strong, advanced economic power. The development of science and technology depends on people. The number and quality of those in the labour force that have a good grasp of science and technology is an important criterion for measuring a country's economic development. The task of training scientists and technicians and putting them to work plays a decisive role not only in terms of present levels of construction but also with regard to long-term economic development. During the ten years of chaos, intellectuals were universally branded 'the stinking ninth category' and suffered discrimination and oppression. Many scientists and university professors were branded 'academic reactionaries' and underwent severe criticism and attack. Scientific and technological development suffered severe disruption and many sectors which since 1949 had been struggling hard to reach advanced international standards, began to fall behind once again. The ten years of catastrophe wreaked havoc on education in particular. The policy of stopping classes in order to 'create revolution' led to a de facto curtailment of teaching activities and a number of institutions of higher education were turned into battlegrounds. The 'two basic appraisals'[1] that determined the line on education and the 'Leftist' policies that were drawn up according to them made it extremely difficult to proceed with normal personnel training. It was not until 1982 that students began once again to graduate from tertiary institutions having undergone a relatively conventional course of instruction. Thus the intervening period stretched for as long as 15 years. The result was that around 1 million

1 In 1971, the National Conference on Educational Work was dominated by the 'Gang of Four' and put forward the following argument: 'In the 17 years after liberation, the proletarian line on education was not implemented fully and the bourgeoisie seized power from the proletariat. The world-view of the majority of teachers is fundamentally bourgeois.' This critique was later abbreviated to the 'two basic appraisals'.

university students and 2 million polytechnic students that should have been trained received no training whatsoever and this has caused a serious imbalance within scientific and technical education and economic development. Moreover, a void stretching for over ten years has appeared in the composition of our scientific and technical work force. In whichever economic managerial sector you care to choose (in either scientific or commercial enterprises) there is a clear shortage of administrative and technical personnel between the ages of 30 and 40. This poses serious problems of succession in our skilled work force. This shortage is even more serious than a shortage in material production and is far more difficult to compensate for. The hard lessons that we learnt during the 'Cultural Revolution' have taught us us that the training of skilled personnel is a strategic task. When deciding on a strategy for economic development, we must give high priority to fostering talented workers. While focusing on the development of our material resources, we must also give full consideration to developing skills and intelligence. As a consequence of the ten years of chaos, the quantity and quality of skilled workers in many different professions and sectors are far from adequate to meet our needs for economic construction. We need to make use of various different methods and channels to rapidly build a skilled work force for economic construction. These methods should include the re-training of those who have already qualified as scientists and technicians as well as making bold decisions to employ young scientists and technicians. In this way, we should be able to recoup, at least in part, some of the losses that we incurred and sow the seeds for China's future economic prosperity.

6. Controlling population growth in a planned and systematic way is a matter of basic national policy and there is no room for complacency

Men and women are producers and represent the primary ingredients for our social forces of production. Population growth can help us organise a vast and powerful working army that will intensify and expand production. It can also promote economic development by creating an enlarged domestic market for the consumption of various kinds of products and commodities. However, a person is a consumer of daily necessities from the day he or she is born until the day he or she dies. Before the age of maturity and after the age of retirement, the individual is a pure consumer who makes no contribution whatsoever to social wealth. If population is allowed to grow too fast, an excessively large proportion of annual national income growth will be wasted on meeting the needs of the 'new' members of the increased population. This will both limit the growth of accumulation and have a negative impact on raising the consumption levels of the population as a whole. It is also likely to put severe pressure on the development of facilities for employment, education and health as well as the construction of housing, communications and other urban public utilities. An even more serious problem is that population reproduction is unlike the production of material goods where any disequilibrium resulting from overheated production can be promptly and actively controlled through various different regulatory mechanisms. If population is allowed to grow without restraint, the consequences will have to be borne by the whole of society. This means that whatever angle you care to take, population development is in greater need of planned and systematic control than economic development.

China is the most populous nation in the world and its vast population is one of its basic national characteristics. However, for a relatively long period of time, we did not pay much attention to this factor and the way in which it constrained economic development. We finally began to confront the problem in the 1960s and great emphasis was placed on family planning work. However, virtually no one took an interest in this matter during the ten years of chaos due to the structural paralysis that reigned at all levels of administration and the rising wave of anarchy. And even when people did start to deal with the issue again later on, it was very difficult to put any concrete measures into practice. The outcome was that population was allowed to spiral out of control at the same time as material production was being attacked and destroyed, and over the ten year period, population grew by almost 200 million people. Moreover, because the population index has grown by such a large extent, the absolute increase in population remains extremely large no matter how hard an attempt is made to control the birth rate. The level of development of China's productive forces has always been relatively low and this limits the amount to which national income can be increased every year. Thus, this blind rise in population means that after funds from the new increase in national income have been used to satisfy the consumption needs of the new increase in population, the amount of money that can be devoted to the pursuit of construction is extremely low. It has therefore become even more difficult to raise the standard of living for the population as a whole and this has inevitably had an impact on economic development. If we do not deal properly with the problem of employment, it is likely to become a serious social issue. Therefore we must always bear in mind the harsh lessons that we have had to learn concerning population control. From now on, whatever the circumstances may be, we must always remember that China's vast population is one of its basic national characteristics. The extent to which we are able to control population effectively will play a large part in determining our rate of economic development and improvements to our standard of living. We must make the adoption of tough measures, the implementation of family planning and the strict control of the population a matter of basic national policy and maintain this stance well into the long term.

7. It is only by maintaining a policy of openness and liberalisation that we will be able to accelerate our socialist modernisation and construction

Our basic political strategy is to rely on our own strength to develop socialist construction. However, China's socialist development is not, and cannot be, independent from the rest of the world. International exchange is a constant and necessary condition for economic construction. Since a basic feature of large-scale modernised production is the expansion of exchange, it is not enough for us to merely expand our domestic market, we must also expand outwards from domestic exchange towards international exchange. We need to build links with the international market, expand foreign trade, attract advanced technology, utilize foreign capital, and develop various channels of international economic and technical co-operation. Within all these spheres, it is important to exploit our own advantages and employ the principle of equal exchange to make up our deficiencies. This should not be seen as an obstacle to our national independence. On the contrary it will boost our own capacity for self-strengthening and self-renewal and advance the progress of the Four Modernisations. During the 'Cultural Revolution', the efforts of Mao Zedong and Zhou Enlai helped to build bridges between China and capitalist countries of the West, and economic exchange grew between China and the USA and China and Japan. The exploitation of various beneficial forms of foreign exchange played an important role in attracting advanced facilities and equipment to China and this has helped to promote our economic construction. However, during the ten years of chaos, the 'Gang of Four' branded learning from Western practice and the attraction of Western technology as 'worshipping all things foreign'. They picked on the 'snail incident' and the 'boat-buying incident' to attack the State Council for promoting 'national betrayal' and 'fawning and obsequious behaviour'. This placed huge obstacles in the path of continued international economic exchange. China cut itself off from the increasingly active and dynamic international economy and thereby squandered a precious opportunity for developing its own domestic economy. This greatly delayed the advance of the Four Modernisations.

Our practical experience shows that in order to promote socialist construction, we must stand on the side of self-strengthening and renewal and resolutely oppose the infiltration of corrupting ideas from abroad. However, as far as our economic work is concerned, our most urgent requirement at the moment is to break through the constraints of 'Leftist' thinking that has propagated a closed-border ideology and stultifying rigidity, and resolve to carry through our policy of opening to the outside. We should fully exploit our own national advantages and do our utmost to get even more of our products on to the international market. We need to reflect on our historical experience, and achieve rapid mastery of the skills necessary to expand external trade and international economic and technical co-operation under increasingly complex conditions of international exchange. We must make full use of the advantageous conditions that exist in our coastal regions and continue to expand and strengthen links and co-operation with all those countries and individuals who are prepared to conduct economic and technical exchange with China on an equal footing. We need to diligently study and digest the experiences of other countries and attract their advanced technology in order to accelerate China's socialist modernisation and construction.

Building socialism is a great, new historical enterprise for mankind. Under the leadership of the CCP for over 30 years, our exploratory steps along the road towards the construction of socialism in a country like China with its huge population and widespread poverty have already produced unprecedented results. We have amassed a wealth of practical experience and overcome many difficult obstacles. Our task now is to make a careful review of the course we have travelled and come up with an accurate summary of our historical experience. This is vital if we are to continue to uphold the Four Cardinal Principles, make progress with bringing order out of chaos in terms of our practical work on the economy, avoid repeating the mistakes of the past and improve our construction of socialism with Chinese characteristics.

Since 1949, a succession of radical changes have occurred within our forces of production, relations of production, economic base and super-structure. The links between these different sectors, including the connections between every sector of the national economy, are extremely complicated. Nevertheless, historical development occurs in line with theory and logic. We therefore need to make a careful analysis of our historical materials to determine the optimum way to apply the standpoints, views and methods of Marxist-Leninism and Mao Zedong thought. We must eliminate the false and retain the true and proceed from the surface to the inner essence in order to attain a clear and accurate grasp of all the complex links and mutual relationships. We need to unearth the major threads of development and uncover the objective rules for historical development. Our discoveries should then be drawn together in a body of written work of scientific and economic history. This is an arduous and complicated task and will require the efforts of large numbers of people over a long period of time.

Document 2.2

'The important issues involved with China's strategy for economic development'

LIU GUOGUANG

Chinese Social Science, 1983, No. 6

In September 1982, the Twelfth Party Congress put forward a programme to comprehensively develop socialist modernisation and construction and strive to raise China's economy to a new level. Part of this programme was in the form of an array of plans and policies and strategic measures to set key targets and develop key strategies for economic construction until the end of the century. The thinking behind these strategies was a concrete manifestation of Deng Xiaoping's proposals to advance according to China's actual circumstances, follow the path of Chinese-style socialism, and achieve the preliminary target of realising a comfortable standard of living by the year 2000. In early 1980, Deng Xiaoping pointed out that 'in the sphere of economic development, we are searching for a path that corresponds to China's specific reality and that will help us accelerate our progress while at the same time saving resources' [*Selected Works of Deng Xiaoping (1975–1982)*, p. 210] 'Our Four Modernisations are Chinese-style ... If we manage to increase the value of national production to US$1000 per capita by the turn of the century, then that can be considered a comfortable standard of living [*Ibid.* p. 223]. At the end of 1980, in his discussion about the path and concrete measures that China should take to achieve modernisation, Deng Xiaoping stated that we must 'continue to cast off the yoke of rigid convention, both old and new, and achieve a clear and accurate grasp of the mutual relationships between the various factors that comprise our national characteristics and our economic activities' [*Ibid.* p. 315]. This requires us to conduct research into a strategy for economic development. The thinking behind the strategy for economic development put forward at the Twelfth Party Congress reflected the results of research and debate conducted by Chinese economists and academics over a number of years. It also represented a great impetus to conduct further research into a strategy for economic development in China. It is an important task and responsibility for Chinese economists to investigate every aspect of economic development strategy in China. This must include research into China's national characteristics, a thorough consideration of our historical experience, learning from practice in other countries, conducting theoretical analyses and linking them closely to practice, and putting forward a number of practicable recommendations.

I

The phrase strategy for economic development has been popular in China for a number of years now. However, the concept strategy has a more familiar ring to it when used in conjunction with revolutions or wars. Many years have passed since Mao wrote famous works such as *On Protracted War* and he stated: 'Matters of strategy relate to research into war as a whole and the rules of war; All of those factors which are concerned with every aspect and every stage of war can be considered to represent war as a whole' [*Selected Works of Mao Zedong*, Vol. 1, p. 159]. Military strategy governs war as a whole and takes precedence over military technique.

Our strategy for economic development in the medium to long term (for example, 5 years, 10 years, 20 years) should be designed according to an assessment of all the factors and conditions affecting economic development.

We should proceed from an appraisal of every aspect which has a bearing on economic development as a whole. We must consider and set targets for economic development, define our focal areas of attention, and plan the stages through which we must pass. We also need to develop a series of effective plans and important strategic measures which will enable us to achieve these goals. All of this relates to the overall, long-term and far-reaching nature of economic development. In this sense, although we have not tended to use the term strategy for economic development in the past, we have still investigated these kinds of problems in practice. The research we have previously conducted into a strategy for economic development has manifested itself in the designated line for economic development over a relatively long period and an array of important plans and policies. The only problem is that this research has been sporadic and has lacked self-awareness. It is only through the rise in the concept of a developmental strategy in recent years that research into this issue has achieved its rightful status.

At the end of the 1970s, a number of economists in China, particularly those researching the economies of other countries and the international economy, began to use the term strategy for economic development. In the early 1980s, Yu Guangyuan proposed studying a strategy for social and economic development and this received attention and provoked reaction from many quarters. In February 1981, a number of organisations including the Centre for Economic Research at the Chinese Academy of Social Sciences, the State Scientific Committee Policy Research Centre, the Office of the Special Taskforce to Modernise Technology, Economics and Management, the Chinese Centre of Research into Science and Information Technology and the National Association of International Economics, published a joint communique convening the first seminar on the issue of a strategy for social and economic development.

The seminar has been convened at fixed intervals in Beijing for over two years now and 15 meetings had already been held by June 1983. Its main topics of discussion have included: the meaning and methods of researching a strategy for development; making connections with China's basic national characteristics and determining strategic targets and strategic methods; how to merge current economic adjustments with future economic development; the scale of construction and sources of capital; a strategy for agricultural development; a developmental strategy for external economic relations; a strategy for scientific and technological advancement; learning selectively from development strategies in other Third World countries; future research and studies; etc. This seminar has played an active role in encouraging Chinese academics and economists to conduct research into the issue of a developmental strategy. Now this issue represents a new sphere of enquiry within economic research. It has not only been acknowledged and approved, it has also attracted the attention and support of a growing number of economic theorists and practitioners as well as social scientists, natural scientists, and technical scientists. This shows that researching the issue of a strategy for economic development is an urgent requirement for China's modernisation and construction.

Over the last three years we have introduced foreign theories and learnt from the experience of other countries while simultaneously carrying out a comparative analysis. We have conducted research which takes account of China's specific national features and explored strategies for economic development that have Chinese characteristics. Unlike other developing countries, China's strategy for economic development is guided primarily by Marxist thinking and must embody socialist principles, benefit the consolidation of the socialist system, and promote its superiority. At the same time, it must take account of China's national characteristics, namely that China is a huge country with a vast population and a fragile base. It is therefore not possible to blindly imitate the style and methods of development adopted by other countries. As Deng Xiaoping pointed out in his opening words of the Twelfth Party Congress: The basic conclusion that we have reached through an examination of long-term historical experience is that we must combine the universal truths of Marxism with China's concrete reality, follow our own path and build socialism with Chinese characteristics.

In the course of investigating and debating China's strategy for development, people have posed the following problem: Is it possible to imagine the creation of a Marxist developmental economics? Some people believe that while it is necessary to research ways in which a strategy for socio-economic development can act as a system of policies for socialist development, it is not necessary to establish an independent discipline of Marxist developmental economics. This is because the socialist aspects of Marxist political economics in particular are concerned amongst other things with the theory of social reproduction. In this way, the theoretical basis for establishing and determining a strategy for socialist development of the economy and society is already provided. This kind of reasoning is justifiable to some extent, since if we leave behind the entire body of Marxist political and economic theory, particularly with regard to the way in which it guides social reproduction theory, then we will be unable to carry out accurate research into strategies for socio-economic development. However, Marxist political economics are important aspects of research into basic economic theory. Developmental economics, on the other hand, is guided by political economics and relates to every area of economics and professional economics as well as population, territory, ecology, science and technology etc. It is inter-disciplinary, marginal and multi-faceted and therefore belongs within the realm of research into applied economic theory. The former cannot completely incorporate or substitute for the latter. With the guidance of Marxism, a developmental economics which uses the features of developing countries as an object of research can obviously provide a direct theoretical basis for conducting research into strategies for economic and social development. In the actual process of research, however, these two are intimately linked together. To conduct extensive and thorough-going research into problems with a country's strategy for development (for example, China's strategy) can provide an important practical and strategic basis for establishing a theory of developmental economics. This means that it is also logical to proceed from a study of strategies for economic development in order to later establish a Marxist developmental economics.

II

Since the Third Plenary Session of the Eleventh Party Congress at the end of 1979, the formulation and implementation of policies of adjustment, reform, consolidation and improvement have led to a great change in China's strategy for economic development. The substance and implications of this change have become the subject of hot debate among Chinese economists. This debate has occurred alongside research into the ways in which other countries have addressed strategic problems with regard to economic development. This has naturally encouraged some people to cite strategic changes in economic development that have occurred in developing countries and to take the view that the changes in China over recent years resemble those that have taken place in many other developing countries. In other words, China has moved away from a so-called traditional development strategy, which chiefly aims for high rates of growth in the value of national production, and towards a so-called new development strategy, which is principally aimed at satisfying people's basic needs. However, since China is a large, socialist, developing country, its evolving strategy for economic development still has many of its own unique features. China's previous strategy for economic development was by no means immutable and frozen, it went through a number of important changes. If we ignore the period just after 1949 when China's national economy was in a state of recovery and recuperation, our economic development from 1953 to 1978 can be divided into four major strategic periods:

1. The First Five Year Plan (1953–1957)

Our strategy for economic development over this period is reflected in the general line for the transition period that was put forward in October 1953. The First Five Year Plan is the concrete implementation of this general line and its strategic targets include: the step-by-step realisation of socialist industrialisation; the gradual socialist transformation of agricultural and handicraft industries as well as capitalist commerce and industry; and raising the material and cultural level of people's lives based on the development of production and improving labour productivity. The strategic measures adopted to achieve the above targets were: to prioritise the development of heavy industry and encourage the appropriate development of light industry and agriculture; to focus our financial and material resources on the development of 156 key engineering projects to act as a backbone of basic construction; to manage effectively the relationship between construction and daily life, and between accumulation and consumption; to pay close attention to an aggregate equilibrium etc.

Practice shows that our strategy for economic development during the First Five Year Plan was correct. The main targets that were set in the First Five Year Plan were for the most part attained in advance of time and results exceeded all expectations. The annual average value of industrial and agricultural output grew by 10.9% and national income increased by 8.9%; the increases in output from agriculture and industry, heavy industry and light industry were generally proportionate; economic returns were relatively good and there were clear improvements in capital tax and interest rates and in the labour productivity of State Owned Enterprises; people's standard of living improved and the incomes of farmers and urban workers rose. Co-operativisation was initiated for agriculture and handicraft industries and a system of public-private co-operative management for capitalist industries was introduced. In this way, we basically managed to achieve the socialist transformation of the means of production that used to be under a system of private ownership. The whole process was completed in less than five years, despite the fact that it was originally scheduled for a longer period of development that was to cover three Five Year Plans. This led to a number of flaws and errors in our work and before long people became impatient for quick results.

2. The Great Leap Forward (1958–1960)

At the end of the First Five Year Plan, the slogan 'Surpass Britain and overtake the USA' was put forward. The output of steel became a key target and before long this had been developed into a policy of taking steel as the key link. This was closely followed by the promotion of the Three Red Flags, namely, the General Line, the Great Leap Forward and the People's Communes. The former strategy of steady development was soon overtaken and replaced by a rash strategy characterised by hasty planning and an impatience for quick results. The main aims of this new strategy were to blindly attempt to accelerate the Great Leap Forward and to mould the relations of production in line with the slogan: 'One Big; Two Public'.[2] In practice, the everyday lives of the population were deemed of secondary importance. The main strategic measures of that time were: to smelt large quantities of iron and steel in an attempt to triple annual production in 1958; to engage in wholesale communisation by abolishing private plots of land and individual market trading; to raise the rate of accumulation and increase the scale of basic construction; to emphasise the role of mass movements at the expense of an overall balance; to abolish piece-rate wages

2 The People's Communes would be good if they were large in scale and public in ownership. (Ed.)

71

and remuneration by denigrating the principle of distribution according to work.

Practical experience shows that this kind of strategy was wrong. It could only be sustained for three years and from the second half of 1960, it became necessary to make corrections and adjustments. Nevertheless, the negative effects of this strategy persisted for a period of several years. Over the whole period covered by the Second Five Year Plan, there were only minimal increases in the total output value of industry and there were actual reductions in both the total output value of agriculture and national income; there was a major drop in economic returns causing great damage to people's livelihoods. All of this could be reduced to one simple fact: a serious imbalance in the proportionate relationships in the national economy.

3. The period of adjustment (1961–1965)

Our mistakes brought us to our senses. At the beginning of the 1960s, a plan to adjust, consolidate, replenish and improve was formulated, and this made real changes to our strategy for economic development. At around this time, several members of the CCP Central Committee put forward a number of important ideas concerning our development strategy. For example: since agriculture is the basis for the development of our national economy, our planning work should be conducted according to an agriculture/light industry/heavy industry hierarchy; in developing commodity production, we must respect the Law of Value and use economic methods to regulate the economy; our scale of construction must be in line with our national strength, and we must give equal consideration to people's livelihoods and national construction; the overall balance of the economy must be managed properly, especially the balance between material assets, financial assets and credit; etc. These ideas were to have an important bearing on the strategy for economic development that was later put into practice. The strategic targets at that time were: to adjust the proportionate relationships in the national economy and give priority to agricultural recovery; to adjust the relations of production, introduce a three-tier system of ownership with the Production Brigade as the base within the People's Communes and overcome the winds of communism and egalitarianism; and to forcefully suppress accumulation in order to guarantee a basic standard of living for people. The strategic measures that were adopted to achieve these targets were: reducing investment in basic construction; increasing revenue, reducing expenditure and striving to achieve a balance between finance and credit; bringing inflation under control and stabilising market prices; streamlining the work force, reducing the size of the urban population and giving full priority to agriculture; making corrections and adjustments to enterprises and closing some factories and mines; etc.

These economic changes soon bore fruit. Between 1963 and 1965, the gross output value of agriculture increased by an annual 11.1%, the gross output value of industry grew by 17.9% and national income rose by 14.5%. Economic returns were clearly improving and a number of economic indicators reached unprecedented levels. People's incomes increased and their standard of living improved. We had finally passed through the stage of serious economic hardship that had been caused by a number subjective and objective factors. And yet, generally speaking, this change in our economic development strategy was implemented through necessity and there was no option other than to carry out our practical work in this way. As far as its theoretical underpinnings were concerned, however, the hypothesis concerning the Three Red Flags continued to hold sway for a relatively long period of time. This means that we had still not fully solved the problems with the guiding philosophy behind our basic strategy. Thus, as soon as things began to take a turn for the better, we repeated once again the mistakes of the Left.

4. The ten-year period of internal chaos (1966–1976)

Policy changes and adjustments were bringing economic recovery and further development as China entered its Third Five Year Plan. It was originally envisaged that the basic tasks of the Third Five Year Plan were as follows: to put great efforts into developing agriculture in an attempt to provide everyone with basic subsistence levels of food, clothing and everyday items; to appropriately strengthen national defence construction and develop advanced technology; to strengthen basic industry and develop communications, commerce, and educational and scientific institutions to a corresponding level. However, with the start of the Cultural Revolution in 1966, economic construction came under political attack and it became impossible to carry out the strategic plans mentioned above. What actually happened during the ten years of chaos was as follows: as far as economic construction was concerned, priority was given to war-preparedness and strengthening the construction of the three lines; in our economic work, priority continued to be given to heavy industry and taking steel as the key link; in connection with the relations of production, the slogans 'endless transition' and 'cutting off the capitalist tail' were put forward;[3] as far as people's livelihoods were concerned, wages were frozen, the so-called 'rights' of the capitalist class were rejected, and egalitarianism was promoted; in our economic relations with other countries, the so-called blind worship of all things foreign and fawning and obsequious mentality were criticised and China began to operate a closed-door policy.

This was an incoherent and chaotic strategy for economic development devised under the guidance of Leftist thinking. Even though the resistance and efforts of large numbers of officials and ordinary people meant that the economy continued to grow in fits and starts, we still incurred great losses.

3 These were slogans to justify egalitarian income payments and abolition of interest payments to former capitalists. (Ed.)

Over the ten-year period, the rate of production development fell and in some years, agriculture, industry and national income registered negative growth. Once again, serious imbalances appeared in the proportionate relationships between accumulation and consumption, industry and agriculture, and heavy industry and light industry. In particular, there was a serious drop in economic returns and many economic indicators did not measure up to their levels during the First Five Year Plan. There was a reduction in workers' real wages and very little increase in farmers' incomes.

For a number of reasons, we continued to make the mistake of being impatient for quick results for the three years following the smashing of the Gang of Four in 1976. This exacerbated the proportionate imbalances that already existed. It was not until the Third Plenary Session of the Eleventh Party Congress that we began to set things right and bring order out of chaos. Soon a new policy of adjustment, reform, consolidation and improvement gradually began to bring our strategy for economic development back on to the correct path.

It is clear from the historical analysis above that China's strategy for economic development has undergone a number of changes in the past. Sometimes it was more or less correct, and at other times it was seriously flawed and misguided. When our strategic policies were correct, the national economy experienced vigorous growth, people's standard of living began to improve and the socialist system was consolidated. However, when our strategic policies were defective, economic development was held back, it became impossible to raise people's standard of living and the socialist system was weakened. This means that it is not advisable for us to follow the example of other developing countries and use the term the traditional, old strategy to sum up and encapsulate our changing strategy for economic development over 20–30 years. While it may be true that China's economic development has been beset by a number of negative factors, China has not been the victim of long-term problems such as unfair income distribution, chronic unemployment, persistent inflation, rising foreign debts etc that have been the inevitable consequences of traditional development strategies in many other developing countries during the course of their industrialisation. Or rather, if China has suffered from these problems, then they have only been localised or temporary phenomena. On the other hand, while many developing countries are now recommending the adoption of new strategies to deal with the problem of satisfying the basic needs of their people, such as nutrition, health, education etc, China has already achieved remarkable results in finding solutions to these problems during its previous course of development. This is recognized by all impartial experts and commentators outside China. Many accounts, including the report by the World Bank on China's economy, acknowledge that in its previous development, China has been able to both achieve rapid industrialization and satisfy the basic needs of its population. In fact, in the thirty years since the founding of the People's Republic, we have basically managed to build a self-contained, independent and intact national economic system. With heavy industry as its base, it has essentially succeeded in providing subsistence levels of food and clothing to one billion people.

This proves that some elements were certainly correct in China's past strategy for economic development. These elements can help to give full rein to the superiority of the Chinese socialist system and achieve results that have not yet been achieved by non-socialist developing countries. In our account above, we have explained some of the achievements of China's economic development and also detailed some of the serious setbacks that have occurred in the course of our economic construction. Most of these setbacks are inseparable from the erroneous Leftist thinking that has reigned time and again since the Great Leap Forward of 1958. Our mistakes have mainly been to demand too much of economic construction, to be extremist in our policy-making, to pursue rates of growth above all else, to excessively increase our scale of investment, and to exceed the capabilities of our national strength. The consequence has inevitably been economic contraction. Our previous history of one step forward, one step back has incurred great losses and wasted long periods of time. It has also had a damaging effect on people's motivation. All of this has affected our ability to give full rein to the superiority of the socialist system and made it difficult for us to raise returns on economic construction. Improvements to people's standard of living have not matched the work and effort that people have put in.

Since the Third Plenary Session of the Eleventh Party Congress, our strategic attempts to restore order and stability to the economy have centred around changing our old practices and methods that were developed under the guidance of Leftist thinking. Having gained a greater understanding of China's national characteristics, we have started down a new road that should produce greater economic returns and more material benefits for the population. This is a great historical turning point in China's strategy for economic development. Generally speaking, this fundamental change in strategy can be encapsulated in a few main points:

1. As far as our strategic targets are concerned, we have shifted emphasis from our past policy of stressing the single-minded pursuit of economic growth towards paying more attention to satisfying the increasing material and cultural needs of the people based on economic growth. Economic growth is important – without economic growth, we would have no material basis upon which to improve people's standard of living. However, pursuing economic growth for its own sake, placing economic growth above all other strategic targets and treating the lives and livelihoods of the people as of secondary importance is a biased and one-sided policy. It is even more mistaken to damage people's livelihoods for the sake of economic growth. Although, generally speaking, economic growth has not been slow in the past, it has still not been in line with the material benefits that people have enjoyed. This must be

regarded as mistaken strategy. The strategic targets for economic development put forward at the Twelfth Party Congress called for people's material and cultural standards of living to be brought up to a comfortable level based on a trebling of the total output value of industry and agriculture. This reflected the fundamental economic rules of socialism and the unity between developing production and raising people's standard of living. These aims were clearer than any strategic targets that had been set in the past and this made it much easier to mobilise the masses to strive to achieve them.

2. As far as the rate of economic development and returns from economic development are concerned, we have switched from concentrating solely on pursuing high rates of growth towards making raising economic returns a central task. While the rate of economic development is important, it is biased and one-sided to stress the rate of growth at the expense of economic returns. In particular, pursuing unrealistic rates of growth will have a negative effect on economic returns and the inevitable consequence will be not high, but conversely, low rates of growth – even to the extent that the desired rate of growth becomes unattainable. In the past, China's economic development advanced at a certain rate but it was by no means stable and featured great peaks and troughs. In recent years, growth has been maintained at a comparatively normal rate but this has not yet led to real and visible improvements in economic returns. The national economy has not been able to transform itself completely from an unhealthy to a healthy cycle and this has held back progress in the fiscal economy. The target proposed by the Twelfth Party Congress to treble the total output value of industry and agriculture is based on the premise that we can continuously improve economic returns. This means that if we steer away from raising economic returns, trebling output loses it real significance. On the other hand, if we do not manage to raise economic returns, then it will be difficult to realise our goal of trebling output. It is worth noting that because of this problem, many people have not changed their ways of thinking and either consciously or unconsciously, they frequently tend to fall back on the old idea of pursuing output value and rates of growth above all else. This means we must continue to stress economic returns and strive to focus all of our economic work on raising economic returns.

3. In dealing with the relationship between balanced and unbalanced development, we have changed our policy from a one-sided emphasis on the key issues while ignoring equal development to a combined emphasis on grasping the key issues and promoting equal development. In our economic development it is necessary for us to focus on certain weak links or key links and concentrate our energies on improving them. This will stimulate the development of other sectors. However, it is biased and one-sided to place undue emphasis on one particular sector (e.g. our past emphasis on heavy industry, or even the narrow emphasis on iron and

steel within heavy industry) and give no support to other products and lines of production, especially agriculture and light industry. The outcome of such a policy is a proportionate imbalance and further advances will become difficult to achieve. The Twelfth Party Congress singled out agriculture, energy and communications, and education and science as key strategic areas for economic development. Problems in these areas were to be solved based on a policy of maintaining an overall balance and this would then promote a relatively rapid growth in the production of consumer goods and stimulate the development of the economy as a whole. Clearly this new policy was different from our past strategy of unbalanced development which took steel as the key link or placed a one-sided emphasis on the development of heavy industry.

4. In our methods for expanding reproduction, we have moved away from a blind reliance on extended development through new construction projects towards paying greater attention to methods of latent development which focus on exploiting the hidden potential of existing enterprises through consolidation, reorganisation and technical innovation. We should channel the necessary funds and initiate key construction projects to eliminate the weak links, strengthen our infrastructure, develop new sectors and make gradual adjustments to our distribution. However, it is biased and one-sided to continue with our previous policy of regarding new construction projects as the only means of expanding reproduction, and take the view that it is possible to develop the economy just by setting up new areas of business. We already have tens of thousands of enterprises in existence. Since we have ignored the importance of technical innovation for a long period of time, facilities and equipment in these enterprises have become old and out-moded, production techniques have fallen behind, product quality is poor, wastage is high, and latent potential remains untapped. All of this has seriously impeded our task of raising economic returns. While guaranteeing the maintenance of key construction projects, the Twelfth Party Congress also stressed the importance of technical innovation. This means that it is not enough to rely solely on extension to expand reproduction, it is also important tap the latent potential of existing enterprises. We must pursue of policy of minimum investment for maximum yield. This ties in closely with our task of trebling the production of agriculture and industry with the prerequisite of improved economic returns.

5. In the sphere of developing both material and human resources, we have moved away from the past policies of emphasising the construction of a material and technological base at the expense of developing human resources, particularly levels of knowledge and expertise. This has been replaced with a new strategy of placing an equal emphasis on material and human resources. Men and women are the most important factor of all our forces of production and levels of knowledge, scientific and

77

technical expertise, and grasp of modern systems of administration and production are playing an increasingly important role in our economic development and modernisation. In the past we paid scant attention to expertise and ostracized intellectuals. This caused considerable damage to China's economic development. While continuing to stress the importance of material assets, the Twelfth Party Congress also emphasised the role of human resources and cited education and science as examples of key strategic areas. It also gave importance to the development of knowledge and expertise. In this way, we will be able to make effective improvements to our levels of technology, administration and production and ensure the further development of the economy. We must give top priority to investing in expertise. This is also a basic policy of reaping maximum yield from minimum input.

6. In dealing with the relationship between our internal and external affairs, we have moved away from our past policy of isolationism and moved towards a strategy of openness to the outside world. As a great socialist country, China must rely mainly on its own endeavours and self-strengthening to effect its own modernisation and construction. This goes without saying. However, our past experiences with blockades, embargoes and breaches of contract by other countries have given rise to biased and one-sided notions of self-strengthening in many people 's minds. This is the background to our actual adoption of policies of isolationism and self-sufficiency. These policies have restricted out own development. No country possesses all the necessary natural resources and technology to develop its social forces of production to the levels that are necessary today. This is particularly true for developing countries which suffer from a lack of capital, technology and other assets. Implementing a policy of openness to the outside world and expanding economic and technological exchange with other countries has promoted our own economic development and boosted our capacity for self-strengthening. The Twelfth Party Congress's affirmation of this new strategy of openness is an important move to accelerate China's economic development.

7. In line with all the changes detailed above, we have also had to transform our systems of economic administration and management. We have moved away from our past policies of a blind pursuit of large-scale and public economic forms and their resultant over-centralisation as well as the notion that all must eat from the same rice bowl towards a more pluralist economy centred around state-run enterprises. It is now possible for different economic forms to coexist which combine collective and individual rights and the advantages of both the planned and market economies. We have put new systems into place which are based on the principle of distribution according to work and material benefits. These changes have done much to boost enthusiasm and motivation from all sides and have facilitated the development of

commodity production and commodity exchange. In this way, they have helped to realise the strategic goals for the economy as a whole.

All of the changes and transformations mentioned above have moved China's strategy for economic development onto a new path. This new strategy exhibits Chinese characteristics: not only does it differ from so-called traditional strategies of economic development practised in certain countries, it also differs from so-called flexible strategies of development practised in other countries. For instance, China's new strategy is concerned with both economic growth and people's everyday lives; it encourages the pursuit of wealth through labour while at the same time preventing the growth of a wide gap between the rich and the poor; it promotes openness to outside influences and the active use of foreign capital while at the same time taking pains to ensure that China does not become mired in foreign debt. The comfortable standard of living that we propose does not only mean that people's basic daily needs are satisfied, it also means more enrichment within people's lives. This enrichment includes rational and full employment, stable prices, and the protection of the environment. These are goals that have not yet been achieved by many other developing countries all over the world. China's new strategy for development differs even more from strategies for economic growth that operate in developed countries. For example, our aim is to develop appropriate levels of consumption, rather than the high levels of consumption (in other words, squandering and waste) that have taken hold in the West; we want to place more emphasis on the all-rounded development of each person and demand higher levels of intellect and culture as well as a heightened sense of public security (a much lower crime rate etc). To sum up, China's new strategy for economic development cannot be said to be based on any foreign models of development.

Document 2.3

'The spirit of the age reflected in Deng Xiaoping's theory on the essence of socialism'

XU CHONGWEN

Chinese Social Science, 1995, No. 2

When Deng Xiaoping put forward his theory of socialism with Chinese characteristics, he solved a primary and fundamental problem by identifying exactly what socialism is. In his summary of China's practical experience with socialism over the past 20 or 30 years, he pointed out several times that 'we were not properly aware of this issue in the past' and 'we did not manage to gain a complete grasp of it'. This means that one of the most important lessons we have to learn is that 'we must achieve an accurate understanding of this problem'.

At the same time as highlighting this issue, Deng Xiaoping also managed to explain and solve problems from various angles and on various levels through a continuous exploration and summation of past practice. In his Southern statement ['nanfang tanhua'] of 1992, Deng brought all of these theories together, transforming them into the over-arching laws and essence of socialism. He stressed that 'the essence of socialism is to liberate and develop the productive forces, eradicate exploitation, abolish social polarisation, and achieve the ultimate goal of a common prosperity' [*Selected Works of Deng Xiaoping*, vol. 3, p. 373].

It is important to point out that under the new historical conditions of a world-wide shift away from war and revolution towards peace and development, Deng Xiaoping applied his theories to every aspect of the essence of socialism by using the criteria of whether or not it promotes the socialist development of our social and productive forces. This is how Deng's theory took on the unique characteristics of the times and thereby made a great, epoch-making contribution to scientific socialism.

1. Changes in the international order and our attempts to bring all of our national advantages into the foreground

Deng Xiaoping's theory on the essence of socialism reflects the contemporary themes of the world as it moves away from revolution and war towards peace and development.

At the beginning of the 20th Century, Lenin had a good grasp of the historical transformation from capitalism to imperialism and the international move away from the peaceful development of capitalism towards armed conflict between imperialism and proletarian revolution. He led the October Revolution which paved the way for a new era in the history of mankind and transformed socialism from theory into reality. After the Second World War, the practice of socialism had spread from one single country to a number of different countries.

However, there have been a number of further changes in the world order since the middle of the 20th Century. After the Second World War, the face of international politics became polarised into two camps, which was closely followed by a tripartite division into the Three Worlds. This finally developed into a new stage where East-West North-South relationships became the most prominent features. When a Japanese business delegation visited China in 1985, Deng Xiaoping pointed out that: 'There are two major issues in the world today that must be tackled according to a universal strategy – one is the issue of world peace, and the other is the issue of the economy, or rather, development. The question of peace is an East-West issue, while the question of development is a North-South issue.

This can all be summed up in the four words: East, West, North, South'
[*Selected Works of Deng Xiaoping*, vol. 3, p. 105].

As far as questions of war and peace between the East and the West are concerned, the post-war development of the world economy, especially the globalisation of production and capital, led to an unprecedented level of mutual interdependence between developing countries. They were therefore forced to search for methods other than war to resolve their mutual disagreements. This bolstered the forces of peace in the world over and above the forces of war, thereby helping to prevent the reality and possibility of another world war. As far as questions of the economy or development between the North and the South are concerned, movements of national independence passed through the stage of fervent revolution and then began to break new ground by striving to eliminate poverty through social and economic development. However, the kind of unequal and unjust economic relations that had been formed under conditions of colonialism represented a serious obstacle to the economic development of the countries of the South. 'The current state of the world is such that the North is developed and rich while the South is undeveloped and poor, and there is an ever-growing gap between the two. The South wants to escape from its poverty and under-development and the North also needs the South to develop, otherwise where will the North find markets for its products?' [*Selected Works of Deng Xiaoping*, vol. 3, p. 96]. In this way, although the world is still far from peaceful, and hegemony and power politics continue to exist, it is still the case that the contemporary themes of the world are clearly moving towards peace and development.

These new trends in the world have changed the forms of expression of the objective law that socialism will inevitably replace capitalism. This has meant that the notion that war leads to revolution and revolution brings an end to war that existed between the two world wars has given way to the idea that socialist countries should use the superior qualities of economic growth and the comprehensive development of society to motivate the broad masses of the people. In this way, the whole of mankind will be able to see the unique inevitability of socialism and its superiority over capitalism.

Changing world trends have also transformed the forms of coexistence and struggles between socialist countries and capitalist countries. This has effected a shift away from a single-minded competition for military superiority towards an attempt for a more rounded superiority in terms of a country's national assets as a whole, particularly a competition for economic and scientific superiority. This new atmosphere of struggle and competition has been characterised by the British weekly *Foreign Affairs Report* as a Third World War: 'the victorious nations in this war will not be those with the greatest military might, but those with the highest quality work force, the highest rates of productivity, the most skilled designers and the most astute long-term investors.... Wise strategists are no longer concerned with bullets, battleships and tanks – no matter how necessary these weapons are – they are planning the large-scale market and investment projects that have not yet been fully developed and that will ultimately be the most profitable'. Even the Chairman of the US Senate Intelligence Committee, who is a conservative when it comes to military affairs, recognised this change in circumstances. He gave the following warning to the American people: 'If the US cannot fit in with the new world order built on the foundations of economic strength rather than military might, it risks losing its international pre-eminence' (*New York Times*, 4 April 1990).

Under the current circumstances of world change and transformation, it is becoming increasingly important for socialist countries to absorb and learn from all the cultural fruits of mankind's social creativity and perpetuate and accelerate the healthy development of our social forces of production. It has also become important to use this as a basis for raising people's standard of living in order to attain a more favourable position than capitalist countries.

Deng Xiaoping's theory on the essence of socialism incorporated these international changes and took into consideration the great challenge that socialism is currently facing. The contemporary features of his theory are as follows: the precondition of every aspect of socialism must be that it benefits the development of our socialist forces of production. Deng Xiaoping stressed that 'it is essential to emancipate our minds, even to the extent that we question what it is that we call socialism; In discussing socialism, we must always remember that its primary target is to develop our forces of production – this is very important. In the final analysis, increases in national income depend on the development of our forces of production. This is the standard that outweighs all other standards. Empty talk about socialism is no good, and people will not be persuaded by it'. ['*Selected Works of Deng Xiaoping*' Vol. 2, pp. 312, 314].

2. Liberating and developing our forces of production must be incorporated within the essence of socialism

The concept of socialism originally arose as an antithesis to the idea of individualism. In particular, it emerged as a means of correcting some of the worst malpractices associated with early capitalist society. Socialist philosophy was based on the idea of co-operation and the collective management of society to achieve wealth and happiness for the masses as a whole. A specific requirement was to reform social systems to guarantee social harmony and raise the standard of living for the lowest social strata. Therefore, the socialism envisaged by early socialists was constrained by an emphasis on social equality.

Marx and Engels transformed socialism from a hollow theory into an important scientific model and incorporated within socialist theory the idea that the development of the productive forces should act as the decisive factor that stimulates social development. They clearly stated that: 'The boundless forces of production characterised by modern industry are an important condition for the liberation of labour'; they pointed out that the two real conditions for eliminating alienation are both predicated on the large-scale growth and development of the forces of production; they indicated that the division of labour in society can only be eliminated when 'the productive forces have developed to the extent that the system of private ownership and the division of labour become real constraints'; they stated that only by developing the forces of production and creating the material conditions for production can we 'build the concrete foundations for a higher level society based on the principles of the overall and free development of each individual'; they emphasised that a communist society based on the principle of 'from each according to his ability, to each according to his needs' is to be realised through the development of the productive forces by each individual making full use of all sources of collective wealth. It was for these reasons that the *Communist Manifesto* made rapid growth in the aggregate forces of production a crucially important task after the seizure of power by the proletariat. Moreover, Marx and Engels used elements of contrast to prove their common thesis. They pointed out that if an attempt were made to attain social equality without developing the forces of production then 'this would only lead to the rise of widespread poverty; and conditions of extreme poverty will lead inevitably to a renewed struggle for basic daily necessities. This means that all of the old and decayed practices are likely to re-emerge and gain a new lease of life.'

By arguing in this way, Deng Xiaoping made the development of the productive forces part of the very essence of socialism. His theory can be traced back to the thinking of Marx and Engels detailed above where they highlighted and analysed both positive and negative aspects of the question. It was at once both a legacy and a development of basic Marxist theory.

Nevertheless, at the same time, Deng Xiaoping's introduction of the development of the productive forces into the essence of socialist theory was also a great achievement that reflected the spirit of the age. This was because when Marx and Engles envisaged the outbreak and victory of socialist revolution, they were focussing on a number of major developed capitalist countries. This meant that their sights were mainly set on clarifying the advanced development of the productive forces and their basic function as a means to emancipate labour, eliminate alienation, the division of labour and class distinction, and provide the necessary conditions for the transition from socialism to communism.

After capitalism entered the stage of imperialism, the rule that economic and political development do not occur at a balanced rate meant that socialism was first to emerge in Russia: the weak link in the imperialist chain. Thereafter, socialism won a series of victories in several European countries which were relatively undeveloped in terms of both culture and economy. A number of major capitalist countries continued to exist and develop. Under these circumstances, a new issue arose that Marx and

Engels had not dealt with: socialist countries needed to surpass capitalist countries with regard to the development of their forces of production. It was for this reason that Lenin constantly stressed that after the proletariat had successfully managed to seize the reins of power, 'it was necessary to give priority to the fundamental task of building an economic system that surpasses those that exist in capitalist societies; this fundamental task equates with raising the rate of labour productivity'. 'Communism is using advanced technology as well as a willing, self-aware and united work force to develop rates of labour productivity that are higher than in capitalist systems.'

Under the guidance of Lenin's philosophy, the period after the October Revolution saw the rapid growth and development of the Soviet economy. This was all the more striking when compared with the international economic crisis that was overwhelming capitalist systems at that time. However, since the Soviet model was a highly centralised and a military state that had been created through war and revolution, it was beset by a number of flaws and defects, despite the fact that it has played a very positive historical role. For example, it placed one-sided emphasis on the development of heavy industry at the expense of light industry and agriculture; it could not link the development of the forces of production with raising the standard of living of the population and could not guarantee the stable and balanced development of the national economy. It gave no consideration to the level of development of the productive forces and artificially and prematurely introduced a unitary system of ownership, which impeded the development of the forces of production, constrained the existence and development of a relationship between commodities and money, and created a serious shortage of some products and a great surplus of others.

The rejection of market mechanisms in favour of the introduction of a planned economy by mandatory targets destroyed incentives for enterprises and workers and hampered attempts to improve standards of economic administration and management. Also, its high degree of centralisation and reliance on methods of administrative coercion blurred the distinction between Party and Government and allowed the Party to substitute itself for government. This led to a wilful ignorance of the construction of socialist democracy and prevented the grass-roots levels of society from exercising their right to participate in national policy-making and planning. It thus became impossible to give full rein to the superiority of the socialist system and former excellence dropped inexorably towards mediocrity.

As a result of this, by the time that the world was moving towards peace and development after the Second World War and developed capitalist countries were embarking on the rapid development of their productive forces through the new technological revolution, the Soviet Union was experiencing consistent falls in its rate of economic growth. In China, however, two tendencies emerged which merely equated socialism with peace and harmony, and characterised socialism as the way towards the attainment of a utopian paradise of egalitarianism. In fact these two ideas were mistaken and premised on little more than a common poverty. The emergence of these tendencies reflected the fact that, while people aspired to surpass capitalism, they had not yet fully grasped the need to exert long-term efforts to develop the forces of production. This created an artificial separation between social fairness and efficiency, and between the productive forces and production itself, that were connected in Marx's original view of socialism. The fundamental tasks of raising efficiency and developing the productive forces were therefore neglected in favour of a one-sided emphasis on transforming the relations of production and bringing about social peace. It was mistakenly believed that these objectives were what socialism was really about. During the Cultural Revolution, the Gang of Four took these mistaken tendencies to even further extremes, putting forward malicious slogans such as: 'It is preferable to have a poverty-stricken form of socialism' and 'It is more important to have the bare essentials of socialism'. This plunged the national economy into a state of lethargy until it was on the verge of collapse.

It was against this backdrop that Deng Xiaoping, holding firmly to the world shift from war and revolution to peace and development, highlighted the superiority that socialism needed to achieve over capitalism and emphasised the critical importance of the development of the productive forces for the consolidation and development of the socialist system: 'The superiority of the socialist system is reflected in its capacity to facilitate the development of the productive forces at a rate inconceivable under the old feudal system. It also makes it possible to satisfy the ever growing material and cultural requirements of the people.' 'If the rate of development of the productive forces in socialist countries cannot match similar rates in capitalist countries over a relatively long period of time, then how can we talk about the superiority of socialism?' [*Collected Works of Deng Xiaoping*, Vol. 2, p. 128]. 'Adhering to socialism primarily means casting off the shackles of poverty and backwardness and focussing all our efforts on developing the productive forces to realize the inherent advantages of socialism over capitalism.' [*Collected Works of Deng Xiaoping*, Vol. 3, p. 224]. The superiority of socialism over capitalism 'must be manifested in various ways, but must primarily be reflected in the rate and results of economic development. For without this condition, everything else is just empty posturing' [*Collected Works of Deng Xiaoping*, Vol. 2, p. 251]. This was Deng's basic motive for bringing the development of the forces of production into the realm of the essence of socialism. It was also because of this that Deng highlighted the construction of socialism with Chinese characteristics, imbued it with a rich array of contemporary features and defined it broadly as 'the kind of socialism that promotes the uninterrupted development of the productive forces' [*Collected Works of Deng Xiaoping*, Vol. 3, p. 328].

The development of the forces of production and achieving superiority over capitalism is not only a critical issue for socialist countries. It is also gaining increased currency among non-Marxist socialists in capitalist countries. For example, in an interview with a reporter for *The Los Angeles Times* in 1993, the President of Greece and leader of the Pan-Hellenic Socialist Party, Papandreou, was keen to point out that: 'If we cannot develop our forces of production in this age of brutal competition among world economies, then we will not be able to maintain the rights and interests of our workers and the welfare of our population. Socialism has always emphasised justice and fairness, but in the 1990s we must focus more attention on competition. One of the factors behind the decline of socialism in Europe is that socialists have not understood that if we fail to win the battles of economic competition, we will have no means of attaining our socialist objectives. If we fail to boost production and merely stress fair distribution, we will end up with nothing at all to distribute. It is vital to improve our forces of production if we are to safeguard the salaries and welfare of our work force as a whole' [*Hong Kong Kuaibao*, 28 October 1993].

According to one school of thought, the factor that encapsulates the essence of socialism should be the relations of production rather than the forces of production, and the main goal of socialism should be the all-round development and liberation of the people, rather than the development of the forces of production.

When the social relations of production spontaneously develop in line with changes in the forces of production, it is certainly true that the relations of production as a whole will take on the characteristics of a certain kind of social formation. However, when development has occurred to the extent that people are consciously beginning to reform society, particularly in those economically and culturally under-developed countries where socialism has taken hold, it is not possible for the relations of production alone to express the full essence of socialism – they merely reflect a kind of incomplete socialism that is purely concerned with striving to catch up with other countries economic and cultural levels. If we ignore the basic task of developing the productive forces and define socialism purely in terms of the relations of production, then we will not be able to use socialism as a cornerstone for promoting the development of the forces of production. This will prevent us from achieving superiority over capitalism and from creating the necessary preconditions and foundations for the transition to communism. Moreover, it may also lead to the kind of development that has often occurred in socialist countries in the past, in which the productive forces are ignored in favour of a one-sided emphasis on the pursuit of greater and higher socialist relations of production. This eventually leads to erroneous tendencies which hamper the development of the productive forces. It is only by following Deng Xiaoping's advice and combining the liberation and development of our forces of production with the eradication of exploitation and polarisation in our relations of production that we will be able to give full play to the true essence of socialism and prevent the re-emergence of the erroneous practices detailed above.

It is even more unreasonable to contrast the all-round liberation and development of the population with its own precondition – the high-level development of the forces of production. The facts of the matter are just as Engels pointed out – it is only on the basis of the accelerated development of the forces of production that 'all members of society as a whole can achieve their similar and appropriate levels of development '. It is also only on this basis that 'everyone will have enough leisure time to inherit things of genuine value from history in terms of culture, science, art, social intercourse etc. and transform all of this from the sole products of the ruling classes into the common prosperity of society as a whole, thereby promoting its further development. This means that it is sheer nonsense to suggest that placing the development of the productive forces towards the top of the socialist agenda in order to increase levels of common prosperity is tantamount to encouraging the pursuit of consumerism. It is Deng Xiaoping's incorporation of the productive forces within the essence of socialism that has facilitated the development of the productive forces.

In the past, Marxists have had a tendency to stress the need to liberate the forces of production from capitalist oppression and exploitation. They have tended to believe that under socialist conditions, it is merely necessary to develop the forces of production. However, practical experience shows that even in a socialist society, an economic system that does not conform to the need to develop the productive forces will also hamper their development. Before it is possible to develop the productive forces, it is first necessary to liberate them through the reform of the economic system. The criteria that must be used when considering this reform are whether or not they are likely to promote the development of the forces of production, rather than whether or not they allow the development of socialist relations of production that are larger in scale, more public and more pure. On the basis of his historical account of our experience of socialist development, Deng Xiaoping stressed the need to adhere to the socialist system and put forward policies to liberate our productive forces and reform the specific mechanisms that restrict their development. He stated that: 'After a basic socialist system has been established, we still need to make fundamental reforms of the economic mechanisms that restrict the development of our productive forces. We must begin to build a socialist economic system that is full of vitality and energy and boost the development of the forces of production. This kind of reform also represents the emancipation of the productive forces. In the past, we have only been concerned with developing the forces of production under socialist conditions. We have never talked about the necessity to liberate the forces of production through reform. This has created an incomplete picture. We need to pay attention to both the liberation and the development of the forces of production' [*Selected Works of Deng Xiaoping*, Vol. 3, p. 370].

3. The institution of a socialist market economic system to liberate and develop the forces of production

The spirit of the age illustrated in Deng Xiaoping's theory on the essence of socialism is not only manifested in his incorporation of the liberation and development of the productive forces within the essence of socialism; it is also reflected in his idea to abandon the narrow ideology that suggests that either a planned or a market economy should be viewed as the basic building block of society, and in his decision to establish a socialist market economic system in order to further liberate and develop the productive forces.

After the success of the October Revolution, the planned economy played an undeniable historical role in promoting the development of the socialist forces of production. However, along with continual improvements in levels of economic development, the structure of the economy became increasingly complex and the shortcomings of a planned economy became ever more apparent, for a planned economy suppresses business vitality and worker motivation and this restricts the development of the productive forces. The facts were just as Deng Xiaoping stated: 'Making everything part of the planned economy will restrict the development of the productive forces. Combining the planned economy with a market economy will facilitate the liberation of the productive forces and accelerate economic development' [*Selected Works of Deng Xiaoping,* Vol. 3, pp. 148–149]. And yet, why is it that, having realised this point through their own practical experience, a number of socialist countries have still not begun to make practical use of the planned and market economies in a way that benefits the development of the socialist forces of production, and have still not managed to find practical and effective ways to combine the two economic systems? One basic reason for this arises from the tendency to regard the planned economy and the market economy as fundamental social systems. The belief that a planned economy is socialist while a market economy is capitalist is an ideological straitjacket, and criticism of market socialism has obstructed the progress of reform.

It was in reaction to this that Deng Xiaoping made his Southern Statement of 1992. Before making positive comments on the essence of socialism, he made the following statement: 'Expanding the role of either the planned or the market sector is not a simplistic decision between socialism and capitalism. A planned economy is not equivalent to socialism – planning is also part of capitalism. Similarly, a market economy cannot be mapped simplistically onto capitalism – markets also exist within a socialist system. Planning and the market are both economic tools' [*Selected Works of Deng Xiaoping,* Vol. 3, p. 373].

In that case, how could the simplistic idea that planning and the market equate with basic social systems have emerged in people' s traditional ways of thinking? The reasons are as follows:

During capitalism's early historical development, the institution of private systems of ownership without any state intervention, guidance or control led to the development of an imperfect market economy, which brought about cycles of serious and damaging economic crises. This was reflected in social phenomena such as the growing impoverishment of the proletarian classes as well as increased rates of unemployment and bankruptcies. In addition to this, Marx and Engels hypothesised that socialism would win a succession of victories over the major capitalist countries that had achieved a high level of development in terms of their productive forces. Thus, they used abstract methods to predict future trends of social development and envisaged that: 'producers would engage in the work of society according to principles of shared and rational planning'. Lenin developed further the idea that a planned economy and a market economy should be regarded as two contrasting social systems. He said: 'While the market economy continues to exist and while the influence of money and the power of capital is maintained, no law in the world will succeed in eradicating inequality and exploitation. It is only by establishing a large-scale and socialised planned economy that all land, factories and tools can be returned to the ownership of the working classes. Only then, will we be able to eradicate all forms of exploitation'.

However, Marxists must always be concerned with seeking truth from facts. They always develop theory according to the limits of practice and correct any imperfections or flaws in theory by testing it against practice.

On the question of the relationship between capitalism and planning, Marxists were forced to correct their assumption that there was no role for planning within capitalism by the emergence of trusts at the end of the 19th Century. In his 'Critique of the Draft Guiding Principles of the Social Democratic Party of 1891', Engels criticised the fourth paragraph of the introduction to the guiding principles which talked about the disappearance of planning with the rise of capitalism and private production. He strongly stressed that this sentence had to be revised because, 'if we take into consideration the stock companies and the trusts that monopolise and control all sectors of industry, then not only does private production cease to exist, the argument that there is no planning also becomes untenable'. Some time later, in April 1917, Lenin gave a speech in which he also stated that 'as far as our understanding of capitalism is concerned, if we disregard the function of trusts and say that there is no role for planning within capitalism, then this is completely unsatisfactory ... planning now plays a direct role within capitalism and various forms of planning have emerged'.

On the question of the relationship between socialism and the market, despite Lenin's acceptance of the traditional idea that socialism destroys the commodity economy that he espoused after the victory of the October Revolution, Lenin did change his way of thinking and methods when the time came for putting new economic policies into practice. This was because 'economic competition based on the use of the market to satisfy the needs of the masses will occur between socialism, which must be built through the adoption of new economic policies, and capitalism which always threatens to re-emerge'. Lenin merely regarded commodity

89

production, the market economy etc. as a means of strengthening ties between workers and peasants, and as a means to realise the transition to socialism. In essence, however, he still believed them to be capitalist, for he stated that 'circulation means the freedom to trade and that, in turn, means capitalism' and 'commodity exchange and freedom to trade signify the inevitable emergence of capitalists and capitalist relationships'.

Stalinist models of socialist construction that were formed after Lenin's death abolished the commodity economy and the market system. In a book entitled *The Economic Problems of Socialism* written in 1952, Stalin confirmed that under the two forms of socialist ownership, it was inevitable that commodity production and commodity exchange would continue to exist. However, he also denied that enterprises under the ownership of the whole people were units for the production of commodities, that capital goods were also commodities, and that the Law of Value played a regulatory role within the sphere of production. In the 1950s and 1960s, Mao Zedong affirmed that commodity production and commodity exchange still had an active role to play within socialism and indicated that there was a close connection between the fate of commodity production and the level of the social forces of production. He stated that to prematurely abandon commodity production would be to violate objective laws and pointed out that closely linking commodities and socialism was unlikely to lead to the re-emergence of capitalism. However, in the 1970s, Mao Zedong retreated to his belief that there was very little difference between a socialist commodity system and capitalism. It was therefore necessary to limit its development through the dictatorship of the proletariat. This belief held sway right up until Deng Xiaoping's meeting with the American Deputy Editor of the *Encyclopedia Britannica* and others on 26 November 1979, when Deng stated: 'It is inaccurate to say that a market economy is purely limited to capitalist societies and that a market economy is, by its very nature, capitalist. Why can't socialism develop its own market economy – this would certainly not equate with capitalism.' It was only then that we managed to escape the narrow patterns of thinking that had branded a market economy with the stamp of capitalism.

Why is it that a market economy developed under socialism cannot be equated with capitalism? According to Deng Xiaoping, this is because the market economy comprises relationships between elements under the ownership of the whole people, between elements under collective ownership, and between joint enterprise between China and capitalist foreign countries. Nevertheless, the whole system in essence is socialist – it is a product of socialist society. Therefore, using the market economy as a means to an end will not affect the entire socialist system and will not lead to a re-emergence of capitalism. Deng Xiaoping's arguments laid the ideological and theoretical foundations for using a socialist market economy to reform the economic system and accelerate the liberation and development of the productive forces.

While socialist countries may decide to make use of the market economy as a means to develop their social forces of production, there is no obligation on them to develop carbon copies of market systems that operate in capitalist countries. Indeed, despite the usual features of a market economy, a socialist market economy remains tightly bound to the basic socialist system. It is developed under the guiding leadership of the Communist Party with its main activities under public ownership and with the expansion of common prosperity as an overriding objective. These characteristics mean that a socialist market economy can work more effectively than a capitalist market economy in terms of the relationships between general and sectoral management, short-term and long-term operations, planning and the market, macro-economic regulation and micro-economic operations, raising economic efficiency and achieving social justice.

It is likely to take a number of years of hard effort, experimentation, creativity and practical assessment before we can successfully develop and establish an effective socialist market economic system in China. However, practice has undoubtedly proved that Deng Xiaoping's theory on the essence of socialism has facilitated the development of the social forces of production under the socialist system and we now have great latent potential to achieve superiority over capitalism. In the United Nations *1993 World Economic Report* a comparison was made between the methods adopted by China and those adopted by the former Soviet Union and East European countries. The *Report* emphasised that: 'The large-scale privatisation that has occurred within most East European countries as well as Russia and other countries of the former Soviet Union will continue to provoke a downwards slide in their economies and there is already evidence of social unrest.' In contrast, rapid economic growth in China 'is not the result of the whole-scale privatisation of state-owned assets. Although it would appear that the accumulation of wealth is a major motivating factor for entrepreneurs, the facts show that there is no necessary link between this and a spirit of creativity or rights to private ownership.' On 7 September 1994 *Hungary News* published an article entitled 'The New Economic Strategy' in which it was stated that: 'Of all the former socialist countries, only China has been successful'. The reason for this is that 'China has not immediately destroyed the socialist structure and replaced it with a market economy, but has gradually built up a market economy while leaving the political and economic structure relatively intact. This has meant that over 15 years, production in China has not merely maintained its former level, it has grown at an unprecedented rate. Similarly, the standard of living has not fallen, but risen at a rate faster than any country that has followed the capitalist road'.

4. Focusing attention on promoting the development of the productive forces, while making public ownership and distribution according to work implicit within the elimination of exploitation and polarisation

Deng Xiaoping's theory on the essence of socialism specifically highlighted the need to eliminate exploitation and polarisation with respect to the relations of production and broke away from the traditional practice of defining socialism in terms of the system of public ownership and distribution according to work.

Some people separate these two aspects and regard them as opposing forces. Others believe that since public ownership and distribution according to work have not been specifically defined as innate characteristics of socialism, it follows that they are not essential features of socialism. Still more people hold to the view that the system of public ownership and distribution according to work must be defined as the very essence of socialism.

All of these disparate views are misguided. In reality, making a common prosperity through the elimination of exploitation and polarisation our ultimate objective means that we have to uphold public ownership and the principle of distribution according to work in our socio-economic system. In fact, these are two sides of the same question: if we were to replace public with private ownership and distribution according to work with distribution according to capital, how would it be possible to eliminate exploitation and polarisation, and achieve our ultimate goal of common prosperity?

This is the reason why Deng Xiaoping has always given great weight to these two sides of the socialist relations of production. At times he has spoken of these two factors as two extremely important aspects of socialism itself: 'There are two aspects of socialism that are of the utmost importance: a basic reliance on the system of public ownership and the prevention of polarisation' [*Selected Works of Deng Xiaoping*, Vol. 3, p. 138]. At other times, Deng has regarded them as the two basic principles that must be upheld through the duration of the reforms: 'As we proceed with our reforms, we must continue to uphold two basic principles: the leading role of public ownership in our economy, and the need to develop our economy along the lines of common prosperity by preventing polarisation' [*Selected Works of Deng Xiaoping*, Vol. 3, p. 142].

Given the utmost importance of public ownership and distribution according to work, why do we not explicitly define them as innate characteristics of socialism, instead of treating them as pre-conditions and guarantees by making them implicit within the elimination of exploitation and polarisation? It should be pointed out that here lies the crux of Deng Xiaoping's new understanding based on his summation of our historical experiment with socialism. It reflects yet another contemporary feature of his theory on the essence of socialism.

The Communist Manifesto summed up the underpinnings of Communist Party theory as 'the elimination of private ownership'. However, according to basic Marxist principles, transforming the relations of production and achieving a system of public ownership must proceed according to whether or not it facilitates the development of the forces of production. Private ownership is a source of exploitation, alienation, and inequality, but it by no means follows that the socialisation of capital goods at any time and in any form is necessarily in harmony with facilitating the development of the productive forces. If we engage in a blind pursuit of ever more pure and socialist relations of production that are ever increasing in scale without first establishing what the level of our productive forces will be after the socialist system has been established, then the ultimate consequence will be the destruction of production. This is particularly true in a country like China, which is rather under-developed in terms of its economic and cultural levels.

In fact, leading members of the Communist Party including Mao Zedong became aware of this after China's socialist transformation had been achieved. As a result, Mao advocated the maintenance of the individual economy within certain limits to supplement the state-run and collective economies. He also suggested that it was possible to engage once again in capitalism even after capitalism had been abolished; underground factories should be legalised and brought above ground to provide legitimate forms of employment; investment by overseas Chinese should not be confiscated for periods of 20 or 100 years; and distribution should occur according to the principle of giving equal consideration to the state, collective and the individual. In a speech at the 8th Party Congress, Chen Yun put forward some important [balanced] policies such as: allowing the state-run and collective economies to take centre stage while the individual economy remained as a supplementary adjunct to some extent; planned production to be the main focus, but free production determined by the market to play a supplementary role, within the limits of what planning would allow; the state market to play the main role, but this to be supplemented to a certain extent by the free market. It was purely the result of the pernicious development of Leftist ideology that these correct policies were not successfully realised.

After the Third Plenary Session of the Eleventh Party Congress, Deng Xiaoping summed up China's historical experiment with socialism and made this analysis the basis for establishing a series of fundamental criteria against which to test every aspect of the reforms. These criteria were: whether or not [any reform] facilitated the development of the forces of production within a socialist society; whether or not it helped to boost the strength of socialist countries as a whole; and whether or not it helped to raise the standard of living of the population. He advocated the maintenance of state-ownership as the main focus as well as the common development of other components of a diversified economy. He established a system of income distribution that was centred on distribution according to work and that gave precedence to efficiency, while giving due consideration to fairness. Over 15 years of reform, China's economy has developed at a remarkable rate that has attracted world-wide attention. An important factor behind this growth has been the institution of these new policies that have been developed according to China's specific circumstances.

Therefore, the move to make public ownership and distribution according to work implicit within the principles of eliminating exploitation and polarisation, and to define the latter as one of the fundamental characteristics of socialism, was a measure designed to concentrate people's attention on promoting the development of the socialist forces of production. It both upholds the basic principle that socialism should maintain a system of public ownership and distribution according to work, and reflects the need to judge whether or not our reforms help to promote the development of the productive forces. It does not simply focus on the degree of public ownership and distribution according to work in themselves as a means of establishing specific forms of public ownership and distribution under different circumstances and over different periods of time. (For example, during the initial stage of socialism it was only possible to implement methods of allocation and structures of ownership centred around public ownership and distribution according to work).

5. Translating localised prosperity into common prosperity is the only way to develop the social forces of production and raise people's standard of living

The contemporary aspect of Deng Xiaoping's theory on the essence of socialism is also reflected in his proposal that wealth should expand from a small section of the population and a limited number of regions, to a state where, eventually, the goal of common prosperity is achieved. This is the way to promote the development of the social forces of production and raise people's standard of living.

In contrast to the polarisation between rich and poor that exists under capitalism, 'the greatest advantage of socialism is common prosperity. This is manifested in the very essence of socialism' [*Selected Works of Deng Xiaoping*, Vol. 3, p. 364]. The historical experience of socialist countries illustrates that common prosperity cannot be achieved by following the course of egalitarianism since widespread impoverishment will destroy the motivation of the masses and the development of the socialist forces of production. The only possible course of development is to increase the wealth of certain regions first and then move on to achieve the ultimate goal of common prosperity. Deng Xiaoping stressed that 'we will adhere to the socialist road and our basic goal will continue to be the realisation of common prosperity. However, we cannot pursue equal development. Our previous adherence to egalitarianism and eating from the same bowl led in practice to common backwardness and shared impoverishment. This caused us great damage. The first task of our reforms is to destroy egalitarianism and notions of eating from the same bowl. This is the correct course of action for today' [*Selected Works of Deng Xiaoping*, Vol. 3, p. 155].

According to one school of thought, making the socialist market economy a model for reforms to the economic system in order to liberate and develop the forces of production will necessarily produce a growing gap between people's incomes, leading ultimately to exploitation and polarisation. This therefore runs contrary to our policy of eliminating exploitation and polarisation and achieving our ultimate goal of common prosperity.

It is true that a market economy will engender vigorous competition between enterprises and individuals. Under certain conditions, this will increase the gaps between levels of income and standards of living among different individuals and different regions. It could also foster the spread of exploitation and polarisation within sectors of the economy which are not under public ownership. However, the operation of the socialist market economy in China is closely linked to the basic target of developing production and achieving common prosperity. Moreover this is to be attained under a political system reflecting the People's Democratic Dictatorship under the leadership of the Communist Party, a structure of ownership centred around public ownership, and a system of allocation based on distribution according to work. All of this means that under conditions of fair and legitimate competition, we will be able to keep within rational limits any differences in income induced by variations in labour and operations. We can also allow the private economy to take a subordinate position in the wider economy so that it can perform a supplementary role without allowing any exploitation or polarisation to endanger the national economy as a whole. More importantly, the benefits that a socialist market economy will bring in terms of liberating and developing the productive forces and strengthening public ownership will lay the material foundations for the elimination of exploitation and polarisation and the attainment of our ultimate goal of common prosperity. Deng Xiaoping stated that our 'systematic utilisation of foreign capital and partial development of the individual economy are both dependent on the general requirement of developing our socialist economy' [*Collected Works of Deng Xiaoping*, Vol. 3, p. 142]. This means that 'absorbing foreign capital and permitting the existence and development of the individual economy are basically contingent upon furthering the development of the productive forces and strengthening the state-owned economy. It is only by giving pride of place to public ownership within our economy that we will be able to avoid polarisation' [*Selected Works of Deng Xiaoping*, Vol. 3, p. 149]. Therefore there are no grounds for separating these two aspect and treating them as opposing forces.

What then is the practical path of development that we must follow in order to reach our final goal of common prosperity through the initial creation of wealth among certain people and certain regions?

Our primary method is through imitation by example: if some people achieve great results, increased incomes, and improved standards of living through their own hard work, then this will inevitably act as a great force of encouragement spurring others on to follow their example. This will invigorate the entire economy with continuous waves of development and allow every ethnic group throughout the country to achieve relatively rapid increases in wealth [*Collected Works of Deng Xiaoping*, Vol. 2, p. 152].

A second method is by stipulating that the more advanced sectors have a duty to help the less advanced: we must impose constraints on those sectors of society that enjoy initial increases in wealth through the collection of income tax. At the same time we must encourage those who become prosperous fastest to make voluntary contributions to educational or infra-structural projects. While this kind of voluntary action should be encouraged, it is no longer appropriate to make excessive use of such examples as propaganda. As far as different regions are concerned, we must ensure at the appropriate time that those regions that become wealthy the fastest are obliged to pay more tax to support the development of impoverished areas. We need to conduct serious research into the questions of when and on what basis this issue should be resolved. If we start taxing regions too early, it could jeopardise their vitality, and if we impose taxes too late, it could lead to polarisation. Deng Xiaoping envisaged that 'we must emphasise these problems and come up with solutions by the turn of the century when we have brought everyone up to a comfortable standard of living. Until that time, developed regions must continue to develop and offer maximum support to under-developed regions by paying extra taxes and transferring their technology' [*Selected Works of Deng Xiaoping*, Vol. 3, p. 374].

In addition, we can also use the powers of Party and Government organs to transfer wealth and materials and adopt poverty-relief measures to provide support and aid to less advanced regions so that they can begin to achieve rapid development.

We need to devote our energies once more to strengthening the construction of a socialist spirit and a socialist culture in order to provide strong ideological guarantees for the correct development of a socialist civilisation in the material sense, and a firm ideological basis for a smooth transition from selective prosperity to common prosperity. We must sweep away all constraints that are purely a matter of ideology.

In the fifteen years between 1979 and 1993, the total value of China's GDP grew at an average annual rate of 9.29%. This was far in advance of the 6.1% recorded between 1953 and 1978. After price factors have been deducted, the value of urban and rural incomes grew at an annual 6.34% and 8.47% respectively, outstripping by far the 2.2% registered between 1953 and 1978. These objective facts clearly illustrate that allowing certain sectors of the population and certain regions to achieve prosperity first will influence, help and motivate other regions and other sectors to follow in their footsteps. This is not only the essential way to achieve common prosperity, it is also the only way to develop the social forces of production under socialism and raise people's standard of living.

6. Deng Xiaoping's theory on the essence of socialism is a clear reflection of the spirit of the age and will encourage the development of socialism in a more healthy direction

How can we recognise the essential elements of socialism? This is an important question that has a bearing on the success or failure of socialism. In the modern world, the essence of socialism is that democratic socialism is a mixture in which socialism is subsumed by bourgeois democracy, on the [theoretical] basis that democracy and human rights are not only means to the realisation of socialism but are also the ends of socialism itself. That is to say that the aim to establish both a democratic economy and a democratic society. This kind of reasoning has prevented the social democratic parties of the West from putting into practice a socialist agenda since they cannot overcome capitalism. Even if they manage to win power, they are only administering a capitalist society for the sake of the bourgeois classes.

In keeping with the world transition from war and revolution to peace and development, Deng Xiaoping made a comprehensive summary of the historical development of socialism in China and used this as a basis for making the advancement of the development of the socialist forces of production an important criterion for further progress. He analysed the questions concerning the essence of socialism and applied this criterion to every aspect of these essential components. He used his findings as a basis for his new theory on the essence of socialism that clearly reflects the spirit of the age. Not only has this revitalised the development of socialism in China in the direction of the final goal of shared wealth and common prosperity, it will also serve to show the people of the world the inevitability of socialism and the advantages of socialism over capitalism. By the middle of the 21st Century, when we have achieved the third-stage strategic targets for our socialist modernisation, 'we will have even clearer evidence of the advantages of the socialist system over capitalism. This will show the direction of the struggle for three-quarters of the world population and provide even greater proof of the accuracy of Marxism' [*Selected Works of Deng Xiaoping*, Vol. 3, pp. 195–196]. 'This not only provides a path of development for Third World countries which contain three quarters of the world population, it will also, more importantly, show all people of the world that socialism is both inevitable and superior to capitalism' [*Selected Works of Deng Xiaoping*, Vol. 3, p. 225].

Document 2.4

'Some issues relating to the theory of the socialist market economy.'[4]

LIU GUOGUANG

Economic Research, 1992, No. 10

During the upsurge in the study of the speeches which Deng Xiaoping made on his Southern Tour, one of the issues which has been of great interest, and

---

4 This paper is the text of the author's introductory lecture, given on 19 September 1992, in a series of lectures on 'Reform, opening and economic development in the 1990s', given under the joint auspices of the Organisation and Propaganda Departments of the Central Committee, the Chinese Institute of Science and Technology, organs and working committees directly under the Central Committee and Central Committee state organs and working committees.

which everyone has been eagerly discussing, has been that of the socialist market economy. The issue is not actually a new one. As long ago as 26 November 1979, when he gave an interview to the deputy chief editor of the American *Encyclopedia Britannica*, Deng said, 'It is definitely incorrect to say that the market economy is limited to capitalist society and refers to the capitalist market economy. Why can't socialism have a market economy? The seeds of a market economy were sown as early as the period of feudal society. Socialism too can have a market economy.' In 1985, when receiving a delegation of United States industrialists, Deng reiterated this view. Early this year, in the speeches he gave during his southern tour, he made comprehensive and penetrating statements on the issues of planning and the market, inspiring us to consider further the question of a socialist market economy. Deng's series of statements on planning and the market have been an important component of the establishment of the theory of socialism with Chinese characteristics, and we need to study them carefully, grasp them properly, and put them into effect in the reform and development of China's socialist economy.

There are two issues I would like to address in what follows: one is to say something about the circumstances surrounding the discussion of theoretical questions relating to the socialist market economy over the last few years, and to describe the protracted evolution of an understanding of the issues of planning and the market (including such concepts as a planned economy, a commodity economy and a market economy); the other is to discuss my own understanding, from studying the speeches which Deng made during his southern tour, of some central questions in the theory of the socialist market economy.

All the changes which have been brought about by our economic reforms – the multiplicity of alterations to the system of ownership, the marketisation of the bulk of the economy, the fostering of the market itself, the fact that the government now also has to manage the economy through the market, and so on – all of these are manifested everywhere in the constant expansion and intensification of market-oriented reforms. Market orientation of this sort is of course not based on a system of private ownership, but on a system of public ownership, and is not oriented towards a blind and anarchic market, but towards a market system which is under macro-control and regulated in a planned way. Are the enormous advances and achievements in the reform of China's state economy over the past twelve or thirteen years, ultimately the fruits of reinforcing administrative mandatory plans or the fruits of expanding the role of market mechanisms and remoulding mechanisms from the traditional planned economy in line with the requirements for developing market mechanisms? The answer is clearly the latter. Why have the coastal areas of southeast China developed more rapidly than China as a whole over the last ten or more years? Why, though both are on the coast, has Guangdong developed more rapidly than Shanghai? One very important reason is that market-oriented reforms have gone much further there.

In the past, many comrades disagreed with or fought against market-oriented reforms, and there were two main reasons for this: the first was that they believed market orientation meant having a market economy, and a market economy used always to be seen as capitalist; the second was that they believed a number of negative phenomena which appeared in the Chinese economy, such as the market chaos, income disparities and inflation of 1988, were caused by the emphasis on market forces. Since Deng Xiaoping's speeches on his southern tour this year, the first reason has ceased to exist. As to the second, some comrades believe that such negative phenomena are unavoidable in the early stages of reform and when first developing a commodity economy, and were due not to over-development of the market but to the fact that the market was not yet developing *enough* and had not really started to mature and the government's macro-control of the economy had not managed to keep pace with it. These phenomena occur during periods of transition, not because there is too much reform but because there is not enough. To rid ourselves of such negative phenomena and problems in our economic life, we must continue to implement market-oriented reforms which are subject to macro-control and planned guidance, and carry them through to the end.

Next, I shall say something about the discussions concerning the question of a socialist market economy.

There has been prolonged discussion of this question ever since the reforms began, and articles about it have proliferated recently, after Deng Xiaoping's speeches, and the general secretary's speech at the Party School. They all take a positive line, however, and no dissenting voices have been heard, whereas for a long time previously there was debate between different views. In April 1979, at the start of the reforms, a meeting was held in Wuxi, to discuss the law of value in a socialist economy, and at this meeting the concept of a socialist market economy was put forward. Some people agreed with it, others did not. It was then, too, that the idea of combining a market economy with a planned economy emerged. When the Central Committee pointed out, at the Third Plenary Session of the Twelfth Central Committee, that China's economy was a planned commodity economy, and delegates were engaged in studying the resolutions of the Third Plenary Session of the Twelfth Central Committee on reforming the system, an elderly economist from Guangdong suggested that if the theory were carried a little further, a socialist commodity economy could also in fact be called a socialist market economy. Other delegates said that there was no need to distinguish the concepts of a commodity economy and a market economy, but that a distinction should be made between a socialist market economy and a capitalist market economy. Opposite opinions also emerged at this time. One professor said that the concept of a market economy had a fixed meaning in the western literature, and that the three principles for a market economy system had been clearly laid out in the writings of Japanese economists. The first was that private ownership of property was sacrosanct; the second was the principle of contractual freedom; the third was the principle of personal responsibility. It was obvious that the typical market economy, as interpreted in western works on economics, was a capitalist market economy. He then went on to say that he believed that 'a socialist, planned commodity economy is not a market economy'. Debates of this sort continued for a long time, until the State Council approved Guangdong province as a pilot region for comprehensive reforms in 1988. Economists in Guangdong, wanting to make some preliminary theoretical explorations, held a conference to discuss questions relating to the market economy in the primary phase of socialism, and these questions were explicitly raised. At this conference a common view was reached that, since there were capitalist market economies in the world based on the system of private ownership, there should also be socialist market economies based on the system of public ownership; that since there had once been free market economies without planned regulation and control, there ought also to be planned market economies subject to macro-control. We should look carefully into the socialist market economy, implement one and develop it. In the second half of 1988, two more important national academic discussions were held, one a theoretical discussion on the reform of the national economic system held at the end of October, and the other a theoretical symposium held in December to mark the ten years since the Third Plenary Session of the Eleventh Central Committee of the CCP. At both these meetings it was proposed that the concept of a commodity economy should be developed a step further, into the concept of a market economy, and it was also suggested that there was an urgent need for us to establish a theory for a socialist market economy. All these things occurred before the political disturbances of early 1989. They were more or less consistent with the trends in theoretical circles of the time, mentioned above, vis-à-vis issues of planning and the market. At that period, two views existed in theoretical circles, but more and more comrades were leaning towards an emphasis on the commodity economy as the more important of the two aspects of a socialist planned commodity economy, and gradually the numbers of those using the concept of a market economy began to increase.

After the spring and summer of 1989, as criticism of the ideological tide of bourgeois liberalisation centred on the advocacy of privatisation was quite rightly growing in the field of economics, criticism of the socialist market economy approach also began to appear in some internal documents. In public discussions, however, there was still a dispute between the two different points of view. One of them held that the market economy position was unacceptable. One writer, in a piece entitled *What is a market economy?* on 17 June 1989 stated that the market economy was a relatively standardised concept with particular connotations, that it was based chiefly on the system of private ownership, that decision-making was highly decentralised and that all economic activity was controlled by the 'unseen hands' of market forces. He believed that because some western nations have linked together a market economy, private ownership and capitalism, many politicians and scientists in socialist countries were not simply being careless when they referred to developing a socialist commodity economy as 'having a market economy'. To talk about developing a commodity economy is fine, but that does not mean having a market economy. He said that the term 'socialist market economy' meant nothing more than using the capitalist market economy as a model for socialist economic reforms. Briefly, then, such a view links the market economy, the planned economy and the socialist system together and asserts that the market economy is capitalist, and that if socialism operates a market economy it is being capitalist. Of course there were still some people who did not agree with this idea, believing that the issue of a market economy cannot be linked to the socialist system, and that the market economy is merely a synonym for a modern commodity economy or a modern monetary economy. Some economists maintain that the essence of China's economic system reforms consists of the substitution of resource allocation based on a market economy for resource allocation based on administrative orders, and in this sense, it is permissible to call a socialist commodity economy, a socialist market economy. Both views continued to exist.

Let us now look at how Xue Muqiao, one of the older generation of economists, treated this issue. He told a journalist from the Shenzhen *Special [Economic] Zone Times* on 11 January 1991 that in-depth research on the relationship between a planned economy and a market economy was needed. He said the old idea that the former was socialist and the latter capitalist, was an approach which was extremely unhelpful when it came to the intensification of the reforms. As to whether a market economy and market regulation are two essentially separate things, he believed that has yet to be discussed. He considered that even if the two can be equated, neither can be equated with capitalism. As long as the system of public ownership of the means of production remains central [to our economy], we cannot say it is a capitalist market economy. Therefore it is still the system of public ownership which differentiates it, and not the market economy. Xue added that 'this issue has not reached maturity, and there are still several areas of theory which are possibly regarded as off-limits. In scientific research, there ought to be no areas which are off-limits: free and serious discussion of this question should be permitted, not avoided.' Discussion, and even confrontation, between different views is normal and helpful, and essential if we are to gain a deeper awareness. Discussion of the two differing views on the socialist market economy continued right up until the beginning of this year, when Deng Xiaoping went on an inspection tour of the south and made public his penetrating opinions. He said that a market economy is not the same as capitalism, since socialism too has markets; that a planned economy is not the same as socialism, because capitalism too has planning. Since he made these speeches, the view that planning and the market, planned economies and market economies, belong to separate systems has started to disappear. But one more process is necessary in order to solve this problem perceptually once and for all. This is not only with regard to the perception of a market economy: it is difficult to change even the old perception of a commodity economy. At the start of the reforms, it was acknowledged that socialism must develop commodity production and exchange, but the concept of the commodity economy was not deemed acceptable, because it was thought that a commodity economy meant a system of private ownership, and generally speaking a commodity economy could not but be a capitalist one. It took several years, from the Third Plenum of the Eleventh Central Committee to the Third Plenum of the Twelfth Central Committee, to change this perception. Changing theoretical concepts is very difficult. When Sun Yefang proposed the concept of socialist profit the same year he ran into similar difficulties.

During the 1980s we put forward the theory of a planned commodity economy, which helped to promote the implementation of economic reforms and development in China. In the 1990s, because our reforms, especially the market-oriented reforms, have gone so deep, we need a new theory, the theory of the socialist market economy. The emergence of this theory will certainly help to further the intensification of our reforms and development.

Since planning and the market are both economic measures, why are we now changing, or developing, the concept of a socialist planned economy into the concept of a socialist market economy?

The reason I spoke just now about why we should make the transition from a 'socialist commodity economy' to a 'socialist market economy', was that I wanted to show clearly that the crux of China's economic reforms is that planned allocation is being replaced by market allocation as the principal method of resource allocation. But there is one issue here that needs to be clarified: since both planning and the market are methods of economic regulation, and whether there is more of one or more of the other bears no relation to the social system, why can we not combine the two, while still retaining the structure of a *planned* economy, rather than insisting on combining them within a *market* economy structure? That is to say, why does the principal method of resource allocation have to be changed from planned allocation to market allocation? This question involves a comparison of the respective implications and respective merits and demerits of the two methods of resource allocation. It should be said that, after many years of implementation and observation, the issue is becoming much clearer.

In fact, planned resource allocation and market resource allocation each have good points and bad points. Planned allocation is ordinarily what occurs when the government acts in accordance with pre-established plans, and depends largely on administrative orders for its implementation. Its great strengths are that it can concentrate forces (i.e., resources) to accomplish major projects, and that it is possible to coordinate economic development with an eye to the interests of society as a whole. But the main drawback of planned allocation is that, because of limitations in the formulation of the plans and in the grasp of information and cognitive ability of the decision-makers, (and such limitations are unavoidable if one considers the positions they hold and the interests they represent), the planned allocation method cannot but suffer from bias and rigidity, and thus it may frequently restrict economic activity and work against the optimised allocation of resources. Market allocation usually works in accordance with the demands of the law of value, by adapting to changes in the relationship between supply and demand, and giving full play to the mechanism of competition. Its strength lies in the fact that it can promote the survival of the fittest, coordinate the relationship between supply and demand and allocate limited resources to the best combination of links by means of sensitive price signals and the usual pressures of competition. But market allocation too has its drawbacks: regulation through the market is characterised by spontaneity, blindness and hindsight. Market regulation either struggles or is completely powerless, for instance, when it comes to ensuring the overall balance of the economy, preventing dramatic economic disturbances, rationally adjusting major economic structures, preventing great disparity and polarisation between rich and poor, and protecting the environment and natural resources.

Since we can see that there are advantages and disadvantages to both planning and the market, it is up to us to make best use of the good points of each and avoid the bad ones, learning from the strong points to make up for the weak ones, and applying the two in combination. But we have not so far answered the question of why we should replace a planned economy with a market economy. I believe that this is a question not of conviction, nor of emotion, but of positivism. This means that if we want to answer the question, we must disentangle ourselves from abstract theoretical considerations of whether the market economy and the planned economy can be dubbed socialist or capitalist, and should take a realistic look at how the operating mechanisms of these two sorts of economy have performed in the world economic arena throughout history, and show which of them is the more effective method of resource allocation, under which conditions, and which of them is the more effective overall.

A look at history will also make us conclude that the planned economy is not to be written off at a stroke. It has its own particular sphere of application and under certain historical conditions is more effective [than the market economy]. And what are the historical conditions under which the planned economy is more suitable? First, when the standard of economic development is relatively low and construction is on a fairly small scale (for example, the First Five Year Plan, when there were 156 construction projects); second, when the economic structure and the industrial structure are relatively simple (as when non-public ownership elements were abolished and the development of heavy industry was paramount); third, when development goals are quite simple and focused (as in a war-time economy, a strategic economy, or when even the provision of food and clothing is problematic); four, when major emergencies, other than war, occur (e.g., an exceptionally serious calamity or economic crisis); five, when a country is closed off from the outside world and has to be self-sufficient. Under these conditions, it is better to have a planned economy, and such an economy will be very effective. But once there is a higher level of economic development, and construction is on a larger scale, once the economic structure and the industrial and product structures become more complex, and the goals of development are normalised and multiplied (when those goals are the satisfaction of the multifarious demands of the people in their lives, and the overall strengthening of the nation, centred on science and the economy), once opening up towards the outside world begins gradually to internationalise the economy – under these conditions, a planned economy in which resource allocation is chiefly implemented by administrative planning is less and less suitable, and it needs to move as soon as it can towards becoming a market economy in which resources are allocated chiefly by the market. This is precisely the situation, and the task, which China now faces. During the eighties, China's economy took a huge step forward, and during the nineties we must grasp this great opportunity to speed up development by building on the optimisation of the structure of production and improving quality benefits; we must carry our opening up a step further, move towards international markets and participate in international competition. This requires us to place more stress on, and give full scope to, the guiding role of the market in resource allocation, and to establish a new system of socialist market economics. On such a foundation, we can better combine planning and the market as regulatory devices. In resource allocation, let the market handle whatever it can handle properly; if the market cannot manage it, or if it cannot manage it properly, it should be managed by the government by means of policy and planning. A modern market economy does not reject government intervention and planning guidance, it actually has to draw on them for support, and rely on them to compensate for the deficiencies of the market itself. This is something which we must never forget as we make the switch from a planned economy to a market economy.

If the concept of a market economy is not peculiar to one particular system, why do we need to add the attribute 'socialist' to 'market economy'? What are the features which distinguish a socialist market economy from a capitalist market economy?

Some people overseas have also asked the question, surely it is enough for China to have a market economy – why does it have to be socialist? Either they have their own motives for asking this, or else they do not understand that both the aim and the content of China's market-oriented economic reforms are the improvement of the socialist system itself, not the blind imitation of western market economies. People overseas ask this question in the belief that there is no difference, as far as operating mechanisms go, between the market economies in the two social systems. If you tell them that there *are* differences, these are seen as being caused not by a problem with the market economy itself, but by differences in the basic characteristics of the two social systems. This is why some of us maintain that we should speak about 'a market economy under socialist conditions', or 'under a socialist system', rather than 'a socialist market economy'. There is, I believe, some truth in this view, but for the sake of brevity, let us agree on the term 'socialist market economics' to indicate 'market economics under a socialist system' or 'under socialist conditions'. Besides this, it is common for some general categories to exhibit specific characteristics when reflected in concrete objects, and quite normal for a specific attribute to be added to a general category. For example, this happens with such commonly-used concepts as 'socialist modernisation' and 'socialist enterprise'. When referring to a market economy under socialist conditions, there is no harm in using the term 'socialist market economy', because the socialist market economy and the capitalist market economy do have things in common, as well as each having specific features of its own. Even among capitalist market economies, the German market economy cannot be equated with the French market economy, nor the Japanese market economy with the US market economy. This is even more the case with the market economies of socialist countries, which of course have differences and special characteristics which are not the same as those of capitalist market economies. We have already touched frequently in this paper on what the socialist market economy and the capitalist market economy have in common, for instance, the function in resource allocation of the law of value, the relationship between supply and demand, price signals, mechanisms of competition, etc. The differences are for the most part due to the fact that a market economy cannot get away from the constraints of the social system in which it exists. The features which differentiate a socialist market economy from a capitalist market economy are determined by the essential characteristics of the socialist system, and particularly by the close links between such an economy and the basic economic system of socialism.

The most important basic characteristics of China's socialist system, as far as the political system is concerned, are the leadership of the Communist Party and the political power of the people. This power, overall, does not pursue the selfish interests of any particular groups or individuals, but has as its aim the service of the people as a whole. In the basic economic system, the ownership structure is principally public ownership (including state ownership and collective ownership), which is supplemented by individual ownership, private operation and the foreign investment economy. Different systems of ownership can take different forms to combine operations, and each element of the economy and each form of enterprise enters the market, competes on equal terms and develops alongside the others. The leading role of the state-owned economy must be fulfilled through market competition. Corresponding to the ownership structure, the principal basis of the socialist system of distribution is distribution on the basis of work, supplemented by distribution on the basis of other production factors, with both productivity and fairness taken into account, and rational application of market mechanisms to increase the distance between them and to stimulate productivity, while at the same time many regulatory devices are applied to even out unfair distribution and gradually achieve prosperity for all. These basic characteristics of the socialist system cannot but have a major influence on the workings of a market economy, by injecting into it greater awareness and greater attention to public welfare. Due to the leadership of the Communist Party, and the fact that we have a basic foundation of public ownership, and the goal of prosperity for all, we have a better chance, in operating a socialist market economy, of being conscious at the outset of combining the interests of society as a whole with those of its parts. In such areas as handling the relationships between planning and the market, between flexibility at the micro-level and coordination at the macro-level, and between stimulating productivity and bringing about social justice, we should also be able to achieve better results than a capitalist market economy and perform more satisfactorily. We are very confident indeed of this, because these are things which can be achieved through persevering with comprehensive reforms.

The establishment of a socialist market economy system is an extremely complex piece of systems engineering, and involves the reform of numerous interlinked and important areas. The first of these areas is the reform of business mechanisms, especially the transformation of the management systems in state-owned large and medium-sized enterprises. Here, by rationalising property rights relationships, we must bring about the separation of government and business, push enterprises towards the market and make them into true corporate entities and competitors in the market, responsible for their own managerial decisions, their own profits and losses, their own development and regulation. Second is the cultivation and improvement of market mechanisms. Not only do we need to develop a commodity economy, we must also cultivate a production factor market and speed up the establishment of price mechanisms in which prices are determined principally by the market, at the same time bringing in standardised and scientific market regulations and management systems. Third is the setting up of social income distribution mechanisms, and a system of social guarantees, which meet the requirements of a market economy while also abiding by socialist principles. Fourth, a macro-control system and macro-control mechanisms should be set up, founded on market forces, and government intervention in enterprises should be correspondingly reduced. There should be a move away from the old micro-management system, under which there is direct control of the money, goods and personnel of an enterprise, towards a macro-management system where the emphasis is on good planning, coordination, supervision and service, through property tax, banking and industrial policies etc. A change in the function of the government is crucial here, because without it, reforms in all the above-mentioned areas will be hard to carry through in greater depth. Each of the reforms in these areas is a complex piece of systems engineering in itself, and thus I shall not go into them in detail here. I shall merely sum up by saying that the establishment of a socialist market economy is not something which can be achieved overnight, but a process which will take a long period of hard and painstaking work. It will require the whole Party, all of our people and all sections of society to work together and, building on the basis of the market-oriented reforms achieved in the past ten or more years, to continue to explore boldly, to have the courage to take risks, to sum up experience at the right time, and thus enable the transformation of our new economic system to move forward smoothly. In this way we can greatly expedite the process of establishing socialism with Chinese characteristics, and bring about the early accomplishment of the second and third of our strategic goals in the economic development of our country.

(The author is Deputy Director of, and research fellow at, the Chinese Academy of Social Sciences) (Editor: Zhan Xiaohong)

Document 2.5

'Deng Liqun criticises Deng Xiaoping, praises Jiang Zemin'[5]

YUEH SHAN

Cheng Ming, (Hong Kong), 1 August 1999

I [Deng Liqun] attend today's symposium marking the 78th founding anniversary of the party with a heavy heart, and my strength has fallen short of my desire. Practice has proved, and will continue to prove, that the theory of centring around class struggle, which was upheld during the era of Mao Zedong, was the cause of China's economic collapse, as well as the cause for the backwardness of our country and the impoverished life of our people; while Deng Xiaoping's 'central theory of centring everything around the economy and placing money above politics' has brought about disaster to our country and our communist party. The corruption and degeneration of the communist party has shaken the foundation of its leading status, there is a lack of unity and solidarity among our people, and the party is heading towards the road of destruction. The problem currently

---

5 These remarks are given as verbatim from a speech by Deng Liqun delivered at a symposium sponsored by the Chinese Communist Party Secretariat on 29 June 1999.

faced by the communist party is not just a problem in certain departments and regions where certain leading cadres have lost their political bearing and become degenerate; but a problem with the entire party – that our Marxist political party has ceased to exist except in name, and a problem with the contingent of leading cadres who have lost their faith and become disillusioned. Where is our country heading? Our party is already on the brink of a virtual degeneration and collapse today, and it will prove a severe historic test to our leading body as to whether our party can make reflections on the status quo. Rebuilding a Marxist communist party is the heartfelt desire and the sense of responsibility of every communist soldier and everyone who believes in communism.

Is Comrade Deng Xiaoping's theory a development and enrichment of Marxism, or is it a revision, deviation from, and betrayal of Marxism; is it keeping with or divorced from China's social and national conditions? Practice has proved that Deng Xiaoping's theory is, in essence, a combination of an Asian capitalist social and economic entity with the political entity of the Soviet Union in the late 1970s. It is true that Deng Xiaoping's central theory of centring everything around the economy and placing money above politics has brought certain material benefits to the people, yet it has failed to win corresponding support from the people, or to strengthen the coherent force among the people. Quite the contrary, all kinds of contradictions in society have intensified; and the spearhead of such contradictions is now directed at the party and the government, and at the leadership of the communist party. From ministries and commissions at the central level to local governments, grassroots units, and rural areas, the organism of the party has already become rotten, which will give rise to crises in the country's political situation and will lead to the collapse of the leadership of the communist party. This is the cost and the failure of Deng Xiaoping Theory.

3

Creating a Market-oriented Industrial and Economic System

INTERDEPENDENCIES AND LINKAGES

Four major features have emerged out of China's economic reform during the past two decades. The first is encapsulated in the transformation of a centrally planned, Soviet-style system of resource allocation to a decentralised, market-orientated, western-style economy. The second reflects changes in ownership, from a system that was overwhelmingly dominated by state-ownership in industry to a myriad of forms, involving direct government control, joint-stock corporations, cooperatives, private undertakings, and Sino-foreign joint ventures. The third feature embraces the national price system: prices fixed by the state (including those for farm procurement) are now essentially a matter of the past, having been largely replaced by free market prices. The final aspect of China's economic reform, which is considered separately in Chapter 7, is captured in the strategic opening of the economy to the outside world.

The first three features are closely linked. In the light of western experience, market transactions presuppose the existence of a social-legal foundation based on private property rights that facilitates and legitimises the turnover of privately owned goods and services. Where they exist, government-owned corporations (railways, aviation, public utilities, etc.) are normally also subject to the same set of market regulations as the much larger number of their private counterparts. In such circumstances, free market prices prevail and are signals of the willingness of private economic units to engage in transactions, whether demand or supply orientated. If, however, central planning and control mechanisms are introduced into this framework, the outcome is to undermine market prices and nullify private ownership. Germany's wartime experience provides a good illustration of this. The Nazi Government's mobilisation in support of armaments construction of large, privately-owned machine-building and chemical conglomerates, against their owners' interests, left private property rights a legal fiction, devoid of any operational significance.

Such organisational interdependence points to the need for a simultaneous, comprehensive solution in implementing economic reform in China. This kind of 'total' solution was indeed at the heart of the 'shock therapy' or 'big bang' approach adopted in Russia, and also characterised the abortive '500-day programme', previously formulated by Yavlinsky on behalf of Mikhail Gorbachev. Yet the Chinese approach – often referred to as 'incrementalism' and aptly described by Deng Xiaoping in terms of a metaphor ('crossing the river by feeling for the stones') – has been quite different. It is essentially an 'unbalanced' strategy, in which successful experimental reforms become proven models, and peripheral industries gradually encroach on the core. Through a transitional process, the core element – central planning itself – is transformed under the impact of market-orientated reform, which gives way to a comprehensive dismantling of the system. This kind of creeping decentralisation has also characterised ownership and price reforms in China.

THE INCREMENTALIST APPROACH

In the twenty years since 1979–1980, China has largely completed the process of economic reform. By virtue of the incrementalist approach embodied in it, it is a process that has not only been characterised by conflicts of interest and resource claims, but at times has experienced major setbacks and retreats. Not until the early 1990s did Deng Xiaoping formulate his own grand vision and thereby tilt the balance towards accelerated systemic marketisation.[1]

The incremental approach is highlighted in two lengthy periods of reform experiments. The first began in 1984–1985, when the Soviet-style system was formally divided into a dual framework comprising a market-orientated sector and a planned sector, and – simultaneously – a phased, generic trimming of the scope of industrial mandatory planning was introduced. Alongside a centralised, but premature attempt (1988) to float almost all prices, these decentralisation efforts contributed much towards eliminating the monopolistic overhang that has been part of the very fabric of China's State Owned Enterprises (SOEs). The upshot was rampant inflation, culminating in the political upheavals of June 1989 and, in 1990, the backlash to reforms.

At the juncture of 1989–1990, it seemed that the previous 'decade of confusion' was abruptly about to end and give way to an inexorable reversal to even more extreme forms of central planning and orthodox Marxist ideology. In the event, however, Deng Xiaoping's own draconian injunction in 1992 gave rise to the second major period of even more robust economic reforms. Out of this emerged the ambitious imperative of establishing a 'socialist market-economic system', involving the even wider

1 Reference to the chronology appended to this chapter will serve to highlight the main stages of the reform process in China. See also Y.Y. Kueh, Joseph C.H. Chai, and Fan Gang (Ed.), *Industrial Reform and Macroeconomic Instability in China*, Oxford, 1999, chapters 1 and 14 for further elaboration of pre-1997 reforms.

opening of China's door to the outside world in order facilitate inflows of foreign investment and higher levels of trade, and the attempt to expose all SOEs, large and small, to the dictates of the market. The marketisation drive clearly benefited from carrying Deng's imprimatur. But it may also have been subtly driven by the desire of the Chinese government to comply with GATT requirements, which embodied a decentralised economic régime free of state manipulation.

There is a marked difference between the first and second periods of decentralisation. In the latter, with mandatory output targets mostly eliminated (see table 3.1), the earlier two-track system had converged into one that was wholly market-based. Not only did this make it very difficult to restore comprehensive, centrally-determined bureaucratic physical controls; it also served to reinforce the national strategy of seeking to assimilate China's economy into the global economic system. Thus, indirect regulation through appropriate fiscal and monetary policy instruments subsequently assumed increasing importance. Indeed, as the experience of prolonged deflation in the late 1990s of demonstrates, these instruments may have been used to excess.[2]

With the benefit of hindsight, the process of incremental reforms seems to have grown out of a master blueprint that was formulated as early as 1984 and called for a gradual transformation of the Chinese economic system from mandatory planning to 'guidance' planning (French-style planification), and eventually to a wholly market-orientated economy. Of all the changes that have taken place over the years, the 1987 CCP National Congress's redefinition of the role of government *vis-à-vis* the market (regulatory), and of the market relative to the enterprises (guiding)[3] would seem to have been critical. In effect, they provided the policy context in which the abortive initiative to implement comprehensive price liberalisation, made by Deng himself, was introduced. But the major setback of 1989–1990 apparently did not invalidate the 1984 blueprint as a means of charting the reforms towards the intended destination of a market-based system with macroeconomic regulation.

2 Interpretations vary on the causes of the prolonged deflation. They all revolve around the massive accumulation of savings deposits (over 6,900 billion *yuan* – around 80% of GDP in 1999) by both urban and rural residents in China – these, in turn, reflecting depressed consumption expenditure. One view attributes this phenomenon to increased economic uncertainty and family vulnerability resulting from rapid economic reforms. The fear of being laid-off without adequate social security provisions for health care, children's education, or simply making consumption ends meet demands precautionary savings. Another view finds an explanation in inadequate financial intermediation to help channel idle funds into productive investment outlays. Whatever the true explanation, notwithstanding an increase in the savings propensity was initially motivated by high interest rates for saving deposits (in order to combat inflation), sucessive interest rates reductions (the latest and biggest – in June 1999 – from 3.78% down to 2.25% on one-year deposits), as well as a new levy on interest income (1999), there have been few signs of a significant rise in consumer spending.

3 See Chronology.

Creating a Market-oriented Industrial and Economic System

Table 3.1 Phasing out central planning and allocation by SPC, 1979–1998

	Mandatory planning in industry		Commodities subject to 'unified distribution'					
	Total no.		Total no.		As % of total output			
	by product categories	As % of GVIO	by categories	Steel products	Timber	Cement	Coal
1979			259	77.1	85.0	35.7	58.9
1980	120	40.0					
1984				62.3	44.3	24.1	49.0
1985	60	20.0	24				
1987	60[1]						
1988	50[1]						
1990			19	41.6	30.7	13.1	50.4
1991				40.7	25.9	11.0	52.5
1992	59	11.7	19	34.3	19.5	6.9	49.5
1993	36	6.8	12	19.9	9.9	4.5	49.2
1996			13[2]				
1998	12	4.1	5[3]	0	0	0	

Note: [1] These targets were set in 1984–1985. Similarly, it was intended that industrial products subject to control by the various branch ministries would be drastically reduced from 1900 categories in 1979 to 380 by 1985.
[2] These constituted a mere 2% of total output.
[3] These included crude oil, petroleum products, coal, natural gas, and automobiles; but then only parts of the products within these five categories are subject to control.

Sources: Y.Y. Kueh *et al.*, op. cit.; and Wang Mengkui, (Ed.), *The Chinese Economy in the 20-Year Transition*, Beijing, 1999, pp. 280–283.

But in its present form, in several important respects the Chinese system still bears the hallmarks of an incomplete transition to a fully-fledged market economic system – hallmarks that are often referred to as 'Chinese' or 'socialist' characteristics. If we are to obtain a full picture of the emerging Chinese economic system, we should examine these more closely.

A MARKET ECONOMY *SUI GENERIS*

The 'socialist' characteristics of the new Chinese economic system can be defined quite easily. Nor is there doubt that in important respects, the system closely reflects the reality of 'Chinese' economic conditions. But for the time being, it remains a matter of speculation whether these special 'characteristics' can eventually be translated into a universally recognisable free market system.

The single most important factor that gives the present Chinese market economy its unique or *sui generis* character, with its socialist overtones, is the continuing pre-eminence of its industrial SOEs. As of 2000, some 65,000 SOEs (including new joint-stock corporations in which the state has a controlling stake) still unaffected by successive rounds of outright or quasi privatisation continue to control a critical mass (28%) of national GVIO.[4]

These SOEs had all experienced two important property rights reform: first, the trial expansion, in 1979–1984, of managerial autonomy (*kuo quan*); the second, the separation (1985–1992) of 'management' rights (*jingying quan*) from the rights to 'ownership' (*yongyou quan*). The ultimate goal of these changes was to free China's SOEs from the political and administrative tutelage by the state. It was not, however, until 1992, when the 'Deng whirlwind' first began to blow across the country, that even the more important and powerful SOEs – especially large and medium-scale SOEs (some 17,000 of them as of 1998) – were encouraged to merge, as circumstances dictated, into multi-enterprises groups (*qiye jituan*) or chaebol-like conglomerates.[5] This was contrary to hitherto strictly demarcated industrial-departmental and territorial spheres of competence or property rights distinctions (state versus collective, or domestic versus foreign ownership). But the new conglomerates have clearly been expected to assume the business forms of companies having limited liability or, even more significantly, of joint-stock corporations, in which the state would hold a controlling stake (and for which the Shanghai and Shenzhen stock markets had, in 1990–1991, almost simultaneously been established).[6]

The campaign to incorporate SOEs into a joint-stock system gained momentum in 1994. In October 1997, it was endorsed by the Fifteenth CCP National Congress, where it was the main thrust of policy designed to end the perennial search for an 'ownership' solution that would facilitate

4 In 1992, on the eve of massive marketisation, the corresponding figures were 103,000 and 48%. In fact, the relative quantitative decline also partly reflects the reclassification, especially since the early 1990s, of many larger SOEs into the new categories of share-holding corporations (*gufenzhi jingji*) and Sino-foreign joint ventures, in which the state still retains, to a greater or lesser extent, a non-controlling share. This is in addition to the accelerated privatisation of small unprofitable SOEs – through selling, merging, leasing or in the guise of commissioned management – since the late 1980s. Another major reason for the reduced GVIO share of SOEs is the rapid expansion of TVEs. For virtually every year since the mid 1980s, TVEs' output has grown significantly faster than that of SOEs. Many TVEs have even been able to intercept raw material supplies to SOEs and have effectively encroached on their market shares.

5 The term 'chaebol' (of South Korean origin – *caifa* in Chinese) refers to such internationally renowned brand names as Hyundai, Daewoo, and Samsung. Prior to the spectacular collapse of some of these huge conglomerates in 1998–1999 under the impact of the Asian financial crisis, the Chinese targeted chaebols as a model for emulation in SOEs reforms. I benefited from a discussion with Professor Chang Xiuze, Executive Deputy Director of Economic Research Institute of the State Development and Planning Commission, PRC, during his visit to Lingnan University in Hong Kong on 20 January 2000; see also his feature article in *Ta-kung Pao* (*Impartial Daily*), Hong Kong, 23–25 November 1999.

6 Following the debut of the familiar Tsingtao Brewery on the Hong Kong Stock Exchange in 1991, large SOEs have sought, successfully, public listings in Hong Kong, New York and elsewhere.

the establishment of a 'modern enterprise system' (*xiandai qiye zhidu*), incorporating western-style corporate governance. At the Fourth Plenum, convened in late September 1999, the campaign was further elevated as the only tenable path to fulfilling the long-run 2010 vision of 'combining public ownership with the market economy (in an effective way)' and 'enabling enterprises of different ownership forms to compete with one another on a fair basis'.

Nevertheless, in the midst of the corporatisation drive,[7] the new variants of SOEs continue, as did their predecessors, to be 'custodians of state priority'. Specifically, the government at various levels still retains the authority to make key appointment and remuneration decisions, as well as major investment decisions. This clearly is contrary to the dictates of orthodox western-type corporate governance. What is more, today's Chinese SOEs still monopolise or otherwise control many crucially important economic activities or 'pillar' industries, including rail transport, civil aviation, telecommunications, power generation, petrochemicals, chemicals, metallurgy, machine-building, automobile, and electronics, as well as banking and finance. Taken together, these add up to a highly integrated industrial system of strategic importance to national development – one that cannot easily be broken up and made wholly subordinate to market forces.

Furthermore, in the wake of the recent bold initiative, launched at the National People's Congress in March 2000, to focus developmental efforts of the entire country on western interior regions in order to promote the second wave of national development, it is likely that the state's role will be further enhanced, in order to facilitate the massive, concentrated transfer of capital and technology, and provide the necessary logistical physical support from relevant major coastal industries. How and whether this policy orientation is eventually compromised by increased competition from the expected influx of western investors following China's entry into the WTO is of course a separate issue.

The role of the state in China's economic transition has manifested itself in many other ways. Foremost among these has been the new approach to price regulation and control of major commodity prices, through the establishment of buffer reserves and risk-hedging funds at both the central and local government levels. This has embraced – quite uncharacteristically from the perspective of an advanced western-style market economy – a wide range of commodities, including grain, edible oil, cotton, and even chemical fertilisers, which hold the key to stabilising agricultural output in China.

---

7 By early 2000, about 10% of all SOEs had been 'corporatised', presumably with a 'modern enterprise system' (MES) in place. According to a State Statistical Bureau survey made in 1998, of 2,562 large SOEs classified as having national strategic significance, 1,943 (75.8%) had established a MES. Of these, 612 (31.5%) had been reorganised into joint-stock corporations, and 768 (39.5%) into companies with limited liability. The remaining 563 (29%) retained sole proprietorship status. Clearly, corporatisation has mainly impinged on the larger SOEs: see Wang Mengkui, *op. cit.*, p. 87.

Finally, in order to strengthen and enhance macroeconomic control, both fiscal and monetary policy instruments demand constant refinement if they are to cope with many new and crucial variables that have emerged. Attention should be drawn to three of these. First, are the increased inflows of foreign capital and the trade surplus, which together may translate directly into base money supply. Second, are the 'non-standard' wage payments made by foreign-invested enterprises (FIEs) over and above income received and investment made by the millions of TVEs and urban collective undertakings that constitute now rather a substantial share of aggregate demand. Third and last are most input materials imported by FIEs and other sources, which serve significantly to enhance aggregate supply. In short, this new macroeconomic setting marks a sharp departure from the past, when central planning dictated that the government's main task in providing for national financial equilibrium was simply to ensure that the total supply of consumer goods, valued at officially fixed relative prices, matched the national 'consumption fund' (itself strictly circumscribed by officially set industrial wage norms and farm procurement prices). Clearly too, the days have gone, when, in the wake of a major supply disruption (perhaps due to a poor harvest), the government could simply resort to strict rationing in order to suppress inherently exploding inflation.

In general, the incrementalist approach that China has adopted during the last two decades in order to create a market-orientated economic system has fared remarkably well. This incrementalist experience is in sharp contrast to the catastrophic disorder, which followed the espousal of 'shock therapy' in Russia under Boris Yeltsin. In China, inflation has been kept within a tolerable range and, remarkably, GDP growth has been sustained at a rate of well over 9% p.a. for the entire 20-year period. It was only ten years ago, when Russia's GDP was more than twice the size of China's GDP. Today, it is one-third smaller.[8]

Appendix

Chronology of industrial enterprise reform

1979 • Enterprise fund, financed by permitted profit retention, set up in SOEs (State Owned Enterprises), as a conduit for incentive bonus awards and small innovative investment outlay; central planning and management framework remained unaltered, however.

---

8 From 1991 to 1996 alone, Russia's GDP fell by 45% – far greater than the 25% wartime reduction in GNP, or the 30% loss in the US GNP occasioned by the Great Depression of 1929–1933. Between 1991 and 1996, the general price level in Russia rose 6188-fold, with annual inflation peaking at an astonishing 2,600%, compared with the Chinese peak of 22% (1994).

1980 • Some 6600 pilot SOEs selected for reform experiments; mostly of large-and medium-scale, accounting in total for 60% of national gross value of industrial output (GVIO) and 70% of all industrial profits earned.

1983 • Initial experiment launched for replacing compulsory profit delivery by SOEs with income tax payments (*ligaishui*); state appropriations (non-interest-bearing) converted into bank loans (*bogaidai*) for financing fixed asset investment.

1984 • A 10-point decree announced in May for extending SOEs' decision-autonomy – as a precursor to the major reform blueprint promulgated in October, envisaging 'guidance' (*zhidaoxin*) planning to fare alongside and eventually replace conventional mandatory control with physical input and output targets:

• two-track system (*shuangguizhi*) emerged, allowing SOEs to operate for both the plan and the market in production, investment, and pricing.

• Commune and Brigade enterprises renamed Township and Village enterprises (TVEs) and given new mandate for satisfying both consumer and producer demands; rapid proliferation subsequently throughout China.

• Soviet-style monobank system split into two-tier structure; mandatory loan quotas nonetheless still imposed by Central Bank (People's Bank of China) on the specialised state banks (agriculture, industry and commerce, investment, and foreign exchange).

1985 • Significant wage reform linking total wage bill to realised profit and allowing SOEs to shape internal wage system; floating wages introduced.

• Renewed policy call for 'invigorating' large – and medium-scale SOEs.

• Industrial products under mandatory planning by State Planning Commission (SPC) and those controlled by branch ministries, as well as commodities subject to 'balancing' and 'unified distribution' by SPC, all began to be phased out from 1985 onwards.

• First major attempt made at price liberalisation (in contrast to previous rounds of readjustments officially made within the framework of set prices), causing the first wave of inflation (8.5% in 1985, 6.0% in 1986 and 7.3% in 1987).

1986 • Small SOEs began to be sold off, or more generally, leased out initially to collective and private individuals under the guise of commissioned management; new status, organisation, and modus operandi thus becoming similar to TVEs and numerous urban collective undertakings.

• Continuous twin-expansion of 'high consumption' and 'high investment' despite renewed recourse by government to administrative fiats for controlling inflation.

- China applied for admission to GATT (reorganized into World Trade Organization (WTO) in 1994).
1987 • Industrial 'contractual management responsibility system (*chengbao jingying zerenzhi*) generally adopted by large- and medium-scale SOEs.
- Key policy slogan 'let the government regulate the market; let the market guide the enterprises' enshrined in the 13th National Congress of the Chinese Communist Party (CCPNC) communique.
1988 • Abortive attempt made in summer to achieve comprehensive price liberalisation in line with Deng's famous injunction that it was 'better to endure a sharp, sharp bout of pain than suffer long, lingering pain'.
- Disastrous bank runs and panic buying in major parts of the country in summer and autumn.
- Inflation surging to record high of 18.5% for the year.
1989 • Political upheavals in 'Tiananmen Square' targeting *guandaoye* (officials colluding with SOEs to illicitly redivert centrally allocated production materials to the market for profiteering from highly inflated prices).
- Inflation staying at high of 17.8%.
- Double (fiscal and monetary) squeeze policy, initiated in late 1988, enhanced to combat inflation.
1990 • Hectic re-centralisation by way of renewed bureaucratic-physical-allocative control, coupled with continuous 'double-squeeze', leading to 'crash landing'; inflation decelerating to 2.7% in 1990 and 2.9% in 1991, and hence severe recession well into 1991.
1992 • Deng Xiaoping proclaimed, in conjunction with his famous 'South China inspection tour' in early spring, bold move to further open up China both geographically and institutionally.
- Creating a 'socialist market economy' now made a national strategic goal at the 14th CCPNC held in October.
1993 • Mandatory industrial output targets for SOEs drastically reduced amidst the marketisation drive.
- Renewed decentralisation and relaxation in bank loans and credit control prompted inflation to accelerate to 13% from 5.4% in 1992.
- Zhu Rongji, then Vice-Premier, introduced, in July, a 16-point programme to attack inflation, including: compulsory bank loan recall and subscription quotas for treasury bonds, advance approval for any new capital-raising schemes, strict separation of 'policy' loans from commercial loans (to guarantee adequate fund supply to priority sectors), a moratorium on price reform in the second half of 1993, and perhaps more importantly, the introduction of flexible interest rate readjustments by the People's Bank to attract savings deposits (in order to address a growing

'disintermediation' crisis caused by funds circulating freely outside the formal banking sector (*tiwai xunhuan*) for cashing in high market interest rates).

1994
- Wide-ranging reforms in finance and taxation, money and banking, and foreign exchange systems initiated in late 1993 compromising, nonetheless, Zhu's programme to result initially in yet another round of even higher inflation (21.7% in 1994 and 14.8% in 1995). (Other contributing factors include massive rise in food prices, wage hikes, and favorable trade balance translating into base money expansion).
- Specialised banks converted into commercial banks proper, with enlarged business portfolio overlapping with each other's specialty.

1996
- New platform now largely in place for applying western-type fiscal and monetary policy instruments to regulate macroeconomic aggregates and instability for a 'soft landing'; inflation successfully phased down to 6.5%.
- Producer goods subject to 'unified distribution' by SPC now consistently reduced to a mere 13 categories, making up a mere 2% of GVIO.
- Prices determined by markets now embracing 80% of producer goods, 85% of agricultural products, and 95% of industrial consumer goods.

1997
- Inflation decelerating into negative consecutively for more than 25 months from October 1997 through late 1999;[9] interest rates reduced by eight rounds from September 1996 well into 1999, with a view to stimulating consumption and investment expenditure for sustaining high GDP growth (8.8% in 1997).
- 15th CCPNC, convened in October, decided to convert major SOEs into joint-stock entities with modern, western-type corporate governance.

1998
- New banking regime adopted for regulating lendings by commercial banks with prescribed asset-liability ratio rather than credit volume quotas.
- GDP growth hardly affected by Asian financial crisis; realized with a remarkable 7.8% for the year under fiscal and monetary policies with 'appropriate tightness' (*shidu congjin*).
- Continuous supply glut with negative inflation prompted scholars and officials to speak of a 'farewell to the economics of shortage' à la Kornai, (i.e. the phenomenon of pervasive supply shortage conditioned by tight centralised allocation in all Soviet-style economies).

9 This refers to the general (social commodity) retail price index; for consumer prices the comparable monthly decline began from April 1997, and for producer goods prices as early as April 1996. By November 1999, there was still no signs of a reversal.

1999 • 4th Plenum of the 15th CCPNC held in September, with the 'Decision on some key problems concerning SOE reform and development' promulgated, deliberating the envisaged role of public ownership and SOEs in the market economy through 2010.
   • Breakthrough in Sino-American negotiations over China's entry into WTO, paving the way for the Chinese economic system to be further assimilated to the western model.

Document 3.1

'The role of the State in the Socialist Market Economy'

SHE JIANMING

Modern Enterprise Herald, Vol. 5, 1997, No. 5.

In 1992, the Fourteenth National Congress of the Chinese Communist Party set a reform target for building a socialist market economic structure. It aimed at making the market play its fundamental role in the allocation of resources under state macroeconomic control. At this point China's reform and opening-up policy and economic development entered a new historical period. The functions of government must also be further reformed in order to meet the requirements of a developing socialist market economy.

In the present stage, the economic functions of the Chinese Government are embodied mainly under the following eight headings:

(1) To formulate long-term plans and industrial policies for economic and social development and put forward strategic development goals to guide the readjustment of the industrial structure

The *Ninth Five Year Plan for National Economic and Social Development and the Outline of Long-Term Goals for 2010* is China's first plan for the medium and long terms under conditions of a developing market economy. Compared with the eight preceding Five Year Plans, this plan has greatly reduced content of a mandatory nature and related quantitative targets. It has put forward, with stress, the main goals, basic principles, guidelines and strategic policies for national economic and social development. Among these are the goals for readjusting and optimising the industrial structure and related policy measures. This plan for the medium and long term gives prominence to its macroeconomic, strategic and policy character. In general, it is a plan of a character that guides and predicts. The targets of government macroeconomic control set forth in the plan will guide enterprises in making business decisions and in carrying out microeconomic activities, but they are not binding. The industrial policies, structural readjustments, and major development projects proposed by the plan will be given financial support by the state or granted loans according to policy. The State will also use various economic levers and economic policies to ensure their realisation, taking into consideration market competition and changes in supply-demand relations. Since the beginning of the 1990s, the Chinese Government has successively formulated and promulgated outlines of industrial policies for the 1990s; instructive catalogues for use by foreign industrial investors; and industrial polices for the automobile industry. The industrial policies for the machine-building, electronics and construction industries are now being formulated.

(2) To strengthen and improve macro control in economic operations

An important government function is to strengthen and improve macro control in economic operations. China is now in a period of transition of its economic structure. Structural contradictions have stood out due to heavy employment pressure. The prices of major commodities and services have not yet been rationalised. The market system is still in a relatively low stage of development, while risk and self-restraint mechanisms of State Owned Enterprises have not yet been fully established. And there are many factors which can lead to inflation. Therefore, it is especially necessary to strengthen and improve macroeconomic control. The experience over the past few years has further proved this point. Due mainly to investment inflation, commodity retail prices increased by 13.2% in 1993 and further by 21.7% in 1994. Faced with this situation, the Chinese Government decided to check inflation and regarded it as the primary task of macroeconomic control. It adopted a series of policy measures to strengthen and improve macroeconomic control, which achieved significant results. The rate of increase in retail prices fell back to 14.8% in 1995 and further to below 6.5% in 1996. On the other hand, economic growth in these two years maintained the higher rate of around 10%. Thus, a 'soft landing' was achieved. This indicates that the ability and effectiveness of the Chinese Government in exercising macroeconomic control to regulate the market economy has risen steadily.

The Chinese Government exercises macro control mainly in accordance with a macroeconomic control target. In setting this target, the Chinese Government employed four indicators which are in common use internationally. These are the economic growth rate, the inflation rate, the balance of international receipts and payments, and the employment rate. Apart from these, it added several other indicators in accordance with China's actual conditions, which are the fixed assets investment rate, financial receipts and payments, the rate of increase in currency supply, and the natural growth rate of the population. It regarded the proper handling of the relationship between reform, development and stability in promoting a sustained, rapid and healthy development of the national economy as the basic theme of macroeconomic control in the present stage, so as to combine the achievement of a basic balance of the economic aggregate with the optimisation of the industrial structure, and to combine the control of the demand pull with an increase in effective supply. In choosing the forms and means of macro control, it made greater use of such economic means as credit, taxation, interest rate, exchange rate and price controls, as well as legal means. It exercised mainly indirect control, supplemented by administrative measures when necessary. At the same time, it strengthened the monitoring and forecast of macroeconomic movements and activities, correctly analysed and assessed the economic situation, and properly adjusted the intensity, timing and focus of macroeconomic control.

(3) To cultivate a market system and supervise market operations

In the course of transforming China's economic structure, the Chinese Government has all along played an important role in forming, developing and perfecting a market system. Since the beginning of reform and opening up 18 years ago, all kinds of commodity markets have developed rapidly. Finance, labour, property, technology and information markets, as well as markets for other essential factors of production have sprung up, and a competitive and open market system has begun to take shape. In reforming the price management system and price formation mechanism, the Chinese government adopted the form of combining adjustment and deregulation of prices and step-by-step advancement. At present, about 80% of the purchasing prices of farm produce, about 90% of the prices of consumer goods and about 80% of the prices of means of production are formed by the market. As a result of the smooth implementation of the price reform, the gravely distorted price parity relationship is becoming rational, and there has been no major turbulence in economic operations and in people's livelihood. The Chinese Government has also stepped up its work in making laws and regulations for the market. It has formulated, or is formulating, a series of laws and regulations aimed at protecting fair market competition, regulating economic behaviour on the market, maintaining market order and improving market regulation and control. It has actively developed intermediary organisations to play their service, communication, notary and supervisory roles for the market. At the same time, in order to enhance market monitoring and set up and perfect a market information transmission and feedback system, the State has drawn up circulation plans to reflect the total demand and supply of major commodities for the whole economy and the flow directions of these. It has set up systems for ordering some of the major commodities and putting them on the market, as well as an import and export regulation system, in order to regulate market supply and demand and ensure market stability. In addition, it has preliminarily established a major commodities reserve and price regulation fund system and a food and non staple foodstuff risk adjustment fund system to cope with major regional natural disasters and other emergencies.

(4) To accelerate infrastructure construction and improve the investment environment

Government functions in this respect are mainly manifested in four areas:

First, policy formulation. For the energy industry, it has called for attention to be paid to both development and energy saving. First priority is to be given to the latter and efforts are to be made to readjust the energy consumption structure. Energy development is to take electric power as the core and coal and charcoal as the base. Great efforts are to be made to exploit petroleum and natural gas, and to develop new energy sources as well as renewable energy sources. These policies have played an important guiding role in the rapid development of China's energy industry in the past more than 10 years.

Second, centralisation of planning. The government has put into force comprehensive plans for the development of communication and transportation facilities. With emphasis on strengthening the capacity of railway transportation, it has brought the superiority of many means of transportation, including highway, water, air and pipeline transportation, into full play, and built a comprehensive transportation system. It has enforced centralised planning on the layout for regional communications and transportation, laying stress on the key points. It has achieved an initial result in easing the 'bottlenecks', which have seriously impeded communications and transportation for many years, and at the same time promoted the economic development in central and western China.

Third, concentration of investments. Over the past 10 years and more, the Chinese Government has persistently attached importance to investments in infrastructure development. It not only has treated this as a priority for direct government investments and loan investments by state banks, but also has made every endeavour to mobilise various social capitals to invest in it. The State made arrangements for 284 major infrastructure development projects during the Eighth Five Year Plan period, representing 27% of the total number of large and medium-sized capital construction projects. These involved investments of 391.5 billion yuan, 54.7% of total investments in large and medium-sized capital construction projects for the same period. Among them, investments in posts and telecommunications development projects completed during the period amounted to 232.9 billion yuan, nearly 12 times the investments made under the Seventh Five Year Plan, representing an annual growth of about 72%.

Fourth, policy support. The State has successively set up construction funds for electric power, railway, posts and telecommunications, highway, civil aviation and port projects. It has readjusted several times the prices for infrastructure, which were on the low side. Apart from maintaining a steady increase in indirect financing, it has carried out experiments on direct financing by means of stocks, bonds and equity financing. It has made explorations of different forms of joint investment by various investment entities. It has gradually eased restrictions on direct foreign investment in infrastructure projects, and carried out experiments on 'BOT' and other forms of project financing. All these policies and measures have produced positive effects in quickening infrastructure construction.

(5) To promote the structural transformation of State Owned Enterprises and strengthen the management and supervision of state owned assets

Since the beginning of reform and opening, along with the rapid development of non state owned economy, the proportion of the state owned economy in the aggregate of the social economy as a whole has declined year after year. Nevertheless, its leading role in the state economy has not changed. Its leading role is even more conspicuous in the electric power and petroleum sectors of the energy industry; in the railways, ports, civil aviation and posts and telecommunications sectors of the infrastructure; and in such important sectors of manufacturing industry as automobile, electronics, petrochemicals and metallurgy. According to statistics gathered during the national campaign to revalue the stocks and assets of enterprises, in March 1995 total assets of State Owned Enterprises accounted for 65% of the total assets of all enterprises in the economy; jobs provided by them accounted for 67% of total urban employment; and the amount of money turned over to the state accounted for 60% of the total state revenue. Proceeding from the actual conditions in China, the Chinese Government will uphold for a long time the policy of developing the leading role of the state owned economy with the public ownership system as the mainstay. Therefore, an important function of the Chinese Government is to supervise and control State Owned Enterprises.

After more than ten years of reforms and explorations, government supervision and control of the State Owned Enterprises mainly involve two things, which must be done well. The first job is to promote the structural transformation of the State Owned Enterprises. The objective is to set up a modern enterprise system with 'unequivocal property rights, clearly-defined powers and responsibilities, separation of government functions from those of enterprises, and scientific management' as its basic characteristics. Specific policies and measures are now being adopted to help State Owned Enterprises solve problems left over from the past. These include problems such as debt ratios being too high, social burdens being too heavy, and staff redundancy as well as practical problems arising from enterprise reform, reorganisation and transformation. They will also spur enterprises to strengthen their management and to become real market competitors. The second job is to strengthen supervision and management of the State Owned Enterprises. In accordance with the principle of separating government's investment management function from its investment function, and of separating its social economic management function from those of state property ownership, we are establishing a state property investor and a corporate assets system adapted to the market economy as well as a system that combines unified state ownership, government supervision at each level, and enterprise operational independence.

(6) To perfect the social distribution mechanism and set up a sound social security system

Under conditions of giving full play to the basic functions of market mechanisms in the allocation of resources, we need to perfect the social distribution mechanism by firmly adhering to the principle of the coexistence of various modes of distribution with distribution according to one's work as the main mode, giving first consideration to efficiency, but at the same time taking fairness into account. The Chinese Government has all along attached importance to the question of perfecting the social distribution mechanism, and at the same time playing its irreplaceable role in maintaining fairness. Since the implementation of reform and opening up, the Chinese Government has, as a first step, made major readjustments in the relations of distribution under the planned economic system. In recent years, in light of the crucial problems existing in the realm of distribution, it has adopted a series of policy measures of a regulatory character. For example, through deepening the reforms in the financial and taxation systems and in the distribution system of enterprises, it has strengthened the restraining mechanism for wage distribution and regulated the relations of distribution between the State, the enterprises and individuals. By means of readjusting the prices of farm products and other reforms [government] has also regulated the relations of distribution between urban and rural areas and between workers and peasants and, through stepping up the collection and management of personal income taxes and readjusting the distribution policy, it has regulated the interest relationship among the social constituents. The Chinese Government has drawn up a 'help-the-poor' program for the Eighth Five Year Plan period and adopted a series of policy measures. It is anticipated that, by the end of this century, it would have basically solved the problems of 65 million poverty-stricken people. The Chinese Government has started to implement a preferential policy on major development projects in Central and West China and is vigorously encouraging economic integration and technical cooperation between the eastern, central and western regions in order to promote a harmonious development of the regional economies.

Over the past ten years and more the Chinese Government has also carried out active explorations as to how to promote reform in the social security system. In the mid-1980s, it started to reform the endowment insurance program. By the end of 1995, staff members and workers of enterprises in cities and towns participating in endowment insurance plans totaled 89 million people, representing 75% of the total number of enterprise staff and workers, while people taking up endowment insurance plans in rural areas numbered 51 million. Since the beginning of the 1990s, the Chinese Government started to reform the unemployment insurance system. By 1995 the number of employees and workers participating in unemployment insurance plans reached 95 million. Over the past few years a total of six million unemployed people were provided with unemployment relief, while some three million were helped to find other jobs. Meanwhile, reforms in the medical insurance system for employees and workers have begun to produce effects in the past 10 years, while reform in urban and rural social welfare and social relief systems and efforts to provide special care to and to resettle disabled servicemen and family members of revolutionary martyrs, have also made remarkable progress. Through the combined efforts of the government at all levels and various social circles, a social security system comprising social insurance, social welfare, social relief and special care for and resettlement of the disabled servicemen and martyrs' family members, and a social security structure integrating mutual assistance in society and personal savings accumulation protection have gradually taken shape. Practice proves that the government's positive role in developing social security undertakings has helped maintain social stability and protect the interests of labourers, and has created a favourable social environment for economic development.

(7) To implement a sustainable development strategy to promote harmonious economic and social developments

China has the largest population in the world. Notwithstanding its vast territory and comparatively rich natural resources, per capita resources are much lower than the world average. Moreover, its resource utilisation rate is low, while waste and destruction of resources have given rise to very serious environmental and ecological problems. In the light of this situation, the Chinese Government has all along regarded the control of population growth and protection of the environment and ecological equilibrium as its basic state policies, and as the inescapable responsibility of the government at all levels. In particular, after the United Nations Environmental Development Convention passed the resolution on the 'Global Agenda for the 21st Century' in 1992, the Chinese Government made a commitment and took the lead in formulating a sustainable state-level development strategy in light of its actual conditions – *China's 21st Century Agenda – A White Paper on China's Population, Environment and Development in the 21st Century.* This document serves as a guiding document for government at all levels in formulating long-term plans for the development of the national economy and social development.

(8) To promote economic exchange and cooperation with foreign countries and encourage domestic enterprises to participate in competition on the international market

We are in an age in which our economic life is becoming increasingly internationally and globally oriented. Scientific and technological progress and economic development now transcend national boundaries, bringing closer together different countries and different peoples. Looking at the trend of economic development in the world today, one finds that economic coordination between governments of various countries is essential, whether in strengthening the global multilateral economic system, in setting up an integrated regional economic organisation, or in developing bilateral economic and trade relations and promoting international cooperation between enterprises. A government not only has to be an active promoter of, but also the initiator and participant in its country's economic exchange and cooperation with other countries. Since the beginning of the 1980s, China has regarded opening up to the outside world as a basic national policy, and elevated this policy to an unprecedentedly high strategic plane. The government has done a large amount of work to promote development of economic relations with foreign countries and to develop international economic cooperation. This has helped maintain a tendency of rapid development in foreign trade, in the utilisation of foreign capital, and in economic and technical exchanges with foreign countries. In accordance with the requirement for adapting China's developing socialist market economy to international practices, we have persistently carried out reform and readjustment in economic structures and policies involving foreign interests. At the same time, we have made efforts to improve the investment environment and create still better conditions for China's enterprises to develop foreign trade and attract foreign investment by stepping up infrastructure development, training personnel with pertinent expertise, raising administrative efficiency, and regulating market behaviour.

We also intend to further open up the agricultural, energy, transportation and other basic industrial and infrastructure sectors to interested foreign parties, and will also open up the financial, insurance, commercial and foreign trade domains in a measured way. Proceeding from the actual conditions in China, the Chinese Government has stepped up contacts and negotiations with international economic organisations and foreign governments and signed a large number of multilateral and bilateral economic and trade cooperation agreements. Domestically, it has actively created conditions by means of introducing macroeconomic policies related to financial and monetary affairs, foreign trade and industrial development to pave the way for Chinese enterprises to enter the international market and engage in fair competition. It is known to all that the Chinese Government has persistently endeavoured to join the World Trade Organization and promoting economic cooperation and trade liberalization in the Asia-Pacific Region.

II

We have made many useful explorations on how to change government's economic functions. Nevertheless, generally speaking, the question of how the government should properly discharge its economic functions under conditions of a market economy is still new to us. In practice, quite a few problems still exist. The main problems are:

First, the question of separating government functions from those of the enterprise. The government is still intervening in business of enterprises more than it should and it has intervened in matters which should have been decided upon and taken care of by the enterprises themselves. This is mainly because we still lack specific and clear-cut regulations separating the functions of government as owner of state properties from its overall responsibilities to society and the economy; the functions of administrative management of state assets from the functions of making use of these assets; and the proprietary rights of the investor from the property rights of the enterprise as a legal entity. The question of how to continue the reform of the government structure, how to set up a new state property operating and management system and how to change the operating mechanism of State Owned Enterprises in accordance with the requirements of a developing socialist market economy, all remain unresolved both in understanding and in practice. The State Owned Enterprises need government assistance to solve the many problems left over from the past. On the other hand, some State Owned Enterprises are overly dependent on the government. All these problems are still pending resolution.

Second is the question of centre-local relationships. China is a big country with a large population and complex conditions. Its resources are unevenly distributed and its economic development is not balanced. Giving the localities necessary powers so that they can be flexible in making policies adapted to local conditions and can actively and creatively develop the local economy has helped enhance the vitality of the economy as a whole. However, it has also brought about some problems. Some localities give too much consideration to local interests and are not conscientious in implementing central policies and guidelines. [This failing] has even given rise to the phenomenon of lower-level authorities dealing with policies from higher authorities in arbitrary ways, and of not enforcing [central] laws and prohibitions. What should be dealt with in a centralised way by central authorities is not effectively centralised and excessive decentralisation exists in certain aspects. As a result, there exist in some regions the [problems] of duplicated industrial structures; development influenced by [the old slogans] of 'large and comprehensive' or 'small and comprehensive'; and carving up the market.[10] All these are unfavourable to economic development in the whole country and to the forming of a unified market. Therefore, an important question that requires urgent solution at present is how to rationally divide economic management powers between the central and local governments, and how to clearly define each other's powers in

10 These slogans refer to policies that encouraged large, State Owned Enterprises to be fully vertically integrated in all aspects of production and a similar policy by which localities also had a full range of local industries facilities. These policies caused loss of economies of scale and specialisation. (Ed.)

handling day-to-day affairs, as well as financial powers and policy making powers, in order to achieve unification of powers and responsibilities. As far as possible, the solutions to this question should be based on regulations and law.

Third, the question of the sphere and degree of government involvement in the market. We have made it clear that, in resources allocation, the basic role of the market should be brought into play. We must resolutely leave it to the market to allocate those resources that should and can be allocated by the market. But the actual situation is that, from the subjective market point of view, State Owned Enterprises have not really become independently-operated economic entities responsible for their own profits or losses and capable of self-development and self-regulation. From the objective market point of view, the market for means of production is still being cultivated and the prices of a small number of products still follow the two-tier system; while the markets for essential factors of production, such as the financial, labour, property, technology and information markets, are not yet adequately developed. The transaction procedures of the commodity market and the market for production factors are still quite confused. Orderly market competition is only just taking shape, while price forming mechanisms and price regulation systems are still not sound. These situations are restraining market mechanisms from playing their role effectively and hence for the present and immediate future, government must exercise control in kind over a very small number of commodities. It must institute examination and approval procedures for major investment projects in the competitive fields. It must exercise control on the asset liability ratio of banks and at the same time control the scale of credit loans. It must support economic activities with necessary administrative means. However, it remains a difficult problem for the government to determine properly the sphere and degree of government intervention, such that it will not affect the forming of market signals and the deepening of reforms, and in a way that can be readjusted in time upon as conditions change and in ways that enable us to bring the role of market mechanism into play.

We have made a good start on exploring the government's economic functions under conditions of a socialist market economy. We encounter some problems at present but we will solve them gradually by continuing to draw on the experience of foreign countries and assimilate the views of Chinese and foreign experts, persisting in carrying out reforms and constantly making explorations.

Document 3.2

'The question of assets and property rights in the transformation of State Owned Enterprises to the shareholding system'

DUAN YIPO

Development in Economics, 1997, No. 4

China started to transform its State Owned Enterprises to the shareholding system in 1984. By the end of [last] year 3,523 State Owned Enterprises had been converted to joint-stock limited companies, representing 55.7% of the total number of joint-stock companies. Their total share capital amounted to 286.5 billion *yuan* of which the state-owned shares were 180.2 billion (62.9% of the total share capital) and subscribed shares amounted to 106.3 billion (37.1%). Assets and interests attributable to state-owned shares were 243.3 billion *yuan*, 5.8% higher than the net value of assets invested by the state. Practice proves that operating the State Owned Enterprises on the shareholding system is an important way to change the operating mechanism of State Owned Enterprises and set up a modern enterprise system. However, the problems existing in the transformation of State Owned Enterprises to the shareholding system must not be neglected.

1. Problems in the transformation of State Owned Enterprises to shareholding based systems

Viewed from the perspective of assets and property rights, the problems in the transformation of State Owned Enterprises to the shareholding system are mainly the following:

1. Installations of 'shell' or nominal shareholders when non-operating assets are stripped from joint-stock companies. The problem of enterprise-run communities exists universally in China's State Owned Enterprises. In the course of their development over a long period of time, these enterprises accumulated an enormous amount of non-operating assets of a social or welfare service character. Viewed from the nature of these funds, they were invested by the state and should be recorded in the books as state capital and be entitled to after-tax profits distributed by the enterprises. However, from the theoretical point of view, capital funds should be used by the enterprises for the reproduction process. Yet these non-operating assets have not participated in the reproduction process of the enterprises. If they are entitled to profit distribution as state-owned shares, the interests of corporate shares, individually-owned shares and foreign-owned shares are bound to be affected. For this reason, it is necessary to restructure the assets of the

former State Owned Enterprises and strip the non-operating assets from the joint stock companies, so that the main production establishment of the enterprises is separated from social burdens. Nevertheless, many State Owned Enterprises have, in the course of restructuring their assets, installed 'shell' shareholders. That is, they invest the main assets for production and management (generally accounting for more than 75%, and some even more than 90%, of net assets) into the joint-stock companies, but retain a small part of net assets which are non-operating or in an unhealthy state of operation for the original enterprises, which are basically 'shell' enterprises, or 'holding companies' converted from the original enterprises. As holders of state-owned shares of the joint-stock companies, they are entitled to the profits and interests due to those shares. There is no distinction between these 'shell' shareholders and the joint-stock companies in their accounts, while their leading members mutually hold concurrent positions. This practice not only separates the owner of state assets (the State) from a joint-stock company through the use of an unqualified investor ('shell' shareholder) thereby stripping state-owned shares of effective control, and providing conditions for the enterprises to make use of restructuring to avoid paying debts (by unloading the debts onto the original enterprises) or to stem and divide profits of state-owned shares, but is also liable to put state shareholders under the control of non-state shareholders in a joint-stock company, or even cause a State Owned Enterprise to become a subsidiary of a joint-stock company.

2. The practice in defining the property rights of an enterprise, of designating state-owned assets as collectively-owned assets, enterprise assets or assets of retired employees and workers, or of giving employees and workers shareholders an obligation to pay for the shares, while not actually paying for them. The current situation is that when large and medium-sized State Owned Enterprises proceeded to transform themselves into shareholding companies, because of relatively tight state control with relatively standardised rules set for the defining of property rights and the installation of stock rights, the losses of state-owned assets and state-owned interests have been minimised. However, when transforming themselves into the shareholding system, cooperative share system, or instituting the system of leased or contract operation, or offering themselves for sale, small-scale State Owned Enterprises in some localities especially in some counties and county-level cities, have defined property rights improperly and installed stock rights indiscriminately. The phenomenon of violating regulations in dealing with assets has been common. This has resulted in losses of state assets generally amounting to 30%–50% of the net value of state assets of these enterprise. For example, when 27 State Owned Enterprises in a county-level city of a certain province carried out the structural reform, out of the net state asset value of 47.07 million *yuan*, they only converted 18.19 million

yuan worth of state assets into state-owned shares, and changed the rest into enterprise assets, bonus assets, and assets of retired personnel. They even quantified a portion of the assets (14.02 million *yuan*) and distributed it to employees and workers.

3. The relations between owners of property rights are unclear and state shares exist in name only. The state is basically the sole owner of China's State Owned Enterprises. After the transformation of State Owned Enterprises to the shareholding system, the ownership of enterprise property rights has been changed from sole ownership by the state to multiple ownership, and the entitlement to the profits and interests of the enterprises has also changed from one-party entitlement to multiple-party entitlement. The capital of these enterprises not only comprise state-owned shares, but also corporate shares, individually-owned shares, and foreign-owned shares. For this reason, to define the rights and interests among the interest parties correctly and fairly is a very important factor in transforming State Owned Enterprises to the shareholding system. As seen from China's reality, the question of who represents the state-owned shares has not been truly solved up to the present. Some government organs vie to become holders of state shares, yet they are unwilling and unable to bear the liabilities and risks that state shareholders are supposed to bear. For example, some state shares are held by the Administration of State-owned Assets, which appoints agents to act for it; some by local governments, which designate a certain organ to manage the stocks; some by designated departments of local governments or corporations converted from those departments; and some by the board chairman or the general manager of the joint-stock company acting on behalf of the state. But whoever they are, the combination of responsibilities, rights and interests remains an unresolved problem. The agents for state shares cannot bear the responsibilities they are supposed to bear. Neither do they have any direct interest in the joint-stock companies, hence the non-existence of an interest mechanism. On the one hand this situation renders the state stocks as merely nominal. It has led to unreasonable distribution by the joint-stock companies. They either will not distribute bonus issues or bonuses to the state shareholders, or distribute or issue to them less than they are entitled to. Or they let bonuses due to state stocks to remain in arrears, or make use of them by paying very low interest or no interest at all. On the other hand, when a government department as the proxy of state shares plays a direct role in the management of an enterprise, it restores a situation in which the functions of government are not separated from those of enterprises. This goes against the principles [we are following in order] to set up a modern enterprise system.

4. The supervisory and control system for state-owned assets is not perfect. To institute the shareholding system does not simply mean that enterprises have a direct avenue to raise funds for, more importantly, it

will give rise to a series of changes in management structures and operating mechanisms. However, due to various subjective and objective reasons, internally there are still the following problems: (1) Shareholders' meetings exist in name only. Since state shareholders occupy the predominant position, votes by 100,000 shareholders can be overruled by one single vote of the Board chairman; (2) Senior staff are still appointed administratively. Board members, managerial staff, and chairman of the supervisory committee are still appointed or dismissed directly or indirectly according to the mode of the planned economy. Consequently, enterprises can hardly play their role as the mainstay of the market; and (3) China's joint-stock enterprises have their own unique and independent leadership and management systems composed of the three institutions which combine the old and the new, i.e. the Board of Directors, the General Meeting of Shareholders, and the Supervisory Committee. Because the organisational structure of enterprises is still administratively-oriented, there are too many management levels with overlapping functions, interconnected duties and unwieldy organizations. Incidents of trespassing on each other's authority, taking wrong positions and failing to take responsibility often occur, and irregularities often find expression in day-to-day operations. Externally, the problem is that although there are regulations to supervise and control the operation of joint-stock enterprises, they are not fully implemented and detailed rules governing specific measures are lacking. Also, there is no effective and authoritative mechanism to supervise and control the enterprises. In reality, the joint-stock enterprises have no supervision and control except by themselves.

2. Causes of current problems

There are multiple reasons for the emergence of the above-mentioned problems. They are analysed below from the viewpoint of assets and property rights concerns.

1. The management authority of state-owned assets is not clearly defined and the behavior of state shareholders does not conform to rules and standards. The holders of state shares can neither exercise their rights as such, nor protect the rights and interests of state shares. One of the purposes of transforming State Owned Enterprises to the shareholding system is to make definite the property rights of enterprises. However, in many of the joint-stock enterprises in China today it is not yet clear who represents the state to manage the state-owned stocks. As a consequence, many departments and organs are anxious to become, or have become, the management party of state-owned stocks. This has given rise to a phenomenon of decentralized leadership in management work, with those having management authority arguing back and forth and making things difficult for each other. Consequently, the state shares of many

joint-stock companies are held by the management departments or organs of the original enterprises. Because the functions of social and economic management and of managing state-owned assets are all concentrated in these departments, they often effectively substitute [old system] administrative management for [new system] equity management, resulting in a failure to separate the functions of government from those of enterprises, and in the dislocation of responsibilities, rights, and interests. This does not conform to the requirement for regularisation of the management of state-owned stocks. Neither can it protect the legitimate interests of the state stocks. Some state shareholders, therefore, exist in name only. There are many instances where board chairmen and general managers of companies are appointed by government departments. Many agents of state shareholders appointed by local enterprises are holding several concurrent positions. They are agents of state shareholders, as well as board chairmen and general managers of joint-stock companies. And they are also individual shareholders holding a majority of stocks. Such irrational personnel arrangements are bound to give rise to unreasonable interest conflicts. In making decisions on major issues having a bearing on the interests of stockholders, such as profit distribution, capital increases and the issue of new stocks, the companies often consider mainly the interests of the individual shareholders and the companies themselves, without giving real consideration to protecting the interests of the state as the major shareholder. An even more serious state of affairs is that some people, taking advantage of their concurrent positions, exercise the rights of shareholders in their individual names. They have no scruples in sacrificing the interests of state shareholders to satisfy the interests of non-state shareholders and foreign shareholders.

2. In transforming the shareholding system, enterprises attach importance to fund raising and make light of the duty of changing [administrative] mechanisms. The shareholding system sets great store by mechanism conversion. However, in implementing the system, some people set their aim at raising funds and issuing stocks, and pay little attention to changing the operating mechanisms. They often retain the same staff, the same set of organizations, and the same pattern of management. Under the conventional system, there is no requirement for preserving capital funds, nor is there a motivation to provide returns on investments made by state asset owners. The mentality is that of 'eating from the big pot' provided by the state. A considerable number of State-Owned Enterprises have obviously not changed this concept after the transformation. From the point of view of some joint-stock company operators, staff benefits and common shareholder benefits are inflexible and must be made good, but the benefits of the state are flexible and its bonuses can be denied and debts owed to it need not be repaid. Some enterprise operators have formed the habit of making arbitrary decisions and are

unwilling to be under the control of shareholders, especially the state shareholders. So in implementing the transformation, they racked their brains to create things such as 'shell' shareholders to free themselves from the control of state stockholders and achieve the purpose of managing themselves independently.

3. The reform of the state assets management system lags behind and hinders the progress of reforming State Owned Enterprises. Practice proves that if the reform of the state assets management system lags behind, it will be unable to reform the State Owned Enterprises. There is no way to merge a state assets management system that is adapted to the planned economic system with a modern enterprise system that is adapted to the market economic system. Over the past two years, with the deepening of enterprise reform, there has been a rapid increase in the number of State Owned Enterprises being designated as pilot enterprises for transformation to the shareholding system, as well as in the scale of their assets. Nevertheless, supplementary reform measures have failed to keep pace with this development. In particular, the reform of government organs which bears heavily on the management of state-owned stocks in the joint-stock companies, and of the state assets management system, has been slow. In practical work, how are government functions going to change? how are the parties in charge of state asset investments organized and how do they operate? how are state assets allocated and restructured for optimum effect? and how are operating budgets for state assets constructed? All these important questions have remained unanswered. Besides, the state assets management departments existing at present are relatively low-ranking. They have only a small staff and lack the authority and necessary means for effective operation. Additionally, the Law on State Assets has not yet come into being. All these are institutional obstructions to the management of state-owned stocks. They constitute weak links in experimental work on the enterprise shareholding system and a deep-rooted cause impeding the development of joint-stock enterprises.

3. Three problems that must be solved to prevent the shareholding system from being distorted

1. We must accelerate the pace of changing government functions and reform the state-owned assets management system. A three-level state-owned stocks management model adapted to the socialist market economy and following specified standards should be established. That is there should be a state-owned assets management organisation at the state level; an investment organisation authorised by the state (that is, the unit or shareholder holding state stocks); and a joint-stock company with state assets holding the controlling share or an equity participant. The state-owned asset management organisation performs the duties and

functions of an owner on behalf of the State Council and exercises supervision and control over the unit holding state-owned stocks in a joint-stock company. The unit holding state stocks exercises the rights of a stockholder in a joint-stock company in accordance with state stock management requirements. Great efforts must be made to promote the reform of government organs and the state assets management system, so that the functions of government and those of enterprises are truly separated, and likewise the body in charge of state assets supervision and management and the body in charge of business operations, asset management and production management are also truly separated. Necessary steps should be taken now to change the situation of too many people making decisions in the management of state-owned stocks and yet of no one bearing the responsibilities. It should be made clear that the department in a government establishment with exclusive duties to manage state-owned assets is the exclusive agency for the management of state-owned stocks. In the reorganisation of State Owned Enterprises into shareholding enterprises and in the operation of the shareholding system, it represents the state to perform the duties and functions of a state stocks management agency. The department (or corporation) authorised by the State Council to supervise and control state assets in a specific industry should divide its responsibilities and functions internally and designate an organisation to exercise exclusive management over the state-owned assets (state-owned stocks). This organisation should accept professional guidance from the state assets management authority.

2. The question of setting up shareholders units properly and strictly keeping the behavior of shareholders within bounds.

   (a) It is necessary to conscientiously study the views on the formation of units to play the role of state shareholders. The forming of entities authorised by the state to take charge of state asset investments should be expedited. Before the investment entities are formed, the state assets management department and competent departments of the original enterprise should jointly exercise shareholders' rights in an acting capacity. The installation of 'shell' shareholders should not be permitted, those which have already been installed should be removed within a limited period of time.

   (b) In accordance with the principle of the party controlling the cadres, the requirements of the standard mode of management and the stipulations of the Company Law, it is necessary to set up a personnel management system that is conducive to strengthening the management of state-owned stocks and safeguarding their rights and interests. The party's organisation department should, working in concert with the state assets management department and the competent department of the enterprise, examine and determine the candidates for leading positions in the state stock holding unit and make appointment or dismissal according to standard procedures.

The holders of state-owned stocks should have the power to select enterprise managers. Agents of state stock holders should be appointed according to regulations. They may not take up positions as board chairman or general manager of a company.

(c) The behavior of shareholders and shareholders' agents should be kept within bounds in accordance with the principle of combining responsibilities, rights and interests, so that they can truly represent the will of the state in exercising shareholders' rights. For shareholders or their agents who fail to safeguard state interests or even undermine the interests of state-owned stocks, the state assets management department should have the power to terminate them and hold them liable to any administrative and legal responsibilities.

3. To promote the responsibility system in asset management and set up a sound micro-management model for state-owned assets. The essential points of a responsibility system for asset management are: asset value maintenance and increase assessment indicators; risk policies for benign expansion of assets and rational policies of solution to the problems left over from the past; the term of liability for assets management; rights and obligations of both parties; concrete methods of rewards for persons responsible for the operation of state assets, etc. This will set the standards for rights and obligations between the state asset owner and the operator, and institutionally define the responsibilities for the utilisation of state capital in business. A *Law of State-owned Assets* should be formulated as quickly as possible in order to provide definite solutions to a series of urgent problems concerning the management and operating systems for state-owned assets; the establishment of state assets management organs and their responsibilities and functions; operating budgets for state-owned assets; and assignment of property rights. All of this will create a favourable environment for the state assets operators to utilise state capital in business. It is necessary to get rid of capital sediments and activate state-owned assets. It is necessary to carry out equity transactions and reorganisation of the equity market and promote the flow of state-owned and corporate capital in a planned and measured way. It is necessary to ensure through institutional arrangements that state-owned assets are not left idle or locked up, but are put on the market for optimal disposition, so that state asset operators can have ample scope to show their talents. In accordance with the needs to raise capital, both structural readjustment and the reorganisation of equity [holdings] should be carried out in a timely manner, thereby giving stockholding an active rather than passive role.

Whether regular and effective management can be exercised on state-owned stocks in the joint-stock enterprises is one of the basic yardsticks to measure the success or failure of the transformation of State Owned Enterprises into the shareholding system. Along with the deepening of reforms, to strengthen the management of assets and property rights of the joint-stock enterprises is not only conducive to preserving and increasing the value of state-owned assets, but can also [be the means] to recover part of the investments made by the state in the course of reforming enterprises, especially the medium-sized and small ones, in order to increase their capital and technological input into the large-scale enterprises and promote the restructuring of state-owned asset inventories. From now on, state management of State Owned Enterprises and state-owned assets will, to a considerable extent, be changed to the form of property rights or equity management.

Document 3.3

'The emerging new Chinese price system and price control'

SUN XIANGYI

Price Theory and Practice, 1997, No. 8

Since the Fourteenth National Congress of the Chinese Communist Party, China has opened up wider to the outside world; its national economy has developed rapidly; the people's livelihood has improved steadily; and reforms for the purpose of setting up a socialist market economy have made significant progress. However, in its economic life, some problems and contradictions have for a while been very conspicuous. In particular, the inflation which started in 1993 has for some time seriously thwarted the healthy development of China's economy as well as its social development. In view of these contradictions and problems and after a careful assessment of the situation, the Party Central Committee and the State Council made a major decision on deepening reforms and strengthening macroeconomic control. They regarded checking the inflation as the key to correctly handling the relations between reform, development and stability, and as the primary task of macroeconomic control. The price control authorities at all levels implemented in earnest the policies and measures of the Party Central Committee and the State Council and carried out price reforms in a positive manner. After five years of unremitting efforts to strengthen macroeconomic control and check the inflation, they have achieved remarkable results and accumulated valuable experiences.

I A price formation mechanism with the market as the determining factor has been basically set up

After the Fourteenth Party Congress set the target for building a socialist market economic system, China accelerated the pace of building a market-oriented economy. It has exerted great and unremitting efforts in deepening price reforms with emphasis on changing the price formation mechanism. During that time, the state authorities liberalised the prices of most agricultural and sideline products and those of means of production and allowed them to be regulated by the market. The increase in the proportion of prices that are subject to market regulation has thus accelerated correspondingly. In view of the steady rise of inflation since the beginning of 1993, the state authorities also made a timely readjustment of its price reform strategy, shifting its emphasis to building and perfecting a price macro-control system. On the one hand, they made positive and steady efforts to promote the formation and maturity of a market price formation mechanism; on the other hand, they summed up the experience and lessons of price reforms in previous years. While stepping up indirect regulation and control of prices, they reinstated the practice of the government fixing the prices or directing the formation of prices on certain individual, important farm products and means of production, which had previously been liberalised. This played a positive role in checking price upsurges and stabilising production and circulation. By 1996, the prices of social commodities that were regulated by the market accounted for 88.8% of total retail sales, up 35.8% from 1991; while prices that were fixed by the government or formed under government direction accounted for 8.8% and 2.4% respectively, down 21% and 14.8% respectively from 1991. Meanwhile, the prices of means of production regulated by the market took up 77.9% of total sales, up 41.5% from 1991, whereas those fixed by the government or formed under government direction took up 15.6% and 6.5% respectively, down 29% and 3.4% respectively. On the other hand, market-regulated purchasing prices were applied to 78.6% of total purchases of agricultural and sideline products in 1996, up 27.6% compared with those in 1991, while purchasing prices fixed by the government or formed under government direction were applied to 17% and 4.4% of such purchases respectively, down 8% and 19% respectively. By comparison, the Commonwealth of Independent States and some East European countries adopted the method of 'shock treatment' in price reform, in an attempt to realise market-regulated price formation overnight. Even though they had paid very heavy prices, the degree of market regulation of prices attained by these countries is still far lower than that attained in China. Even in comparison to countries with a market economy, the degree of price liberalisation in China is still relatively high.

By firmly adhering to the price reform concept of combining step-by-step reforms with breakthroughs in key sectors; taking small but uninterrupted steps; combining regulation with liberalisation; and gradually straightening out the price structure, China has achieved initial success in setting up a price formation mechanism with the market as the main determining factor, thus creating the conditions for the ultimate establishment of a price system adapted to the socialist market economy.

II The situation in which prices of basic commodities are on the low side has improved markedly

The prices of basic products of China's agriculture and basic industries such as energy and transportation have, for a long time, been on the low side. This is an important factor that has led to an irrational price system and has inhibited the development of these basic industries. Since the Fourteenth Party Congress, while exerting unremitting efforts to change the price formation mechanism, China has intensified price readjustments in a planned and measured way.

First, it has increased the purchasing prices of grain and cotton by a relatively big margin, thus reversing the condition in which the prices of agricultural and sideline products have for a long time been on the low side. A comparison of prices in 1996 and 1991 shows that the state authorities have raised the grain purchasing prices by 213% and cotton purchasing prices by 133%. Since the beginning of this year, the fixed purchasing price and protective price of grain have been higher than the market prices. This phenomenon indicates that the situation over the past several dozen years wherein agriculture has provided industry with means of accumulation through price scissors between industrial and agricultural products has gradually changed to a situation wherein industry feeds agriculture instead. This is an important change of historical significance.

Second, the prices of basic products of such basic industries as energy and transportation have been raised appropriately, thus significantly easing the contradiction wherein the prices of basic products are on the low side in relation to prices of downstream products. In 1997, the prices of electricity, aviation services, coal and charcoal and crude oil are higher than those in 1990 by 179%, 194%, 142% and 271% respectively; while passenger and freight tariffs of railroads are higher by 52% and 147% respectively.

The smooth implementation of these structural readjustments in prices has played an important role in changing the situation of the prices of agriculture, energy, transportation and other basic industries being on the low side; promoting the rationalisation of the price structure in China; supporting agricultural development; relieving the 'bottlenecks' of energy, transportation and telecommunications; promoting the structural readjustment of industry; stimulating the momentum for national economic development; and increasing financial revenues and lowering expenditures. In particular, the increase in grain purchasing prices by a big margin has aroused peasants' enthusiasm in growing and selling grain, thus reversing the situation wherein agriculture lingered on for several years without making any advance. It has played a significant role in promoting agriculture and developing the rural economy.

III A price regulation and control system stressing indirect regulation and control Is gradually taking shape

In the course of checking the inflation, to meet the requirements for developing a socialist market economy, the Chinese authorities have further improved and strengthened the means of price regulation and control, in order to enhance government capability to control market prices and to gradually form a price regulation and control system combining the use of economic, legal and necessary administrative means, with economic means playing the main role.

As far as economic means are concerned, China has initially set up a reserve system for important commodities that have a bearing on state plans and people's livelihood, as well as a reserve regulation and control system at both the central and local levels. Reserves at the central level include such important commodities as grain, edible vegetable oils, edible sugar, pork, salt, tea for frontier markets, cotton, good quality chemical fertilisers, material for agricultural films, pesticides and processed oils. Specific reserves to be kept in localities are to be determined by local authorities according to actual conditions.

Apart from building up commodity reserves, China has at the same time gradually set up several systems of price risk funds and price regulation funds as described below:

1. Food Price Risk Fund. This is a special fund used by central and local governments to stabilise grain market prices; to subsidise part of the peasants who have to buy grain back from the market at higher prices for their own consumption; to maintain a normal order of grain circulation; and to exercise economic regulation and control. Money for the central Food Price Risk Fund comes from state budget appropriations, while money for local Food Price Risk Funds comes from subsidies allocated under the state budget and from local budgetary appropriations.

2. Processed Oils Price Risk Fund. The prices of imported processed oils allocated for domestic consumption are fixed at the same level as ex-factory prices of domestically-processed oils. Any surplus resulting from the disparity between the prices of imported processed oils and the prices fixed for domestic consumption is deposited into a special account, and any deficit is made up by a subsidy paid out of this special account, which is operated under the joint supervision of the price control and auditing authorities. This special account is used exclusively to offset the impact of changes in imported oil prices on the prices of domestic products.

3. Chemical Fertilisers Price Risk Fund. Any surplus resulting from the disparity between the prices of imported fertilisers allocated for domestic consumption and the imported cost of same is deposited into a special account, and any deficit is offset by a subsidy paid out of this account. The Fertilisers Price Risk Fund is managed by the China Agricultural

Means of Production Corporation and the Agricultural Resources Companies in the provinces, and is utilised under the supervision of price control authorities.

4. Price Regulation Fund. This Fund has been established in most large and medium-sized cities across the country. According to preliminary statistics compiled in 20 provinces and autonomous regions at the end of 1996, 168 out of 201 prefectures and cities and 633 out of 1,302 counties have set up price regulation funds. Apart from a general fund, various localities have also set up special funds according to specific conditions, respectively for chemical fertilisers, gas, water, agricultural resources, electric power, steel, copper, salt, vegetables, textbooks, coal, oils and houses. Some localities having the necessary conditions have formulated local laws and regulations on the basis of past practices, in order to institutionalise and standardise the sources, utilisation and management of price regulation funds.

As far as legal means are concerned, China has stepped up its market and price legislative work and has persisted in managing prices according to law. It aims to gradually bring price management into the legal orbit, to promote market competition and to set up a regular order for pricing. Since the Fourteenth Party Congress, it has successively promulgated the *Regulations Concerning Clear Marking of Prices on Commodities and Services* for implementation across the country; and the *Provisional Regulations on Stopping the Practice of Reaping Exorbitant Profits*. It has taken the first steps to institute a supervisory system on the prices of the basic necessities of life and basic services for the people, and launched a campaign with a great fanfare against fraudulent and profiteering practices to protect the interests of the vast numbers of consumers. The standing committees of People's Congresses and governments of various provinces, autonomous regions and municipalities directly under the Central Government have also formulated local laws and regulations according to local conditions. For example, the Jiangsu Provincial People's Congress Standing Committee has promulgated the *Price Management and Supervision Regulations of Jiangsu Province* while the Hunan Provincial People's Government has promulgated its *Methods of Market Regulation and Price Management of Hunan Province*. These rules and regulations define the responsibilities and ways and means of the government in regulating and controlling market prices and govern the pricing practice of producers and business operators. In practice, they have produced satisfactory effects. Additionally, work on drafting a Price Law in accordance with the legislation plans of the National People's Congress (NPC) has been stepped up. The *(Draft) Price Law* has been passed in principle at the 56th executive meeting of the State Council and has been submitted to the NPC Standing Committee for discussion and examination. It is hoped that it will be promulgated within this year. With the Price Law as the core, a project to build a legal system for prices has gone into full swing.

As far as administrative means are concerned, these primarily include further perfecting and implementing a target-oriented responsibility system for price regulation and control; ensuring the realisation of a regional equilibrium in grain; a provincial governor responsibility system for the supply of rice; and a city mayor responsibility system for the supply of vegetables. The State and some regions have also adopted the method of announcing monthly commodity price indexes as a means to check and supervise price movements and to ensure the smooth implementation of various regulatory and control measures adopted by the Party Central Committee and the State Council.

IV Efforts to check inflation achieve significant effect

In dealing with the serious inflation which started in 1993, the Party Central Committee and the State Council promptly made an important decision on deepening reforms and strengthening and improving macro-economic control, and adopted a series of effective macro-control measures. The emphasis in 1993 was on rectifying the financial order. In 1994, major steps were taken to reform the macro-control system. In 1995, the primary task of macro-control was to resolutely check the inflation, which was also regarded as the key to correctly handling the relations between reform, development and stability. In 1996, with the inflation having been initially brought under control, further controlling inflation remained the primary task of macro-control, with timely and appropriate adjustments of the strength of such control. These wise decisions and effective measures of the Party Central Committee and State Council have enabled China to win the battle against inflation while maintaining an appropriate rate of economic growth. According to statistics, the rate of increase of China's commodity retail prices fell from 21.7% in 1994 to 6.1% in 1996, and that of consumer prices from 24.1% to 8.3%. Between January and July 1997, the accumulated commodity retail price index and consumer price index rose by 1.6% and 3.9% respectively. For 32 consecutive months since November 1994, the rate of price increases has fallen successively. China's economy in the last two years has formed a favourable development trend of 'high growth and low inflation', signifying that, after several years of macro-control, China's economy has successfully achieved a 'soft landing'.

China's remarkable achievement in bringing down the inflation has extremely important economic and political significance. It has drawn favourable comments both at home and from abroad. The drop in the rate of price increases has created conditions to stop the practice of providing value-guaranteed subsidies, lowering twice the bank interest rates for deposits and loans, and adjusting the strength of macro-control in a timely manner. It has played a positive role in bringing about a benign economic cycle and laid a good foundation for the smooth implementation of the Ninth Five Year Plan. It has also played a positive role in setting people's minds at ease, stabilising society and creating favourable economic and social environments. The success in bringing down the inflation also indicates that our Party and government have become even more mature in the process of transformation to a socialist market economic system, and that their ability to exercise macroeconomic control has been further enhanced. This point is of still even more important and profound historical significance.

V Experience accumulated in price management work under the new situation

Since the Fourteenth Party Congress, China has gone through five years of trials and hardships in carrying out price reform and macro-control, and has achieved successes that have drawn worldwide attention. More importantly, it has gained rich and valuable experiences that will help doing a good job of future work in price management and keeping prices basically stable under socialist market economic conditions. To sum up these experiences in real earnest will have important practical significance for further promoting unity of thinking and understanding, strengthening self-consciousness, minimising blindness in actions, and enhancing the ability to exercise macro-control on prices. In sum, these experiences are mainly embodied in three areas:

1. *Price management also needs to be strengthened under socialist market economic conditions*

For a period of time, there prevailed in society a one-sided understanding about price management under conditions of a socialist market economy. For a while erroneous points of view, such as 'prices formed by the market need no state control' and 'government can simply wash its hands once prices are liberalised', spread unchecked. As a consequence, in the course of structural reform some localities dismembered or weakened their price management functions at will, causing instability among the ranks of price administrators and a slackening of market price management.

Faced with the stark situation of soaring commodity prices and the lessons learned from the once relaxed price control, since 1994 price management authorities at various levels have, under the leadership of the Party committee and government at the corresponding level, unified their thinking and understanding. They have come to understand that price liberalisation under conditions of a market economy does not mean that they can wash their hands of price management, and that prices formed by the market do not mean that they need not be regulated and controlled by the State. Instead, they should take the new situation into account, and constantly improve and perfect price management. They should do a good job of price management work in all aspects.

2. To bring down inflation requires comprehensive treatment

Commodity prices are a concentrated expression of the national economy. In the final analysis, fluctuations in the general level of commodity prices are determined by macroeconomic conditions as a whole, and are a reflection on commodity prices of the relationship between economic operations and economic conditions as a whole. The fundamental cause of inflation is disequilibrium in the economy as a whole, hence the way to deal with inflation is to achieve an overall economic equilibrium. It requires controlling excessive demand on the one hand, and increasing effective supply on the other. Only through a comprehensive approach can we achieve the ideal effect.

In the past, we also tried to deal with inflation in the manner of the 'soft landing', but without success. This time we achieved a remarkable success in bringing down the inflation without causing sharp fluctuations in the economy chiefly because the government, in exercising macroeconomic control, attached greater importance to a comprehensive approach. Even though at present it still has to make some use of administrative measures, in most cases it has adopted the form of indirect regulation and control. It has accumulated a considerable amount of successful experience in the comprehensive utilisation of economic policies and means, such as by using financial, currency, and interest levers, and by building up reserves and regulating imports and exports.

3. Price reform comprises the transformation of the price-forming mechanism, rationalising the price structure, and strengthening the regulation and control system

Before the Fourteenth Party Congress, China's price reform emphasised price regulation. After the Fourteenth Congress decided to set up a socialist market economic system, the emphasis switched to liberalisation. This amounted to a 'destruction' of the price management system under the traditional planned economic system. After 1994, as China concentrated its efforts on the central task of checking inflation, the emphasis of price reform was again switched to strengthening and perfecting price regulation and control mechanisms, with the focus on setting up a new price management system which is adapted to the requirements of a socialist market economy. This indicates that China's price reform has entered a new stage of 'establishment' following the 'destruction'.

Where there is 'destruction', there is 'establishment'. 'Destruction' means reform, so does 'establishment'. We have learned lessons in the past from 'destruction' only, but no 'establishment'. Therefore, when we say that we have basically set up a price-reforming mechanism with the market as the determining factor, it does not mean that we have achieved complete success in price reform. The main content of future price reform will be for government to [increasingly] exercise price regulation and control in diversified forms and in systematic, scientific and standardised ways. Price reform is a long-term and arduous task.

All in all, China's achievements in price reform and macroeconomic control since the Fourteenth Party Congress have attracted worldwide attention. China has accumulated rich and valuable experiences in price management under conditions of a socialist market economy. Summing up the past and looking to the future, we have ample reasons to believe that, by holding high the shining banner of comrade Deng Xiaoping's theory of building socialism with Chinese characteristics, and under the guidance of the spirit of the Fifteenth Party Congress, China's price management work will certainly be able to make new contributions to the work of the whole Party and the whole country in general and win new honours for the people.

4

Industrial Change and Technological Upgrading

INTRODUCTION

Economic reform in China in the past two decades has impinged upon Chinese industry in a number of ways. First, has been the remarkable policy shift in emphasis from heavy to light industry to cope with rising consumerism. Second, increased decentralisation of industrial management, including price liberalisation, has triggered wide-ranging inter-industrial readjustments and led to severe restructuring difficulties in major industries. Third, the influx of new industries from abroad in response to inexorable rising demand is something totally alien to the conventional Soviet-style industrial setting of pre-reform China. Fourth, but not least, has been the rapid build up of pressures for technological upgrading and the transfer of new industrial technology from overseas, in response to enhanced international competition.

The process of industrial reorientation has consistently followed the overall market-oriented reform. However, in parallel to the institutional reorganisation (still far from complete) industrial restructuring has been persistently constrained by the legacy of central planning. The translations in this chapter discuss the predicament faced by the Chinese government from two contrasting perspectives: light versus heavy industries on the one hand, and new versus old industries on the other. The problems involved are highly complex and vary across industries. This introduction provides an interpretative framework for assessing the issues raised and highlights the pattern of industrial transformation in China and the possible course it might take – particularly in light of the country's imminent entry into WTO.

LIGHT AND HEAVY INDUSTRIES

The reorientation towards greater emphasis on light as against heavy industry was part of the overall Economic Readjustment strategy that took place in the early 1980s. The initial impetus for this came from increased demand reflecting the upward move of farm procurement prices (25%) agreed in late 1978 and the subsequent readjustment in industrial wages as well.[1] These changes signalled an era of 'less-harsh' consumption similar to the Kruschchevian reform after decades of Stalinist austerity. At the same time, the remarkable reallocation of resources that followed left many producer goods industries (machine-building in particular) with idle capacity; and with the two-track pricing system then being adopted, this prompted these enterprises to turn to the market for orders to make up for the deficiency in plan assignments. This indeed should arguably be seen as the origin of the market-oriented reform in China.[2]

Thus, in the past two decades or so, light industry has been consistently growing at a faster pace than heavy industry (14.3% per annum compared to 12.6% per annum see Figure 4.1). This has completely reversed the old pattern of heavy-industry biased growth firmly established prior to 1978.

By the mid 1990s, it appeared that readjustment seemed to have run its cycle and there was a shift towards a more balanced pattern.

Nonetheless, the present Chinese industrial system still bears major characteristics of a transition economy, rather than that of a fully-fledged, market-based one. The bulk of national income earned by both workers and peasants is, in the first place, still subject to monopsonistic control,[3] used by planners for the purpose of enhancing savings and industrial accumulation. The State Owned Enterprises (SOEs), being the custodian of state priority, continue to command the lion's share of national investment funds.[4] But coupled with the new-found managerial autonomy, the upshot has been a quite peculiar industrial system that appears to be increasingly a combination of overproduction and accelerated industrial deregulation. This is true not only in heavy industry, but also in a somewhat less pronounced fashion, in light industry as well.

There are several aspects of this remarkable transformation from the 'economics of shortage' (associated with Soviet-style central planning) to

1 Consistent increases in prices for resale of food grain to urban workers necessarily led to parallel urban wage likes.
2 Amidst the reform experiments conducted throughout all Soviet-style economies in the 1960s and 1970s, this particular measure introduced in China in the early 1980s represented the first attempt ever made to marketise the producer goods sector. This step went far beyond the original proposal of Sun Yefang, the most prominent early reform economist, who sought to confine any drastic decentralisation of decision-making to the 'simple reproduction' (replacement investment) sphere, while retaining all allocative prerogatives for the planners in the sphere of 'expanded reproduction' (new investment).
3 Note that SOEs have remained the single most important industrial employers in a world of mounting urban unemployment pressures in China. State agencies for farm procurement also continue to be the most pervasive customers of the peasants, setting benchmark prices for all major transactions.
4 SOEs currently account for less than 40% of total industrial output, but take up two-thirds of the bank loans extended by the entire state banking system.

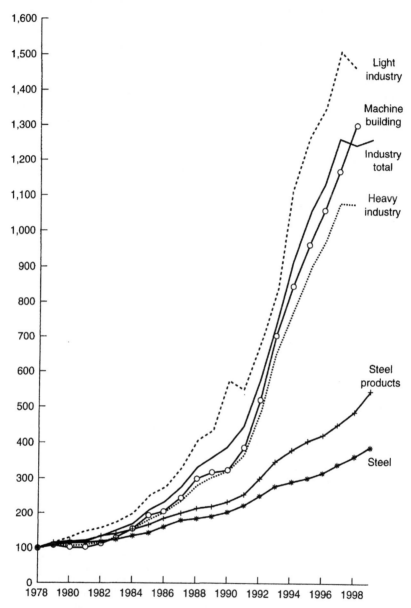

Figure 4.1 Trends in industrial production (gross value of output in 1990 prices), in China, 1978–1999 (1987=100).

Sources: *Zhongguo Tongji Zhaiyao 2000* (Chinese Statistical Abstract 2000), pp. 105 and 108; and *Zhongguo Tongji Nianjian* (Chinese Statistical Yearbook), various issues.

chronic 'supply glut' and consequent fierce price competition and prolonged deflation. First, the drastic price deregulation of 1993/1994 has enabled the SOEs to fully take advantage of the sellers' market position to expand production and supply, without due regard to potential market fragility.[5] Second, in the absence of any significantly enhanced 'budget constraint', all major SOEs have continued to invest in expansion, free of economic pressures to promote technological upgrading or raise productivity. The third point, is that industrial deregulation has helped encourage many emerging local enterprises to compete against the SOEs for both goods markets and input supplies. And, finally, there is clearly a mismatch between increased industrial supply and the capability of the tens of millions of urban and rural consumers to absorb this output. This market predicament appears, therefore, to be more an institutional than a cyclical or macroeconomic problem.

The ramifications of this situation should be clear. With wage costs and prices for essential inputs remaining relatively inflexible (notably raw cotton for the textile industry and coal, petroleum, and electricity for the metallurgical sector), many SOEs have found it increasingly difficult to sustain unwarranted inventory accumulations and associated financial losses, and to service mounting bank debts.[6] More important, chronic financial losses incurred under the new system of economic accountability, have also deprived the SOEs of opportunities for investing in technological innovation. In this context, however, in the case of textiles and clothing, i.e. the lynchpins of light industry, these difficulties have been somewhat mitigated by expansion into overseas markets for low and medium grade products. But in the case of metallurgy, i.e. the pillar of heavy industry, China has now to rely increasingly on imported supplies

---

5 Subsequent to the abolishment of the two-track price system in 1993–1994, prices for steel products rose by 3.5 times compared with the former officially fixed plan prices. At the peak in 1993 the average price for steel products stood at 3000 to 4000 *yuan* per ton, but gradually dropped to less than 2000 *yuan* by late 1999, only to rebound to 2500–2600 *yuan* per ton in April 2000, for reasons which remain yet to be expanded; see *Impartial Daily* (Hong Kong), 27 May 2000.

6 The issue of SOE losses, a topical issue of popular concern among both Chinese and western analysts should, nonetheless, be subject to more careful scrutiny. Take the case of the familiar Anshan Iron and Steel Corporation. As a former Deputy Minister of Metallurgy puts it, the conglomerate used to be a major contributor to state revenue, but its profit has now been increasingly reduced to a minimum, essentially as a result of increased interest payment liability to the state banks, after state appropriations have been converted into interest-bearing bank loans. By contrast, the Baoshan Steel complex in Shanghai which is globally hailed as a new, profitable, and efficient producer, has actually been endowed with generous state investments from the inception. Specifically, if Anshan's debt-asset ratio is applied to Baoshan, the latter's total profit, remarkable as it is, would not even be sufficient to pay for the interest costs incurred. The massive operating losses, as observed with many major SOEs, are therefore deemed by the Deputy Minister himself, as a matter of 'government behavior', having nothing to do with management inefficiency. If this is correct, then obviously Premier Zhu Rongji's celebrated campaign for turning the SOEs' books from red into black by year 2000 has missed the real target. See *Studies on Metallurgy Economy*, No. 13, 5 July 1998, p. 3.

of high-quality steel products to meet the mounting input demand from such new industries as automobiles, while continuing to stockpile unwanted domestic output. Stocks have stood at around 20 million metric tons in recent years. It is interesting to note that high quality and high value-added steel products imported from abroad have recently amounted to some 7.5 to 10 mmt per year, i.e. nearly one-tenth of total Chinese steel output by weight, or one-third by value; while domestic demand lagged persistently behind domestic outputs, leading to calls from the Chinese government for a scaling down of production and for intensified technological renovation.[7]

NEW VERSUS OLD INDUSTRIES

There are two aspects to what may be considered as a new problem for the Chinese industrial system. The first relates to the development and application of new technologies which were, just a decade or so ago, almost totally unknown on the Chinese industrial scene. In this respect, electronics and modern communications and information industries come to mind immediately. The second refers to the radical reorientation of a handful of conventional industries, automobiles in particular, towards an entirely new spectrum of clientele. Thus, while just a few years ago saloon cars were still far beyond the dreams of private individuals, they have now rapidly come into the realms of possibility for hundreds of thousands of urban households, as was the case with colour television, video-recorders, and refrigerators, from the mid-1980s onwards.

Table 4.1 shows that for most electronics products, the pace of growth has indeed been truly extraordinary since the mid-1990s. All urban households now own more than one colour TV (111.5 sets per 100 households), and by 1999 virtually all rural households had either a colour TV (38.24%) or a black and white one. Personal computers are now also rapidly entering into urban Chinese households, as are air conditioners and microwave cookers. Even more impressive are the counts revealing the rapid spread of telephone lines both among urban and rural residents. These have grown at per annum rates of 32% and 48% between 1994 and 1999. The same goes for pagers (36% per annum) and mobile telephones (94% per annum) in the same period. Most spectacularly, users

---

7 A total of 103 small iron and steel plants are to be closed in year 2000, with the help of various administrative fiats, including suspending supply of fuel, electricity, and bank loans, and outright cancellation of business registration, *Impartial Daily*, 26 April 2000. This is part of the overall policy programme of 'aggregate control' (which is also directed against coal and sugar production, among others) for scaling down total steel production from the all-time high of 124 million tons in 1999 to 110 million tons for 2000, in order to facilitate technological upgrading by selected major steel producers. The retrenchment is regarded as a possible factor accounting for the unexpected price upsurge in April 2000; see supra note 5. For an excellent discussion of the imperative for technological upgrading of the Chinese steel industry, with an international perspective, see the article quoted in note 6.

Table 4.1 Sales and growth of major electronics and information technology products in China.

Product	1995		1996		1997		1998		Average annual growth rate (%)
	Sales	Growth rate (%)	Sales	Growth rate (%)	Sales	Growth rate (%)	Sales	Growth rate (%)	
Programme-controlled switchboard (10,000 lines)	1104.00	38.35	1386.00	25.54	2659.00	91.85	3057.20	14.98	42.68
Microcomputer (10,000 units)	75.00	267.60	122.00	62.67	135.00	10.66	262.24	94.25	108.80
Television sets (10,000 sets)	3551.00	24.42	2881.00	-18.90	3232.00	12.18	3225.80	-0.19	4.38
(incl. colour TV)	1876.00	18.06	2081.00	10.93	2481.00	19.22	2656.50	7.07	13.82
VCR (10,000 sets)	163.00	-8.94	234.00	43.56	237.00	1.28	174.30	-26.50	2.36
VCD player (10,000 sets)	65.00		269.00	313.80	960.00	256.90	1200.00	25.00	198.60
CD player (10,000 sets)	49.70	46.18	43.00	-13.50	31.00	-27.90			1.59
Fax machine (10,000 units)	3.03	62.90	5.25	73.30	20.41	289.90			142.00
Telephone sets (10,000 units)	2434.00	27.84	2230.00	-8.38	2358.00	5.74	2821.40	19.65	11.21
Hi-fi stereo (10,000 sets)	552.00	19.74	527.00	-4.53	550.00	4.36			6.52
Kinescope (10,000 units)	3164.00		2510.00	-20.70	2702.00	7.65	3525.60	30.48	5.82
(incl. colour kinescope)	1737.00		1909.00	9.90	2161.00	13.20	2795.90	29.38	17.49
Glass bulb (10,000 units)	2291.00		2120.00	-7.46	3037.00	43.25	3158.60	4.01	13.27
Integrated Circuit (10,000 units)	50382.00	113.70	74322.00	47.52	126422.00	70.10	128608.00	1.73	58.25

Sources: *Chinese Electronic Industry Yearbook* (for 1995, 1996, 1997, 1998); Ministry of Information Technology, 'Electronic Industry Information Network' (January 1999), as quoted in Institute of Industrial Economics, CASS, *China Industrial Development Report 1999*, Beijing, 1999.

of computer networks increased from a mere seven thousand in 1995 to two million in 1997, and are expected to soar to 20 million by the end of 2000.

As for the automobile industry, the most remarkable change is that by 1998–1999 saloon cars took up 32% of total output, compared to only 8% in 1990, while the share of trucks was reduced to only 40% from 71% during the same period, with buses accounting for the balances of 28% and 21% respectively. It is expected that out of the two million vehicles to be produced in year 2000, saloon cars will further increase to more than 700,000, and buses to 550,000,[8] with around 50% of the saloon cars produced to be purchased by private individuals, as compared to only 34% in 1995. Within the share for trucks, there has also been strong diversification in production from medium-sized to heavy, light, and mini goods vehicles, to cope with the changing demands of the economic setting.

The emerging new industries may be distinguished from the old ones in several important aspects.

First, both electronics and automobile industries have been strongly consumer-led in their accelerating expansions. The latter case is obvious, but nearly half of the output of the former also represents consumer electronics, without counting output of basic electronic components. This stands in remarkable contrast to the textile and clothing industries, for example, which until the eve of the economic reforms had remained little more than sectors manipulated by the planners to satisfy a subsistence standard of living.

Second, the share of producer electronics output has nonetheless steadily increased from 22% in 1993 to 38% by 1998 at the expense of consumer electronics, whose share is down from 44% to 34%; the balance being the share of components at 34% and 28% respectively. This underscores the great importance that electronics has assumed in China's attempt to catch up with technological advances in the West by following a route of upgrading conventional industries through electromechanical integration, application of computer-aided modeling and simulation testing, and by increased adoption of electronically-controlled fuel injection in car manufacturing.

Third, being designated as 'pillar' industries of the national economy, both electronics and automobile industries[9] are not only less subject to state 'extortion' through mandatory profit delivery, as was the case in textiles and metallurgy in the past, but both are beneficiaries of state fiscal transfers. A good case in point is the massive integrated circuits (ICs) Project 909, financed jointly by the central and Shanghai governments and launched in the Shanghai Pudong Zone in the name of Huahong (China Rainbow) Microelectronics in late November 1996. This was an attempt to boost the

---

8 *Impartial Daily*, 23 February 2000.
9 The other industries similarly designated include machine-building, petrochemical, and modern communications; the latter being of course closely tied in with the electronics industry as well.

Chinese share of ICs supply (dubbed the 'foodgrain' of the electronics industry) to 30% of the domestic market.[10]

Fourth, again unlike textiles and metallurgy, which have been suffering from massive losses, both electronics and automobile industries – the former in particular – are highly profitable undertakings, and have indeed accounted for the largest share of foreign capital inflow, mostly in Sino-foreign joint ventures. It is not until the past couple of years that a number of Chinese brand names, such as Changhong, Konka, Haier, Haixin, TCL, Legend, and Great Wall, have rapidly developed as national brands for colour TVs, personal computers, and VCDs.[11]

Nonetheless, as the celebrated Huahong ICs project clearly reflects, the present Chinese electronics industry is virtually entirely foreign in origin. Around 80% of China's semiconductor requirements, including memory and microcomponents output, and virtually all sophisticated semiconductors that the Chinese electronics firms need, must be imported.[12] While the more advanced telecommunications equipment, mobile phones in particular, are all dominated by global brands such as as Motorola and Ericsson. The same goes for personal computers as well, and of course for large and medium-sized ones.

Likewise, the entire Chinese automobile industry, which now appears increasingly to be reduced to a few familiar names such as Volkswagen, Audi, General Motors, Peugeot, and Honda, relies almost exclusively on imported technology. And while the rate of 'localisation' of components has become remarkably high in recent years, virtually all new saloons produced in China represent models that are more or less at the mature stage of their life cycles in the West. This includes the much publicised Buick New Century which made its debut in Shanghai in 1999, the Audi A6 produced in Changchun, and the new Honda Accord 2.3 VTI in Guangzhou.[13]

Not only is the technology in both electronics and saloon manufacturing in China dated, but their production represents little more than assembly operations. The spectacular proliferation of VCDs in China from the birth of the industry in 1993 is a typical story. With market access virtually open to any investors, VCD output soared from just 20,000 units in 1994 to more than two million in 1996, and to 10 million in 1997, only to face the cruel reality of being swiftly replaced by DVD from 1998. As a result, the

10 See *The People's Daily*, 29 November 1996, Institute of Industrial Economics, CASS, *China Industrial Development Report 1997*, op. cit. p. 103.

11 According to one international survey, Legend had by early 2000, already surpassed IBM and Compaq to be the largest PC producers in the Asia Pacific region and ranks 13th globally, *Impartial Daily* 4 July 2000, p. C2).

12 See *South China Morning Post* (Hong Kong), 23 May 2000 (Technology section, p. 2). Domestic chip fabrication plants mainly supplies low-end devices used in less sophisticated consumer-electronics products.

13 The only passenger car in China, which may still claim to be entirely of Chinese intellectual property, is the Red Flag, but this is also being rapidly marginalised by the many foreign brands; see Clara Li, 'Battle to keep the Red Flag flying', *South China Morning Post*, 2 July 2000, (*Features*, p. 4).

average VCD price was drastically reduced from some 4000 *yuan* in 1993–1994 to a mere 1000 *yuan* by 1997.[14]

A similar saga was played out in the colour TV sector, as it was in the market for home appliances such as airconditioners, microwave cookers, refrigerators, and washing machines, all of which have all seen spectacular price wars unfolding from time to time among the various popular Chinese brands, as a result of 'supply gluts' from the mid 1990s onwards. This pattern may well all imply enhanced consumer welfare; but the new Chinese industries need to look to more positive ways of developing their own technology to enhance the long-run sustainability of their international competitiveness.

On a more positive note, new Chinese industries such as electronics and automobiles are at least now fully integrated into the competitive market economy. By contrast, the ills of some major conventional industries, textiles and metallurgy in particular, may have to await the full impact of China's accession to the WTO to be go through the process of acquiring and surviving in a competitive market.

WTO IMPLICATIONS

An authoritative State Council analyst has recently stated that the Chinese metallurgy industry is subject to a three-pronged, external attack. First, from international competitors attempting to perpetuate the benefits of large-scale, low-cost imports from China of such resource-based primary products as pig iron and ferro-alloy, leaving China with unsustainable pollution, high energy consumption, and environmental degradation. Second, is foreign 'dumping' onto the Chinese markets of ordinary steel products that are not only 'crowding' out China's own production capacity, but also holding up the technological upgrading of the industry. Third, is the existence of price and non-price competition from foreign producers, as well as deliberate blockading of technology transfer to China, all of which makes it extremely difficult for the Chinese metallurgy industry to develop its own technological capabilities to meet the ever increasing domestic demand for high-quality special steel products.[15]

Viewed this way, it is clear that WTO may do more harm rather than good to Chinese industry, holding down its self-sufficiency rate for the much needed special steel products needed by critical long term future customers such as automobiles, ship-building, railways, and petroleum; and thus preventing it from 'turning from a large into a powerful industry'. The potential impact appears indeed to be particularly serious in light of the fact that the world steel industry currently has enormous excess capacity, with no sign of any significant turn around in the near future.

The Chinese textile and clothing industries have been frequently seen as potential winners through the WTO accession, since they have been star

14 See Institute of Industrial Economics, *China Industrial Development Report 1999*, op. cit. p. 187.
15 See *Studies on Metallurgy Economy*, No. 14, 15 July 1998, p. 8.

export performers since China's opening up to the West, earning consistently one quarter of the country's foreign exchanges. But here again, the actual prospects are ambiguous. For one thing, WTO may serve to perpetuate the country's status as a labour-intensive, low-technology exporter; although there is also the possibility that, with the phasing out of the export quotas guaranteed under the MFA, China's market share may be eroded by developing countries that share the competitive advantage of low labour costs. More seriously perhaps, the Chinese clothing industry has been increasingly relying upon imports of chemical fibre from countries with advanced technology to sustain its export-processing operations. With import tariffs to be lowered under WTO, a large number of existing domestic producers may be rapidly driven out of the scene by international competitors. Moreover, the expected influx from abroad of medium and high-grade apparel may also dash the hopes of many Chinese producers aspiring to compete in the high fashion markets.

As for the automobile industry, it is a foregone conclusion that the forthcoming influx of major foreign car makers into the Chinese market will wipe out by way of acquisition or merger, the one hundred or so local manufacturers, thus reducing the entire industry to a handful of globally known brands. The piling for the foundation of such a new Chinese automobile industry has, indeed, already been completed, with all the prominent German, American, Japanese and French carmakers having taken up the overwhelming share of the rapidly expanding Chinese market through the mechanism of Sino-foreign joint ventures.

In broad terms, therefore, the Chinese electronics and information technology industries represent *faits accomplis*, which the automobile industry seems poised to emulate. Thus the Chinese industrial system as a whole is likely to become one that is fully integrated into the global technological structure but is, nonetheless, a somewhat passive beneficiary, rather than itself a locomotive of globalisation. China's WTO accession seems likely to reinforce this scenario.

Document 4.1

'The iron and steel industry. Some issues to be considered in changing the pattern of growth in the Ninth Five Year Plan'

SHAN SHANHUA, GUAN KEZHEN, WANG XIAOMING

Metallurgy Economics Research, 1996, No. 18

During the Eighth Five Year Plan period (1991–1995), China's iron and steel industry achieved considerable progress in adjusting its product mix, increasing the variety of products in great demand, raising product quality and improving its major technical and economic indicators. However, driven by market forces, scale-generated economic returns have continued to be given primary consideration. Steel output increased by 27.65 million tons during the period, averaging 5.5 million tons annually. The increases in 1992 and 1993 were 9.9 million tons and 7.7 million tons respectively. Stimulated by returns to scale, enterprises further expanded their scales in pursuit of quantitative growth. Starting in the latter half of 1993, the state intensified its macro-control, and adopted measures to impose strict control on the scale of fixed asset investments and to limit the growth of money supply. This brought about a radical change in the supply and demand relationship on the steel market. The market for many steel products changed from seller's to buyer's, and a situation arose wherein supply was in excess of demand. Some enterprises suffered declines in returns or even losses for a long period of time because their products were not suited for the market while production cost was high and sales were sluggish. The deep contradictions of the steel industry arising from its extensive management system were gradually brought to light. Many enterprises came to realise the necessity of changing their growth pattern, and made efforts in this direction when they worked out their Ninth Five Year Plans. Three major enterprises – the Anshan Iron and Steel Company, the Wuhan Iron and Steel Company and the Capital Iron and Steel Company – adjusted their plans for achieving a 10 million-ton capacity in favour of a lower output. They are using their limited funds to optimise product variety, increase efficiency and improve environmental protection. This has brought about fairly good results. However, looking at the industry as a whole, two prominent problems still exist in the Ninth Five Year Plans drawn up by various enterprises.

First, some enterprises still pursue quantitative growth and regard it as their development priority.

The Chinese National People's Congress (NPC) set steel output at 105 million tons in its Five-Year Plan for National Economic and Social Development. China's present steel-smelting capacity exceeds 100 million tons, while its steel output was 93 million tons in 1995. This means that the steel industry only has to add about 15 million tons to its capacity during the Ninth Five Year Plan period to meet the NPC target. However, the arrangements now being made by enterprises show a tendency of increasing their scales by varying degrees. If the key enterprises increase their capacity by about 10 millions and local backbone enterprises by about 15 million tons, the total added capacity would have exceeded the state plan. This shows that, in formulating their Ninth Five Year Plan, some enterprises still had not changed their guiding ideology and mentality. In pursuit of scale, some local backbone enterprises went so far as to increase their production capacity by 30%–50%. Some individual enterprises even doubled their capacity. Certain increases in capacity are necessary if the increases are brought about by the application of new technology or by increasing the variety of products in great demand. But some are unnecessary from the national perspective. For example, many new electric furnaces have been built in areas along the lower reaches of Yangzi River, adding over 5 million tons of new capacity. The enterprises operating these furnaces generally produce steel materials of average quality. Besides, the supply of steel scraps and electricity in those areas is very tight.

Second, the scale of investment is too large while funds are extremely short.

Fixed asset investments in China's iron and steel industry during the Eighth Plan period came to 156 billion yuan. Based on the arrangements the enterprises have made, total investments for the Ninth Five Year Plan will be in excess of 300 billion yuan, doubling the amount for the Eighth Five Year Plan. Such a scale of investment is obviously too large. Both the state and the enterprises themselves can hardly afford it.

The iron and steel enterprises are currently facing a marked decline in economic returns. At the end of 1995, loss-making key state enterprises and local backbone enterprises numbered 25, their debt ratio being 56% and gross liabilities exceeding 331 billion yuan. If enterprises with a lower debt ratio – such as Baoshan, Handan and Anyang Steel Works – are excepted, the average debt ratio would be 61.5%. The debt ratio of more than one-half of the key iron and steel enterprises was higher than 70%. Moreover, the industry's economic returns showed a further declining trend in the first quarter of 1996. As Chinese steel products have already entered the international market and the prices of most varieties have been adjusted to international levels, steel prices are not expected to fluctuate heavily in the next several years. Yet there are still differences in the prices of coal, electricity, transportation and other upper-stream products with those of their international counterparts. They will gradually come to a par around 2000. Therefore, no major improvement in the economic conditions of the iron and steel enterprises are to be expected. The inadequacy of funds raised by the enterprises themselves will be a prominent contradiction in implementing their Ninth Five Year Plan.

In view of the situation described above, it is absolutely necessary for iron and steel enterprises to adjust their Ninth Five Year Plan in order to facilitate a change in the growth pattern of the steel industry. Based on our initial understanding of the guidelines of the 5th NPC, we give our opinions below on some of the issues requiring attention in effecting a change of the industry's growth pattern.

1. To stress variety and quality and make persistent efforts to effect a change from scale-generated returns to variety and quality-generated returns

For China to change from a country with a large steel industry to a country with a powerful steel industry, it is first of all necessary to increase the variety and improve the quality of steel products. At present, however, some iron and steel enterprises are stressing variety and quality in name only, while in deed, they are working on expanding their production scale. They believe that it is quicker to achieve a growth in benefits by increasing output than by increasing variety and improving quality. Such an idea is derived from a planned economic system, which needs to be rectified as quickly as possible. To gain a share of the market amid intense competition, we can only rely on product marketability, high quality and low cost. It is hard to sell products of low or average quality. An expansion in scale may not bring about any benefits at all. With an increased cost of energy, products of low added value will gradually lose their market competitiveness. This point is fully testified by the fact that, over the past two years, while a considerable number of enterprises had their economic benefits slashed by a large margin, the profits of enterprises capable of manufacturing high-quality products and products in great demand, such as the Baoshan and Fushun Steel Works, have continued to grow significantly.

During the Ninth Five Year Plan period, the steel industry should find ways to satisfy the needs for special steel products by key sectors of the national economy, particularly steel and stainless steel products needed by the automotive, electric power, petroleum, railways and shipbuilding sectors. Measures should be adopted to raise the country's self-supporting rate in these sectors, and capture this part of the market as soon as possible.

(1) Steel products for automobiles

The self-supporting rate of steels for automobiles is an important indicator of the level of development of a country's steel industry. At present, China relies mainly on imported steels for its sedan cars, such as galvanized plates, which must be of very high quality. Currently, even products of the Baoshan Steel Works, which boasts of the highest level of equipment, can hardly satisfy consumers' requirements.

It is estimated that, in the year 2000, about 2.5 million tons of steel products will be required for use in sedan cars. Among them, medium plates will account for 1.5 million tons, of which 70%, or about one million tons, will be extremely difficult to produce. During the Ninth Five Year Plan period, it is necessary to upgrade the cold-rolling mills, galvanizing equipment and other relevant facilities in the Baoshan, Wuhan and Benxi Steel Works, so that they will be able to supply 600,000 tons of deep drawing galvanized plates for use in sedan cars at the end of this century, thus achieving a 60% self-supporting rate. About 180,000 tons of high-grade gear steel will also be needed for sedan cars in the same time frame. Arrangements are now being made to build gear production lines at the Daye and Fushun Steel Works. It is estimated that, by the year 2000, they will be able to produce 120,000 tons of gear steel, thus achieving a 65% self-sufficiency rate.

(2) Special steels for the electric power industry

It is estimated that, by 2000, the electric power industry will need 1.4 million tons of cold-rolled silicon steel sheets, 270,000 tons of high-pressure boiler tubes and 210,000 tons of high-pressure boiler plates. Steps will be taken during the Ninth Five Year Plan period to increase the production of cold-rolled silicon plates at Wuhan, Baoshan and Taiyuan Steel Works, so that by 2000, they will have a combined production capacity of 1.02 million tons, meeting about 73% of the required quantity. Great efforts will be made to upgrade and perfect the 100,000-ton high-pressure boiler tubing production line at Baoshan Steel Works during the period, and measures will also be taken at the Shanghai Steel tubing Plant and the Qiqihar Steel Works to create a 210,000-ton high-pressure boiler tubing production capacity, thus achieving a self-supporting rate of about 75%. High-pressure boiler plates are generally over 50mm thick. Apart from developing the production capacity of the Wuyang Steel Works, the post-processing operation at Anshan Iron and Steel Company's wide and thick plate rolling mill will also be transformed. It is estimated that the self-sufficiency rate of high-pressure boiler plates will reach 30% by 2000.

(3) Special steel products for the petroleum industry

It is estimated that the petroleum industry will need 1.4 million tons of special piping in 2000. These will include one million tons of casing pipes, 300,000 tons of oilpipes, and 100,000 tons of drilling tools. Steps will be taken during the Ninth Five Year Plan period to exploit the potentials of the seven pipe mills operating in five existing production enterprises, so as to increase their production capacity to 763,000 tons, or about 50% of the required quantity.

(4) Special steel products for railways

Heavy rail requirements for 2000 are estimated to be 1.7 million tons, including 500,000 tons of full-length quenched rails. Also needed will be 240,000–260,000 tons of wheels and 30,000 tons of wheel rims. Steps will be taken during the Ninth Five Year Plan period at Baotou, Panzhihua, Wuhan and Anshan Steel Works to increase heavy rail output to 1.65 million tons, including 550,000 tons of full-length quenched rails. This will basically meet the requirements in terms of variety and quantity. At present, the Ma'anshan Steel Works has the capacity to produce 160,000 tons of wheels and 50,000 tons of rims. The Ministry of Railways has plans to build two cast steel wheel production lines during the Ninth Five Year Plan period, which will have a capacity of 100,000 tons. In general, China's production of wheels and rims will be enough to meet its 2000 needs.

(5) Special steel products for the shipping industry

Ship plates required for 2000 are estimated to be 2.3 million tons. This can be met domestically as during the Ninth Five Year Plan period, the medium plate mills at the No.3 Plant of Shangrao Steel Works and at Anshan, Wuyang and Handan Steel Works will be transformed and fitted with a full range of equipment on a priority basis.

(6) Stainless steel products

The requirements for stainless steel products in 2000 are estimated to be 920,000 tons of stainless steel sheets, 41.86 tons of which will be cold-rolled thin sheets. Since the current annual output of cold-rolled stainless steel sheets is less than 50,000 tons, supply will fall heavily short of demand and will have to depend mainly on imports. During the Ninth Five Year Plan period, priority will be given to transforming the cold-rolled plate mill at Taiyuan Steel Works to increase its output capacity to 100,000 tons. A stainless steel coiling project with a designed capacity of 400,000 tons will be built at the No. 3 Plant of the Shangrao Steel Works, but will not be ready for operation until after 2000. Once these two projects are operative, the shortage of cold-rolled sheets will be basically solved.

China now produces 12 million tons of steel products in 115 varieties that are up to advanced international standards in physical quality. It is anticipated that the quantity of such products will reach about 30 million tons by 2000, accounting for one-third of the country's total output of steel products. This will greatly enhance the competitiveness of Chinese steel products on both the international and domestic markets.

To improve product quality, it is necessary to conduct concrete analyses on specific enterprises. For the country as a whole and within the permissible scale of investment, it is necessary to pool funds to solve the shortage of steels for automobiles and of stainless steels on a first priority basis. This is because, to a certain extent, steels for automobiles reflect the image of the variety and quantity of a country's steel products. During the Ninth Plan period, it is necessary to pool financial and technical resources to upgrade the production lines at the Baoshan and Wuhan Steel Works. The successful implementation of this measure will supply more than 50% of the steel plates needed for the manufacture of sedan cars. On the other hand, it is also necessary to speed up the development of the stainless steel industry to change the current situation in which the industry is dependent on tariff protection to offset price differences between domestic and international products.

160

2. To save energy and lower consumption through scientific and technological means is the road to survival, development and better returns

The backward technology and equipment of most of China's existing iron and steel enterprises is the main cause of their inferior products, heavy energy consumption and high costs. Energy consumption is the main factor affecting the cost of steel production. In 1995, China's steel industry consumed 129 million tons of standard coal, accounting for about 10% of the country's total energy consumption. The average composite energy consumption per ton of steel was 1.516 tons of standard coal. This is 30%–40% higher than the per-ton-of-steel energy consumption in developed countries, after taking in account the influencing factor of statistical discrepancies. Herein lies the industry's latent capacity. In order to survive, develop and make better yields, the industry must save energy and cut down consumption and regard this as its primary task in the future.

It is estimated that, around the year 2000, the price per ton of standard coal will rise from the present 510 yuan to about 600 yuan. Currently, energy cost already accounts for 25%–30% of the iron and steel enterprises' production cost. As in future China's energy prices will have to match those on the international market, the prices for coal, petroleum and electric power are bound to go up further. Consequently, the production cost of steel products will also continue to increase. To offset the increased cost, it is preliminarily estimated that China's steel industry will have to reduce energy consumption from the present 1.516 tons of standard coal per ton of steel to below 1.32 tons of standard coal. This will lower the cost for producing say 100 million tons of steel by 11.5–12 billion yuan. To achieve this goal, it is necessary to replace out-of-date technology with modem technology. This will take 5–10 years.

To realise the goal stated above, the first thing to do is to draw up an overall energy consumption plan for the steel industry. This requires a scrupulous analysis of the present state of energy consumption in order to set the consumption indices for various sectors, and to work out the energy-saving goals and measures.

During and beyond the Ninth Five Year Plan period, the steel industry must give priority to developing the following six items of advanced technology, which will substitute for the present backward production technology and play a significant role in achieving the goal of "saving energy, cutting down consumption and making better yields".

One, to promote the development of completely continuous casting and high-efficiency continuous casting technology and strive to raise the continuous casting ratio from 47% in 1995 to over 75% in 2000. At present, with 247 operating continuous casters, China boasts of having the largest number of continuous casters in the world. Its output of continuous casting billets in 1995 was 43.75 million tons, ranking third in the world. However, its continuous casting ratio was below the world average, which was 72.6% in 1994. In order to catch up with the world's advanced level in continuous casting technology, to accelerate the optimisation of the technological structure in steel production, to effectively transform the structure of continuous casting and casters to a structure geared to efficient and intensive operation, and at the same time to avoid massive and repetitive building of low-level casters, great efforts must be exerted during the Ninth Plan period to promote the development of completely continuous casting and high-efficiency continuous casting, and to incorporate hot-filling and hot-feeding in the continuous casting projects. Based on a steel output of 105 million tons for the year 2000, the higher continuous casting ratio will raise the output of steel billets by 2.3 million tons and increase the yields by over two billion yuan.

Two, to replace open hearth furnaces with converters. China presently possesses an open hearth furnace steel production capacity of 14 million tons. Its open hearth furnaces are mainly located in the Anshan, Wuhan and Baotou Steel Works. Steel smelting by open hearth furnaces is characterised by high consumption of energy and refractory materials, low labour productivity and poor economic returns. It can hardly match continuous casting and it obstructs optimisation of the technological structure. If all open hearth furnaces in the metallurgical system were replaced with the technologically more advanced converters, the industry would be able to save energy equivalent to about 1.7 million tons of standard coal (including some 700,000 tons of heavy oil), and 260,000 tons of refractory materials. The resultant higher continuous casting ratio would also increase the output of steel billets by about one million tons.

Three, to do away with cupola smelting. China's present cupola smelting capacity is estimated to be around 7.5 million tons. The iron-smelting furnaces are mainly located in several blast furnace top pressure power generation, converter gas recovery, and reheating furnace comprehensive energy-saving technology. Efforts should also be made to promote energy optimisation models and energy management centers for enterprises. Energy conservation management work should be carried out in all sectors of production operations to reduce gas diffusion and make better use of recovered residual heat. This is a very important aspect in lowering the energy consumption of iron and steel enterprises.

3. To tap the potentials of existing enterprises, dampen their desire for scale and quantitative expansion and attach importance to increasing variety, upgrading quality and lowering consumption. No new mills should be built during the Ninth Five Year Plan period

The development of the iron and steel industry during the Ninth Five Year Plan period should focus on tapping the potentials of and transforming the ten major iron and steel enterprises, centering around increasing their product variety, improving product quality and lowering consumption.

The Baoshan Steel Works is the most important base as far as variety is concerned. It plans to complete its third-phase expansion project during the Ninth Five Year Plan period, which will increase its output of galvanized plates by 400,000 tons, cold-rolled silicon plates by 325,000 tons, cold-rolled plates by 1.05 million tons and hot-rolled plates by 1.139 million tons. All these items are in very short supply at present.

The Wuhan, Anshan and Capital Steel Works have all shelved their plans for expanding the scale of their steel production to 10 million tons. They will concentrate their resources on transforming and developing their plate mills. Projects to be undertaken by the Wuhan Steel Works will include transforming its cold plate mill, the second phase project for silicon steel production, a 300,000-ton galvanizing line, and a second tandem rolling mill. The Anshan Steel Works will carry out its 1.7-meter tandem rolling mill transformation project and the No.2 plate billet continuous caster enterprises in Shanghai, Tianjin and Qingdao. Cupola smelting not only wastes energy and increases costs, but also causes environmental pollution. Cupola smelting should be eliminated step-by-step in the next ten years by building blast furnaces or molten iron reduction equipment in those enterprises. This technological improvement will save about 1.3 million tons of coke, cut down iron wastage by 260,000 tons and lower production cost by about 1.5 billion yuan a year.

Four, to promote the use of blast furnace coal powder injection technology. This technology can be applied at three levels: for local backbone enterprises and key enterprises where conditions are not good, the amount of coal powder injection should be 100 kilogram (kg) per ton of iron, for key enterprises with a bigger deficiency in coke but better conditions, the amount should be 150 kg per ton of iron; and for a few large blast furnaces, the amount should be 200 kg per ton of iron. To realize this goal, it is estimated that the amount of coal powder injection for blast furnaces in the whole country should have reached 13 million tons by 2000, an increase of 9 million tons from that in 1995. This will lower the cost of pig iron by over one billion yuan.

Five, to substitute ultra high-power electric furnace-external refining-continuous casting-continuous or semi-continuous rolling technology for the backward small ordinary-power electric furnace-die casting-cogging-horizontal rolling technology presently used in special steel manufacturing plants. Preliminary plans call for completing the technical transformation of key special steel manufacturing plants during the Ninth Five Year Plan and Tenth Five Year Plan period. The new technology will greatly lower power and electrode consumption and increase the rate of finished products. It will bring about significant economic returns.

Six, to promote the application of new energy-saving technology and strengthen energy conservation management work. Further efforts should be made to promote the application of advanced energy-saving technology that has proven to be effective, including dry coke quenching, project at its No. 3 Smelting Plant. The Capital Steel Works will work on its 2160 continuous hot caster project and No. 2 Smelting Plant transformation and refitting project.

The Baotou Steel Works will focus on its full-length heavy quenched rail project and the first phase of its sheet billet continuous caster project. The Benxi Steel Works will refit its 1676 cold-rolled plate mill with a full range of equipment, transform its 1700 continuous hot caster and build a new plate billet continuous caster. The Taiyuan Steel Works will complete its 100,000-ton cold-rolled electric motor silicon steel plate mill transformation project and its 100,000-ton cold-rolled stainless steel plate mill expansion project. The Panzhihua Steel Works will complete the transformation of its continuous hot plate caster, and its RH vacuum processing, large square billet continuous caster and heavy rail residual heat quenching projects. The Tangshan Steel Works will be able to start its project to expand its production capacity to 5 million tons during the Plan period, yet it may consider to carry out its cold-rolled plate project first.

As the ten major steel works concentrate their resources on projects related to products that are in short supply, their steel smelting capacity will increase by about 7 million tons accordingly (the third-phase project of the Baoshan Steel Works alone will increase the capacity by about 2.5 million tons).

According to our understanding, local iron and steel enterprises are even more inclined to expanding their production scales during the Ninth Five Year Plan period. Some localities and enterprises built new electric furnaces to produce ordinary steel products. Some local backbone enterprises added to their existing long-flow-process production capacity certain electric furnace short-flow-process capacity. These practices have given rise to more problems, such as shortage of steel scraps, tense electric power supply and poor economic performance. It is, therefore, necessary to tighten the grip on the development of local enterprises during the Ninth Plan period. Strict control must be exercised on new projects. In particular, the building of new electric furnaces with a short flow process must be subjected to tight macro-control.

The 2000 targets for growth in steel output and capacity can be fully met by tapping the potentials of and transforming the existing steel works. The building of new steel works planned for the Ninth Plan period, including the Beilun Steel Works, can be put off for the time being.

4. In accordance with the principle of doing what is possible, to reduce appropriately the scale of fixed asset investment and use limited funds on key projects

Based on the development plans submitted by various iron and steel enterprises, total investments in the Ninth Plan period will be in excess of 300 billion yuan. As the situation stands, it would not be easy to raise so much capital. Therefore, it is necessary to set priorities on development projects. Funds should be spent, on a priority basis, on increasing product variety, improving quality and cutting down consumption. The scale of fixed asset investment should be compressed appropriately. It is proposed that steps be taken in the following five directions:

First, projects carried over from the Ninth Five Year Plan should be sorted out in real earnest. Funds should be concentrated on ongoing projects which conform to the two basic changes, so that they can be completed and put into operation as quickly as possible. Projects with poor returns or those incurring losses after completion must be terminated without hesitation. Only by greatly reducing the scale of investments in carry-over projects can funds be made available for projects that will save energy, lower consumption, increase variety and improve quality.

Second, all iron and steel enterprises should only do what is within their ability to raise funds for development, and adjust their development plans for the Ninth Five Year Plan period accordingly.

Third, at an appropriate time, the departments in charge of the iron and steel industry should convene a national forum of iron and steel enterprises to review the implementation of their Ninth Five Year Plan Year Plans. This will enable them to have a good grasp of the overall situation and avoid blindness in action.

Fourth, in view of the fact that the development of the iron and steel industry involves heavy investments over a long period of time and yet its returns are low, the state needs to support the industry in terms of funding and policy considerations so that it can realise its Ninth Five Year Plan development goals. Credit finds and preferential policies should be granted to the most urgent and important projects.

Fifth, competent authorities should pay serious attention to the problem of massive construction of electric furnaces by the localities to expand their production capacities, and take necessary steps to put it under macro-control.

Document 4.2

'China's textile industry: from size to strength'

LI CHANGMING

China Industrial Development Report 1997, Chap. 11

In recent years China's textile industry has intensified its structural readjustment. It has at the same time achieved considerable growth. The output of its main products are the biggest in the world and it has always been among the top performers among China's various industries and trades in terms of export earnings.

However, as a representative traditional industry, textiles is up against growing pressure and challenges in both domestic and foreign markets. It is faced with the problem of how to effect a change from size to strength [and to do this] through further structural readjustments and upgrading of the industry under the new conditions of structural reform and the policy of opening up to the outside world.

1. The development of China's textile industry

(1) Fast and sustained development

China's textile industry enjoyed a period of excellent growth during the first 18 years of reform and opening up. This is testified by the output figures of its main products for 1995. Chemical fibres output at 3,529,500 tons, 12.4 times that of 1978; cloth, 26.02 billion metres, 2.4 times; yarns, 5,423,000 tons, 2.3 times; wool fabrics, 663.97 million metres, 7.5 times; silk fabrics, 3 billion metres, 4.9 times; clothing, 8 billion pieces, 11.9 times (See Table 4.2). As for production capacity [as distinct from actual output] the textile industry ranks first in the world in respect of cotton spinning, cotton cloth, silk fabrics, clothing, knitwear and printing and dyeing capacities; and is second in respect of chemical fibres, wool fabrics, wool spinning and ramie and flax yarn. The industry employs some 15 million staff members and workers, one-sixth of China's total industrial employment. The industry 's annual output value amounted to 645.569 billion *yuan* in 1994, one-sixth of China's total gross industrial output value (GVIO).[16] Currently, the industry's annual profits and tax payments account for about one-tenth of the total industrial profits and tax payments for the whole country. It can be seen from the above data that the textile industry carries a big weight in China's national economy.

(2) Rapid growth in textile exports

Since the implementation of the reform and opening up policy, products of China's textile industry have achieved remarkable progress in international trade. In 1970, China's exports of fibre products, textiles and clothing accounted for 2.6%, 2.7% and 2.4% respectively of the world total exports. By 1992, these percentages had risen to 10.2%, 7.4% and 12.8% respectively. In 1980, China's exports of fibre products ranked 7th among eight principal export countries and regions in the world. They then rose steadily to take up the second position in 1992 (see Table 4.3). China's exports of textile products have occupied the first position in the world in terms of volume since the beginning of the 1980s. In terms of value, with

16 GVIO is a standard measure of output in the Chinese statistical system. It is the sum of outputs of all branches and enterprises, therefore neglecting the problem of 'double counting'. However the value of the measure for growth and other estimates is considerable. (Ed.)

Table 4.2 Major products of China's textile industry, 1978–1996

Year	Chemical Fibre (000 tons)	Cloth (billion metres)	Yarn (000 tons)	Hand Knitting Wool Yarn (000 tons)	Wool Fabric (million metres)	Silk (thousand tons)	Silk Fabric (billion metres)	Apparel (billion pieces)
1978	284.6	11.03	2382	37.8	88.85	29.7	0.611	0.673
1979	326.3	12.15	2635	44.4	90.17	29.7	0.663	0.744
1980	450.3	13.48	2926	57.3	100.93	35.4	0.759	0.945
1981	527.3	14.27	3170	76.5	113.08	37.4	0.835	1.008
1982	517.0	15.35	3354	92.5	126.69	37.1	0.914	0.985
1983	540.7	14.88	3271	102.1	142.91	36.9	1.003	1.004
1984	734.9	13.69	3219	110.0	180.49	37.6	1.178	1.106
1985	947.8	14.67	3535	125.9	218.16	42.2	1.449	1.267
1986	1017.3	16.47	3978	149.1	251.86	47.1	1.501	2.527
1987	1175.0	17.30	4368	204.1	265.40	51.9	1.602	2.260
1988	1301.2	18.79	4657	224.4	286.11	51.5	1.711	2.911
1989	1478.2	18.92	4767	249.9	279.63	52.3	1.628	3.003
1990	1648.2	18.88	4626	237.9	295.05	56.6	1.712	3.175
1991	1910.4	18.17	4608	282.5	311.43	60.7	2.406	3.384
1992	2111.2	19.05	5014	350.6	337.91	73.3	2.524	4.266
1993	2268.7	19.69	5014	344.6	352.52	92.4	2.836	6.368
1994	2803.3	21.13	4895	439.6	419.00	106.4	3.128	7.816
1995	3529.5	26.02	5423	513.8	663.97	113.4	3.000	8.000
1996	3343.9	17.48	4900	414.3	375.02	78.9	3.296	5.136

Source: Almanac of China's Textile Industry 1995 and China Statistical Yearbook 1996.

Table 4.3 China and Hong Kong among the world major fibre product exporting countries (in billion US$ and ranking)

Countries/ Region	1980 Value	Rank	1985 Value	Rank	1990 Value	Rank	1991 Value	Rank	1992 Value	Rank
Hong Kong	6.75 (5.57)	3	9.74 (5.38)	1	23.62 (11.44)	1	27.73 (12.03)	1	31.04 (12.20)	1
China	4.25	7	5.29	7	16.89	4	20.81	3	25.29	2
Italy	8.74	2	9.70	2	21.33	2	21.14	2	22.40	3
Germany	9.10	1	5.77	6	20.38	3	20.69	4	22.21	4
S. Korea	5.16	5	7.00	3	14.08	5	14.72	5	14.98	5
Taiwan	4.21	8	6.00	4	10.12	7	11.83	6	11.68	6
France	5.72	4	5.87	5	10.73	6	10.59	9	11.52	7
USA	5.07	6	3.13	8	7.60	8	8.92	8	10.10	8

Note: Figures in brackets under 'Hong Kong' are export value net of re-exports.
Sources: Studies on Textile Economy, No. 6, 1994.

exports worth 25.29 billion US dollars in 1992, China surpassed major textile export countries such as Germany and Italy to take up the world second position. It would have taken the first position if the amount of re-export trade through Hong Kong were adjusted. The world market share of China's textile products has also been increasing steadily. Exports of raw silk and cotton cloth ranked first in the world, taking up a 90% and a 20% share of the world market respectively. The textile industry has become a leading industry in China, and is second to none in terms of export earnings. Between 1978 and 1994, China's textile exports grew at an annual rate of 18%, far exceeding the 10% growth rate for worldwide textile exports. In 1978, China's textile exports amounted to 2.431 billion US dollars; in 1993, the figure went up to 27.13 billion US dollars or 11 times that of 1978. In the years 1995–1996, China's exports of textiles and clothing accounted for over 13% of the world total export figures for same. For the 11 years 1986 to 1996, the average annual exports of Chinese textile products accounted for more than one-fourth of China's total exports. From 1989 to the present, net annual export earnings of textile products exceeded 10 billion US dollars. Aggregate export earnings since 1980 amounted to 138.2 billion US dollars. These earnings, while partly consumed by the industry itself, have provided strong support for the development of key sectors of the national economy.[17] It can be said that the textile industry has made significant contributions to China's national economic construction and to its opening up to the outside world.

17 This refers to the fact that China is a major importer of textile raw materials and intermediate products, including man made fibers. (Ed.)

The vigorous development of the textile industry and the increasingly important position it occupies in China's international trade indicate that, for a very long period of time, the textile industry will continue to enjoy broad development prospects and absolutely will not become a 'sunset industry' like those in the developed countries. This is because China has not completed its industrialisation process and, according to the common law of industrialisation, light and textile industries invariably play a leading role in the industrialisation process. The textile industry is one of a few industries in China that are placed in advantageous positions. It is playing an irreplaceable role in capital accumulation, employment and foreign exchange earnings. The Fifth Plenum of the Fourteenth Chinese Communist Party Central Committee called for developing the machine-building, electronics, petrochemical, automotive and communications industries into pillar industries of the national economy as quickly as possible. Although the textile industry has not assumed the status of a pillar industry, its importance is obvious and undeniable whether in terms of its relative weight in the industry as a whole, or in terms of its competitiveness on the international market. While investing the main portion of its funds into automotive and other pillar industries, China absolutely cannot ignore the development of its textile industry. It should provide necessary funds to help the textile industry solve problems that require an urgent solution, in order to further accelerate its development.

2. Problems of the textile industry

(1) Falling economic returns, heavy losses

The textile industry economic returns have been declining steadily since 1989 as a result of heavy increases in the prices of raw materials (such as cotton and fibres) and rising labour cost. Take 1992 for example, the rate of profits and taxes to capital of China's spinning and weaving, chemical fibre and garment industries was 6.25%, far lower than the 9.45% average for all industries in the country. Moreover, the economic returns to urban textile industries were also below the average level of returns to the textile industries of the whole society. Starting in 1991, the whole cotton spinning and weaving industry has been making losses. Its losses grew heavier in 1993 as [raw] cotton prices increased further. The situation became increasingly serious in 1995 and 1996 as economic returns continued to decline further. Statistics showed that, in the first quarter of 1996, 2,103, or 64.17%, of the 3,277 state-owned textile enterprises listed in the budget were making losses, amounting to 30.05 billion *yuan* in total, which is equivalent to the amount of losses for the whole year of 1995. From January to May 1996, among the 1,129 state-owned textile enterprises in 38 major cities, 707 or 62.62% were making losses, involving a total amount of 2.44 billion *yuan*. Between 1980 and 1990, China's textile industry achieved an average annual growth rate of 10.27% in GVIO, yet profits and taxes realized per 100 *yuan* of asset value dropped by an annual average of 10.08%. Nevertheless, total profits and taxes realised in those years maintained a 2% annual growth thanks to the increase in the number of newly-built projects. By 1995, the industry GVIO had risen by 13.95% annually on an average, yet the realisation of profits and taxes per 100 *yuan* asset value had shown an average decline of 12.25%. This indicates that the industry could no longer maintain a growth in profits and taxes by relying on newly-built projects.

(2) Severe excess inventories. More enterprises working below capacity and more shutdowns

According to statistics for the first quarter of 1996, the output of cotton yarn and cotton cloth of the 3,277 State Owned Enterprises listed in the budget rose by 30% compared with that for the corresponding period of 1995. More than 1,000 enterprises had operations suspended or part suspended. Some 700 enterprises were unable to pay wages. Over 500,000 workers were removed from their work posts, some 20% more than the number for the corresponding period of 1995. Those remaining at their posts were paid only their basic salaries. In the face of increasing raw material and labour costs, textile enterprises in general found themselves in difficult positions. The State Owned Enterprises were caught in a greater plight due to the heavy burden of an increasing number of retired personnel whom they must take care of.

(3) Weak competitiveness and a fall in net foreign exchange earnings

In recent years, textile products and clothing have earned more and more foreign exchange, yet the rate of net foreign exchange earnings has continued to fall. [i.e. exports minus imports of materials etc. needed by the industry]. For example, the net foreign exchange earning rate of textile products and clothing in 1986 was 69.3%, but it fell to 60.3% in 1990 and then sharply to 43.7% in 1992. The main cause of the fall is weak competitiveness on the international market resulting from rising costs of cotton, chemical fibres, wages, water and electricity and heavy increases in prices of imported raw materials. In recent years, imports of chemical fibre raw materials and materials for making the outward side of garments increased rapidly. Imports of the latter accounted for more than 30% of the import quota for the entire textiles system, surpassing the amount of exports of same. For a long time China's textile industry relied on its low cost advantages, and developed itself rapidly centering on quantitative growth. However, since 1993 its low cost advantages began to taper off. This is because the ex-factory prices of raw cotton have increased at an average annual rate of 37.84% and are now even higher than the prices on the international market; the prices of chemical fibres, which account for 30% of the raw materials used by the textile industry, have also increased steadily; while the costs of energy and other means of production have likewise been adjusted upward repeatedly. In more recent years, with the increase in wages year after year, the low labour cost advantage in China has been constantly weakened. Besides, China's productivity at present is still significantly lower than the international level. In foreign countries, the cotton spinning industry employs some 100 people to operate 10,000 spindles. In China we have to employ about 400 people. Moreover, the rate of tax reimbursement for exports has been lowered, which also increases the export cost. Another factor unfavourable to China's exports is that international trade protectionism is raising its head again, while China's commitment to take steps to meet the requirements for admission into the World Trade Organisation also weakens the advantages of its textile exports correspondingly. In the meantime, the peripheral countries and regions are developing their exports rapidly, using their low cost advantages and preferential measures. They have become China's strong competitors on the export market. Pakistan cotton yarn exports have surpassed China by a large margin, taking up a 39.49% share of the world cotton yarn exports in 1991. The proportion of textile products in China general trade as a whole has been on the decrease year after year. In 1994, it accounted for 59.28% of the total volume of general trade. It fell to 54.34% in 1995 and further to 42.92% in 1996.

(4) Substantial readjustments required to resolve sharp structural contradictions

For a long time China's cotton spinning and wool spinning industries, like other traditional industries, have been faced with the problem of excessive low-level production capacity but insufficient high-level production capacity. In the traditional garment industry, this is manifested in a surplus in aggregate output, overproduction of medium and low-grade goods and serious underproduction of textile products for fashion and industrial uses. Structural problems of the textile industry are epitomised in the following three aspects:

First, the technological structure is falling behind. Only 15% of its existing 3.6 million wool spindles are up to advanced international level. 500,000 outmoded spindles need to be eliminated. China's cotton spinning capacity in 1995 was around 41 million spindles, of which over 10 million spindles were obsolete. The finishing process in printing and dyeing has always been a weakness of China's textile technology. Only 6% of the existing finishing equipment is up to advanced international level, while 60% is on extended service beyond their normal service life. Finishing and special finishing techniques are falling even farther behind the international level.

Second, the product mix does not suit market requirements. The structure of China's textile industry is not adapted to the changing international trends of textile production, nor to the structural changes in international and domestic market demands. The proportion of textile products for industrial use in the overall production of textile products in the developed countries will rise from the present 30% to 50% by 2000, and their proportion in international trade will also rise from about 13% at present to over 40%, whereas in China they still only account for about 10% of the total domestic fibre output up to this time, falling far behind market requirements. In terms of quality and technological content, textile products exported by China are obviously inferior to those exported by [competitor] developed countries. The foreign exchange earnings per ton of fibre manufactures exported by Germany and Italy in 1995 exceeded 20,000 US dollars, whereas those exported by China earned only 10,000 US dollars.

Third, the scale structure of enterprises is backward. Most of China's textile enterprises are relatively small in scale. They do not meet the requirements for an economy of scale. For example, the aggregate production capacity of the some 470 existing chemical fibre enterprises is three million tons, or less than 10,000 tons per enterprise. Among them, 330 are small enterprises, with an aggregate production capacity of 700,000 tons, averaging only some 2,000 tons per enterprise.

3. Major development tasks

In order to extricate itself from the present predicament and to achieve a new and remarkable progress, it is crucial for the textile industry to carry out structural readjustments. On this, everybody seems to share a common view. However, progress during the most recent years has been quite slow, whether in capacity readjustment by means of cutting down the number of spindles, or in structural readjustment by means of moving spindles from the 'east to the west'. Here there is a question that needs to be resolved first of all. It is necessary to have a correct understanding of the role of the textile industry in national economic construction and to correct the erroneous view that traditional industry is a 'sunset industry'.

Whether in the earliest-developed England and France, or in the late-developed Japan and Korea, the textile industry has invariably played the role of a capital accumulator and foreign exchange earner in the course of achieving industrialisation. China is still working hard for its industrialisation. In this stage the role of the textile industry is that of a prerequisite [to further development in other industries]. This is determined by the common law of economic development, and by the current stage of China's economic development. China is rich in labour resources. At present we have a surplus labour force of about one hundred million people. On the other hand, we are extremely short of construction funds. To absorb a great mass of the labour force and to accumulate funds through the development of the textile industry conforms perfectly to China's resource situation. This is the fundamental reason why, despite its numerous problems, the textile industry has been able to make significant progress over these years, whereas some capital-intensive industries have failed to compete with their foreign counterparts although China has exerted great efforts and invested huge amounts of funds in their development. We should see from this great contrast the important role the textile industry is playing. Without a doubt, to drop the textile industry is to give up our [natural comparative] advantage.

The textile industry has a history of several hundred years. It is unquestionably a traditional industry. But a traditional industry is not a sunset industry. The textile industry is both an old industry and an evergreen industry. Generally speaking the textile industry in developed countries is withering and is gradually being replaced by automotive, electronics, computer and other 'sunrise industries'. However, we must also see that even developed countries are still continuing to develop high-grade and sophisticated textile products and are reaping considerable profits therefrom. China, as a developing country with a large population, is not the same as the developed countries. With more than 1.2 billion people needing to be fed and clothed, its textile industry will never be like the setting sun on the domestic market. Besides, its textile industry is still holding an edge on the international market. What needs to be changed, however, is its product mix to match the changes of demand for better quality and more sophisticated textile products. In the course of this structural change, what is like the setting sun is not the industry itself but its outmoded technology and product mix. For this reason, the key to developing the textile industry lies in structural readjustments to get rid of 'sunset' technology and products. With new technology and higher quality products, the textile industry will shine again.

(1) Readjustment of the technological structure

The technological structure of China's textile industry is out of proportion with the leading position the industry occupies in the world. China's machinery is in a fairly backward state. It lags not only behind those in the developed countries like the United States, Japan, Germany, Italy and England, but also considerably behind some developing countries such as Pakistan and Indonesia. For example, although China owns 33.7% of the total number of weaving machines in the world, most of them are the relatively backward shuttle looms. In 1994, the ratio between shuttleless looms and shuttle looms in China was 1:23. This may be compared to a ratio of 1:3 in Japan, 1:0.3 in the United States, 1:7 in Indonesia and 1:1 in Pakistan. The numbers of water-jet looms and air-jet looms owned by China are smaller than those owned by Japan, the United States, the Republic of Korea or even China Taiwan Province (see Tables 4.4 and 4.5). At present, while spinning and weaving technologies are advancing in development by leaps and bounds and electro-mechanical integration and computer technologies are being employed on an extensive scale in foreign countries, China has made only slow progress in transforming its spinning and weaving equipment. Less than 20% of its equipment is up to the level of the 1980's. New-technology equipment accounts for only 16%, while

Table 4.4 Cotton looms of major textile industrial countries and regions, 1994 (000 units)

Countries/Regions	(A) Shuttleless Loom	(B) Shuttle Loom	ratio of B:A
India	6.3	145.8	23.14 : 1
Japan	39.5	113.0	2.86 : 1
S. Korea	33.0	7.0	0.21 : 1
Taiwan Province	19.0	6.2	0.33 : 1
Pakistan	10.0	10.0	1.00 : 1
USA	65.4	18.0	0.28 : 1
Russia	141.7	13.3	0.09 : 1
Germany	7.4	0.5	0.07 : 1
Italy	13.4	2.0	0.15 : 1
U.K.	6.3	0.3	0.05 : 1
Indonesia	26.0	182.0	7 : 1
China Mainland	**36.0**	**845.0**	**23.47 : 1**
World	710.2	1903.4	2.68 : 1

Source: *Almanac of China's Textile Industry 1995.*

Table 4.5 Jet weaving looms by country (region) (000 units)

Countries/Regions	Type of Jet Looms	1990	1993
Japan	WJL	25.0	25.5
	AJL	18.0	20.0
S. Korea	WJL	25.0	40.0
	AJL	3.0	4.5
Taiwan Province	WJL	25.0	33.0
	AJL	8.5	14.0
U.S.A	WJL	6.0	6.0
	AJL	18.6	19.5
U.K.	WJL	3.7	4.0
	AJL	1.0	1.2
Italy	WJL	3.0	3.2
	AJL	7.4	7.6
France	WJL	3.8	3.8
	AJL	3.8	4.0
Southeast Asia	WJL	5.7	13.1
	AJL	5.3	9.2
China Mainland	WJL	6.5	17.0
	AJL	3.0	6.0

Note: WJL refers to Water-jet Loom and AJL refers to Air-jet Loom.
Source: *Almanac of China's Textile Industry 1995.*

40% of the equipment from the 1950s and 1960s are still operating beyond their life expectancies. Even some pre-Liberation equipment is still operating in some enterprises.

In recent years, the textile industry was given some impetus by imports of advanced technology and equipment from abroad. During the Eighth Five Year Plan (1986–1990), China increased its technological investments in the textile industry to 71 billion *yuan*. The imported equipment, including gripper looms, automatic bobbin winders, and blowing-carding-drawing units, promoted the industry technical transformation. However, technological imports were also fraught with problems, the main ones being lack of unified planning resulting in duplicated imports, and insufficient attention to digesting and absorbing the imported technology. Because of this, innovations deriving from these imports were out of the question. China, for instance, has imported dozens of high-speed dacron spinning lines, but has done little serious research to digest and absorb them. As a result, it has failed to keep pace with other countries in technological advancements.

At present, the textile industry is extremely short of competent technicians. According to a survey on the knitting industry, there were only 430 university and secondary technical school graduates in 58 enterprises, representing only 3.9% of the total number of their staff and workers. *Among them, 15 enterprises did not have one single university or secondary technical school graduate.* (Ed. ital). Textile enterprises were unable to keep competent technicians because of their poor pay resulting from heavy operating losses. Moreover, the quality of the industry staff members and workers is generally quite low. Many of its first-line workers came from rural areas with hardly any technical training. With these people at the work posts, it is hard to ensure product quality.

Whether or not the textile industry can cope with future competition on the international market depends to a large extent on its technological structure. In the remaining years of this century, we must resolutely carry out further readjustments on the industry technological structure under unified planning and, by giving priority to key projects in making investments, totally change the backwardness of the technological structure.

(2) Readjustment of the product mix

In recent years, China stepped up the development of its chemical fibre and garment industries, and made a certain amount of progress in readjusting the product mix of the textile industry. By 1996, the proportion of chemical fibres in the total consumption of textile fibres had reached about 45%, while ready-made garments made up over 55% of domestic clothing goods. On the other hand, the proportions of combed yarn and cloth woven by shuttleless looms had risen to 14.5% and 15.3% respectively. Nevertheless, the product mix remains a crucial problem keeping the textile industry from effecting a change in its growth pattern.

At present, the textile industry has a surplus primary processing capacity, but insufficient capacities in high-grade processing, fine processing and deep processing, as well as in chemical fibre production. The large proportions taken up by roughly-finished and low added value products coupled with the relatively low proportion of intensively and deeply processed products have, on the one hand, led to excessive competition of medium and low-grade textile products on both the international and domestic markets; and, on the other hand, resulted in a very low international and domestic market share for high-grade textile goods. This has adversely affected economic returns and foreign exchange earnings. Moreover, there is also a sharp contradiction between insufficient raw materials and surplus processing capacities. For example, China's chemical fibre output is gravely inadequate and one-third of its requirements have to be imported, which requires an enormous amount of foreign exchange. Between 1980 and 1992, the number of China's cotton spindles rose by 2.35 times, but the demand for cotton yarn increased only by 84%. The surplus in spindle capacity is obvious. China started to cut down spindle capacity in 1992, but the spindle figures for 1992, 1993, 1994 and 1995 at 41.89 million, 41.31 million, 41.57 million and 41.17 million respectively, indicate that after several years of effort, there is still a surplus primary processing capacity of about 10 million spindles. Fundamentally speaking, the slowness in structural readjustments reflects the slowness in structural reform. This indicates that effective means of regulation and control are still lacking in industrial management. It also indicates that the textile industry is faced with an extremely arduous task to change its pattern of extensive growth. [i.e. growth based on output expansion rather than qualitative improvement and market adaptation].

Along with the modernisation of the industry and the industrialisation of high and new technologies, the textile industry is also undergoing a profound change. Textile goods are being developed not as simple means of livelihood but to meet multiple [consumer] requirements. Specifically, textile products are expanding their development in three areas. One is clothing. The development in this area is advancing towards clothing for functional and health purposes, which require higher technological contents. Another area is textiles for fashion purposes. The development in this area keeps pace with people desire for comforts in life. It is advancing rapidly towards serialisation and high-grade development, with an increasing demand for high-technology contents. The third area is textiles for industrial purposes. This kind of textiles has opened up a new territory for the textile industry, which is no longer a low-technology industry but one involving low, medium and high technologies. The technology required in manufacturing a shuttleless loom is by no means lower than that required for the manufacture of a high-class saloon car. On the other hand, the production of special fibres and composite materials involves the application of the most up-to-date technologies. At present, clothing accounts for 75% of China's textile products; textiles for fashion purposes 17%; and textiles for industrial purposes less than 8%. In the United States, the percentages for corresponding goods are 40.5%, 37% and 22.2% respectively; and in Japan, 35%, 30% and 34.5% respectively. It can be seen from the above figures that the 'threefold' development of the textile industry is an international trend. It also indicates that there are broad prospects for China's textile industry if it readjusts its product mix.

Whether in England and the United States, or in Japan and Korea, the textile industry was supported by preferential measures in its development stage. Even today, when the textile industry in those countries has shown signs of gradual withering, it is still being given appropriate protection in terms of subsidies for the procurement of cotton and other raw materials. Therefore, to ensure a healthy development of China's textile industry, an overall readjustment of its product mix should be carried out with intensified efforts. At the present stage, it is most important for China to adopt a macro industrial policy to provide correct guidance to the industry and to introduce to it effective management on the basis of the market economy.

(3) Readjustment of the regional structure

The purpose of readjusting the regional textile industry structure is to give full scope to the relative advantages of different economic regions. The strategy of 'moving spindles from the east to the west' is to develop high added-value, finely and intensely-processed, and export-oriented products in the coastal regions and key cities and to move primary processing capacities to the hinterland. Over the past two years, 850,000 spindles had been or were being thus transferred, including 550,000 spindles to Xinjiang. Apart from those for cotton textiles, the regional production structures for silk cloth, wool fabrics, printing and dyeing, and garments are also under readjustment.

The 'moving of spindles from the east to the west' should not be confined to the transfer of personnel and equipment alone if readjustment of the regional structure is to achieve the desired effects. Instead, it should accomplish the purpose of integrating the optimal restructuring of assets with the structural readjustment of enterprise scales, and of integrating the readjustment of the technological structure with the readjustment of the product mix. In the course of implementing this 'moving spindles from the east to the west' strategy, outmoded products and backward technology must be resolutely eliminated. In this sense, the movement is a process of selecting the superior and eliminating the inferior, through which to achieve the purpose of upgrading product quality and technology and adjusting the scale of enterprises. On this basis, the funding and technological advantages of the coastal regions and key cities, and the manpower and raw material advantages of the hinterland can both be brought into play. A rational distribution of the industry can thus be realised, with the regional structures supplementing each other for the common cause of development.

4. Prospects and outlook of the textile industry

The world demand for textile products is growing at a steady pace. As shown in Table 4.6, in 1995 the world ultimate quantity of fibre consumption was 41.2 million tons. In the next few years, due to the increase in population and economic growth, fibre demand will increase at the average rate of 2.4% annually. By 2000, the quantity required will reach 46.50 million tons. The world per capita fibre consumption will rise from 7.1 kilograms in 1995 to 7.6 kilograms in 2000.

A comparison between various countries and regions shows that Asia will register the fastest increase in consumption. By 2000, Asian fibre consumption will account for nearly 40% of the world total consumption. The demand for chemical fibres in Asia will also grow at the rate of 6.45% annually, more than 2% higher than the world average growth rate. Its proportion in the world total consumption will increase to 41.8%

According to estimates shown in Table 4.6, China's fibre demand from now to 2000 will increase at a rate of 4.79%, which is higher than the world average growth rate. Its demand for chemical fibres will be as high as 8.44%. The proportion of China's fibre requirements in the world overall requirements was 16.9% in 1995, rising to 19% in 2000; and that of its chemical fibre requirements was 16% in 1995, rising to 19.7% in 2000. China's average *per capita* fibre consumption will increase markedly, from 5.8 kilograms in 1995 to 7 kilograms in 2000. China will become the world biggest fibre and chemical fibre consumer country, with its total requirements exceeding those of the United States.

It can be seen from the above analysis that both the international and the domestic markets offer broad prospects for the future development of China's textile industry. The industry will continue to develop at a fast pace so long as its product mix can keep abreast with the changes in market demand.

On the other hand, we should also see from Table 4.6 that, although the growth rate of China's textile industry is comparatively higher, that of the Republic of Korea, India and even the ASEAN countries is very close to or even higher than China. This indicates that, in its future development, China will be faced with strong challenges from its Asian neighbours.

Table 4.7 compares the import tariff rates of some countries and regions for major items of fibre products. It shows that China's tariff rates are, in general, higher than those of most countries and regions, and are lower only than those of Pakistan and India. That is to say that the fact that China's exports are far greater than its imports is not unrelated to the high import tariffs. China has greatly reduced its import tariffs since 1 April 1996. With the gradual fulfillment of its commitments in connection with its application for admission into the World Trade Organisation (WTO), China will further lower its import duties on textile products. This means that, in international trade, China's textile products will be up against greater external pressure. On the other hand, along with the return of Hong Kong in 1997, the textile quota for Hong Kong will very likely be

Table 4.6 Forecast fibre and chemical fibre demand of major countries and regions of the world (000 tons)

Countries/ Regions	1995		2000		Growth rate (%) (1995–2000)	1995		2000		Growth rate (%) (1995–2000)
	Fibre Demand	World Share (%)	Fibre Demand	World Share (%)		Chemical Fibre Demand	World Share (%)	Chemical Fibre Demand	World Share (%)	
Asia	15,300	37.1	18,500	39.7	3.86	6,900	37.5	9,400	41.8	6.15
Japan	2,900	7.1	3,100	6.6	1.09	1,600	8.8	1,800	7.8	1.68
S. Korea	800	1.9	1,000	2.1	4.43	500	2.5	600	2.8	6.64
Taiwan Province	400	1.0	500	1.0	3.55	300	1.8	400	1.8	4.08
ASEAN	1,100	2.7	1,400	3.0	4.82	400	2.2	700	2.9	9.58
China Mainland	7,000	16.9	8,800	19.0	4.79	3,000	16.0	4,400	19.7	8.44
India	2,300	5.6	2,800	6.0	3.91	600	3.2	900	4.1	9.24
Western Europe	9,400	22.7	10,000	21.5	1.27	4,200	22.6	4,700	20.8	2.35
Eastern Europe	4,200	10.2	4,700	10.1	2.06	1,500	8.0	1,900	8.3	4.72
America	10,500	25.5	11,400	24.5	1.63	5,100	27.7	5,700	25.2	2.22
USA	7,400	18.0	8,000	17.3	1.57	3,800	20.5	4,200	18.8	2.31
Other	1,800	4.5	2,000	4.3	1.65	800	4.2	900	3.9	2.64
World	41,200	100.0	46,500	100.0	2.42	18,400	100.0	22,500	100.0	4.09

Source: Japanese Association of Chemical Fibre Industry (Investigation Committee), Environmental Changes to the Japanese Chemical Fibre Industry and their Impact (Chinese translation), 1996.

Table 4.7 Comparison of import tariff rates of some countries and regions for major fibre products in 1994 (per cent)

Type of Products	Japan	USA	Europe	Canada	S. Korea	Taiwan	China	Indonesia	Pakistan	India
(Pure) Cotton Yarns	2.8	7.8	6.0	12.5	8.4	4.5	25.0	15.0	50.0	65.0
Cotton Grey Cloth	4.4	9.0	10.0	15.0	8.0	7.5	45.0	25.0	90.0	65.0
Polyester/Cotton Blend Fabric	8.0	17.0	11.0	25.0	8.0	7.5	80.0	30.0	90.0	89.75
Wool Yarns	3.2	9.0	3.8	12.5	8.0	7.5	50.0	10.0	30.0	65.0
Knitted Cotton Underwear	11.2	21.0	13.0	25.0	8.0	12.5	60.0	40.0	90.0	65.0
Knitted Polyester Coats	14.0	34.2	14.0	25.0	8.0	12.5	80.0	40.0	90.0	65.0
Men's Machine Knitted Woollen Trousers	11.2	21.0	14.0	25.0	8.0	12.5	80.0	30.0	90.0	65.0
Women's Machine Knitted Cotton Trousers	11.2	16.4	14.0	25.0	8.0	12.5	60.0	40.0	90.0	65.0

Source: Almanac of China's Textile Industry 1995.

incorporated into the overall quota for China, which will result in China's share of the overall quota being greatly reduced. For the sake of Hong Kong's prosperity and peaceful and stable transition, China is bound to give priority consideration to measures that would ensure Hong Kong textile exports. These unfavourable factors will have an impact on inland China. It is therefore necessary that the Chinese textile industry step up its structural readjustments with increased efforts, and optimise its industrial structure and product mix as quickly as possible. On this basis, the industry can strive to consolidate its existing international markets, and explore the new markets in the Middle East, Russia, Latin American and the Asia-Pacific region. By diversifying its markets and making full use of its international and domestic markets, the textile industry will be able to achieve further progress in development.

Document 4.3

'The automobile industry: on the threshold of a brilliant turn'

ZHAO YING

China Industrial Development Report, 1997, Chap. 10

I Brilliant record in the 1990s

Since the beginning of the 1990s, China's automobile industry has made considerable progress. During the Eighth Five Year Plan (1991–1995), the industry made brilliant achievements in the following areas:

1. Rapid growth in value and quantity of output

The Gross Value of Industrial Output (GVIO) of China's automobile industry rose rapidly from 46.8 billion *yuan* in 1990 to 210 billion *yuan* in 1995. Its proportion in the national GVIO also rose from 1.6% in 1990 to 3.5% in 1995. The industry's GVIO went up further to 230 billion *yuan* in 1996. In 1990, the industry manufactured 509,000 vehicles of all types. The number jumped to 1,452,600 in 1995 (see Table 4.8), and further to 1,542,800 in 1996.

The average annual growth rates of China's automobile industry in terms of GVIO, quantity of output and profits and taxes were all over 20% during the Eighth Five Year Plan. Thus, the industry witnessed its most rapid growth in output in its history. Because of its rapidly increased output and the improved quality of its products, its share of the domestic market rose from 80% in 1990 to 94% in 1996. It has, to a considerable extent,

Table 4.8 Automobile production in China, 1990–1996 (1,000 units)

Year	Total	Trucks	Off-road Vehicles	Light Vehicles	Buses	Saloons	Chassis
1990	509.2	269.0	44.7	44.3	23.1	42.4	90.5
1991	708.8	361.3	54.0	53.3	42.7	81.0	122.8
1992	1061.7	460.2	63.3	61.7	84.5	162.7	199.1
1993	1296.7	623.1	59.2	57.0	142.7	229.6	171.7
1994	1353.3	613.1	72.1	70.3	193.0	250.3	169.1
1995	1452.6	571.7	91.7	89.7	247.4	325.4	161.8
1996	1490.0					390.0	

Source: China Automotive Industry Yearbook 1996 and *The People's Daily* 5 April 1997 for the two 1996 figures.

satisfied the needs for China's economic construction, social development and national defense.

2. Notable increase in overall strength

During the Eighth Five Year Plan, the automobile industry invested 580.1 billion *yuan* in its development, doubling the aggregate total of investments in the preceding 40 years. Investment priorities were state projects carried over from the Seventh Five Year Plan, with a switch of emphasis to saloons and parts and accessories. Consequently, the saloon industry registered a remarkable growth, with its output increasing at an annual average of 23% in volume and 32% in value. The annual automobile production capacity has increased to two million cars. The value of the industry fixed assets rose from 28.03 billion *yuan* to 96 billion *yuan*. Automobile exports reached $US650 million in value. Trucks manufactured by the China Number One Automobile Factory, the Dongfeng (East Wind) Automobile Corporation and other manufacturers made their way into the international market on a scale of around 1,000 vehicles each. In 1996, more than 5,000 medium trucks were exported by the China Number One Automobile Factory. Before 1995, a number of important state projects successively passed acceptance tests conducted by concerned state departments and organisations. These included medium and light vehicle projects of the China Number One Automobile Factory; medium and heavy-duty vehicle projects of the China Number Two Automobile Factory; the Steyr (Si Tai-er) heavy vehicle Project of the Heavy Vehicles Industrial Corporation; the Iveco (Yi wei-ke) light vehicle project of the Nanjing Automobile Industry Corporation; the heavy vehicle project of the Ordnance Industry Corporation; and the auto-engines projects of the Jiang Ling Automobile Company and the Qing Ling Automobile Company, and parts and accessories projects for main types of vehicles. The projects that have not been completed during the

Eighth Five Year Plan will be fully completed and launched into production in 1997. These include the Volkswagen Project of the China Number One Automobile Factory; the Shen Long Project of the Dongfeng Automobile Corporation, and the Xia Li Project in Tianjin, all for saloons and their accessories. With the completion of these projects, the major manufacturing enterprises of heavy, medium, and light vehicles, minicars and saloons will have preliminarily reached the economic scales specified in the industrial policy. These backbone enterprises will lay the foundation for the development of the automobile industry in the Ninth Five Year Plan. They will, at the same time, provide favourable conditions for the industry to readjust its industrial structure and optimise its organization according to the industrial policy.

3. Higher degree of concentration in production

With the heavy input of funds from both central and local sources, the backbone enterprises of the automobile industry have achieved faster progress, as well as a higher degree of concentration in production. At the end of the Eighth Five Year Plan, all of the enterprises manufacturing the three main types of vehicles – saloons, buses and trucks – have achieved a production concentration ratio of over 80%, with the exception of three enterprises among the front-ranking manufacturers of light buses and trucks, which achieved a production concentration rate of less than 60%. On the other hand, the three front-ranking enterprises manufacturing heavy trucks and minibuses have achieved a production concentration rate of over 90%.

4. Massive imports of new technology

Up to the end of the Eighth Five Year Plan, the automobile industry brought in from abroad 313 kinds of advanced technology. These included 26 kinds of technology for the building of whole cars; 30 kinds of technology for the manufacture of motorcycles; 25 kinds of essential assembly technology; 153 kinds of technology for the manufacture of parts and accessories; and 79 other kinds of technology. It set up some 350 joint-equity enterprises, bringing in 1.5 billion US dollars worth of foreign capital. All this was done during the Eighth Five Year Plan, resulting in greatly raising the level and quality of the industry products.

5. Increased product variety, enhanced production development capability

To meet the diversified requirements of the automobile market, the automobile manufacturing enterprises have paid great attention to new marketable products. Up to the present, the industry has developed some 120 types of vehicles of six main categories, including trucks, buses, saloons, cross-country vehicles, dumpers, and motor tractors; and some 750 types of special-purpose vehicles, including vans, tank trucks, special dumping trucks, bunker cars, and vehicles for special operations. During the Eighth Five Year Plan, funds spent by major automobile manufacturing enterprises on research and development increased by varying extents in proportion to their volume of sales. They have acquired initial capabilities to develop medium trucks, and have launched cooperative projects to develop saloons (a pilot project being the Santana 2000). Large conglomerates have started to employ CAD/CAM technology and dynamic simulation test technology in development and testing. Considerable progress has been made in digesting and assimilating imported technology. Some imported technologies have been successfully disseminated within the industry. The research and development of auto parts and accessories has also made a certain degree of progress.

II Main problems of the automobile industry

1. The deep-rooted problem of scattered investments and redundant construction remains unresolved

The problem of scattered investments and redundant construction has been with the automobile industry for dozens of years. Although the Chinese Government Department in charge of macro economic control has made persistent attempts to solve this problem through administrative and economic means or even through the enforcement of industrial policies, the results have fallen short of expectations. At present, China's automotive industry has 122 factories manufacturing whole vehicles, ranking first in the world in number (see Table 4.8). However, their total output is less than the output of the Fiat Automobile Company (1.55 million vehicles in 1995) (see Table 4.9), which ranks ninth among the top ten automobile companies in the world. Under their Ninth Five-Year Plans, 20 provinces, municipalities

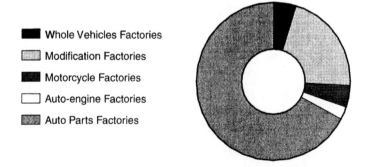

■ Whole Vehicles Factories
▨ Modification Factories
■ Motorcycle Factories
□ Auto-engine Factories
▨ Auto Parts Factories

Figure 4.2 Classification of China's Automobile Manufacturers at the End of 1995 (number of factories and percentage)

Source: *China Automotive Industry Yearbook 1996.*

and autonomous regions in China list the automobile industry as their pillar industry, which will be given priority support. This is bound to aggravate the situation of scattered investments and redundant construction.

The main cause of the problem is that the government at various levels is still the main investing body. This situation makes it impossible to invest limited available funds in key enterprises in a concentrated way in order to achieve optimum effect. This point is borne out by the norms adopted by various provinces in having stocks listed on the stock exchanges. Except for the China Number One Automobile Factory and the Si Huan Automobile Company, all other automobile manufacturing enterprises that have gone public are of small or medium scales. This also makes it impossible to have funds distributed in an optimum way on the capital market.

2. Poor returns to scale economy

Because of spread-out investments and redundant construction, few enterprises of China automobile industry reach the needed economic scale. Even several years from now, only some enterprises will have entered the threshold of an economic scale production. The automobile industry is still far from being able to realise the benefits of scale economies. China's automobile manufacturing enterprises are lagging far behind their foreign counterparts in this respect (see Tables 4.9 and 4.10).

By comparing the two tables, we can see clearly that China's automobile industry is still far from reaching the economies of scale. Because of this, the costs ands prices of its products are high and quality is poor, hence they lack

Table 4.9 Output of the world's top 10 auto manufacturers in 1995 (units)

			Vehicle Output	
Ranking	Company Name	Country	All	Saloons Only
1	General Motors	USA	4,368,621	2,515,136
2	Ford	USA	3,453,669	1,395,710
3	Toyota	Japan	3,171,277	2,557,174
4	Peugeot	France	1,823,488	1,694,101
5	Volkswagen	Germany	1,765,339	1,370,714
6	Chrysler	USA	1,721,245	576,846
7	Nissan	Japan	1,713,982	1,508,922
8	Renault	France	1,665,658	1,385,261
9	Fiat	Italy	1,550,039	1,550,039
10	Mitsubishi	Japan	1,327,553	908,874

Note: Figures do not include the output of the overseas subsidiaries of these companies.
Source: *China Automobile Statistics 1996*, Ministry of Machinery, (Automobile Section).

Table 4.10 Output of China's top 10 auto manufacturers, 1995 (units)

Ranking	Company Name	Vehicle Output
1	China Number One Automobile Corporation	182,258
2	Shanghai Dazhong (Volkswagen) Automobile Corporation Ltd.	160,070
3	Dongfeng Automobile Corporation	141,228
4	Tianjin Automobile Industry Group	133,885
5	Yue Jin Automobile Corporation	82,318
6	Beijing Jeep Automobile Corporation, Ltd.	80,151
7	Chang An Automobile Company, Ltd.	70,070
8	Liu Zhou Compact Automobile Factory	50,407
9	Beijing Light Vehicle Company, Ltd.	50,061
10	Harbin Ha Fei Automobile Manufacturing Company	45,331

Source: *China Automotive Industry Yearbook 1996.*

competitiveness on the international market and find it hard to make their way into Chinese homes on a massive scale.

3. Low level of specialisation

The situation of 'big and self-contained' or 'small and self-contained' exists to a varying extent in Chinese automobile factories manufacturing whole vehicles. Their level of specialisation is low. In recent years, large enterprises have lowered their self-manufacturing rate considerably. The China Number One Automobile Factory and the Dongfeng Automobile Corporation have had many of the assembly parts, spare parts and accessories manufactured by outside establishments and have oriented their parts and accessories production toward the whole industry. Nevertheless, compared with large foreign corporations, their self-manufacturing rate is still high and their level of specialisation is still low.

4. Backwardness in technological development

The biggest problem faced by China's automobile industry is the weak technological development capability of its manufacturing enterprises and their low level of research and development. At present, these enterprises are only able to digest and assimilate imported technology. They still do not have the capability to develop technology independently and they have little technological reserve. The amount of product development funds available to some large foreign automobile companies in proportion to their sales value is far higher than that available to Chinese automobile enterprises. For example, the average annual product development funds at the Ford Company is 2.894

billion US dollars, representing 3.3% of its sales value; that of the Toyota Company is 2.26 billion US dollars, 4.4%; that of the Honda Company 1.121 billion US dollars, 4.96%; that of the Fiat Company 4.4 billion US dollars, 11.58%; and that of Volkswagen 1.169 billion US dollars, 3.52%. On the other hand, product development funds allocated to major Chinese automobile manufacturing enterprises during the 1990s amounted to less than 1% of their sales value. The annual sales value of the China Number One Automobile Factory is around 20 billion *yuan*, yet the annual average of funds expended on product development during the 1990s amounted to less than 0.5%. It can be seen from this comparison how far China's automobile industry is lagging behind in research and development.

Except for medium trucks and light vehicles, Chinese automobile enterprises have only just begun their research and development on other types of vehicles, especially on saloons. Their means of research and development and testing are anything but perfect. They are lagging far behind in computer-aided development. While major foreign companies have attained a high degree of maturity in computer applications in modelling, structural analysis and simulation tests, the Chinese automobile industry still remains in the initial stage of development in this respect. Its auto parts and accessories research is lagging even farther behind, while its research in electronic equipment for automobiles has just got started. Moreover, the industry lacks high-calibre scientists and technicians.

Because the industry has not yet created its own development capability, international corporations, which have set up joint ventures in China for the manufacture of saloons, have continued to play a dominant role in the production and development of saloons. Almost all major saloon manufacturing enterprises in China are Sino-foreign joint-equity companies. These joint-equity enterprises are controlled by the foreign parties through their technological dominance. As a matter of fact, it is not the wish of the foreign partners for China's automobile industry to form its own scientific and technological development system. They are willing to bring to China, for production only those models of vehicles that are already in the mature stage of their life cycles.

5. Shortage of funds

At present, China's automobile manufacturing enterprises can hardly accumulate capital on their own. Most of the backbone enterprises are quite heavily in debt. With the introduction of the new tax system, the tax burden of the automobile manufacturing enterprises has increased. Although their economic returns decreased in the last two years of the Eighth Five Year Plan, they still paid taxes directly to the state amounting to 30.144 billion *yuan*, 11.739 billion *yuan* more than the amount of profits they earned for the same period. The tax:profit ratio was 6.2:3.8. With their involvement in some important development projects, the enterprises have, beyond any doubt, experienced great difficulties. The industry requires an input of approximately 140 billion *yuan* (including basic circulating funds) during the Ninth Five Year Plan. The maximum amount of state loans obtainable is 55 billion *yuan*; the remainder must be raised from other sources. As pointed out above, there is as yet no way to smoothly channel funds into the backbone automobile manufacturing enterprises. For this reason, it will be quite difficult to raise the necessary funds.

6. Slow development of the parts and accessories industry

The slow development of the auto parts and accessories industry is a long-standing problem of the automobile industry. Some changes were made in recent years, but the overall situation of lagging behind remains unchanged. Compared with foreign countries, the development lag in respect of some components and parts is even greater. Examples are electronically-controlled gasoline injectors, antilock braking systems (ABS), and safety airbags, the development of which has just got started in China. Due to the lack of massive outputs of low-cost, serialised and high-quality components and parts, the cost, standard and quality of production of whole vehicles in China have been greatly affected, and the progress in using domestically-made parts in the construction of imported models has been retarded.

7. Low-level products

Leading products of China's automobile industry at present are largely those brought in by foreign corporations, which are products of the late 1970s and early 1980s and are in the mature stage of their life cycles. Only a few are products of the mid and late 1980s. On the whole, they are about 15 years behind those of the United States of America and Japan. The lag in respect of components and parts is even greater. The MTBF (mean time before failure – a key quality indicator) of the industry's leading products – saloons and medium trucks – was over 5,000 kilometres in 1995. That of other types of vehicles had not even reached this level. The MTBF of medium trucks manufactured by the developed countries is over 10,000 kilometres; that of light vehicles and saloons is much higher.

8. Disorderly market

Since the beginning of the 1990s, China's automobile market has remained in chaotic conditions due to the influence of local protectionism. To protect their own automobile enterprises, local governments introduced certain 'local' policies, imposing restrictions on the marketing and use of automotive products not manufactured locally. For example, some cities imposed the rule that minibuses cannot be used as hired vehicles; some cities restricted the use of saloons as hired cars; some cities restricted the use of certain types of saloons according to their engine displacements; still some cities levied surcharges on increased capacities of vehicles. From marketing to operation, cars are required to pay many taxes and fees, in some cases more than 20 kinds. The market price of one Citroen AX (Fu Kang) saloon is 124,600 *yuan*. Tax paid in the course of manufacture is 10,600 *yuan* or 8.5% of the market price; sales tax is 35,200 *yuan* or 28.2%; pre-registration tax paid by the buyer on top of the price is 62,200 *yuan* or 49.8%. Total payment by the buyer on delivery of the car is 186,800 *yuan*. Even Jiefang (Liberation) and Dongfeng trucks have to pay taxes and fees amounting to 31.9% of the market price. In addition, users have to pay highway tolls, which are charged at random. The procedures for buying a car are also quite complicated. The invoice requires as many as nine official seals. The buyer of a new car has to go through 13 procedures. This state of affairs seriously impairs fair competition on the Chinese automobile market, and hinders the sales of automobile products. In view of this situation, the General Office of the State Council specifically transmitted the State Planning Commission 'Opinions on Revoking Local Restrictions on the Use of Economy-Type Saloons'. However, it will take time to restore order in the Chinese automobile market.

III On the threshold of a crucial turn

As discussed above, China's automobile industry has made considerable progress, but it also faces a host of important problems hampering its development, which cannot be overlooked. The industry will have to exert great efforts in order to develop itself into a pillar industry capable of withstanding international competition. We can say that China's automobile industry is now on the threshold of a crucial turn. What it will do between now and 2010 will determine its destiny.

1. Signs of a forthcoming crucial turn

1. The truck market is becoming mature. For a long time in the development of China's automobile industry, there existed the problem of 'scarcity of heavy trucks and shortage of light trucks.' This problem, however, has been basically solved through developments during the Seventh and Eighth Five Year Plans. China now has a full range of cargo-carrying vehicles including heavy, medium, light and miniature trucks. Trucks will still have broad prospects in future, but the pace of their development tends to become relatively steady. The period of high-speed development such as that during the time when there were shortages in heavy and light trucks, is over. Another sign of a mature truck market is that the market for medium trucks has become saturated. Medium trucks are the main product of China's automobile industry, which have the advantages of a scale economy and the capability of independent development. Since 1994, however, there has been a steady decline in the sales volume of medium trucks in proportion to the total sales volume of

automobiles as a whole. Their market share has been gradually eroded by heavy trucks, light trucks and vehicles for farming purposes. Since the beginning of the 1990s, the proportion of medium trucks in the total output of automobiles decreased at an average annual rate of 14.39%. In 1996, the proportion dropped further from 25.81% to 14.49%. This trend conforms to the common law of development of the international automobile industry, in that the development of trucks tends to grow faster at both ends, i.e. heavy and light models. This is also a stage the industry must go through in rationalising its product mix.

The gradual maturity of the truck market is also reflected by increased competition. Intensified competition leads to the merger of powerful corporations. A significant example is the merging of the Jin Bei (Golden Cup) Automobile Company in Shenyang, which was once listed as one of the top eight automobile enterprises in China, into the China Number One Automobile Factory. With the truck market becoming mature, it becomes necessary for truck development to switch its emphasis from quantitative expansion to quality upgrading. It also becomes necessary for the automobile industry to switch its development emphasis to saloons.

2. The saloon industry grows rapidly. It can be seen from Table 4.11 that, in a sharp contrast to the truck industry, the saloon industry grew rapidly during the Eighth Five Year Plan. During that period the output of saloons increased to 1,023,800 units, representing 85.35% of the total automobile output since the founding of the People's Republic (in 1949) and registering an average annual growth rate of 47.89%. Correspondingly, the demand for saloons on the Chinese automobile market also rose rapidly, with the pattern of demand showing a diversifying trend. The strong demand for saloons has aggravated the competition between the domestic automobile industry and foreign automobile corporations on the China market.

3. Domestic production of major imported models is being realised. During the Seventh Five Year Plan and Eighth Five Year Plan, China's automobile industry greatly raised the level of its main automobile models through the application of technology brought in from abroad. At present, the industry is able to produce, almost completely domestically, the major imported models of automobiles (see Table 4.11).

With the domestic production of major imported car models being gradually realised, a sharp question has been brought forward: What is the next step? Should we continue to rely on imported technology or should we find a way to develop our own capabilities? In essence, this is a question of whether or not the automobile industry should take the road of independent development, and if the answer is affirmative, then how? This question has become even more acute because most of the major imported models of automobiles were already in the mature stage of their life cycles at the time when they were brought in, and, after 5–10 years of

Table 4.11 Production localisation rate (PLR) of China's main imported vehicle models, 1995

Ranking	Model & Brand	Imported Enterprise	Foreign Enterprise	Local Content %
1	Santana Basic Model	Shanghai Dazhong (VW) Automobile Corporation	Volkswagen, Germany	88.56
2	Santana 2000	Shanghai Dazhong (VW) Automobile Corp.	Volkswagen, Germany	63.84
3	Cherokee CX1	Beijing Jeep Automobile Corp.	Chrysler, USA	82.26
4	Cherokee CX8	Beijing Jeep Automobile Corp.	Chrysler, USA	83.31
5	Cherokee CX1-D	Beijing Jeep Automobile Corp.	Chrysler, USA	50.88
6	Charade 7100	Tianjin Automobile Industry Group	Daihatsu, Japan	89.23
7	Charade 7100U	Tianjin Automobile Industry Group	Daihatsu, Japan	85.36
8	Peugeot 505SW8	Guangzhou Peugeot Automobile Co. Ltd.	Peugeot, France	84.00
9	Peugeot GL	Guangzhou Peugeot Automobile Co. Ltd.	Peugeot, France	78.20
10	Audi C3V6	China Number One Automobile Corp.	Volkswagen, Germany	40.86
11	Jetta	China No.1-VW Automobile Corp.	Volkswagen, Germany	62.35
12	Citroen AX	Dongfeng Automobile Corp.	Citroen, France	26.18
13	Alto	Chang An Automobile Co. Ltd.	Suzuki, Japan	64.56
14	Skylark	Guizhou General Aviation Industry Corp.	Mitsubishi Heavy Industries, Japan	46.49
15	Steyr	China Heavy Automobile Group	Steyr Motorentechnik, GmbH., Austria	93.44
16	Iveco A40.10	Yue Jin Automobile Group	Iveco, Italy	76.77
17	Iveco A30.10	Yue Jin Automobile Group	Iveco, Italy	62.93

efforts to produce them domestically, the products have become even more outmoded.

4. Private purchases show an increasing trend. The pattern of demand on China's automobile market showed a diversifying trend during the Eighth Five Year Plan. The proportion of purchases by township and town enterprises, private enterprises and private individuals in the total sales volume of automobiles has grown bigger and bigger. In 1984, total car ownership in China was 2.6 million units, of which 174,000 cars or 6.9% were in private possession. By 1995, private possession of cars had increased to 12.5 million units, accounting for approximately 23% of total car possession. Purchases by private individuals in 1995 accounted for 33.8% of total car sales. More than 80% of the medium trucks sold were bought by private individuals, who were also the main buyers of minicars and light passenger cars. In 1996, the number of cars bought by private individuals in Beijing exceeded the number bought by official users. Saloons have become the favorite purchase of private purchasers.

It can be seen from the above analysis, that China's automobile industry has entered the threshold of a crucial turn. The law that dominates the development of the automobile industry in the world is manifesting itself in the development of China's automobile industry. Generally speaking, from now till 2010, China's automobile industry will go through several, major changes: a change in emphasis from trucks to saloons; a change from quantitative expansion to a combination of qualitative and quantitative improvements; a change from relying mainly on imported technology to self-development; a change from relying mainly on official purchases to relying mainly on private purchases to suit the requirements of a diversified market; and a structural change in the industrial organisation from a structure of scattered and overlapping organisations, to a structure of large conglomerates with significant advantages scale economy, which will be formed through competition and mergers. These changes will be inevitable and are independent of man's will. Whether or not these changes can be effected satisfactorily will determine the destiny of China's automobile industry. This is because not much time is left at the industry's disposal to pursue its development.

2. Increasingly harsh external pressure and challenges

1. The scope in which the state affords protection to the automobile industry is becoming smaller and smaller. From 1 April 1996, the state readjusted downward its import tariffs by a large margin, and the import tariffs on automotive products were also readjusted correspondingly. Among them, the import duties on gasoline-driven small saloons, cross-country vehicles, and minibuses have been lowered from 150% to 120% for those with displacement higher than 3.0 litres, and from 110% to

100% for those with displacements of or below 3.0 litres. The import duties on diesel-driven small saloons, cross-country vehicles and minibuses have been reduced from 150% to 120% for those with displacements higher than 2.5 litres, and to 100% for those with displacements of and below 2.5 litres. The import duties on gasoline-driven trucks with a gross weight of 8–14 tons have been lowered from 50% to 30%. A uniform tariff rate of 50% is imposed on auto parts and accessories with the exception of some specified items. Despite the reduction of import tariffs, the present rates still embody a degree of protection for the automobile industry. However, we must envision that, with the date for China's eventual admission to the World Trade Organization drawing nearer and with the progress in trade liberalization within the scope of APEC, the scope in which the state affords protection to the automobile industry by means of import duties is becoming smaller and smaller. We cannot expect the state to always protect the automobile industry at the expense of other industries each time it readjusts its import tariffs downward. Viewed in this light, China's automobile industry should have a sense of urgency in effecting the changes with a greater speed.

2. Foreign corporations step up their challenges on the China market. The fact that the automobile industry has taken up a bigger share of the domestic market reflects an increase in its strength. Nevertheless, a careful analysis shows that one cannot be so optimistic about the situation. First, its increased market share is attributable partly to state protection of the domestic market. Second, some of the vehicles sold on the domestic market were assembled with imported parts. Between 1980 and 1995, China imported 687,000 sets of CKD components and parts for automobiles, of which 566,000 sets were for saloons. Moreover, China still imports a considerable number of automobiles annually, and its imports of automobiles greatly surpass its exports (see Tables 4.12 and 4.13). It can thus be seen that China's automobile industry still lacks competitiveness on the international market.

At present, China is regarded by international automobile giants as the last big market pending exploitation. They try to make their way into the China market by all conceivable means. They enter the China market not only by means of setting up joint-equity ventures, but they have also started to adopt the strategic measure of buying stocks on the capital market. For example, in 1995 the American Ford Corporation bought stocks of the Jiang Ling Automobile Limited Company; the Japanese Isuzu Corporation bought corporate stocks of the Beijing Station Wagons Limited Company (to the extent of holding a controlling share); and the Japanese C. Itoh Company Limited bought state-owned stocks of the Beijing Light Vehicles Limited Company. As China opens up further, major international automobile corporations have stepped up their competition on the China market, employing an increasing number of ways and means and launching

Table 4.12 Total vehicle imports of China, 1980–1995

Year	All Vehicles (units)	Goods Vehicles (units)	Passenger Cars (units)	Auto Parts (US$1,000)	Total Value (US$1,000)
1980	51,083	26,101	19,570	62,990.0	616,120
1981	41,575	20,770	14,013	35,941.0	305,364
1982	16,077	7,730	1,101	60,802.0	25,118
1983	25,156	8,445	5,806	135,762.0	432,592
1984	88,743	28,047	21,651	166,517.0	1,048,212
1985	353,992	111,492	105,775	288,484.0	2,936,899
1986	150,052	64,570	48,276	277,085.0	1,954,595
1987	67,182	17,554	30,536	418,850.0	1,214,310
1988	99,233(26,907)	14,201(1,694)	57,433(24,407)	339,130.0	1,612,400
1989	85,554(31,043)	12,587(1,598)	45,000(20,560)	347,500.0	1,327,320
1990	65,430(24,176)	18,395(3,003)	34,063(18,136)	437,400.0	1,202,933
1991	98,454(56,466)	18,578(4,628)	54,009(40,004)	582,630.0	1,659,923
1992	210,087(127,222)	42,005(7,162)	115,641(88,114)	870,716.0	3,535,235
1993	310,099(130,402)	72,935(7,684)	180,717(111,059)	970,657.0	5,351,430
1994	283,060(144,981)	68,269(3,349)	169,995(135,580)	687,944.0	4,714,826
1995	158,115(116,783)	12,073(11,286)	129,861(105,497)	854,690.0	2,575,498

Note: (1) 1980 figures are from foreign trade yearbook statistics as supplied by the China Automobile Import and Export Corporation to China Automobile
Corporation General Office; the 1981–1994 figures are from the yearbooks of the Chinese Bureau of Customs and Excise.
(2) Whole vehicles imports include unassembled units (figures in parenthesis); value of auto parts include vehicle bodies.
(3) 1992–1994 import values cover engines, motorcycles and trailers. The figure for engines include some generators not used for motor vehicle or
motorcycle.

Source: China Automotive Industry Yearbook, 1996.

Table 4.13 Total vehicle export of China, 1980–1995

Year	All Vehicles (units)	Good Vehicles (units)	Passenger Cars (units)	Auto Parts (US$10,000)	Motor Vehicles (US$10,000)
1989	2,676	2,063	6	4,772	8,031
1990	4,431	3,254	73	8,170	12,784
1991	4,108	2,253	789	10,138	15,284
1992	63,752	243	914	12,395	30,615
1993	11,116	4,534	2,866	17,165	42,422
1994	18,648	10,234	1,698	24,580	51,520
1995	17,747	9,070	2,529	37,609	72,138

Note: Export figures are from Customs and Excise statistics which do not include foreign exchange earnings generated from the domestic market. This differs from the measurement adopted in the previous statistical yearbooks.
Source: *China Automotive Industry Yearbook 1996*.

promotional campaigns one after another. In view of this situation, China's automobile industry must build itself up as quickly as possible.

As discussed above, the period between now and 2010 will be crucial to the future of China's automobile industry. It will determine whether the industry can establish itself independently among the automobile industries in the world, or be reduced to an appendage to large foreign corporations. The automobile industry must wage an all-out struggle within that limited period of time. There is no other way out.

IV. Development prospects and strategy

1. Development prospects of China's automobile industry

It is anticipated that, by the year 2010, China will be in the forefront of the world in terms of annual automobile output and car ownwrship. It is estimated that by 2000 China will have 18–21 million cars in possession, as against annual demand of 2.5–3.0 million cars; and by 2010, the number of cars in possession will be 44–50 millions with annual demand of 5.5–6.5 million. The projected output of the automobile industry for 2010 will be 6 million cars, including 4 million saloons; and projected gross industrial output value will be 1,098 billion *yuan* (calculated at 1990 prices). The added value of the automobile industry will be about 440 billion *yuan*, representing about 3% of the Gross National Product of that year. 350,000–400,000 automobiles will be exported in that year, earning US$6.6 billion worth of foreign exchange. By 2010, the automobile industry will have its own development capabilities, and will be producing a relatively complete range of automobiles. Its manufacturing technology will have reached the contemporary international level. By then, the industry will have become a pillar industry of China's national economy. Judging from the industry growth potential, it is possible to realise the projected targets listed above. However, the industry will have to exert its utmost and the state will have to adopt policies that are favourable to the industry. Otherwise, it will be extremely difficult to realise the above goals.

2. Near-term strategy for accelerating the growth of the automobile industry

1. Broaden the fund-raising avenues for the industry's backbone enterprises. The key to developing the automobile industry is to adopt a capital fund allocation policy which favours the backbone enterprises, so that they will be able to develop at a faster pace. This calls for broadening various fund-raising avenues. First, consideration should be given to absorbing foreign financial capitals such as investment funds. Financial capital cares more for the rate of return on investment than for production and technological control. This suits the pattern of the industry's future development. Workable plans in this area should be studied in real earnest. Secondly, consideration should be given to setting up industrial development funds in China. Thirdly, arrangements should be made on a priority basis to have stocks of backbone automobile enterprises listed on both domestic and international stock exchanges. Fourthly, the financing companies of the existing groups of automobile enterprises should be allowed to expand their scope of operation, so that they can play a greater role in arranging finance for these groups. Fifthly, the large enterprise groups should be authorised to issue technical transformation bonds.

2. Encourage enterprises to form mergers and conglomerates to accelerate the structural rationalisation of industrial organisations. The departments administering the automobile industry have worked hard to change the phenomenon of scattered investments and redundant construction, but with little tangible effect. It appears that this problem will have to be resolved through market competition, which will force enterprises to merge and form conglomerates. What the state can do to accelerate this process is to comply with the demand for market competition. Some mergers have now taken place in the automobile industry. In these cases, the government played a coordinating role, enabling the mergers to be completed at a smaller cost and within a shorter period of time. In future, the government can give an impetus to such mergers by means of sensible administrative intervention. It can also introduce some preferential policies in favour of the merging enterprises, such as reducing or remitting certain liabilities, helping redundant personnel of merged enterprises find new jobs, and providing facilities for the transformation of the merged enterprises.

3. Give vigorous support to enterprises making auto parts and accessories. It is necessary to prop up the enterprises making auto parts and

accessories with great efforts, especially those producing key components and parts of high quality, so that they can develop in the direction of mass production and specialisation to serve the whole industry. Consideration should be given to relaxing the conditions for setting up cooperative and joint-equity ventures with foreign parties. For example, the ratio of shares held by the Chinese side may be lowered appropriately, and consideration may even be given to allowing foreign manufactures of auto parts and accessories to set up factories in China which are entirely owned by them. In making investments, the state should change the former practice of giving greater preference to engines than to parts and accessories, and allow a greater increase in funds invested in enterprises making parts and accessories, in order to achieve a 1:1 ratio in investments between engines and parts and accessories.

4. The state should encourage enterprises to carry out research and development in cooperation with foreign enterprises and research organizations. The state should assemble forces to carry out research on certain important new technologies such as auto engines driven by new energies and electronic products for use on automobiles. Such research activities, however, should be conducted by large enterprise groups to avoid the old practice of scientific research and production each going their own way.

5. Conscientiously implement the automobile industry industrial policy. The many policies and measures provided for in the industrial policy of the automobile industry need to be brought into effect in real earnest. The problems encountered in implementing the industrial policy should be carefully studied, in order to ensure that the industrial policy truly plays a in role of guiding and promoting the development of the automobile industry.

6. Make further efforts to put the automobile market in order and promote the formation of a unified automobile market. The state should formulate a unified market policy and revoke the 'local' policies formulated by various localities. Earnest efforts should be carried out to sort out the many different taxes and fees imposed on automobile sales, with a view to lowering the costs of purchase and use of vehicles. The procedures involved in private purchases of automobiles should be simplified. Arbitrary levy of fees on the purchase and use of automobiles should be prohibited by legislation. Laws and regulations should also be formulated with respect to the sales and after-sale services of automobiles, to protect consumers' interests. It is suggested that the state substitute a fuel tax for the surcharge now imposed on vehicle purchases. If it is difficult to do so at present, then the state should change the surcharge to a tax to be levied according to the tonnage of cargo-carrying vehicles, the seating capacity of buses, and the mean sales price of saloons. Tax reductions should be effected in the near term until the consumer tax on automobiles is ultimately abolished.

Document 4.4

'The burgeoning electronics industry'

XIE XIAOHUA

China Industrial Development Report, 1997, Chap. 7

The level of development of a country's electronics and information industries, which embraces the semiconductor industry, computer and software industries, and modern telecommunications and information services, is an important indicator of its overall national strength. According to figures published in 1993 by the United Nations Industrial Development Organization, 65% of the GNP of all countries of the world is in some way related to electronics technology. Thus, most countries attach great importance to their electronics industry and are developing it at a much faster rate than traditional industries. For example, electronics is the leading industry in the United States and the second largest industry after the auto industry in Japan. It has been promoted as a pillar industry by the Chinese government in recent years. China's electronics industry has witnessed rapid growth along with the acceleration of [the formation of] the information society and the launching of the 'Gold Projects' (including the Gold Bridge, Gold Card, Gold Customs, Gold Taxation, Gold Agriculture, Gold Enterprises, Gold Intellectual Development, Gold Real Estate and Gold Health projects) since the beginning of the 1990s. However, it is also faced with growing competition from leading multinational companies.

I. China's electronics industry in the 1990s

1. Rapid development of the electronics sector

China's electronics industry has been swiftly expanding since the beginning of the 1990s. Calculated at 1990 constant prices, total output value soared from the 1992 figure of 108.68 billion *yuan* to 296.56 billion *yuan* in 1996, or an average annual growth rate of 27% (see Table 4.14 for the output values and growth rate for specific years). The proportion of the output

Table 4.14 Gross value of output and growth rate of China's electronic industry (at 1990 constant price)

Year	1992	1993	1994	1995	1996
Output (RMB 100 million)	1,086.80	1,395.60	1,861.70	2,457.00	2,965.60
Growth Rate (%)	22.60	28.00	33.40	32.00	20.70

Sources: China Electronics Industry Yearbook 1993, 1995; China Computer Daily, 5 February 1996; *Economic Reference Daily*, 23 January 1997.

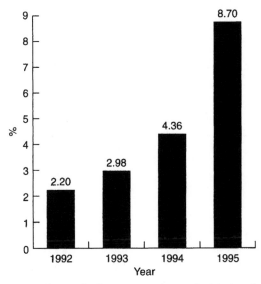

Figure 4.3 Percentage Share of Electronic Industry in National Gross Value of Industrial Output (at 1990 constant prices)

Source: *China Electronic Industry Yearbook 1993*, and *1995*; *Computer World Daily*, 4 November 1996.

value of this sector in the value of overall industrial production has also seen an upward trend (see Figure 4.3), rising from 2.2% in 1992 to 2.98% in 1993, 4.36% in 1994 and 8.7% in 1995.

Economic results of the sector have also shown marked increases along with the rapid growth in output value. Total pre-tax profits have been growing at an average annual rate of 26.6% from 5.882 billion *yuan* in 1992 to 15.3 billion *yuan* in 1996.

2. Rapid export growth

Electronics exports and their proportion in the total volume of Chinese exports have both been on the rise. The sector export value reached US$16.53 billion in 1995, exceeding the value of imports and striking a favourable balance for the first time. The proportion of electronics exports in the total value of exports between 1992 and 1996 is show in Table 4.15.

3. Larger production scale, more rational structure

Since the beginning of the 1990s, China's electronics industry has been steadily developing from a purely manufacturing sector into a modern electronic information industry with the manufacturing of consumer electronics, software production, information services and other industries

Table 4.15 Electronic product exports as percentage share of China's total exports (US$100 million)

Year	1992	1993	1994	1995	1996
Electronic Product Imports	79.85	101.50	134.80	161.00	156.61
Electronic Product Exports	68.72	80.74	123.60	165.30	189.72
China's Total Exports	849.40	917.40	1,210.10	1,487.70	1,510.70
Export Share (%)	8.10	8.84	9.10	11.10	11.90

Note: 1996 figures refer to total for January to November.
Source: *Statistical Yearbook of China 1996*; *China Electronic Industry Yearbook 1993*, and *1995*; *Economic Reference Daily*, 11 and 23 November 1997; *Proceedings of the National Work Conference of the Electronic Industry*, January 1996.

developing side by side. The output volumes of major electronic products have all increased by large margins. China's production of colour televisions, radios, recorders and some electronic components is the largest in the world. Further, the mix of the three major categories of electronic products, that is, capital goods, consumer products and components, is becoming more rational. Between 1991 and 1996, the proportion of capital goods increased from 14.9% to 33.1%, that of consumer electronics dropped from 49.2% to 33.2%, while that of components remained at about 35%, suggesting that the electronic information industry is now better able to provide electronic equipment for national economic construction. Table 4.16 shows the changes in the composition of the sector output value between 1992 and 1996.

4. Greater concentration of capital

With the emergence of large companies, a higher degree of capital concentration has been achieved. In 1995, China's top 100 electronics enterprises, which constituted less than 3% of the total number of enterprises in the sector, was responsible for 46% of the sector's total output value. Sales volume and pre-tax profits accounted for 63.5% and 81.5% respectively of the overall totals. Sichuan Changhong Electric Co

Table 4.16 Gross value of output of China's electronic industry by major categories of product

Year	1992	1993	1994	1995	1996
Producer Goods (%)	19.20	22.00	22.60	26.90	33.10
Consumer Goods (%)	45.80	43.90	42.30	38.10	33.20
Components and Parts (%)	35.00	34.10	35.10	35.00	33.70

Source: *China Electronic Industry Yearbook 1993*, and *1995*; *China Electronics*, 3 January 1997, *China Computer Daily*, 5 February 1996.

Ltd, which headed China's top 100 electronics enterprises, led a drive to slash the prices of colour televisions in the market in 1996. The price cut helped increase the market share of domestic brands to 74.1% by September 1996.[18] The top four enterprises (Changhong, Konka, Beijing and TCL) controlled 55.2% of the colour television market, with Changhong having a 22.6% share. Prior to this, foreign brands held the lion's share of the market. While increasing their market shares, these leading enterprises also attracted most of the capital investment in the sector. This has led to a realignment of assets. For example, Changhong increased its assets through the acquisition of several small colour television enterprises; Konka has absorbed two television manufacturing plants in Heilongjiang and Shaanxi; and Qingdao Haixin has merged with Shuangxi. The larger scale of production has resulted in an obvious increase in the production capacity and competitiveness of these enterprises. The colour television industry owes its success to the opening of the sector to foreign investment in the early 1980s. The import of advanced technologies and production lines meant that the industry could start off with high standards. In the personal computer industry, Chinese manufacturers have also, through years of hard work, finally managed to put an end to the dominance of foreign brands in the Chinese market. The market share of Legend, Great Wall, Tongchuang and other domestic brands increased from 23% in 1995 to over 30% in 1996.

5. Swift expansion of foreign-invested enterprises (FIEs)

China's electronics industry has seen swift development since the beginning of the market-oriented reforms thanks to active international economic and technological co-operation, the introduction of foreign capital and technologies, and the widespread application of modern management methods. The industry has secured US$7 billion in agreed foreign investment and US$4 billion in actual direct investment, and imported over 1,000 technologies over the years. At the end of 1988, there were only 536 FIEs in the electronics sector. By 1994 the number had reached 8,000. The use of foreign capital and the establishment of FIEs has given China's electronics industry a great boost. China's electronics industry was trailing behind and badly needed development, but lacked investment for expansion. The injection of foreign capital eased the shortage of domestic investment and accelerated the sector growth. The output value of FIEs in the total output value of the sector increased from 16.78% in 1992 to 36.04% in 1996,[19] exceeding that of the state sector by 6.5 percentage points. This shows that FIEs are playing an increasingly important role in China's electronics industry. The proportion of the output value of FIEs in the total output value of the sector between 1992 and 1996 is shown in Table 4.17.

18 Source: Survey results from monitoring the business of 106 large department stores in 35 cities by Sai Nuo Co.
19 Statistical figures for the January–October period.

Table 4.17 Share of the three [types of] foreign-funded (Sanzi) enterprises in the gross value of industrial output of the electronic industry (%)

Year	1992	1993	1994	1995	1996
Output (RMB 100 million)	182.37	355.00	532.40	847.70	1,068.80
Share (%)	16.78	24.00	28.60	34.50	36.01

Source: China Electronic Industry Yearbook 1993, and *1995*; *Electronic Trade Promotion Bulletin*, No. 7, 1997, and *China Electronics Daily*, 3 January 1996.

Foreign investment and the establishment of FIEs has also given a tremendous boost to the development of large corporations. Among China's top 100 electronics enterprises, 17 are joint-venture corporations, including 4 in the top 10. Many of the top 100 enterprises are cooperating with foreign firms on a project basis. FIEs have become important constituents of large corporations. Foreign investment has helped improve the economic benefits of the electronics industry. In 1995, there were only 697 FIEs in this sector, accounting for less than 20% of the total number of electronics enterprises. However, their profits totalled 6.09 billion *yuan*, amounting to 62.9% of the sector overall profits. Equity and contractual joint ventures in the electronics industry are all reporting excellent economic results. In the fifth annual selection of the country's ten best joint-venture enterprises, four were in the electronics business. The introduction of foreign capital has also promoted rapid growth in the export of electronic products. In 1995, electronic product exports of FIEs accounted for 56.5% of the total volume of electronics exports, amounting to US$10.49 billion.

China's vast and lucrative electronics market holds immense appeal to international capital and has attracted many multinational companies. While boosting the development of China's electronics industry, the open-door policy has also brought some negative impacts. With their financial strengths and their experience in the market economy, foreign firms have successfully entered the China's market and inflicted heavy casualties on its electronics industry.

II. Challenges confronting the sector

1. Competition from foreign firms

With their financial clout, multinational companies have been able to open up new markets through a combination of marketing strategies, including launching publicity offensives, holding exhibitions, giving press briefings, establishing training centres and appointing agents. They have successfully captured many sectors of the China's market. For example, foreign telecommunications equipment companies have a market share of over 80% in China, leaving domestic equipment with a mere 20% share, in spite of the fact that China's own 04-, 06- and 08-series of digital programme-controlled exchanges are technologically more advanced and cheaper than similar foreign products. Their sales have been retarded because foreign manufacturers have managed to secure many clients through credit offers. In the cellular products market, foreign companies have a 95% share, with Motorola alone controlling 40%–50% of the handset market.

In the computer industry, there is very little room left for Chinese manufacturers because most of the large, medium-sized and small computers in use are imported. Even the personal computer market is saturated with foreign brands. Almost all notebook computers, servers, network products, scanners and inkjet and laser printers sold in China are imported. Since the massive inroads of foreign brands at the beginning of the 1990s, the market share of Chinese personal computers has been on the decline, dropping from 80% in 1988 to 37.8% in 1993, 35% in 1994 and 23% in 1995. This downward trend was not reversed until 1996.

Foreign companies are in general keen on expanding their market share and set great store in image building and product promotion. For example, *Computer World* published a market survey report in its April 1996 issue, citing 3M as the best-selling brand of floppy diskettes in China. 3M widely publicised the results in a bid to further consolidate its lead and prepare the ground for new products. Other foreign firms also launched promotional activities, but Chinese companies did nothing of the sort. The same survey indicated that the quality of leading domestic brands was by no means inferior to foreign products, but none of the Chinese companies made use of the findings to boost their image and push sales. In a modern market economy, a company which does not attach importance to market expansion will lose valuable opportunities in competition.

The predominance of foreign firms in China's electronics sector has, to a large extent, left many domestic enterprises in a deep plight. Some have even been forced to switch to other lines of production. The impact on state enterprises is particularly serious. Between January and October 1996, state enterprises in this sector saw a 58.3% drop in their pre-tax profits compared with the corresponding 1995 period, while output value only edged up 0.8%. During the same period, FIEs registered an increase of 58.7% in output value. By the end of 1996, about 50% of state-owned electronics enterprises were losing money.

2. Failure of the policy to 'Offer Market in Exchange for Technology'

China introduced the policy of 'offering market in exchange for technology' in the early stage of its economic reform in the hope of attracting advanced foreign technologies to upgrade its products. However, foreign firms are always very cautious about technology transfers and will only agree to conditional and gradual transfers in line with China's technological development, in order to control its progress. Key technologies are barred from being exported to China. In many areas, the opening of the market has failed to bring about the transfer of much-needed technologies. Today, China's electronics market is already dominated by competing foreign corporations. If this goes on, China's electronics industry will become dependent on foreign firms.[20]

3. Failure to achieve economies of scale

Since the beginning of the 1990s, multinational electronics companies have been establishing joint-venture or wholly-owned enterprises in China. Motorola has invested US$1 billion in the establishment of production facilities for pagers, cellular telephones and other mobile telecommunications equipment in the Tianjin Development Zone. It has also formed a joint-venture with the Nanjing Panda Electronics Group to produce personal computers. It further plans to invest US$560 million to set up a factory for large semiconductor chips. Nortel and Philips have jointly set up a semiconductor plant in Shanghai. Intel has a US$50 million chip packaging and testing plant in Shanghai. IBM, Compaq and other companies have all established personal computer assembly plants in Shenzhen. In the television manufacturing sector, world heavyweights such as Matsushita, Toshiba and Hitachi, which began by importing complete television sets into China, have moved on to establish joint-venture plants for the production of colour television tubes. More recently they have also established holding companies for the manufacturing of their own brands. A foreign company has even declared that it would edge Chinese colour television manufacturers out of the market in three years. While foreign firms keep injecting capital and enlarging their scale of production in China, Chinese electronics enterprises are trailing behind and are weighed down by problems of duplicated and scattered projects. Take for example the computer industry. China produced 600,000 personal computers in 1996. Even Legend, the largest domestic manufacturer, was only producing 200,000 units. Other big companies were only producing well under ten thousand computers annually. Compaq, IBM and Apple, on the other hand, are turning out over 4 million computers a year. China has over 1,000 software manufacturers which employ about 80,000 people. Among these companies only one employs more than 500 software experts. The majority employ less than 50. Those with an output value of over 10 million *yuan* are already considered leaders. In 1995, software production and information services grossed 14.795 billion *yuan* in revenue (the software market grossed 8.2 billion *yuan*, with China's-made software accounting for a 30% market share). Although this already represented a big jump

20 The policy of 'offering market for technology' was exactly that followed by the Japanese government in its post-war negotiations with IBM. The unity of purpose and control on each side was perhaps a factor in making this a successful policy from which both sides gained. (Ed.)

compared with 4.06 billion *yuan* in 1992, 8.987 billion *yuan* in 1993 and 10.7 billion *yuan* in 1994, it still paled by comparison with IBM software revenue of US$12.949 billion. The revenue figure for Microsoft was US$7.418 billion. India is the world largest exporter of software, with some 120,000 scientists and workers employed by the country's 700-plus software companies. In 1995, revenue from software sales amounted to US$1.2 billion, including US$734 million in exports, 60% of which were bound for the United States. Thus, achieving economies of scale is vital to the survival of China's electronics enterprises.

4. A backward basic electronics industry

Statistical data suggest that electronic products contribute much more to a country's national economy than do products of other sectors. Government statistics show that if the contribution of a unit of rolled steel to GNP is 1, the contributions of other products are as follows: small cars, 5; colour televisions, 30; computers, 1,000; and integrated circuits (ICs), 2,000. This illustrates the obvious importance of IC production to GNP growth. The information industry in all developed countries is based on a powerful microelectronics industry. ICs are already in their fourth generation, that is, very large-scale integration (VLSI). The developed countries are already producing 8-inch chips with lines as fine as 0.35 microns, and are experimenting in laboratories with the production of chips with lines only 0.16 microns wide. However, even the most advanced production lines in China are still producing 4–5 inch chips with lines 3 microns wide. China is lagging behind overall international standards in VLSI technology by three generations, or about 15 years. In 1995, the world IC market grossed US$146.428 billion, with the United States accounting for 40%, followed by Japan (39%), the Asia-Pacific region (12%), and Europe (9%). Chinese chips only accounted for 0.3%-0.4% of the world total in terms of output volume and 0.3% in terms of output value, and only had a 20% share of the domestic market. China not only had to spend over US$1 billion on IC imports, but was unable to achieve breakthroughs in new hi-tech products without the support of essential ICs. The backwardness of its micro-electronics industry has slowed down the growth of major sectors (such as the computer industry).

5. Loss of State assets

Since joint ventures are entitled to policy concessions, in the 1990s many enterprises in the electronics sector have shown a keen interest in seeking joint-venture partners. Without the necessary cash, they have to use land, premises and brand names as capital investment, and they tend to under-value their assets in a bid to lure foreign investment. This has been a major cause of the loss of state assets.

6. Brain drain

For a hi-tech industry such as electronics, having a stable workforce is of crucial importance. China is actually not short of well-qualified people, but many of them have been head-hunted by multinational companies in China which offer attractive pay packages. This problem is particularly serious in the computer software sector.

III Measures for promoting the electronics industry

1. Upholding a policy of 'self-reliance supplemented by foreign assistance'

Ever since it embarked on its market-oriented reforms, China has been drawing on foreign investment and technology to increase its development capability and invigorate its national economy. Foreign companies are willing to export capital and transfer technology to China because they want to secure a slice of the Chinese market, exploit China's cheap labor and reap huge profits. There is a unity as well as a conflict of interest between the two sides. For this reason, China realises that it must implement a policy of 'Self-reliance supplemented by foreign assistance' in order to safeguard national interests while maintaining cooperation with foreign countries.

2. Stepping up development of China's domestic electronics industry

China must increase investment and give greater support to the development of key products vital to the electronics industry as a whole in order to achieve new breakthroughs. In particular, it must increase investment in the development of microelectronic and basic products and strive to narrow the gap with international standards in order to better support the industry. In technology imports, attention must be paid to absorption, assimilation and innovation with a view to developing domestic products. Only in this way will China be able to stop relying on foreign technology, increase the overall strength of its electronics industry, and become more competitive in the international market.

3. Fostering large companies through mergers

China's electronics industry is mainly comprised of small and scattered operations producing similar products. These small enterprises should merge with the better-run operations in order to increase their overall capability. In foreign countries, many big companies have reached advanced world standards and achieved a large scale of operation, but are still striving to increase their competitive edge through amalgamation and mergers. Since China's electronics enterprises are much smaller in scale, it is all the more necessary for them to take the road of mergers in order to survive in a cut-throat market environment. State enterprises in particular must learn from the advanced management experience of FIEs in order to become more market-oriented and competitive. In certain spheres, it is necessary for enterprises to fully open themselves to domestic competitors before opening themselves up to foreign investors, in order to cultivate a sense of competition and increase their competitive edge. In this way, they will not be swept off balance by foreign rivals and be completely out-competed by foreign products.

4. Assigning greater attention to personnel training

Well-trained staff constitute the foundation of enterprises. Chinese enterprises must strive to retain their staff by providing them with regular training, material rewards and other incentives. Only in this way will they be able to stand up to multinational companies and survive the competition.

5. Encouraging the use of domestic products

Policy concessions extended to foreign companies since the commencement of our market-oriented reforms have contributed positively by introducing foreign capital, advanced technologies, and management expertise to our country. However, they have also resulted in an influx of foreign electronic products. The 'Gold Projects' now underway are expected to our country's progress towards an information society. These cross-century projects will involve investments of billions of *yuan* and require huge quantities of computers and other electronic products. Since China's computer industry is relatively weak and its products are not yet competitive, China depends heavily on imports for the items needed for large electronic systems and the 'Gold Projects'. Actually, many of China's electronic products, such as personal computers, are comparable to foreign makes in terms of quality and technological standards. The government should formulate a procurement policy that gives priority to domestic suppliers for like-quality and like-performance as soon as possible. This will not only promote China's own electronics industry but will be an important measure of strategic significance to China's national security.

In World Bank analyses, the proportion of a country's information industry and other related industries in its GNP is taken to be an important indicator of its economic development. This proportion is 60%–70% in developed countries, 30%–40% in newly-industrialised economies and only 10%–15% in developing countries. Developed countries with 20% of world population control 80% of the world's total information by volume, whereas developing countries with 80% of world population only control the remaining 20%. The United States and Japan export one-third of the total global exports of information technology products. At the Ministerial

Conference of the World Trade Organisation in December 1996, developed countries headed by the United States called for negotiations on an information technology agreement with the aim of abolishing tariffs on information technology products before the year 2000. The United States and the West hope to preserve their predominance in information technology, remove obstacles to their access into developing countries, and make these countries dependent on them for information technology. The Chinese government has already made the electronic information industry its pillar industry during the Ninth Five Year Plan and for the next century. However, in a vast country such as China, it is necessary to rely on one own efforts in achieving IT progress. Without a powerful national industry, China will be at the mercy of others economically, and even politically. Without a powerful electronics industry, national economic development and the upgrading of the industrial structure will be greatly handicapped, and this in turn will greatly weaken China's competitiveness in the 21st century.

Document 4.5

'Reinforcing the key role of State Owned Enterprises in the industrialisation of science and technology'

JIANG LÜAN

(Head, Technology and Equipment Bureau, State Economic and Trade Commission)

Strategic Management, 1995, No. 3

The contemporary economic history of the development of science and technology illustrates that a nation's economic strength and international standing is increasingly determined by the degree to which it has developed and applied science and technology. China's levels of science and technology are higher than most other developing countries, including newly industrialised countries such as the Four Asian Tigers. However, our industrial structure and standards of hi-tech industry fall far behind. China's per capita national income remains at around hundredth place in the world rankings and our levels of industrialisation of science and technology, particularly high-technology, are still too low. The main reason for this is our relatively low rate of transformation of the results of science and technology. This means that an urgent prerequisite for our economic development is to find solutions to the problems of accelerating the commercialisation and industrialisation of science and technology and [learning] how to make use of advanced technology to transform our traditional industries.

Enterprises are the mainstay of the industrialisation of science and technology

The essence of the industrialisation of science and technology is the propagation and application of the fruits of science and technology so that we can achieve economies of scale. This requires both market demand and the appropriate environmental conditions, and the material infrastructure.

In the first place, market demand is the necessary pre-condition for using the benefits of science and technology to transform our productive forces. As far as China's present situation is concerned, the main sources of demand for new and advanced technology are likely to be existing state-owned enterprises, particularly those which are large in scale. This holds true for both the transformation of traditional forms of industry and the establishment of new kinds of industry. It could be said, therefore, that the industrialisation of science and technology in China rests primarily upon the extent to which large and medium-sized State Owned Enterprises can absorb the fruits of advanced technology and thereby improve their product structure.

Secondly, the industrialisation of the benefits of science and technology is not only a matter of time. It also requires certain fundamental conditions such as the existence of appropriate technology and capital together with a developed market. The market is the key to whether or not the industrialisation of the benefits of science and technology can succeed. Once introduced, the continued development and application of the benefits of science and technology runs alongside the development of the market.

The transformation of the benefits of science and technology generally happens according to the following sequence: research and development; intermediate testing; initial production; and the ultimate introduction of a new product onto the market. The entire process depends on the market, and investment is required at every link in the chain – the nearer the end of the chain, the larger the scale of investment becomes. Generally speaking, the proportionate ratios of investment at each stage of the production process (R & D – intermediate testing – initial production) are as follows: 1 : 10 : 100. Any rapid changes or fluctuations in the market can mean the success or failure of scientific and technological development and, for this reason, investment in this kind of venture carries with it a certain degree of risk. The entire technological transformation process can only be achieved if enterprises, particularly large and medium-sized enterprises and enterprise groups, are able to bear risk and have the capacity for large-scale production as well as modernised systems of operation and marketing. All of this means that large and medium-sized State Owned Enterprises provide the mainstay for the industrialisation of science and technology.

A similar situation exists in other countries. Products such as Boeing aeroplanes, high-speed motor vehicles, program-controlled telephone exchanges etc, are all manufactured by large companies. Evidence from other countries clearly shows that the industrialisation of science and technology is mainly likely to occur within enterprises that carry a considerable degree of economic weight.

In recent years, China has established special zones for the development of hi-tech industry in many regions. New pilot projects have been set up that promote the integration of industry with research centres and the industrialisation of the institutions of higher education. Methods such as these that rely on completely new initiatives to exploit the advantages of the industrialisation of science and technology have had only a minimal effect on the large-scale transformation of existing state- owned enterprises. An analysis of vast quantities of data and statistics leads us to one conclusion: while the industrialisation of science and technology can be achieved through a variety of different channels, the main bulk of industrialisation must occur within State Owned Enterprises, particularly large-scale enterprises or enterprise groups.

The main problems with the industrialisation of science and technology within Chinese enterprises.

For historical reasons, China's market systems are still not fully established and this wider environment works against the industrialisation of the benefits of science and technology. In addition to this important precondition, there are a number of other problems concerning the industrialisation of science and technology within enterprises in China. The main ones are as follows:

1. To a certain extent, enterprises lack external pressure and internal motivation to achieve technological progress and advancement. On the one hand, this has been created by long-term systemic problems and an excess of market supply over demand. Any losses incurred by enterprises have generally been compensated for by the State. This has meant that enterprises have not had to face the risk of bankruptcy and have lacked the pressure of market competition. On the other hand, the appointment and dismissal of managers of enterprises has been the responsibility of relevant government departments. The activities of businesses are still to a large extent subject to the desires of government departments and to 'short-termism' caused by imperfections in the enterprise responsibility system. This is an objective reason for enterprises lack of motivation and initiative to seek their own technological transformation.

2. The quality of enterprises as a whole is low. Firstly, China's distribution of technical and scientific strength is not rational as far as capacity for technological development is concerned. Over two thirds of our [total] capacity for scientific development is located outside enterprises and there is [overall] a serious lack of high-level scientists and technicians. According to statistics, less than 30% of engineers and scientists engaged in technological development are employed in enterprises. In 1993, there was a total of 18,663 large and medium-sized industrial enterprises in the country and 921,000 people engaged in scientific and technological

activities. Since 414,000 of these people were qualified engineers or scientists it follows that, on average, each large or medium- sized enterprise employed only 22 skilled technicians.

Secondly, only a small number of large and medium-sized enterprises have set up special structures for technological development. In 1993 only 50.9% of the 18,663 large and medium-sized enterprises had established such bodies. Around one quarter of these units suffered from problems such as a lack of proper funding, a shortage of highly skilled technical personnel, a lack of fixed areas of research, and serious defects in their basic facilities. Large and medium-sized enterprises urgently need to undergo a technological transformation in order to promote Chinese traditional industry to a leading position from the point of view of equipment and technical skills. Of the total book value of production equipment in all large and medium-sized enterprises, only around 6% is micro-chip controlled. Our outmoded technology, poor quality raw materials, irrational design, and poor quality workforce all mean that the quality of our industrial output remains poor and productivity is low. Chinese enterprises consume high quantities of materials and energy consumption per unit of output is four or five times higher than in developed countries. In addition, our capacity for information feedback is weak, and our awareness of market competition is poor, particularly with regard to the international arena. It is often difficult for us to accurately determine possible points of entry into the international market.

3. Problems resulting from technology being out of line with the requirements of production have not yet been fully resolved. These problems are primarily systemic ones. Since we designed our systems after the Soviet model, all of our independent research institutions were established outside industry. In developed countries, however, the forces of research are concentrated in universities, while the forces of development are focused within enterprises. Developed countries do not have many independent research institutions. In 1991, six scientists including Yan Dongsheng, the vice-chairman of the Science and Technology Committee of the Chinese People's Political Consultative Conference, conducted a survey of large and medium-sized enterprises in a number of regions [and cities] including Liaoning, Jilin, Shanghai and Guangdong. The survey showed that the problems involved with the two areas of scientific research and production have still not been fully resolved. The reforms to our scientific and technological systems that we have been instituting since 1985 have led to certain benefits with regard to improving the commercialisation of the fruits of science and technology and encouraging scientists and technicians to participate in scientific and technological development and operational activities. However there have been no improvements in the structure of service systems for scientific and technological research and

development as a whole. An after-effect of the various measures that have been introduced as part of our programme of reform to scientific and technological systems is that independent research institutions have become even more self-contained and isolated. Some large institutions and research centres in a number of industrial sectors are not sufficiently motivated to take on major projects and enter the areas of research appropriate to their particular sector. Instead, they tend to devote all their energies to small, short-term, and piecemeal projects that only lead to small increases in production. Statistics from the Ministry of Machinery and Electronics Industry show that there been no increases in scientific and technological cooperation between independent research institutions and enterprises – on the contrary, there is a downwards trend. It is difficult for appropriate research institutions to make inroads into enterprises, and research bodies within enterprises are pressing for more independence. Many are also calling for preferential treatment in terms of government policy-making. The problems that the survey uncovers are very serious.

4. The cumulative effects of investment in large and medium-sized enterprises are not very powerful, and capital investment in the industrialisation of science and technology is insufficient. At present, of the total funds invested in enterprises for technological development, 10% comes from the state and other levels of government, 40% is raised by the enterprises themselves, and 50% is in the form of loans. In practice, the enterprises themselves shoulder the burden of 90% of loan repayment and enterprises have already become the main source of investment. Around 90% of the total profit made by large and medium-sized industrial enterprises is channelled back to central or local government or various government departments in the form of taxes, interest or other costs. Enterprises are left with just 10% of their actual profits. This 10% must also be divided among various different areas with the result that the amount of money that is actually devoted to technological research is very small. This means that it is difficult for enterprises to become key investors through using their own internally accumulated capital. The lack of pressure on enterprises from market competition and the economic profit [incentive] means that it is difficult for the government to implement the policies necessary to promote technological progress within enterprises. In recent years, the state has initiated a number of policies aimed at boosting technological advancement within enterprises. One example is the government decision to allow enterprises to devote more than 1% of income from selling and marketing to technological development. If we take a look at [enterprise] accounts for the last few years, the amount of money devoted to expenditure on research and development represented only 1.4% of marketing income. There are also some enterprises that have the capacity to invest but are unwilling to take the risk because their risk safeguard

systems are not fully developed. The serious lack of capital has become one of the major factors holding back the industrialisation of science and technology.

Strengthening the policies that will enable enterprises to take the lead in the industrialisation of science and technology

The state should adopt a number of effective measures and policies to accelerate the industrialisation of science and technology, strengthen the leading role that enterprises have to play, and deal with the major issues raised above.

1. We need to reform administrative systems within enterprises, transform enterprises operational mechanisms, and begin to establish a modern enterprise system. This is the key to strengthening the external pressure and internal motivation that will encourage enterprises to place more emphasis on technological progress. The only way to make enterprises consider technological advancement as part of their development strategy is to increase the impact of the market on enterprises and raise their awareness of market competition. This will help to accelerate the industrialisation of science and technology.

2. We must devote great efforts to promoting linkages between enterprises and institutions of higher education and scientific institutions. At present, the bulk of China's advanced scientific and technological strength is concentrated within educational institutions and independent research institutes. There are more scientists and technicians in educational institutions than in enterprises. There are over 1,600,000 students attending universities of science and engineering, of whom around 100,000 are engaged in post-graduate research. How can all of this talent and research be put to good use within enterprises and be transformed into the real forces of production? How can we promote the linkage of enterprises with colleges, universities and institutions of science and technology? Over the last two years, the State Committee on Economics and Trade, the State Educational Committee and the Chinese Academy of Sciences have been working together to implement a development project to unite industry, education and research. We have evidence of the success of such projects from other countries. For example, Canada has formed a special industry, education and research committee and in Japan, similar moves have been dubbed the amalgamation of industry, bureaucracy and education. In promoting this kind of work, we are aiming to encourage enterprises, universities and scientific institutions to work together to develop various kinds of collaborative projects. These should be based on the principles of supplementing each other's strengths and weaknesses, relying on each other, sharing the burden of risk, and sharing the fruits of their labours. This will not only help to resolve the problem of a lack of funds within

universities and scientific institutions, it will also increase enterprises' capacity for development and thereby promote the transformation of the benefits of science and technology.

3. We need to offer support to large and medium-sized enterprises and encourage them to set up a variety of different structures for scientific and technological development according to their own requirements and abilities. Practical experience at home and abroad shows that the enterprises that have gained a competitive edge are those that have established their own internal structures for technological research and development. Their objectives in setting up such internal structures are as follows:

a) To effect large-scale increases in the input of research and development into production activities and to solve the problems arising from the disjunction between scientific research and production.

b) To help establish and perfect key mechanisms for the input of science and technology within enterprises, and bring into play the key role of enterprises as a source of technological research and development.

c) To improve the systems for technological development within enterprises, strengthen the capacity of enterprises to develop new products and new production techniques, and raise the capacity of enterprises to promote their own development and competitiveness.

This means that we must place great emphasis on the construction and perfection of mechanisms for scientific and technological development within enterprises. Large foreign companies place great reliance on technological development and conduct research into a wide range of different fields. Some of them are even engaged in research into the kind of technology we are likely to be using 20 or 30 years into the future. IBM spends US$6 billion every year on research and employs over 30,000 people in its research departments. In 1992, Siemens research expenditure reached US$5.3 billion and over 40,000 employees were engaged in research-related activities. [To compare], US$5.3 billion is equivalent to over 40 billion *yuan* at current prices and in 1993, the total sum of money that China's 18, 663 large and medium-sized enterprises devoted to research and development activities reached 24.86 billion *yuan*. The program-controlled public telephone exchange systems developed by the Swedish company, Ericsson, have now spread to around one tenth of the 600 million telephones in use around the world. The same company's mobile telephone systems now hold around 40% of the world market. These two systems have also taken control of one quarter and two thirds of the Chinese market respectively. Ericsson spends an annual total of over US$1.5 billion on R & D and other technological research and this represents 22% of total operational costs. Of the 66,000 people employed by this company 22% are engaged in technological development. (The number of engineers and technicians in large and medium-sized enterprises in China represents just 6.3% of their total work force. The proportion drops to 1.08% if the category is limited to those with university level qualifications or above.) Ericsson has set up three networks to institute a strategy of external development. The first of these is a vast selling and marketing network stretching throughout 88 different countries and regions; the second is a global production network covering 25 countries; and the third is a research and development network which encompasses over 40 different research laboratories and research centres. It is the combination of these three vast networks that have helped this company dominate the world market.

4. We must strengthen the capacity of enterprises for industrial experimentation. The main reason for our poor results in scientific and technological transformation is that our intermediate links are extremely weak. Although this would normally be a matter for enterprises themselves, the State Commission on Economics and Trade has decided that at our current stage of development it is advisable to channel certain funds into supporting the establishment of intermediate testing sites for large and medium-sized enterprises and supporting industrial experimentation for certain key products and technologies.

5. We need to encourage enterprises to attract, digest, and absorb advanced technology from other countries and make it part of our domestic production process. We must support the establishment of bases for the domestic absorption of major items of technological equipment. During the course of the Seventh Five Year Plan, the state organised the 'twelve dragons' project in an attempt to attract and absorb foreign technology. These so called dragons were a series of projects aimed at promoting technological development, transformation, and integration, and the aim was to link them all together to form one long dragon.[21] The actual substance of the initiative was to integrate products, equipment, components and raw materials to form one long dragon that stretched from the design stage to technological processing and industrial production. As far as organisation was concerned, enterprises, research and design institutions and tertiary level colleges were linked together in a similar way to form one long dragon. In 1991 a new eleven dragons project was initiated and this was put into practice one year later. Around 9 billion *yuan* was invested in this initiative, of which 2.5 billion *yuan* was earmarked for the most important project: the domestic production of video recorders. As a major project organised by the State Commission on Economics and Trade, this initiative illustrates the future direction of the industrial development of enterprises.[22]

21 In Chinese festivals, 'dragons' are made up of groups of people *linked* to each other under a dragon-like covering – hence the analogy of the linked projects. (Ed.)

22 The Eleven Dragons referred to here are eleven technological projects aimed at attracting and absorbing new technology in video recorders, textile machinery, extra-furnace refining equipment, copper smelting equipment etc. using the sequence of behaviour mentioned in the text. (Ed.)

6. We must adopt favourable policies to strengthen the financial capacity of enterprises. Central and local government should work together to consolidate the position of large and medium-sized State Owned Enterprises, give a boost to other State Owned Enterprises, and make full use of the major role that State Owned Enterprises have to play in economic development.

7. We need to reform our investment mechanisms and develop new security systems to minimise investment risk. A lack of risk safeguard systems has meant that when enterprise managers make strategic decisions to develop advanced technology, they tend to revert back to low-risk projects that use relatively low levels of technology. In a market economic system, banks are unwilling to invest funds in high-risk, hi-tech projects that have a long cycle of maturity, out of concern for their own economic interests. This means that there is a serious lack of funds for the industrialisation of new and advanced technology. In order to promote reforms to our investment mechanisms, the State Commission on Economics and Trade and the Ministry of Finance have joined forces to set up an Assurance Company for Investment in Technology and the Chinese Economy. If an enterprise comes up with a marketable project whose industrial transformation necessitates the tolerance of a certain degree of risk, the enterprise can approach this new Assurance Company to acquire the necessary guarantees that will allow the enterprise to make use of bank loans. Work in this area is still in need of further development. This will help promote the reform of our investment mechanisms and the institution of new investment risk safeguard systems. It will thereby help to accelerate the industrialisation of advanced science and technology in China.

5

China's Agriculture during the Period of Reform

INTRODUCTION

The central economic issue facing China throughout its modern history reflects the elemental challenge of providing enough food for its population. At the end of the 1950s, it was the collapse of grain production that halted industrialisation and forced a wholesale, if temporary reorientation of economic priorities in favour of the farm sector. Thereafter, population pressure continued to highlight the critical importance of agriculture, especially the food sector. Between 1955–1957 and 1974–1976, average per capita output of grain hardly changed, even though yields showed quite impressive growth.[1] Although post-1978 reforms transformed this situation,[2] agricultural and food issues have remained strategic economic preoccupations of successive Chinese governments. For their leaders, mindful of the catastrophic famine of 1959–1961 and nervous of excessive dependence on imported American food supplies, the old adage – 'agriculture is the foundation of the economy; grain is the cornerstone of that foundation' – has meaning even in a context in which recent grain output growth has generated a comfortable cushion above subsistence requirements. This is the background to a continuing commitment to a strategy of basic domestic food self-sufficiency. A keen awareness by Chinese leaders of the social, even political, implications of agricultural impoverishment is another critical dimension to their continued emphasis on the role of the farm sector in China's future development.[3]

1 Cf. 302.6 kg. (1955–1957) and 305.4 kg. (1974–1976) – a difference of <1%. During the same period, average grain yields grew by 2.6% p.a. 1955–1957 were the last 3 years of China's First Five Year Plan; 1974–1976 were the last three years of Mao's life.
2 E.g., average per capita output of grain rose from 316.6 kg. to 410.5 kg. (a rise of 30%) between 1978 and 1998. Even allowing for higher yield growth (2.9% p.a.) and a slower decline in grain sown area (-0.3% p.a. [1955/1957–1974/1976]), compared with 0.5% p.a. during the 1980s and 1990s, it is clear that slowing population growth contributed most to rising per capita grain output after 1978 (cf. average growth rates for total population of 2% p.a. [1955/1957–1974/1976] and 1.3% p.a. [1978–1998]).

The table on the following page shows basic indicators of China's agricultural performance during the Mao era and offers a comparative basis for assessing the impact of post-1978 reforms.

Contained within these figures and reflecting institutional and planning inefficiencies was a significant legacy of rural poverty. With some exceptions, per capita disposable income in the countryside remained very low – in 1978, averaging a mere 145 *yuan*, compared with 346 *yuan* for urban residents.[4] Rural poverty was to prove the source of some of China's most intractable problems after 1978 and the persistence of low living standards, especially among farmers, has remained a potential threat to China's economic and social stability.

The reform process has affected the agricultural sector more profoundly and comprehensively than any other branch of the Chinese economy. In an article translated in this chapter, Wu Xiang explains the *rural* origins of the post-Mao reforms in demographic and economic terms: it was in the countryside, he argues, that most of China's population still lived and worked, and it was here that the planning system had inflicted the most severe damage.[5] That Chinese farmers were not only more vocal than other groups in demanding reform, but also more active in support of such demands is highlighted in their spontaneous action, which facilitated the widespread re-establishment of family farming throughout the country.[6] The fact that the countryside was where more than 80% of China's population lived and worked (farming alone accounting for 71% of national employment) no doubt encouraged the rural focus of early reforms. As subsequent history demonstrated, farming also faced fewer

---

3 The strategic role of the agricultural and grain sectors, as perceived by Deng Xiaoping and his successors is brought out in the article by Sun Zhonghua and Li Shaohua, translated in this chapter. A much more comprehensive rehearsal of Deng's views on agriculture is given in Chinese Academy of Agricultural Sciences and Ministry of Agriculture (Eds.), *An Investigation of Deng Xiaoping's Thinking on Agriculture*, Beijing, 1998.

4 Joseph C.H. Chai, 'Consumption and living standards in China' in Robert F. Ash and Y.Y. Kueh (Eds.) *The Chinese Economy under Deng Xiaoping*, Oxford, 1996, p. 249.

5 It is not coincidental that agricultural reform should have started in Anhui – a province with a background of institutional experimentation in the farm sector. In another article, Wu Xiang points out that as early as 1977, family farming began to re-emerge in Anhui, and in 1979 contractual arrangements with households spread more widely in the province. Such developments owed much to the reformist zeal of Wan Li (First Secretary of the Provincial Party Committee), although Wan's actions were also prompted by the prior spontaneous reversion to household farming practices by many Anhui peasants. Wu quotes Wan to the effect that 'I believe that the benefits of contracting output to the household outweigh the disadvantages, provided it is conducted on a limited scale'. He adds that in July 1979, the local Party Committee in Anhui '*succumbed to pressure from various quarters* and issued its Document No. 46, which resolved to amend the household contract system' [my emphasis]. See Wu Xiang, *China's Human Resources Development*, 1994, No. 1.

6 Thus, 'the pattern of peasants leading the state was most pronounced in the creation of family farms. The move towards family farms was the reform period's outstanding example of peasant efficacy under a strong state', Daniel Kelliher, *Peasant Power in China: The Era of Rural Reform, 1979–1989*, New Haven and London, 1992, p. 40.

Table 5.1 China's agricultural performance, 1952–1978

	1952	1957	1965	1978
Arable area (m.ha.)	107.9	111.8	103.6	99.4
Irrigated area (m.ha.)	20.0	27.3	33.1	45.0
Agric. machine power (m.kw.)	–	1.2	10.9	117.5
Total sown area (m.ha.)	141.3	157.2	143.3	150.1
Total application of chemical fertiliser (m.tons of nutrients)	0.1	0.4	1.9	8.8
Av. application per sown ha. (kg.)	0.7	2.5	13.3	58.6
Rural population (RP) (m.)	503.2	547.0	594.9	803.2
GVAO (b.*yuan*)	46.1	53.7	83.3	139.7
Av. per capita GVAO (RP) (*yuan*)	91.6	98.2	140.0	173.9
TOTAL OUTPUT (m.tons)				
Food grains	163.9	195.1	194.6	304.8
Oilseeds	4.2	4.2	3.6	5.2
Cotton	2.3	2.6	1.9	2.2
Meat	3.4	4.0	5.5	8.6
OUTPUT PER HEAD RP (kg.)				
Food grains	325.7	356.7	327.1	379.5
Oilseeds	8.3	7.7	6.1	6.5
Cotton	4.6	4.6	3.2	2.7
Meat	6.8	7.3	9.2	10.7

Sources: MOA, 1983 and 1989; *China Statistical Yearbook*, 1999.

entrenched obstacles and was more susceptible to reform than the state-owned industrial enterprises in the cities.[7] But the more fundamental point is that with economic growth still, for the time being, driven by the farm sector, a reinvigorated agriculture held pride of place in Deng's pursuit of the 'Four Modernisations'.[8]

7 The differing nature of the government's responses to urban protest (1989) and rural unrest (early 1990s) highlights the greater perceived threat to social and political stability posed by the highly concentrated and organised urban workforce, compared with its more scattered rural counterpart. Nor is in coincidental that rising urban unemployment associated with SOE lay-offs in the 1990s elicited greater official concern than the emergence of a vastly bigger reservoir of surplus farm labour in the wake of rural reforms.

8 'Poor agricultural performance could wreck the [Four Modernisations] program by undermining both industry and foreign trade. Thus, even though the Chinese vision of modernization focused on industry and advanced technology, Deng's coalition was forced to turn its attention to agriculture as soon as it consolidated power in 1978', Kelliher, op.cit., pp. 49–50.

In 1978, on the eve of the reforms, the institutional legacy of the great collectivisation and communisation campaigns of the second half of the 1950s was still evident. Farmers lived and worked in a collective framework[9] that had changed little for almost two decades. It was a framework that provided them with spurious[10] job security and free access to basic services, including health, education and old age care. Scope for independent economic decision-making was, however, confined to tiny private plots, production in the collective sector being driven by centrally-determined plans, whose implementation was overseen by local cadres. Rural market exchange was minimal and confined to non-essential goods; the distribution of essential products – above all, grain and cotton – was still handled through the state monopoly procurement system, first established in 1953.

Fear of food shortages, hunger and even famine meanwhile bred a psychology in which maximisation of grain output overrode the dictates of farm production based on principles of economic efficiency and comparative advantage. In 1978, the rural sector, which accounted for 84% of China's total population and 71% of employment, was largely co-terminous with *agriculture*, non-agricultural, rural activities being overwhelmingly farm-orientated. A breakdown of rural social value-output for 1978 shows 70% deriving from land-based farming.[11] In the same year, 77% of the gross value-output of agriculture 'proper' originated in crop farming, compared with 15% for animal husbandry, 3% each for forestry and subsidiaries, and 2% for aquatic production;[12] almost two-thirds of cropping GVO derived from grain cultivation alone.

Such was the impact of the reforms during the intervening 20 years that by the end of the 1990s, the agricultural sector bore little resemblance, quantitatively or qualitatively, to what had existed at the end of the 1970s. The collective framework of farming had long disappeared, replaced by 'responsibility systems' that granted farmers a degree of autonomous decision-making unparalleled in China's experience since 1949.[13] Even more dramatic was the Chinese government's announcement in 1985 that, except for a few strategic products, mandatory state quotas would be abolished in favour of free market exchange of agricultural goods. Implied in this decision was a major policy shift from a supply- to a demand-orientated farming system – a commitment to which the government has

9 That is, the three-tier system of Commune, Large Brigade and Production Team.
10 'Spurious' in the sense that although the collective framework maximised employment opportunities, albeit at the expense of low productivity, it also concealed massive underemployment.
11 The remaining 30% was divided among industry (19%), construction (6.5%), commercial activities (3%) and transport (2%) Ministry of Agriculture, *Compendium of Statistics on China's Rural Economy, 1949–1986*, Beijing, 1989, p. 104.
12 Ibid. p. 115.
13 Between 1982 and 1984, the number of rural people's communes fell from 54,352 to 249. At the end of 1984, 98% of all agricultural households had joined 'contract responsibility systems, with payment linked to output'. See Robert F. Ash, 'Agricultural policy under the impact of reform' in Y.Y. Kueh and R.F. Ash (Ed.) *Economic Trends in Chinese Agriculture: The Impact of Post-Mao Reforms*, Oxford, 1993, pp. 19–20.

adhered, sometimes falteringly, ever since. By the early 1990s, 83% of total sales of farm products were at market prices.[14] By 1985, more than 53,000 free markets had been opened in rural areas – a figure that rose to almost 68,000 by the end of 1998. Meanwhile, between 1990 and 1998, the value of grain and oilseed transactions conducted in free markets rose tenfold to 147 billion *yuan*.[15]

No less important was the process of diversification that characterised developments in the countryside in the 1980s and 1990s. The previous near-identity of farming and non-farming rural activities gave way to the emergence of a much more diversified rural economy, mainly driven by the rapid growth of township and village enterprises (TVEs). In 1978, over 28 million workers in 1.5 million TVEs generated a gross value-output of 49.3 billion *yuan* – almost 80% of it deriving from industrial activities.[16] By 1998, employment in TVEs had risen to more than 125 million, associated GVO having registered an average nominal rate of growth of well in excess of 20% p.a.[17]

The figures in Table 5.2, which may be compared with those shown in Table 5.1, seek to capture major dimensions of China's agricultural performance under the impact of reform.

To accept statistical evidence at face value can be dangerous and detailed analysis of China's agricultural performance highlights significant difficulties that have emerged and recurred in the farm sector under the impact of reform. Such qualifications notwithstanding, developments in the 1980s and 1990s do reflect an impressive record of achievement. In terms of comparable prices, agriculture grew, on average, by 5% p.a. during 1978–1998, compared with 2.5% between 1957 and 1978. The annual rate of expansion in total grain output was much closer (2.1%, 1957–1978; 2.5%, 1978–1998). But in physical terms, average annual incremental output doubled between the two periods, from 5.2 to 10.4 million tons p.a., facilitating a marked improvement in per capita output of grain during the 1980s and 1990s. During 1957–1978, average output of grain per head of rural population rose by a mere 6.4%, whereas in the next 20 years, it increased by 46.8%.[18]

---

14 Terry Sicular, 'Redefining state, plan and market: China's reforms in agricultural commerce' in Andrew G. Walder (Ed.), *China's Transitional Economy*, Oxford, 1996, p. 74.
15 State Statistical Bureau, *Chinese Statistical Yearbook*, Beijing, 1999, p. 553.
16 Ministry of Agriculture, *Compendium of Statistics on China's Rural Economy, 1949–1986*, p. 286.
17 The relevant statistics can be found in State Statistical Bureau, *Chinese Statistical Yearbook*, 1991, pp. 378–79 and 1998, p. 420; State Statistical Bureau, *Rural Statistical Yearbook of China*, 1998, p. 297 and 1999, p. 293. It is clear that the average size of TVEs, measured in terms of employment, rose substantially during this period.
18 Between 1957 and 1978, average output of grain per head of *total* population rose from 302 to 317 kg. (a rise of 5%); by 1998, the corresponding figure was 411 kg. (up 30% since 1978).

Table 5.2 China's agricultural performance, 1978–1998

	1978	1985	1995	1998
Arable area (m.ha.)	99.4	96.8	95.0	n.a.
Irrigated area (m.ha.)	45.0	44.0	49.3	52.3
Agric. machine power (m.kw.)	117.5	209.1	361.2	452.1
Total sown area (m.ha.)	150.1	143.6	149.9	155.7
Total application of chemical fertiliser (m.tons of nutrient) (kg.)	8.8	17.8	35.9	40.9
Av. application per sown ha. (kg.)	58.6	124.0	239.5	262.7
Rural population (RP) (m.)	803.2	844.2	916.7	919.6
GVAO (b.*yuan*)	139.7	361.9	2,034.1	2,451.7
Av. per capita GVAO (RP) (*yuan*)	173.9	428.7	2,218.9	2,666.1
TOTAL OUTPUT (m.tons)				
Food grains	304.8	379.1	466.6	512.3
Oilseeds	5.2	15.8	22.5	23.1
Cotton	2.2	4.1	4.8	4.5
Meat	8.6	19.3	52.6	57.2
OUTPUT PER HEAD RP (kg.)				
Food grains	379.5	449.1	509.0	557.1
Oilseeds	6.5	18.7	24.5	25.1
Cotton	2.7	4.9	5.2	4.9
Meat	10.7	22.9	57.4	62.2

Source: State Statistical Bureau, *China Statistical Yearbook*, 1997 and 1999.

Against the background of increasingly severe pressure on the arable land base from both agricultural and non-agricultural sources,[19] even allowing for an extension of multiple cropping,[20] an increasing burden has rested on yield improvements in order to generate farm growth since 1978. In the 1990s alone (1991–1998), average yields of cereals, cotton and major oil crops rose by 18%, 16% and 30%, respectively. Meanwhile, a much more diversified pattern of agricultural production emerged, with the share of crop farming falling from 80% to 61% (1978–1998), compared with rises from 1.6% to 4.5% (aquatic production) and from 15% to 26.5% (animal husbandry).[21]

19 This and other associated issues are explored in detail in Robert F. Ash and Richard Louis Edmonds, 'China's land resources, environment and agricultural production', in R.L. Edmonds (Ed.), *Managing the Chinese Environment,*Oxford, 2000.
20 The MCI rose from 141 (1957) to 151 (1978) to 160 (1996).
21 The share of forestry fell from 3.4% to 2.9% during the same period. Note that these estimates, derived from data in State Statistical Bureau, *China Statistical Abstract*, Beijing, 1999, pp. 87–88, reflect the changing structure of GVAO expressed in real terms.

There were also significant *technical* improvements, which built on a firm foundation established in the Mao era. Between 1957 and 1978, the proportion of arable area effectively irrigated had already risen from 25% to 45%, and it expanded to around 55% by the end of the 1990s. A comparison of rates of growth in the use of machinery and farm chemicals before and after 1978 is misleading because of the tiny base that existed in the 1950s. Suffice to say here that the availability of mechanised power and the application of chemical fertilisers increased fourfold or more after 1978.

With the benefit of hindsight, the ultimate thrust of agricultural reforms since 1979 has been to transform the farm sector from a supply-orientated into a demand-orientated system by making farmers more responsive to market forces. In pursuit of this goal and in order to accommodate conflicting interests, the government in Beijing has had recourse to a variety of policy instruments. The rest of this introduction addresses some of these policy issues and the dilemmas to which they have given rise.

Agricultural investment

Apart from 1963–1965, when farm investment rose to a much higher level in response to the deep agricultural crisis precipitated by the Great Leap Forward, agriculture's share of capital construction and other relevant forms of investment made available by the state remained a little over 10% between the Second and Fifth Five Year Plan periods (1958–1962 and 1976–1980).[22] In the 1980s, however, there was a major contraction in state investment, which was not offset by funding from other sources. Between 1976–1980 and 1981–1985, the cumulative level of investment for purposes of farm capital construction[23] fell by more than 1 billion *yuan*. Even allowing a for a sharp acceleration in the expansion of state-sponsored farm investment in the 1990s,[24] the finding that in 1998, agriculture and irrigation accounted, respectively, for less than 2% and 3.5% of all state construction investment attests to continuing neglect of the farm sector.

Before 1978, the government was responsible for the administration of water conservancy facilities, as well as for funding new capital construction. In the 1980s, in the belief that increasing rural prosperity was a potential source of indigenous funding by individual peasants, the central authorities sought to reduce their role in the provision of irrigation facilities. Although

---

22 The combined share of total state capital construction investment funds allocated to agriculture (including irrigation) fell from 13.9% to 11.8% between 1958–1962 and 1976–1980. During the same period, the proportion of industrial investment directed to the servicing of agriculture rose from 5% to 8.7%. See Statistical State Statistical Bureau, *China Statistical Yearbook on Investment in Fixed Assets, 1950–1995*, Beijing, 1997, pp. 103–107 and 136.

23 I.e., investment in farming, forestry, animal husbandry and fisheries.

24 From 9.1% p.a. (1986–1990) to 24.3% (1991–95) to 43.3% (1996–1998) for direct investment in crop farming, husbandry and fishing; and from 10% p.a. to 28.5% to 42.4% for water conservancy. State Statistical Bureau, *China Statistical Yearbook*, 1999, p. 194.

the government later acknowledged the error of this decision, the level of capital construction investment in irrigation undertaken by the central authorities has remained depressed.[25]

The 1980s and 1990s did, it is true, witness a huge expansion in rural household savings deposits. By 1997, such deposits totalled 913.2 billion *yuan*,[26] or 19.7% of the national (urban and rural) total, and were more than 20 times greater than state capital construction investment in agriculture, including irrigation. Rural savings contained the potential to offset investment deficiencies associated with declining allocations by the state, including local government sources. But the Agricultural Bank and rural credit cooperatives, where most rural savings were deposited, have had a disappointing record in supporting farm investment – a reflection perhaps of the higher returns available from rural industry, commerce and other non-agricultural rural activities. Investment by individual peasants in non-working capital has also been limited, whether because of innate caution in a policy environment perceived to be volatile[27] or an assumption that large-scale fixed investment is a government, not private responsibility. Nor does the prevalence of small-scale farming encourage investment in irrigation – something that may have contributed to a major institutional initiative, designed to set up a 'two-tier operational system' combining decentralised, household-based farming with a collectively-operated 'socialised service system'. Moreover, rural income growth has accrued disproportionately to those engaged in non-farm rural activities, whose penchant to invest in agriculture is likely to be weak.[28]

Property rights

The rural reforms of the late 1970s and early 1980s left property rights unclear.[29] Villagers were all equally entitled to a share in the rights to land within their community, but in the absence of their embodiment in any tangible form, such as a title deed, land ownership was lacking.

Many believe that the absence of free land markets blocks economic efficiency in farming, although tenancy is not necessarily an obstacle to the attainment of scale economies and technical progress, and if land concentration is thought desirable, the associated benefits may be realised through the agency of the local community acting as quasi-landlord. To

25 During 1979–1995, irrigation accounted for a mere 2.9% of all state capital construction investment; in 1998, the corresponding figure was 3.5% (2.1% for new construction). State Statistical Bureau, *China Statistical Yearbook*, 1999, pp. 192–93.
26 Ministry of Agriculture, *Agricultural Development Report, 1998*, Beijing, 1998, p. 19.
27 The threat of re-collectivisation was a one time a recurrent anxiety; quite frequent adjustments in land allocation have also inhibited long-term land investment.
28 Returnee migrants to the countryside have also tended to use accumulated savings for industrial and commercial, not agricultural, purposes.
29 For detailed consideration of the land rights issue, see the article by Jiang Li, translated below.

date, collective ownership of land in China has remained an unshakeable shibboleth. Meanwhile, the absence, until recently, of Chinese membership of the World Trade Organisation (WTO), has meant that partial insulation from international competition and rising relative prices of farm products were capable of generating Ricardian rents. In such circumstances, on grounds of efficiency and equity, it may be preferable that such gains should have accrued to the local community rather than to individual landlords.

Looking ahead, the continuing removal of labour from the land will cause a steady decline in the size of the farm population and work force. If, as their ties with the land weakened, urban migrants and rural non-farm workers felt that having access to land was less important, sales to individual farmers by local communities might facilitate a process of gradual land privatisation. The reality appears to be more complicated. Retention of claims to land use rights has long been an important source of economic security for peasants whose ability to retain a more lucrative non-farm job, whether in an urban or rural setting, cannot be guaranteed.[30] A not unconnected finding, which further undermines the case in favour of firm property rights embedded in a free land market, is that some peasants actually prefer short-term to long-term land contracts.[31] For the time being, there seems little prospect of the government sanctioning the opening of a land market, its preferred approach being to extend land leases to at least 30 years.

The grain sector and food security

If food security were threatened, prioritising the grain sector would make sense. But essential food supplies are not in jeopardy and China has long enjoyed a comfortable cushion above subsistence needs. Given the strong theoretical case in favour of China importing more food and other land-intensive products through increased exports of labour-intensive manufactured goods, it is clear that the continued commitment to a policy of basic food self-sufficiency reflects non-economic imperatives.

The table on the following page highlights the performance of the grain sector in selected years since 1978.

A series of bumper harvests since 1995 is the most notable recent feature of the grain sector's performance and highlights the fulfilment of a per capita output target of some 400 kilograms – a level widely regarded to be consistent with meeting nutritional needs and the dietary aspirations[32] of an increasingly affluent population. From this simple perspective, China has

---

30 E.g., the number of TVE employees engaged in industrial and construction officially fell by 8.4 million between 1996 and 1998. State Statistical Bureau, *Rural Statistical Yearbook of China, 1999*, Beijing, 1999, p. 293.

31 Cf. Jean Oi, 'Two decades of rural reform in China: an overview and assessment', *The China Quarterly*, No. 159, September 1999, esp. pp. 618–19.

32 Including higher demand for fish, meat and dairy produce, all of which place an increasing burden on grain for feed.

Table 5.3 Total and average per capita domestic grain output (Selected years since 1978)

Year	Total output (mill. tonnes)	Average output per head of total population (kgs.)
1978	304.77	316.6
1984	407.31	390.3
1989	407.55	361.6
1990	446.24	390.3
1995	466.62	385.3
1996	480.00	392.5
1997	494.17	399.7
1998	512.30	410.5
1999	508.00	403.5

made marked progress towards meeting its goal of basic self-sufficiency in food grains. Warnings of the apocalyptic consequences of large-scale imports of grain notwithstanding,[33] it is a salutary finding that in no year since 1978 has China dipped below a 95% self-sufficiency rate. In 1997 and 1998, China was a net *exporter* of cereals and associated products – its imports of cereals being less than 0.5% of total grain production in both years.[34] In addition, China's agricultural balance of payments has consistently shown a sizeable surplus and, for the time being, the foreign exchange earnings of non-grain farm commodities are sufficient to finance major purchases of grain from abroad.

Whether such a need will arise remains to be seen. Suffice to say that at the beginning of a new century, the prospects for continued growth are encouraging. Even in the face of further encroachment on arable land, few doubt the capability of scientific and technological progress, including the development of genetically modified crops, to maintain the momentum of recent output expansion. Developments in the second half of the 1990s suggest too that there has been some redress in the regional balance of grain production away from the north (especially the north-east – the main source of incremental output in the late 1980s and early 1990s) back towards central and southern China. Nevertheless, future growth will still be dependent on the ability of northern regions to generate an increasing surplus, which in turn requires effective action by the government in conserving and making more efficient use of severely depleted water resources. Overcoming this critical resource constraint would be a major

33 See Lester Brown, *Who Will Feed China? Wake-Up Call for a Small Planet*, New York and London: W.W. Norton & Co., 1995.
34 The corresponding figure for wheat – China's most important imported grain – was around 1.5%.

achievement and go far towards encouraging optimism in extrapolating from recent growth trends in the grain sector.

Price reform

Despite the proliferation of private markets for farm products, grain and edible oil marketing remained subject to controls throughout the 1980s.[35] By the end of the 1980s, free-market grain sales had only doubled, while those of other commodities had risen four or fivefold. Only in the 1990s did free-market sales of grain and edible oil start to accelerate significantly, rising tenfold between 1990 and 1998 to 147 billion *yuan*. This renewed shift towards commercialisation of grain transactions was partly prompted by the high fiscal cost of government intervention. In particular, the mid-1990s saw many grain responsibilities transferred to the provinces through the initiative of the Provincial Governor Responsibility System, although the trend towards increasing involvement by the *private* sector in handling commercially marketed grain was discontinued in 1998, when the government re-monopolised farmgate grain procurement. The *quid pro quo* was a commitment by central government to maintain a fixed procurement price for grain sales and an undertaking that state grain enterprises would purchase surplus grain at an above-market protective price – commonly at cost plus a 10% margin.

Implementation of these policies generated serious problems. In the wake of successive bumper harvests after 1995, increases in grain output exceeded the rise in consumption, generating excess supply, causing stockpiles to mount and placing an increasingly heavy fiscal burden on the government. A further consequence was the growing reluctance of state grain enterprises to buy grain, especially at protective prices, making it difficult for farmers to offload their produce. Continuing, but inappropriate emphasis on output maximisation was also reflected in neglect of grain variety and quality.[36]

This is the background against which, in May 1999, Zhu Rongji revealed that administrative price protection for grain varieties of poor quality and/or in excess supply would gradually be phased out. The decision foreshadowed further reform of the grain distribution system, designed to facilitate production in accordance with the dictates of the market. Also significant was an announcement (August 1999) that the government-fixed purchase price of cotton was to be abolished.

But the most striking manifestation of the government's determination to create a truly market-orientated grain economy was a subsequent announcement (January 2000) that, for the first time since 1949, efforts should be made to *reduce* the output of staple agricultural products. In

---

35 The discussion that follows is based on research conducted by the World Bank.
36 Viewed from a broader perspective, poor quality also highlighted the discomfiture that impending WTO accession and exposure to competition from more efficient overseas grain farmers was likely to bring.

particular, grain output was to be cut from 508 million tons (1999) to 490 million tons. Henceforth, higher farm incomes would derive not simply from increasing physical output, but from deliberate market-orientated efforts to adjust crop structures and produce more high-quality grains, more grain for processing, and more feed grain.[37]

The regional dimension of farming

Preoccupation with the trans-national implications of China's increasing involvement in the global economy ought not to divert attention from the task – no less important – of viewing its economic development from a *sub-national* perspective. The grain sector is one context in which knowledge of regional developments is critical to understanding changes that have taken place under the impact of reform.[38] Traditionally, the fertile regions of central-southern China have generated the food surpluses needed to meet the needs of grain-deficient areas in the north. This was a pattern that persisted until the early 1980s, but subsequently gave way to a remarkable transformation, as a major shift in the regional centre of gravity of grain production began to take place. By the mid-1990s, the huge grain surplus enjoyed by central-eastern provinces a decade earlier had all but been eliminated, while large deficits had emerged in other southern areas. Only thanks to the above-average performance of northern (especially north-eastern) provinces was the emergence of a sizeable national deficit avoided.

The erosion of the grain base in some southern coastal provinces was part of the background against which the 'provincial grain responsibility system' was instituted in the mid-1990s. From the perspective of the late 1990s, the impact of this initiative has apparently been positive in the sense of mitigating the previous shift in grain output towards the northern half of the country. Whereas between the second half of the 1980s and first half of the 1990s, almost 80% of China's incremental grain output derived from the north, in 1995–1998 the corresponding figure was only 61%. By contrast, outhern China's incremental contribution rose from 22% to 39%.[39] Yet whatever the long-term significance of recent harvests may be, northern

37 Government reports called for the curtailment of production of long-grain, non-glutinous rice in the south, winter wheat traditionally grown south of the Yangtze and spring wheat in the northeast.
38 The regional dimension of grain sector developments in the 1980s and 1990s is explored in some detail elsewhere: see Robert F. Ash, 'Grain self-sufficiency in mainland China: a continuing imperative' in R.F. Ash, R.L. Edmonds and Yu-ming Shaw (Ed.), *Perspectives on Contemporary China in Transition*, Taipei, 1997; Ash, 'The performance of China's grain sector: a regional perspective' in Organisation for Economic Co-operation and Development (OECD), *China in the Global Economy: Agricultural Policies in China*, Paris: OECD, 1997; and Ash, 'The grain issue in China: domestic and international perspectives' in M. Brosseau, Kuan Hsin-chi and Y.Y. Kueh (Ed.) *China Review 1997*, Hong Kong, 1997, which also sets out the regional typology used in all these sources, see esp. ibid., p. 153, note 18.
39 For 1995–1997 alone, the corresponding figures are 56% and 44% in favour of the south.

China is likely to continue to carry the burden of future grain output growth and remain the main source of exports to other parts of the country. The goal of attaining self-sufficiency in central-eastern provinces by the end of the century is an ambitious one, and other southern regions are likely to remain in deficit.[40] Chinese plans are explicit in identifying northern provinces and regions, such as Heilongjiang, Jilin, Henan and Inner Mongolia, as offering the best prospects for future increases in grain supplies.

A vertical regional delineation of China that distinguishes eastern, central and western regions is a useful framework, in which to highlight important structural differences in farming activities between different parts of the countries – differences that have important economic and welfare implications.[41] Relevant indicators suggest that one effect of post-1978 reforms has been to promote rural economic diversification throughout the country, but in varying degrees. For example, rural industrialisation has favoured eastern regions much more than interior provinces, while the decline in the agricultural contribution to rural value-output has also been most marked in coastal areas. Within agriculture, crop farming – the least remunerative branch of farming – has also loomed much larger in central and western China. In short, a smaller proportion of the rural labour force is engaged in high-return rural industrial and other non-farming rural activities in the interior, compared with their coastal counterparts; and of those still primarily engaged in agriculture, more depend on crop farming in central and western China than elsewhere. Just how serious such differentials remain is indicated by data for 1998, which show that the share of TVEs in rural net output was 67% in eastern China, compared with 57% and 41% in central and western regions.[42] In the same year, crop farming's contribution to value-added production in farming 'proper' was 59% and 62% in coastal and central provinces, but 69% in western regions.[43]

Chinese agriculture and the international economy

China's increasing involvement in global markets and its exposure to international competition will pose many challenges for its agricultural sector. In particular, as China enters the WTO, the experience of other East Asian countries, such as Japan, Taiwan and South Korea, suggests that policy-makers will need to exert considerable care in order to obviate

40 In particular, the constraints on grain output growth in Guangdong and Fujian, which together contribute more than 60% of total grain output in the south, should not be under-estimated.

41 This is explored in Robert F. Ash, 'Challenges and opportunities facing the rural sector in China' in Joseph Y.S. Cheng (Ed.), *China Review 1998*, Hong Kong, 1998, pp. 431–53.

42 To state the same broad finding in different terms, the east accounted for 60% of value-added production by all TVEs, compared with 31% and 9% in central and western China, State Statistical Bureau, *Rural Statistical Yearbook of China, 1999*, p. 308.

43 State Statistical Bureau, *Rural Statistical Yearbook of China*, Beijing, 1999, p. 96.

economic and social tensions in the farm sector in the wake of accelerated trade liberalisation.

It is clear that China's accession to the WTO will have a major impact on the farm sector. Some Chinese economists argue that protectionist policies in agriculture will be essential to both the maintenance of food security and the momentum of overall economic development. Such arguments are not persuasive: self-sufficiency and trade restrictions are not an efficient way of protecting farmers' incomes. But it would be idle to ignore the possibility of increasing *demands* for agricultural protectionism, as the negative effects of WTO membership on farmers make themselves felt.

If WTO membership enables China to raise its exports of labour-intensive goods, expanding domestic output in associated industries will generate new job opportunities and may facilitate a transfer of labour displaced from the farm sector. But with the number of farm surplus workers running at between 150 and 200 million, a rapid post-WTO rise in food and other agricultural imports could also impose an unsustainable burden of adjustment on farmers, whose alternative employment opportunities may become increasingly scarce. In any case, the success of any programme of large-scale labour reallocation implies active and costly government intervention in order to co-ordinate and accommodate such changes.

Officially, WTO membership is seen as an opportunity to facilitate the further development of the farm sector and rural economy. First, closer integration in the world economy will support agricultural modernisation by encouraging foreign investment, making possible more effective international agricultural co-operation and facilitating the highly capital-intensive process whereby new scientific techniques are introduced and applied over the entire range of farm activities. WTO accession will also encourage restructuring of the farm sector and generate new sources of farm exports – for example, fruit, vegetables, aquatic and animal-related products – that more closely reflect China's comparative advantage. Through non-discriminatory trade treatment, negotiating and transactions costs of formulating commercial contracts in farm products may be lowered.

Such longer-term gains must, however, be set against what may be significant initial costs for the agricultural sector. In the short run, WTO membership will reduce the profitability, output and income of some farmers by exposing their inefficient and costly production methods to outside competition. The impact will not be the same for all branches of farming, nor, in particular, for all crops.[44] Nor should the *regional* impact of WTO membership be ignored. In the grain sector, different regions will be affected in different ways and degrees. In areas specialising in the production of wheat, maize and soyabeans – especially in north and north-eastern China – the effect of rising imports is likely to be significant, as regions unable to meet feed and other requirements increasingly turn to

44 For example some have argued that the removal of import quotas will have a significant impact on cotton farmers. This is one perspective against which to assess the abolition, in 1999, of state-set purchase prices for cotton.

direct imports of such goods from abroad. The consequences of such changes for farm incomes in these regions could be serious.

Such challenges define the policy response of the Chinese government. Likely measures include the establishment by central and local governments of funds and farm insurance schemes, designed to facilitate adjustments and provide compensation for peasants whose interests are damaged by accession to the WTO. The institution of quality norms and improvements in agricultural marketing arrangements will also assist in upgrading quality and thereby facilitating an increase in farm exports.

Concluding remarks

It would be idle to ignore important continuities in agricultural development that flow across the historic watershed of the Third Plenum of the Eleventh CCP Central Committee (December 1978). Their recurrence throughout five decades of communist rule in China highlight profound dilemmas that have confronted the government in its efforts to promote the rapid and sustained growth of the farm sector in pursuit of the fulfillment of its developmental role.

For example, finding the most appropriate balance between private and public land ownership, or between centralised and decentralised decision-making in agriculture is far from easy. The contrasting experiences of China in the second half of the 1950s and after the mid-1980s highlight critical policy dilemmas, associated with the differing motivations of farmers when they act, on the one hand, as agents of state plans, or, on the other, as individual decision makers. Following collectivisation in 1955–1956, Mao's government found it prudent to allow farmers to retain private plots. No less significantly, following decollectivisation in the 1980s, Deng's government formulated a strategy based on the establishment of a 'two-tier operational system' in an attempt to integrate family-based farming into a framework of socialised services.[45]

Identifying the most desirable scale of farming reflects another policy dilemma. There are strong theoretical and empirical cases in favour of both small-scale, household-based farming and large-scale, collectivised agriculture. But as China's experience before and after 1978 again demonstrates, unqualified policy advocacy of either presents policy-makers with questions to which there is no easy answer.

In China, all these issues are strongly inter-related. With heavy population pressure on a limited arable base, the egalitarian distribution of the rights to land use or land ownership must generate small-scale

---

45 See remarks by Jiang Zemin in Hefei on 28 September 1998, where he is reported to have said' 'The general target for deepening rural economic structural reform is to establish a rural economic structure suited to the development of the Socialist Market Economy, based on the household output-related contract system and supported by the agricultural socialised service system, the agricultural products market system, and the state assistance and protection system for agriculture ...' British Broadcasting Corporation, *Summary of World Broadcasts,* FE/3344, 29 September 1998.

farming. Even if, as in the early 1950s and 1980s, improved incentives are reflected in economic and welfare gains – higher yields and higher personal incomes – other consequences may be less desirable. For example, small-scale farming may impede technical improvements, as well as weakening the ability of the state to fulfil important distributional and other welfare objectives.

Moral economy considerations are also important. A central issue is the nature of élite-mass relations in the countryside, most dramatically captured in the struggle over the disposal of the harvest. To characterise the relationship between state and peasant as that of 'two actors of unequal status' succinctly captures the pattern of clientelist rule in the Chinese countryside.[46] The response to early post-1978 rural reforms throws these entrenched positions into relief by highlighting the growing power of Chinese peasants vis-à-vis the state. If such evidence underlines the constraints on farmers' maneuverability under the former collective framework, the evolving institutional framework of agriculture in the 1990s demonstrates the limits to 'peasant power', not least as new forms of exploitation of farmers emerged, through the issue of so-called 'IOUs' and the imposition of illegal financial levies.

These moral economy dimensions, as well as the policy dilemmas mentioned earlier are an important part of the backcloth against which any assessment of China's agricultural reforms must be made. The heightened economic and social tensions inherent in such dilemmas explain why, despite the declining economic importance of agriculture, the farm sector remains such a sensitive area of concern to Chinese policy-makers at the beginning of the twenty-first century.

Document 5.1

'Why did China's reforms start in the countryside?'

WU XIANG

China's Human Resources Development, 1994, No. 1

[Between 1949 and 1978, China made great progress towards creating an independent and comprehensive industrial system. But rapid industrial development, accompanied by much slower agricultural growth, generated economic polarisation, which showed no signs of abating. As the population continued to grow, many people faced increasing hardship. In particular, large numbers of peasants lived in conditions of poverty, backwardness and even hunger. Far from

---

46 Jean Oi, *State and Peasant in Contemporary China: The Political Economy of Village Government*, Berkeley, California: University of California Press, 1989, p. 128.

everyone sharing in common prosperity, general poverty became the norm. For many years, this reality was not recognized. Only after the upheavals of the 'Cultural Revolution Decade' did people begin to ask whether conditions in China were those of true 'socialism'. Deng Xiaoping's answer – 'poverty is not socialism' – was unequivocal and paved the way for subsequent reforms (Ed.)]

The three 'Third Plenums' that launched and promoted the reforms

The reforms were initiated at the Third Plenary Session of the Eleventh CCP Central Committee (CCPCC). For the next 15 years, GDP grew by 9% a year – a rate of expansion that exceeded all expectations and heralded an economic miracle virtually unprecedented in world history.

The earliest reform successes were achieved in the countryside. After the People's Communes had been replaced by contractual arrangements with households (including the system of contracted responsibilities, with payment linked to output), farmers gained operational autonomy over the use of land and the right to dispose freely of most agricultural products. Feng Yangren's simple statement – 'once a peasant's state quota and collective contribution had been fulfilled, the rest was his to dispose of as he wished' – captured the principle of 'to each according to his effort' and showed the correct way to accommodate the interests of the state, collective and individual.

Such policies won the enthusiasm and inspired the creativity of huge numbers of farmers, resulting in large increases in agricultural production year after year. Between 1979 and 1984, total grain production rose in two consecutive stages to reach over 400 million tons (equivalent to 400 kilograms per head of total population and close to the world average). As a result, China's historical problems of food shortages and hunger were basically solved. Even allowing for significant fluctuations in output, the general health of the farm sector continued to flourish. By 1992, China ranked first in the world in the production of seven agricultural products – grain, cotton, oil-bearing crops, aquatic products, meat, natural silk and fruit – even if in per capita terms, it had still not wholly eradicated poverty and backwardness.

The practice of household contracting[47] might easily be mistaken for the 'individualism' that had defined farming methods before co-operativisation. In reality, however, it represented a new socialist system of farm management, characterised by an integrated two-tier operational system, in which publicly-owned land was managed by the household. The enthusiasm with which farmers greeted the new arrangements is explained

---

47 Here, the text refers to the practice of 'contracting output to the household' (*baochan daohu*), not the more radical form of 'contracting everything to the household' (*baogan daohu*). (Ed.)

by its embodiment of three elements: autonomy, freedom, and material benefit.

The deeper significance of these reforms is that they breathed new life into the rural economy, following a long period of suffocation under the Commune System. Thus, most agricultural products were liberalised and became available on the open market. Factors of production, such as technology, labour and capital, began to circulate freely, facilitating improvements in resource allocation. In particular, farmers ceased to be mere manual labourers and became independent commercial producers. Assuming sole responsibility for profits and losses, they became a mainstay of China's market economy. Without this precondition, China could never have experienced such a rapid expansion of its rural or national commercial economy. As Theodor Schultz, the famous American Nobel-Prize-winning economist, commented: 'Household responsibility systems have become the main driving force behind all the changes in China's rural economy.'

Under the impact of the 'first Third Plenum', accelerated growth of the commercial economy stimulated the enthusiasm of China's peasants, or 80% of the total population. Not even the most perceptive observer could have predicted the chain reaction that resulted. As the reforms spread and intensified, and as the commercial economy expanded, a continuous supply of new talent and new ideas emerged in the countryside. Everywhere, people had high-quality grain to eat, new clothes to wear, and tile-roofed houses to live in.

But the most remarkable development of all was the rapid growth of rural industry (usually referred to as 'township and rural enterprises') and tertiary industry, and the creation of a large number of 'rural cities and towns'. Township and rural enterprises, described by Deng Xiaoping as a 'major new force', have been the second most important rural initiative after household contracting. Their expansion marked the first decisive step towards breaking down the economic and social barriers between the urban and rural sectors. It also posed a strong challenge to traditional models of development and highlighted demands by China's huge rural population to participate directly in the processes of industrialisation, urbanisation and modernisation. New models of industrialisation and urbanisation with their own Chinese characteristics were spawned. These promoted the accelerated growth of Chinese industry and, by facilitating urban and rural reforms, had a beneficial impact on the whole economic system. This was the basis of a new style of 'socialism with Chinese characteristics'.

[The 'Decision on the reform of the economic structure', promulgated at the Third Plenum of the Twelfth CCP Central Committee, defined a socialist economy as a commercial economy with planning, built on the foundations of public ownership. By showing the erroneousness of the view that socialism and a commercial market were incompatible, this was an important break-through and encouraged the shift towards a market system in China. Although the ambiguity inherent in the notion of 'a commercial economy with planning' continued to generate debate about whether plans and markets were by nature socialist or capitalist, the reforms continued until, at the end of 1980s, political upheavals at home and abroad – especially the collapse of the former USSR – intervened.

Early in 1992, the intervention of Deng Xiaoping effectively initiated a new phase of accelerated economic reform and established the theoretical foundation for the development of a 'socialist market economy'. Following the Fourteenth Party Congress, which formally enshrined the establishment of a socialist market economy as the core of China's economic reforms, the Third Plenum of the Fourteenth CCP Central Committee urged the formulation of a comprehensive plan to develop a socialist market economic system. (Ed.)]

The weakest link was the most severely squeezed

A major characteristic of China's reforms is that they were first implemented in the countryside. Why should the first breakthrough have occurred in the countryside?

The answer is simple. The vast numbers that make up the rural population were the most severely affected by the economic system of central planning. Having suffered the greatest losses, they were the most vociferous in their demands for reform. Furthermore, this huge, scattered rural population were the weakest link in the planned economy.

Guided by the spirit of the Third Plenum of the Eleventh CCP Central Committee, the vast rural population had spontaneously begun to experiment with various kinds of arrangements under which earnings were linked to output – experiments that signified the implementation of systemic reforms in agriculture. The structure of the rural economy was relatively simple and subject to fewer external influences than urban industry. As a result, the piecemeal reforms in agriculture did not at first attract much attention. Only later, after they had gained formal government approval and support, did rural reform become a national craze. 'If you deliberately plant a flower, it will not bloom; but if you inadvertently plant a willow, it will provide you with shade' – in other words, actions that appear arbitrary have a kind of inevitable internal logic.

After three years of economic recovery, in 1953 China launched a national programme of large-scale industrial construction, modelled on the USSR, in which priority was given to the development of heavy industry and the implementation of a highly-centralised planned economic system. Heavy industry made great infrastructural demands, offered few opportunities for employment, and required large inputs of capital with long gestation periods. Given China's backwardness and agricultural orientation, the sole source of such funds were 'peasant contributions', extracted through the implementation of a 'unified purchase and sale system' through the maintenance of a scissors differential between agricultural and industrial prices. Farm products, having been purchased at low prices fixed by the state, were sold to urban residents and industrial enterprises at a similarly low price in order to minimize wages and material costs in heavy industry. In this way, the state was able to tax the high profits enjoyed by heavy industry and the use the revenue to invest in further capital construction projects to the benefit of accelerated industrialisation. It is estimated that from initial industrialisation in the early 1950s to the launch of the reforms almost 30 years later, by maintaining the price scissors, the rural population indirectly paid the equivalent of over 800 billion *yuan* in taxes.

But despite its major contribution to industrialisation, the rural population failed to enjoy a fair share of the cultural and other benefits tat industrialisation had brought. Throughout the period in which egalitarianism was so much emphasized, it was the rural population who suffered the most. Although they were allowed to 'eat food from the same bowl', they were never given the luxury of the 'iron rice bowl' that was enjoyed by workers in urban enterprises. Their employment, medical care and welfare were not guaranteed. Rural residents had to bear the full responsibility for all costs related to birth, old age, sickness and death. They were treated like 'second class citizens'. During the initial period of industrialisation, there was a spontaneous migration of people from the countryside to the cities and some rural dwellers found employment as industrial workers. But in the early 1960s, these migrant workers – by now totalling some 20 million – were returned to the countryside. This retarded the pace of urbanisation and impeded the growth of rural industrialisation.

Even more serious was the mistaken 'leftist' ideology that began with fully-socialist collectivisation, was exacerbated by the 'Great Leap Forward', and reached its apotheosis in the 'ten years of chaos' [the Cultural Revolution]. In the countryside, this ideology manifested itself in the 'learn from Dazhai' Campaign. Dazhai – a small mountain village in Xiyang County, Shanxi Province – initially deserved its reputation as a model of hard struggle and construction in a mountainous region. But in 1965, Mao called on agriculture to 'learn from Dazhai' – a slogan that was later adopted by the 'gang of four' in order to advance Dazhai as a so-called 'typical model of continuing revolution under the dictatorship of the proletariat' and promote their ultra-leftist line. In effect, the Learn from Dazhai Campaign sought to 'use the methods of the dictatorship of the proletariat in order to engage in agriculture' and gave rise to the following major hazards:

• **Endless transition.** Emphasis on 'size and public ownership' meant that socialism came to imply ever-increasing scales of production and public ownership. The ownership of factors of production, the scale of communes and brigades, the forms of labour organisation, the methods of administration and management – all were jumbled together. There was blind advocacy of elevating the accounting unit from the production team to brigade and commune levels, regardless of the differing levels of the development of productive forces. The individual economy was rejected and commercial production came under attack. As a result, commercial markets were equated with capitalism and private plots of land and households' sideline activities were abolished in order to 'cut off the tail of capitalism'. Village fairs were branded 'free capitalist markets' and there were exhortations to 'block the capitalist road in order to clear the path for socialism'. 'Cutting off the tail' and 'sealing off the market' became national slogans, creating anxiety and chaos.

• **Chaotic patterns of work.** This was an inevitable outcome of an allocation system based on 'everyone eating from the same bowl'. After the communes were set up, a food supply system was initiated, communal dining halls established, and everyone was allowed to eat free of charge. This system later became unsustainable, forcing communes to retreat to work point-related methods of allocation and 'a three-tier system of ownership based on the brigade'. Work points were calculated according to labour norms. But the norms for farm work were so complicated that it proved impossible to calculate work points accurately. As a result, work points were allocated and recorded inflexibly, leading to frenzied and uncoordinated working patterns. The reward was the same, no matter how hard or how long a person worked.

Such problems were exacerbated by the Learn from Dazhai Campaign, when the allocation of work points was wholly divorced from the quantity or quality of labour input. This invited the passive resistance on the part of commune members, who in the face of the almost random allocation of work points increasingly began to loaf on the job. The working day was long, but work efficiency was very low. Even working for an entire year was insufficient to guarantee subsistence food and clothing. In such circumstances, who could possibly maintain enthusiasm?

• **Confused directions.** The unified integration of commune management and government administration made administration and economics blurred and indistinct. Power was concentrated in the hands of the Secretary, whose recourse to coercion and commandism created an atmosphere in which formalism, deception, exaggeration and egalitarianism could flourish. Regardless of objective conditions, other regions felt compelled to copy initiatives taken by Dazhai, even in the knowledge that such work would be to no avail and would cause serious financial damage. Refusal meant being criticized for not learning from Dazhai.

The system of unified purchases and sales, the People's Communes and the guiding 'leftist' ideology all conspired to ossify the system of rules and regulations in the countryside. Restrictions on the free movement of the rural population became increasingly tight until farmers were completely bound to the land they were born on, with no chance of leaving it. The rural economy suffered great damage, particularly during the Cultural Revolution and the

'Learn from Dazhai' campaign, leaving the rural population in a mental and physical straitjacket. As the Secretary of Heze District Party Committee in Shandong put it to the author in 1980, 'leftist' mistakes in the countryside could be summed up as an obsession with size, public ownership, egalitarianism and unified planning. The inevitable outcome was poverty. People became so poor that they did not even have enough food to eat and had no alternative but to rely on supplies, loans, and relief funds from the state to see them through. Because of the existence of this safety net, everyone tried to claim relief funds. But the more they claimed, the poorer they became, generating a heightened state of dependency. These factors fed on each other to generate a spiralling vicious circle, which destroyed any incentives for farmers – the mainstay of the socialist collective economy.

In 1978, the average per capita net income of farmers was 133.57 *yuan*, compared with 60.62 *yuan* in 1957 (implying an average rate of growth of 2.9% p.a.). More than 90% of this was paid in kind, leaving less than 10% as money income. Some 200 million people still lacked sufficient food and clothing. A contemporary report from one poor region pointed out that farmers had not only been stripped of their property, but had also been robbed of their freedom – these two factors being the main sources of persistent rural poverty since the 1950s. In general, only because of the close ties that had developed between Party and peasants during the [pre-1949] years of struggle and the long period of peace enjoyed by the peasants after 1949, did farmers hold back from taking direct action. As of 1978, the danger was that unless major rural policy changes were introduced, farmers – in poor and more prosperous regions – would rise up and overthrow the entire edifice.

The results of emancipating people's minds and seeking truth from facts

The quiet emergence of household-contracting in 1978–1979 did not mark its first appearance in China. In 1957 and 1959, household-contracting had been adopted quite widely in areas such as Wenzhou (Zhejiang Province), Wuhu (Anhui) and Jiangjin (Sichuan). In 1961, 'responsibility fields' had been introduced throughout Anhui province, although persistent attacks and criticism caused them to be abandoned. But 'not even a prairie fire can destroy the grass; it grows again when the spring breeze blows'. Between winter 1978 and spring 1979, household-contracting emerged on an even wider scale to become the first wave of China's reforms, achieving great success as it spread throughout the country.

This success is largely attributable to the watershed Third Plenary Session of the Eleventh CCPCC. Coming after the 10 years of chaos, this meeting was like the coming of spring after a decade of severe frost and snow. The spring breeze wafted over China and the spring rains began to thaw the frozen earth. The environment had changed, the times had changed: a new era of reform and liberalisation had begun.

[Following Mao Zedong's death, the arrest of the 'gang of four' (October 1976) and the official ending of the Cultural Revolution, endorsed by the Eleventh National CCP Congress (August 1977), paved the way for a reappraisal of China's economic condition. Deng Xiaoping's advocacy of the maxim that 'the only criterion for examining truth is practice' was an important ideological turning point, facilitating a sober assessment of Mao's later years. By 1978, the relaxation of earlier political and ideological constraints offered active encouragement to economic reform. The most dramatic expression of the new thinking was the reformist thrust of the communiqué of the Third Plenum of the Eleventh CCPCC (December 1978). In particular, its advocacy of the 'four musts' – the need to devolve power and enhance enterprise autonomy, to streamline administrative and economic structures, to observe economic rules (including the 'law of value'), and to institute clear lines of responsibilities in economic work – foreshadowed subsequent comprehensive, wide-ranging reforms. (Ed.)]

The 'Draft decision of the CCPCC on some questions concerning the acceleration of agricultural development', adopted at the Third Plenum gave a major impetus to rural reform. It was sent to every province, municipality and autonomous region in the country for discussion and trial implementation. From the perspectives of Marxism-Leninism and Mao Zedong Thought, it summed up the positive and negative features of agricultural production since 1949. It was strongly critical of the 'leftist' errors that had for so long infected the agriculture front, and included the following explicit statement:

'In general, Chinese agricultural development has been slow for almost 20 years. This is incompatible with the needs of the people and the demands of the "Four Modernisations"'.

Such remarks highlighted the central importance of agriculture and placed agricultural issues at the top of the agenda of both Party and people. The seven major 'lessons of experience' mentioned in the 'Draft' were all criticisms of 'leftist' errors that had violated natural and economic laws, robbed production teams and individual farmers of their rightful autonomy, and damaged production incentives. The 'Draft' also included 25 pages of agricultural and rural economic policy, the main thrust of which was as follows:

- The production teams' ownership rights and autonomy should be protected. Neither work units nor individuals should be allowed free access to a team's labour, land, livestock, machinery, funds, products or material resources.
- Private plots and private livestock should be restored to commune members, who should also be allowed to engage in household sideline

production and rural market trading. Farmers should be encouraged to practise such activities in order to boost personal income.

- The state purchase price of grain should be raised by 20%, and the above-quota price increased by an additional 50%. Purchase prices of cotton, oil-bearing crops, sugar, livestock products, aquatic products and forestry products, etc. were also to be raised, as appropriate.

- The base for the monopoly purchase of grain should be reduced and poor regions were to be partly exempted from requisitions and agricultural taxation. Excessive quotas of grain were to be avoided (it was later decided to import 10–15 million tons of grain per year).

- There should be rapid output growth of chemical fertiliser, pesticides, agricultural plastics and other agroindustrial products. The quality of such products should be guaranteed and their purchase price cut, in accordance with lower costs of production (the benefits of which were to accrue to the farmers themselves).

- Subject to prioritising grain production, attention should also be given to cash crops such as cotton, oil-bearing crops and sugar. Grain and cash crop production should be simultaneously developed, as should the various branches of agriculture, forestry, animal husbandry, sideline industries and fishing.

- Encouragement of the establishment of brigade-run enterprises should be enhanced by state policies, such as tax concessions or tax exemptions in accordance with specific conditions.

- Agricultural loans should be increased and agricultural credit at low or minimal rates of interest extended systematically for designated projects and over specific periods.

- The State Council should set up a special committee to conduct overall planning and give special financial, material and technological support to marginal and remote regions, national minority regions and old revolutionary base areas in order to assist in the development of production and removal of poverty.

Such policies contributed much to improving farm incentives, promoting output growth and boosting the rural economy. But historical factors made it impossible to address the problem of distributional egalitarianism; instead, the need to strengthen quota management was stressed and rules were formulated in an attempt to limit household-contracting and prevent farmers from going it alone. In fact, in he wake of years of constant attack and criticism, there was no clear understanding of the differences between household-contracting and 'going it alone'. Contracting output to the household had become equated with following the capitalist road – a misconception that was deeply embedded in people's minds and therefore extremely difficult to correct.

The Draft Decision not only promoted appropriate policies to boost the development of agricultural production, it also rectified the 'leftist' mistakes that had been the guiding ideology for so long. It stressed the importance of proceeding in accordance with China's concrete reality, adhering to natural and economic laws, and guaranteeing incentives for the production team and individual farmers. Thus:

'The main point of departure for reforming agricultural production and the rural economy is to give free rein to the superiority of socialism, and give full play to the enthusiasm of China's 800 million peasants. We must strengthen socialist education in rural areas and pay close attention to the material benefits and political power of the rural population. Enthusiasm will not emerge naturally and spontaneously at all levels of production and administration. Whether or not our reforms can meet the need for the development of China's productive forces will depend on their ability to inspire the enthusiasm of the rural labour force.'

These important words embody the spirit of the Third Plenary Session of the Eleventh CCPCC with regard to the question of agriculture. They provided the guiding ideology for agricultural production and rural work as a whole. The formulation of these clear, precise guiding principles also set out some of the essential preconditions for achieving a new course of agricultural production. China's subsequent experience shows that farmers have benefited materially and enhanced their democratic power. As a result, their enthusiasm has risen continuously.

Document 5.2

'Learning from Comrade Deng Xiaoping's exposition of agricultural problems'

SUN ZHONGHUA AND LI SHAOHUA

China's Rural Economy, 1997, No. 3

Comrade Deng Xiaoping's exposition of agricultural problems was a major part of his theory of establishing socialism with Chinese characteristics. In order to enhance agricultural and rural work, it is extremely important that when they study Comrade Deng's theory of establishing socialism with Chinese characteristics, Party members and cadres who at the agricultural front-line should carefully examine his exposition of agricultural problems. Volumes 1–3 of the *Selected Writings of Deng Xiaoping* discuss China's agricultural problems at length. We believe that what follows captures the main aspects of this discussion.

Agriculture is the foundation and the strategic focus

Volumes 1–3 of the *Selected Works of Deng Xiaoping* show that Comrade Deng viewed agriculture as the foundation and the strategic focus, and placed the resolution of agricultural and rural problems at the top of every work agenda. This way of thinking was a basic starting-point for him in formulating and guiding China's policy of reform and opening to the outside world, and in promoting its economic development.

In 1962, in a discussion of how best to revive farm production, he pointed out:

> If we don't get agriculture right, there is no hope for industry, nor will it be possible to solve the problems of food, clothing and articles for daily use.

In 1963, at a conference on problems in industrial development, he stressed:

> If we rank agriculture, light industry and heavy industry first, second and third, we will be able to promote faster and more effective long-term development. For the time being, the emphasis of our work must reflect policies, which take agriculture as the foundation and which seek to find appropriate solutions to problems relating to food, clothing and articles for daily use.

In the mid-1970s, not long after resuming work, he emphasised that top priority should go to agriculture, pointing out that:

> The modernisation of agriculture is the key to realising the four modernisations.

At the beginning of the 1980s, when formulating the goals of China's development strategy, he commented:

> The prime strategic focus is agriculture, the second is energy resources and transport, and the third is education and science.

He repeatedly urged people not to forget that 'agriculture is the foundation.' In 1990, when talking to a number of responsible comrades from the Central Committee, he again stressed:

> We must address the problems of agriculture. It is easy for rural areas to become rich, but it is also easy for them to remain poor. The land only has to be farmed badly and agriculture will be finished.

Why should agriculture receive such emphasis? Whenever Comrade Deng investigated this question, his analysis generally proceeded from the following premises:

First, making sure that everyone has enough food to eat has always been a major problem for China. Summing up the lessons of domestic construction during the three years of hardship, he said, 'our weak point now is agriculture. Every year there is intense pressure from the addition of another ten or twenty million people who need food, clothing and articles of daily use.' Again in 1982, in a comment on China's economic construction, he stated 'no matter what happens in our country, as long as people have enough to eat, everything else will be easy.'

Second, the development of agriculture is the foundation stone on which the development of heavy industry and of the entire national economy should proceed. Deng pointed out 'unless we make a good job of agriculture, industry will be held back ... If we fail to make a good job of it, we may well hold back the whole of our state construction ... Industrial development, commercial and other economic activities cannot be founded on the poverty of 80% of the population.' Hence, his demand that 'to develop our industrial sector, we must establish an ideology that is founded on agriculture and that serves agriculture ... The more industry develops, the more we must put agriculture first.'

Third, rural development and stability are the basis of national development and stability. In June 1984, at a meeting with foreign visitors, Deng said, 'starting from the reality of current conditions, we are trying to solve the problems of the rural areas first. 80% of China's population live in the countryside, and the stability of China depends primarily on the stability of those 80%. ... To see whether China's economy can develop, we must first see whether the countryside can develop and whether the life of the farmers is improving.'

All these remarks show that Deng's perception of agriculture as the foundation and strategic focus, and his emphasis on resolving agricultural and rural problems before all others were rooted in China's basic situation. His analysis reflected the relationships between agriculture and industry, agriculture and commerce, agriculture and the whole of our national economic development. It was driven by the strategic imperative of overall social stability and economic development.

Deng's analysis reflected the objective laws of economic development and offered a scientific summing-up of the historical experience of China's economic development since 1949. That experience shows that whenever the emphasis has been on agriculture, our economic construction has progressed. Otherwise, it has stagnated or even retrogressed. The major fluctuations in the national economy have all been caused by major fluctuations in agriculture. Whenever the economy has developed smoothly, agriculture has been flourishing. Whenever it has been in difficulties, the problems have started with agriculture. Every economic readjustment has had its origins in the strengthening of agriculture. Hence, Deng's injunction: 'We must consistently get to grips with agricultural problems ... If agriculture takes a wrong turn it will take four or five years to put it right.' We must never forget these words and we must always steadfastly maintain agriculture's fundamental position and give it first priority in our economic work.

The third generation central leadership collective centred around Comrade Jiang Zemin has repeatedly stressed the importance of inculcating all Party members (especially leading cadres) with a proper understanding of Deng's theory of establishing socialism with Chinese characteristics and the need to place major emphasis on agricultural issues in implementing reform and pursuing socialist modernisation. At the Central Conference on Work in Rural Areas held in 1993, Jiang called on 'all Party comrades to make a serious study of Comrade Deng Xiaoping's analysis of agricultural problems, sum up our country's historical experience, and establish even more firmly the guiding ideology that agriculture is the foundation.' Against the background of agriculture having been neglected or weakened during the previous few years, he emphasised that:

> In setting up a socialist market economy system, we must continue firmly and unshakeably to carry out the policy of taking agriculture as the foundation, and we must give agriculture top priority in our economic work. The more we accelerate reform and opening up, the more we must address, safeguard and strengthen agriculture.

In recent years, the Party Central Committee and State Council have frequently held special conferences to study agricultural and rural work, and formulated various policy measures to strengthen agriculture. Provided that all Party comrades and leading cadres have a sound understanding of Deng's thoughts on agriculture as the foundation and strategic focus, and as long as they give proper regard to agriculture and implement all the policy measures of the Party Central Committee and the State Council designed to strengthen agriculture, we can promote sustained agricultural and rural growth and development, and maintain the momentum of reform and modernisation.

The key to agricultural development is to respect the initiative of the farmers, and protect and mobilise their enthusiasm for production

Comrade Deng Xiaoping was the principal architect of China's reforms and open-door policy. A major theme that permeates his thinking on rural reform is the integration of the basic Marxist principle that the relations of production should accord with the level of productive forces, with the realities of the Chinese countryside. He regarded the mobilisation of farmers' production enthusiasm and the development of rural productive forces as the basic parameters of rural reform, and treated the interests and wishes of farmers as the basis on which all Party policies in rural areas should be formulated. These maxims have facilitated the successful pursuit of rural reform in China and will continue to do so. In studying Deng's analysis of rural reform, the points we can learn most from are as follows:

• **The essence of rural reform is the adjustment of rural relations of production, so that they fit in with the level of productive forces in the countryside: this is a reform that has revolutionary significance.** Comrade

Deng noted that, 'from the present perspective, the solution to the problems of agriculture still lies with the relations of production ... As for the most appropriate ultimate form of such production relations, it is probably best to proceed on the premise that whichever form serves most easily and rapidly to restore and develop agricultural production should be adopted; and whichever form the masses want to adopt should similarly be adopted and legitimised.' This view fully embodies the basic Marxist tenet that the relations of production should adapt to the level of the forces of production, and makes clear the basic principle to which rural reform should adhere. After the Third Plenum of the Eleventh Central Committee, the system of People's Communes was abandoned and the household-based contract responsibility system, with remuneration linked to output, was instituted. This accords with the nature of farm production and the level of development of rural forces of production at the present stage. This revolutionary institutional reform removed the systemic obstacles that had previously constrained the development of rural forces of production, and fundamentally transformed the relations of production in rural areas.

• **The basic starting-point for rural reform is to motivate the hundreds of millions of farmers.** Deng observed that 'generally speaking, reform in the countryside means operating the responsibility system, throwing out the system of everyone eating from a communal pot, and motivating the farmers ... The most important thing is to motivate people and transfer rights to lower levels. The reason our rural reforms have been effective is that they have conferred greater autonomy on farmers and given them motivation.' Through the responsibility system, family-run operations have been drawn into the collective economy in rural areas, and a two-tier management system has been created, which combines centralisation with decentralisation and allows the farmers to gain autonomy in production management, thereby greatly enhancing their production enthusiasm. In guiding rural reform, on the premise, the Party has formulated a series of basic policies, designed to motivate farmers. These include: instituting the responsibility system; establishing a wholly integrated two-tier management system that combines centralisation with decentralisation; keeping the system of public ownership as the mainstay, while promoting the overall development of a diversified economy; permitting and encouraging some people to get rich first by honest labour and lawful business operations, with the aim of prosperity for all; never allowing grain production to slacken, while actively developing a diversified economy (including township and village enterprises); rationalising the prices of agricultural products and promoting reform of the product distribution system; and reducing the burden on farmers and helping poorer areas to develop their economies.

• **The basic method and experience of promoting rural reform are to respect farmers' spirit of initiative and their way of putting things into practice, always starting from the actual situation.** More than a decade of rural reform shows how it has constantly been carried forward and deepened by the farmers themselves. Deng Xiaoping had great respect for the initiative of the masses and pointed out, 'farmers are the patent holders of the rural responsibility system. Many aspects of the rural reforms have been created at grass-roots level: we have simply processed and upgraded them to be a guide for the whole country.' Against the background of hesitation and prevarication with which many comrades regarded the responsibility system in the early stages of reform, Deng said, 'the Central Committee's policy is to wait and let them be educated by the facts ... Our policy is to let people watch. Letting them watch is much better than compulsion ... Not getting into arguments is a great discovery of mine. Not arguing means you have more time to do things. As soon as you start to argue, things get complicated and by wasting all your time in arguing you never get anything done. Be bold enough to try something, to rush in and do it, without arguing about it. Rural reform is like that, and urban reform should be the same.' These words of Comrade Deng explain the basic method of rural reform and capture the essence of its success.

• **Basic rural policies should remain stable for a long period of time and be constantly improved.** Ever since the Third Plenum of the Eleventh Central Committee, the Party's basic rural policies have maximised the motivation of the hundreds of millions of China's farmers, accommodating their wishes and their inborn dislike of change. Deng often stressed the need to hold firm to a long-term, stable and unchanging basic rural policy, pointing out (1984), 'if we were to change present policy, it would damage both the state and the people; the people would not approve – and above all the eight hundred million farmers would not approve. If rural policy changed, their standard of living would fall at once.' In 1991, the Eighth Plenum of the Thirteenth Central Committee systematically set out the Party's basic policies in rural areas, and made the explicit proposal that 'we should make the responsibility system, and the two-tier management system combining centralisation and decentralisation, basic institutions of our collective economic organisation in rural areas, maintaining their stability for a long period while consistently seeking to make substantial improvements to them.' Deng approved, stating: 'This Eighth Plenum of the Thirteenth Central Committee has been a good meeting, and has confirmed that the responsibility system in the countryside will not be changed. If it were to change, people would feel uneasy and say that the policies of the Central Committee had changed .... The stability of the basic reform policies in the towns and in the countryside must be maintained for the long-term. We shall, of course, make whatever improvements or repairs are necessary, in line with developments that occur during the implementation of the policies. But we must always remain consistent.'

• **Looked at in the long-term, rural reform and development must make 'two leaps'.** In 1990, Deng proposed the strategic concept of 'two leaps':

246

'From a long-term perspective, Chinese socialist agricultural reform and development must make two leaps. The first is the abolition of People's Communes and institution of the responsibility system. This is a great step forward and should be unswervingly adhered to for a long time. The second leap is to adapt scientific farming methods to the requirements of the socialisation of production, to develop management on a reasonably large scale, and to promote the development of the collective economy. This is another great step forward and will be a very long process.' Deng's thoughts on making the second leap, which had both theoretical and practical significance, showed clearly how rural reform and development should proceed. To make the second leap, it will be essential to raise the level of rural production forces, to promote specialisation and the division of work in the countryside, and to adopt 'scientific farming methods and the socialisation of production'. Complementary requirements are that the organisation of farm production should move towards large-scale management, and that a low-level collective economy should develop into a high-level collective economy. This will take time and we must not be impatient for success. For the time being, we must concentrate our efforts into consolidating and perfecting the first leap, and improving the level of the forces of production. In those few places where the level of production forces is already high, we should actively explore ways of realising the second leap – and the forms it might take – in line with the objective requirements of the development of the forces of production and farmers' wishes.

With the transition of the whole economic system towards a socialist market economy, rural reform now faces a new task: namely, to accelerate the establishment of a rural economic operating mechanism and management system appropriate to the demands of a socialist market economy. Implied in this is the need to cultivate the market as the mainstay, perfect the market system, and enhance both macro-economic control and the protection of agriculture. As we intensify rural reform, we must be guided by Deng's thinking, upholding the basic experience of the first successful reforms in the countryside and respecting the initiative of the farmers, always taking the motivation of the farmers and the development of rural forces of production as the basic parameters of rural reform, and constantly pushing the reforms further.

The main agricultural problems are the grain issue and the need to promote comprehensive rural development

Comrade Deng not only accorded agriculture and the rural economy an important position in the national economic development strategy, but he also highlighted the role of agriculture and rural economic development as a strategic focus and urged comprehensive rural economic development. His analysis reveals the following important findings:

• First, the major agricultural problem is the grain problem. By the year 2000 we must be basically self-sufficient in grain. Comrade Deng had much to say about the special significance of grain issues. As long ago as 1943, when summing up the experience of fighting behind enemy lines in the Taihang Mountain region, he said, 'Experience tells us that whoever has grain has everything.' In 1986, when grain production was slipping, he said, 'I think there are three problems. If we don't properly sort them out, they will affect the development of the whole economy. One is the problem of agriculture – above all, that of grain. ... At present, grain output is growing rather slowly. One expert has argued that with farmland capital construction investment at a low level and farm production in decline, Chinese agriculture is about to enter a new phase of fluctuating output. We should pay attention to this ... and avoid importing large volumes of grain, as we have again been doing in the past few years, because that could affect the speed of our economic development.' Deng's suggestion that the grain issue be placed at the top of the agricultural agenda reflects his strategic vision as a pragmatic politician. As he observed, 'the root of the nation is the people, and the first necessity for the people is food'.

Since the People's Republic was founded – and especially since the espousal of reform – China's achievements in grain production have attracted global attention. Yet the balance remains very delicate. With a growing population and a declining arable area, we cannot afford to neglect grain production even for a second. As Jiang Zemin observed, 'agriculture is the foundation of the national economy, and grain is the bedrock of the foundation ... For quite a while yet – not just in the 1990s, but also for the first 50 years of the 21st century – we will be unable to talk of grain self-sufficiency, let alone claim that we have more than enough to eat.'

In his analysis of the development of grain production, Deng urged comprehensive planning and proposed a development target for national grain production for the end of the [20th] century, and suggested measures whereby the target might be fulfilled. In 1983, he said, 'there must be comprehensive planning in agriculture, and grain production must be increased before anything else. We must calculate precisely how much grain has to be produced by the year 2000, and how many *jin* of grain we need to produce per head in order to be able to claim basic self-sufficiency. It is an important strategic requirement that we should achieve basic grain self-sufficiency by 2000.' In 1986, he issued further instructions in regard to grain planning targets: 'At a rough estimate, by the year 2000, if we reckon a total population of 1.2 billion and average per capita consumption of 800 *jin* [400 kg] annual grain production will have to reach 960 billion *jin* [480 million tons].[48] We will have to produce in excess of ten billion *jin* [5 million tons] more each year from now on if we are to meet this target.' This was the first time that Deng put forward a specific national grain

---

48 In 2000, China's grain output was 467 million tons, implying an average per capita output of 368.6 kg. (Ed.)

output target and an associated required annual rate of increase for 2000. In addition, he referred to measures that would be required in order to fulfil these targets. Thus, 'it will not be easy to raise grain output to the level at which we are self-sufficient, and we will have to work hard on all fronts to determine, within the plan, how we can reach this goal. We must work out what we can do and by how much we can raise production through the adoption of measures, such as increasing fertiliser applications, improving seeds, properly implementing farmland capital construction, controlling pests, enhancing administration ... From a long-term perspective, the grain issue is very important ...'

Deng's rehearsal of grain output targets for the end of the century and of the measures needed to increase production was very accurate. Between 1985 and 1990, the contributions to increased grain output in China were: chemical fertilisers, 32%; irrigation, 28%; improved seed varieties, 16%; new technology, 14%; and pest control 10%. The full potential of all these factors must be tapped in order to fulfil on time the goals of per capita consumption of 800 *jin* [400 kg] and total grain production of one thousand billion *jin* [500 million tons].

• **Second, in order to develop agriculture we must select measures that are appropriate for local conditions and promote diversification of the rural economy.** Deng laid great emphasis on developing a diversified rural economy, while also according priority to grain production. He said, 'agricultural transformation cannot rely on grain alone, it must also depend on diversification. ... The areas that deserve immediate attention are animal husbandry, forestry and fruit growing. With the help of the state in providing fodder and improved breeds, urban suburbs should make great efforts to promote cattle, sheep and chicken rearing and fish breeding. The whole country should focus on the processing of fodder and several hundred modern fodder-processing plants should be set up ... Diversification will facilitate a huge expansion of the commodity economy in rural areas.' This crucial idea of Deng's broke the traditional unitary concept of agriculture and generated the concept of a 'big agriculture', comprehensively developed, in which crop farming, forestry, husbandry and fisheries should advance in complementary fashion. The implications of such integration, accompanied by a division of rural labour and work responsibilities as a commodity economy emerged are far-reaching. If farmers' living standards are to be raised to a comfortable level by the end of this [20th] century, rises in income will have to derive from many different sources, requiring enhanced division of labour and responsibilities, the development of a diversified economy, and expansion of the commodity economy.

In developing agriculture, we must adhere to the principle of adapting to local conditions. Thus, Deng: 'developing production in accordance with local conditions means that where something is suitable for development, it should be developed, and where it is not, development should not be forced. ... Farm diversification means that grain and cash crops should be grown in accordance with the suitability of farming conditions, thereby generating a higher output of both.' Deng's analysis of agricultural regionalisation reflects the basic Marxist tenet of seeking the truth from facts in guiding farm production, as well as embodying the principles of comparative economics. Rural China covers a vast area, characterised by huge variations in natural, economic and social conditions. Guidance of agricultural production must give full consideration to regional characteristics and should always start from the actual situation, using measures appropriate to local conditions.

- **Third, the development of township and village enterprises is the way in which to transfer farm labour, and effect rural industrialisation and urbanisation.** The emergence of township and village enterprises (TVEs) as a new force is a major initiative by Chinese farmers and a successful aspect of China's reformist approach to rural economic development. Deng gave his heartfelt approval to this phenomenon. In June 1987, he said, 'the most rewarding, but wholly unanticipated dimension of rural reform has been the expansion of TVEs and emergence of all sorts of small enterprises, engaging in a wide range of activities and involved in the commodity economy... Annual TVE growth of over 20% p.a. has been maintained for several years and is still continuing.' As productivity rose in the wake of the introduction of responsibility systems, the disguised unemployment that had existed in the countryside for many years became overt, and the need to transfer vast numbers of rural surplus labourers became a serious political, economic and social challenge. Deng recognised the major contribution made by TVEs in absorbing surplus rural labour on a large scale: 'for a long time now,' he said, '70% or 80% of our rural labour force have been tied to the land, with an average of only one or two mu[49] land available per person, and most people not even having enough to eat or wear. But once we started the reforms and open policy, and introduced the responsibility system, the numbers of people engaged in farming fell. What about those who were displaced? Ten years of experience has shown that as long as we motivate the grass-roots units and the farmers, and expand the diversified economy and new forms of TVEs, we can solve this problem. TVEs have absorbed half of the surplus rural labour force.'

Deng also analysed linkages between TVEs and rural industrialisation and urbanisation. He believed that China's countryside must follow the path of industrialisation and urbanisation, with rural enterprises as the mainstay and small towns playing a subsidiary role. In 1987, a propos the development of TVEs, he noted that 'instead of going off to the cities, farmers are setting up lots of smaller, new style towns ... Farmers' enthusiasm is growing, there is an increased variety of farm products, and large numbers of surplus agricultural labourers are being diverted to the new towns and new small and medium-sized enterprises. This, I think, is the road to take. Anyway, we cannot always keep the farmers tied to a

---

49 1 mou is approximately one-fifteenth of a hectare. (Ed.)

small patch of land – if we did that, there would be no hope!' The development of TVEs offers China's rural areas a model of industrialising and urbanising with Chinese characteristics. We must continue along the path pointed out to us by Deng, and bring the civilisation of industry and of the cities into the countryside, ultimately eliminating the differences between the two.

The basic way forward for agriculture lies with science and technology

Deng Xiaoping always stressed the prominent role of science and technology in the development of agriculture. He said, 'the development of agriculture depends first on policy, and second on science. There is no limit to developments in science and technology, nor to the role that they can play ... In the end it may be that science will provide a solution to our agricultural problems.' Deng's discussion of relying on science to revitalise and develop agriculture is a basic guiding ideology behind China's agricultural modernisation and construction. With regard to the practicalities of agricultural work, we should focus on the following three aspects in order to understand and implement Deng's strategic ideology.

• **First, firmly establish the idea that science and technology are primary production forces, the application of which should receive great emphasis.** From the premise of the Marxist theory of the forces of production that he inherited and developed, Deng observed, 'while Marx was absolutely correct to say that science and technology are forces of production, from the current perspective this may not be enough, and we should probably regard them as *primary* forces of production. In future, solutions to agricultural problems will ultimately lie in bio-engineering and advanced technology.' The experience of agricultural development at home and abroad shows that science and technology hold the key to the speed of farm growth, the level of increases in farm production and the transformation of traditional agriculture into a modern farm system. The 21st century will be the century of advanced science, and whoever solves the problems of agricultural science and farming techniques will enjoy a leading position in agricultural development. The history of scientific and technological development embodies a pattern of exponential growth that accelerated with the approach of the modern age. There have been no obvious changes in the agricultural resource endowment of the United States in the past half-century. But between 1929 and 1972, against the background of a declining labour force, scientific research and technological progress in farming contributed 81% of the increase in farm value-output and 71% of the increase in labour productivity. According to FAO-based projections, if people's food needs are to be met in the next twenty years, 80% of incremental output will derive from scientific and technological inputs. With its huge population, shortage of cultivated land, lack of resources and weak agricultural foundation, China will have to rely on scientific and technological advances in pursuit of sustainable agricultural development – which means focusing primarily on expanded reproduction. Although the contribution of science and technology to agricultural production has risen under the impact of reform (during the Seventh Five-Year Plan [1986–1990] advances in farm technology contributed 30% of the increase in grain output; in 1994 alone, the contribution of scientific and technological advances to increased agricultural value-output was 35%), it is still a long way from the 70%–80% contribution to increased grain production in developed countries. By the end of the century, the contribution of scientific and technological progress to farm growth must reach the target of 50%, proposed in the Central Committee and State Council's 'Resolution on Accelerating Progress in Science and Technology'. This is an arduous task, the key to which lies in the comprehensive implementation of Deng's view of science and technology as primary forces of production, and the prioritisation and further utilisation of agricultural science and modern farming techniques.

• **Second, firmly grasp agricultural scientific research, education and dissemination, and follow the path of 'reviving agriculture through science and education'.** 'Economic development depends on science and technology, progress in science and technology depends on skilled personnel, and the training of skilled personnel depends on education'. The three main aspects of implementing 'the revival of agriculture through science and education' are agricultural scientific research, education and dissemination. In 1975, Comrade Deng perceptively warned that 'if scientific research is not given top priority, national construction will be held back. Scientific research is a very important matter, which must be properly discussed.' In 1983, he pointed out that 'there are many articles on agriculture, but we have still not even scratched the surface. Agricultural scientists have put forward many good ideas. We must energetically enhance agricultural scientific research and the training of skilled personnel, and make practical arrangements to tackle key projects in agriculture.' Finally, in 1985, at the National Conference on Science and Technology, he said, 'we must make further efforts to solve the problems of integrating science and economics.' His ideas on scientific research, the training of skilled personnel and the integration of science and economics clearly highlight the main elements of 'reviving agriculture through science and technology' and the direction in which such work should proceed.

At present, agriculture science and farming techniques in China lag seriously behind developments in farm production. This is partly due to the absence in recent years of major technological breakthroughs on a par with the development of hybrid rice, hybrid maize or mulching. But it also reflects the failure to make readily available scientific and technological breakthroughs that *have* been achieved, and the inability to transform research findings into practical production technologies. With a view to providing an effective solution to such problems, Jiang Zemin has issued a clear challenge: 'On the one hand, we must intensify the dissemination and application of appropriate fruits of advanced science and technology; on the other hand, we must enhance research into and the development of major scientific and technological projects in order to ensure that agricultural and the rural economic development maintains its momentum. The focus of scientific and technological work in the countryside must shift to the introduction, demonstration and dissemination of those findings of advanced science and technology that are suitable for use, including the establishment and improvement of different kinds of service organisations for the dissemination of farm technology; to the further stabilisation and expansion of the ranks of scientific and technological workers in rural areas; and to finding new channels for funding and increasing investment in science and technology'.

• Third, enhance the scientific quality of farmers and raise the quality of agricultural scientific and technical equipment, adapting it to the needs of farm modernisation and the second leap. The scientific and cultural level of farmers and the standard of agricultural scientific and technical equipment are basic criteria of farm modernisation. Recent evidence shows that the proportion of China's rural population who are either illiterate or semi-literate has reached 30%. Unless this figure is reduced, the revival of agriculture through science and education, and the modernisation of agriculture will be empty words. In this context, as early as 1977 Deng pointed out that 'reliance on empty words cannot bring about modernisation. We must have knowledge and skilled personnel. Without these, how can we move forward?' Accordingly, we must continue vigorously to promote technological training for farmers and expand post-secondary school vocational technical education, gradually promoting 'green certificate projects' and working energetically to improve levels of farm mechanisation, extend the use of fertilisers and other chemicals, enhance water conservation and bio-engineering, and accelerate agricultural processing work. This is essential not only to enable farm production targets to be fulfilled, but also to realise long-term strategic requirements. From the long-term perspective of rural reform and development, 'the second leap demands the adaptation of scientific farming methods to the needs of socialised production, the development of large-scale management and the expansion of the collective economy.'

The task of implementing rural reforms and development by the end of the century is an arduous one. Under the leadership of the Party Central Committee with Comrade Jiang Zemin at its core, and with Comrade Deng Xiaoping's thoughts on rural reform and development as our guide, we must deepen rural reform, propel agriculture to a new and higher stage, and make an even greater contribution to ensuring the orderly implementation of overall economic systemic reform and the sustained, rapid and healthy development of the national economy.

Document 5.3

'A study of the regional development and distribution of Chinese agriculture'

ZHANG KEYUN

Study Materials for Economic Research, 1995, No. 701

Analysis of current conditions and characteristics of regional development, and the disposition of agriculture in China

There are significant differences in the spatial distribution of agriculture in China in terms of natural resources, environment, the agricultural development base and the farm population. Every region has its own characteristics of spatial distribution of agricultural activities, methods of management and the structure of local farm production.

• **Spatial distribution of agricultural operations.** The spatial distribution of agricultural operations in China is characterised by both a high degree of concentration and a high degree of fragmentation. A 'high degree of concentration' refers to the concentration of important farm products in areas with relatively favourable natural conditions. Such products are mainly produced in Eastern and Central areas, the Sichuan Basin in the West, and on the Northeast Plain (Jilin and Heilongjiang). Important traditional production regions include the middle and lower reaches of the Yangtze River, the Pearl River Delta, the Shandong and Liaodong Peninsulas, the Sichuan Basin, the North China Plain, and the Northeast Plain.

Reference to a 'high degree of fragmentation' highlights regions where a large farm population is engaged mainly in crop cultivation, but where large-scale specialised production has not yet taken hold. Since the regions that produce China's main agricultural products are also densely populated, whereas Western China is sparsely populated, the provinces with relatively high *per capita* output of the principal products (but not aquatic products) tend to be located in Central and Western regions. Large quantities of certain goods – especially cash crops and livestock products – have to be shipped from these regions to the East. This explains why the rate of consumption of agricultural goods is relatively high in the East, while food processing is more developed in the West. It also illustrates the fragmented nature of farm production in China.

• **The spatial dimension of operational scale and returns from agricultural activities.** Except for Shanghai, Tibet, Qinghai and Hainan Island, the agricultural base of every region of China derives from crop cultivation. There are, however, considerable differences in the scale of operations and

Table 5.4 Regional differences in GVAO and RSGVO (1992)

	GVAO	RSGVO
East	436.3 b.*yuan* (= 100)	(= 100)
Centre	297.0 (68)	(40)
West	175.0 (40)	(20)

Table 5.5 Estimates of land productivity and per capita rural income (1992)

	Value-output of cropping per hectare	Average rural per capita income
East	7190 *yuan* (= 100)	1002 *yuan* (= 100)
Centre	4270 (59)	695 (69)
West	4552 (63)	605 (60)

returns from farming in different regions. Generally speaking, agricultural production is most intensive in the East, with Central China taking second place. Cultivation is still relatively extensive in the West.

Agricultural returns conform to a similar pattern, although a comparison of estimates of gross agricultural value-output (GVAO) and rural social gross value-output (RSGVO) (Table 5.4)[50] reveals more pronounced regional differences for the latter than for the former.

Estimates of the productivity of land used for cultivation (the value-output of crop cultivation per hectare of arable land) and of per capita rural income also confirm the persistence of regional differentials (Table 5.5). With both measures significantly higher in Eastern than in Central and Western China, it is clear that there exist quite large differences in agricultural returns between the three major geographical regions.

In 1992, average national agricultural value-output per unit of agricultural labour was just 2669.1 *yuan*: the corresponding figure per unit of rural *industrial* labour was 36,667.7 *yuan* (13.7 times higher), while the average rural social value-output generated per unit of rural labour was 5795.7 *yuan* (2.2 times higher). These wide gaps highlight the major differences in the levels of value-output generated by different activities in rural areas.

There also exist major regional differences in the level of agricultural value-output per unit of labour. Hebei and Guangxi apart, the Eastern region exceeds the national average; by contrast, except for Xinjiang, Inner Mongolia, Jilin, Heilongjiang and Hubei, Central and Western regions fall below this level. The existence of a 9.3-fold gap between the regions with

50 Here and below, data originally included in the body of the text are presented in tabular fashion. (Ed.)

the highest and lowest levels of value-output per unit of labour highlights the regional diversity that characterises the scale of and return from farm operations in China.

Similar regional differences characterise land productivity, which is high in parts of Eastern China (e.g. Shanghai, Guangdong, Beijing, Jiangsu, Fujian and Zhejiang), but much lower in some Central and Western regions (e.g., Inner Mongolia, Qinghai, Ningxia, Gansu, Tibet, Heilongjiang and Shanxi). Productivity in the latter regions is only half that of the national average, while the gap between areas with the highest and lowest levels is some 600%. As early as the beginning of the nineteenth century, the idea that the degree of agricultural intensification tended to vary according to the distance between a particular region and the nearest urban centre was put forward. The pattern of Chinese farming conforms to this rule: agricultural land productivity in regions along the coast and near urban centres is relatively high, but decreases in areas that lie further and further from the coast or cities.

• **The regional structure of agriculture.** Regional agricultural development is largely determined by the structure of farming in particular areas. Between 1990 and 1992, the contribution of crop cultivation to overall agricultural production fell from 54.5% to 50.9% (East), from 63.3% to 60.2% (Centre) and from 59.4% to 59% (West). Given the faster rate of increase in the value-output of forestry, animal husbandry, sidelines and fishing compared with crop cultivation, such figures highlight the structural advantage enjoyed by Eastern regions. An analysis of changes in the internal composition of *rural* social value-output highlights the further structural advantage enjoyed by Eastern China – something that derives from the higher proportion of non-farming rural industry here than in Central and Western regions, as well as the fact that rural industrial growth has far outstripped that of agriculture. In short, the Eastern regions clearly enjoy a distinct advantage in terms of the structure of rural economic activities.

The main problems facing the development and geographical distribution of Chinese agriculture

• **The inadequacy and uneven distribution of natural agricultural resources.** In general, per capita arable land availability in China is limited and there is heavy pressure on water supplies for farm use, especially in the North and in arid and semi-arid regions. The ecological environment of farming is also fragile: water run-off, soil erosion and salinisation reflect indiscriminate tree-felling, and excessive cultivation is also the source of continuing serious problems.

The destruction of natural farm resources and the environment reduces the potential for future agricultural development. In addition to ecological

Table 5.6 Estimates of China's arable area

	Total arable area (million hectares)
1957	111.87
1970	101.13
1980	99.33
1990	95.67
1992	95.40

degradation, statistics point to a continuing decline in China's total arable area (Table 5.6).

These figures imply a contraction by 17.26% in total land availability between 1957 and 1992 (an average decline of some 0.67 million hectares p.a.). China's high man-land ratio means that its per capita availability of arable land is much lower than in developed countries – something that impacts seriously on farm production.

In terms of their regional distribution, natural resources and climatic conditions are far better in the South and East than in the North-west and on the Qinghai Plateau. The South-east enjoys abundant rainfall, plentiful sunshine and high soil-fertility, so that agricultural production here is blessed with exceptional advantages. Such factors constitute the natural basis of regional imbalance in Chinese agriculture.

• **Major regional differences in production conditions and the shortage of agricultural inputs.** Natural factors apart, there are striking differences in agricultural production conditions between different regions. In the East, non-farm economic activities have reached a high level of development, the population is concentrated, there is huge market demand for farm products, and farm inputs are in abundant supply. But China as a whole faces a shortage of such inputs. Moreover, whereas in the initial process of industrialisation in most countries, the investment ratio between industrial and agricultural sectors was about 3.8: 1, in China it was about 6.4:1.

In the Fifth, Sixth and Seventh Five Year Plans [1976–1980, 1981–1985 and 1986–1990], the share of total fixed capital investment allocated to agriculture fell from 10.6% to 5% to 3.4%. In 1992, the per capita value of fully implemented rural fixed capital formation was a mere 219 *yuan*. Insufficient agricultural investment has led to a growing inability to combat natural disasters. In the last ten years, output losses caused by natural disasters have affected,[51] on average, some 34.5 million hectares of land p.a., with over a third of the arable area hit by flooding or drought. In 1991 alone, flooding in the region around the Huai River and Tai Lake caused

---

51 The term used in the original text at this point refers to crop losses of more than 30% below the 'normal' yield. (Ed.)

financial losses of over 70 billion *yuan*, or the equivalent of the total volume of fixed capital investment in irrigation and water conservancy for the previous 40 years. *Regional* imbalances in agricultural investment are striking: in 1992, the average per capita value of realised rural fixed capital assets was 380 *yuan* in Eastern China, compared with 111 *yuan* and 116 *yuan* in Central and Western regions. The use of inputs such as agricultural machinery, electricity and chemical fertiliser was also much higher in the East than in Central and Western regions. In 1992, Eastern China accounted for 49.15% of farm machinery power, 63.9% of rural electricity consumption and 44.6% of fertiliser use.

• **The existence of surplus agricultural labour, its poor quality and major disparities in its regional distribution.** In 1992, China's agricultural population accounted for 78.33% of total population. The farm labour force comprised 340.37 million people (77.7% of the total rural work force), implying average per capita availability of 0.28 hectares of arable land. Because of the low level of farm mechanisation, most labourers remain tied to the land. But it is estimated that there are more than 120 million surplus agricultural workers, implying that labour productivity in farming lags far behind that of non-farming activities.

The last decade has seen an inexorable tide of farm workers, increasingly abandoning agriculture and moving to the cities in pursuit of higher returns. Some 50 million agricultural labourers are estimated to leave their homes to go in search of work every year. They are migrating further and further afield and for longer and longer periods of time. The emergence of this phenomenon is an inevitable consequence of the lower returns available from farming under market conditions. But it has also generated major problems of transportation and public order, as well as having a significant effect on agricultural development. The overall quality of farm labour in China is not high – some 80 million peasants are either illiterate or semi-illiterate. Most of those who leave in search of work elsewhere tend to be those with relatively high levels of education – the backbone of the rural labour force – and their loss exacerbates the low quality of the work force. Moreover, since Eastern China has achieved a higher level of economic development than Central and Western regions, the principal direction of labour migration is from Central and Western China towards the East, thereby intensifying inter-regional differences in agricultural returns. Cultural levels and openness to liberalisation differ greatly between the three regions. In 1992, about 50% of the rural labour force in the East had been educated to junior middle school level or above – 2.5% more than in the Central China and 16.3% more than in the West. The continuing flow and transfer of labour is likely to exacerbate such imbalances.

• **The uneven development of non-agricultural rural activities among regions and the low level of farming technology.** The regional distribution of non-agricultural rural industry is uneven and there are major regional differences in the extent to which such activities are linked to agriculture. Textile and other light industries are mainly concentrated in Eastern China, whereas energy and raw materials industries tend to be located in Central provinces. In general, farming has closer links with textile and other light industries than with energy and raw materials industries. As a result, non-agricultural activities in the East tend to impact more on farming than in Central and Western regions.

Estimates suggest that between 1972 and 1980, around 27% of the increase in GVAO was attributable to advances in farm technology. This figure rose to 35% by the Sixth Five Year Plan [1981–1985], but in the Seventh Plan fell back to 30.4% – 23.8% for crop cultivation, 41.5% for animal husbandry and 45.9% for aquatic production. By way of comparison, between 1929 and 1979, technological advances accounted for 81% of incremental agricultural production and 71% of increased labour productivity in the United States. Such figures highlight the continuing low level of farm technology in China.

• **The decline in agricultural product prices and the downward pressure on farmers' income.** For many years, there has been a large scissors differential between industrial and agricultural product prices. Even allowing for numerous adjustments to agricultural prices under the impact of reform and a rise of 173.9% in the general purchase price index for farm and sideline products (1978–1991), the structure of comparative prices between agricultural and industrial products has, since 1992, become more irrational. Between 1989 and 1992, farm input prices rose by 6.7%, compared with a mere 1.3% increase in the purchase price of agricultural products.... Meanwhile, the absence of effective regulation over supplies of farm products, whether through the market or the planning system, led to 'difficulties in selling grain' on two separate occasions (1982–1984 and 1989–1992). In the wake of these problems came an inter-regional 'agricultural and sideline products war', which pushed farm product prices downwards and caused huge losses to farmers. Farmers have also had to endure increasingly heavy burdens through annual increases in taxes and the like.

Regional analysis shows that rises in farmers' income have been very unbalanced. In 1988, there was an average gap of 47 *yuan* between per capita farm income in Eastern and Western regions. Between the two provinces with the highest and lowest incomes, the gap was 200 *yuan*. By 1992, the corresponding figures were 395 and more than 1,735 *yuan*! This widening gap reflects regional differences in farm production and is a major source of regional imbalances in agricultural development. Because of inter-regional differences in returns from agriculture, farming has become the least attractive form of employment in Western and Central China, and farmers are falling over themselves to join the ranks of migrant workers. In many regions, it is left to the old, the weak and to women to keep agriculture afloat.

Regional strengths in China's agricultural development and the choice of special agricultural development zones

• **Distinguishing regional strengths in agricultural production.** The per capita availability of agricultural products is reflected in commodity rates and regional trading patterns. In Eastern China, farm products have to be transported from Western regions in order to compensate for supply shortfalls. Except for aquatic products, Western and Central China are at a clear advantage in terms of per capita availability of farm products and the leading two provinces for grain, cotton, oil-bearing crops and meat are located in these regions.

These remarks reflect current production conditions in China. However, many regions have latent advantages that are yet to be exploited. Meanwhile, serious problems of soil erosion, desertification, salinisation and drought have prevented the exploitation of China's full agricultural potential.

• **Choosing between regional agricultural planning and integrated agricultural development.** Returns from agriculture are below those of other economic sectors. In addition, there are major regional differences in how farming is arranged, and commodity rates remain low. In order fully to exploit the advantages of different regions and give more impetus to agricultural development, a clear understanding is needed of the key areas and direction of agricultural development in different regions, and of how arrangements for farming should be adjusted.

The Eastern coastal region has a strong economy, good transport, a dense network of towns and cities, favourable environmental conditions and natural resources for farming, a high population density, a high rate of land utilisation, and intensive farm practices. But rising population has encouraged rapid urbanisation, which has seriously encroached on arable land availability. Southern coastal areas are highly susceptible to flooding and typhoons, while drought and seawater flooding regularly affect northern areas. Grain production is erratic and unstable, and there is limited potential to raise output – hence the need for all provinces, except Shandong, Jiangsu and Zhejiang, to import supplementary grain. Eastern coastal China should meet its grain requirements through commodity exchange with other regions, focusing its own efforts producing for urban consumption, such as oil-bearing crops, sugar, silkworms, fruit, flowers and other cash crops, as well as meat, eggs, milk and fish.

This region enjoys high levels of science and technology and a high degree of coastal development. It should establish an intensive system of agriculture that is fully integrated with trade and industry, and accelerate the transition from traditional agriculture to a modernised farm system. Key nodes of development in this region are the Pearl River Delta, the Yangtze Delta, the 'Golden Triangle' of South Fujian, and the region around the Bohai Sea.

Inland Central provinces have a rich and varied natural environment, suitable for producing various cash crops and have great potential for agricultural development. But low temperatures, hail, sandstorms, salinisation and extremes of drought and excessive rain are all serious obstacles to agricultural development. Rich agricultural provinces in this region are frequently affected by natural disasters. In 1991, for example, natural disasters – mainly flood and drought – affected 3.8 million hectares in Heilongjiang, 5.2 million in Henan, 5 million hectares in Anhui, 3.7 million in Hubei, 2.7 million in Hunan, and 1.5 million in Jilin. The dense network of rivers and lakes has contributed much to farm development, but the threat, which it poses through flooding, highlights the need to improve water control. This region is crucially important as a producer of grain, oil-bearing crops, timber and meat products; it is the most important national source of commodity grain; and it enjoys the greatest potential for agricultural development. The Central region should focus its efforts on developing integrated commodity production bases for crop farming, forestry, animal husbandry and fishing; it should raise the output of high quality rice, wheat, maize and soyabeans; through better control of lakes and rivers, it should try to establish an ecological equilibrium in farming. It should take advantage of its superiority in grain production to strengthen the animal feed industry, and make full use of its surface water resources and uncultivated, mountainous regions to develop freshwater fish farming and timber forestry.

Western China has vast tracts of land based on a complex topography. It has quite rich organic farm resources, and its grassy plains are an important national resource. The region has a typical continental climate and contains large areas of desert (including the Gobi Desert) and high mountains; natural conditions for farming are lacking, its economic foundations and communications are poor, and levels of farm output are low. Xinjiang is the only province in the region that enjoys self-sufficiency in grain production. Grain shortages have added to problems of indiscriminate land reclamation and hillside cultivation, and serious difficulties have resulted from the destruction of forest cover – such environmental destruction further limiting grain production. Predatory farming practices have taken their toll on the natural environment and ecological problems are now the key constraint on agricultural development in the West.

Western China must transform its crude farming practices. It should make major efforts to plant trees and grass, extend forest cover, protect grassy plains, and control further desertification. It should focus on forestry and animal husbandry, and develop famous local cash crops. The existing monoculture based on grain production should be changed towards cash crop cultivation, in which it has a comparative advantage.

• **Policy measures to achieve rational agricultural distribution and development.** Agriculture must retain its position as the foundation of the national economy. In the absence of government-sponsored farm support policies and as market-orientated reform intensifies, the low returns available from farming could, however, further erode labour and capital resources available to agriculture. The overall aim of agricultural policy is to remove uncertainty, increase stability and strengthen the farm sector's ability to support the national economy. In turn, this requires the implementation of specific measures, designed to boost agricultural inputs, increase farm incomes and adjust the geographical distribution of farm operations.

The regional division of farm labour must be planned rationally and scientifically, and regional gaps in agricultural development must be narrowed. In line with natural conditions, a preliminary regional distribution of labour has already been achieved for the production of staple products (grain, cotton and oil-bearing crops), and production bases established for their production. Future government farm policies should facilitate the further division of labour in accordance with the principle of exploiting the comparative advantage of each region in order to maximise financially profitable farming in Eastern China, grain, meat and forestry production in Central China, and the development of local specialities and cash crops in the West. The serious problem of urban and industrial encroachment on arable land in the East should be halted. Special protection should be afforded to core commercial production bases of grain and cotton in Central China. Against the background of serious environmental degradation, farm development policies in the West should meanwhile seek to accommodate local ecological demands.

From a national perspective, problems of soil erosion are widespread and China has been beset by a series of natural disasters in recent years, which have caused major losses to life and property. In the face of such environmental problems, government at all levels must adopt effective policies to improve the natural environment and restore the ecological equilibrium. In particular, adequate provision of goods and subsidies should be given to regions along major rivers so that they can regain their ecological equilibrium within a specified time. Environmental degradation not only affects local farming, but also threatens immeasurable damage to agricultural and industrial development in the regions at the lower reaches of these rivers. In recent years, we have established a definite link between agricultural damage caused by flooding and drought, and environmental damage at the upper reaches of rivers. Ecological recovery at the upper reaches of rivers in Western regions should be an important catalyst for agricultural and economic development throughout the country.

All levels of government must make regional agricultural planning a key focus of their work in order fully to exploit the comparative advantage of every region. We must guard against the emergence of 'farm and sideline product wars', caused by regions' headlong pursuit of profit and consequent abnormal rises in product prices. Since the beginning of the 1980s, such wars have broken out among hundreds of different products in different regions, resulting in huge resource waste and serious disincentives for farmers to engage in production. We must eradicate this phenomenon by implementing scientific regional agricultural planning, the provision of prompt and effective information services, and reliance on appropriate administrative and legislative measures. In absolute terms, regional gaps in agricultural development between Eastern, Western and Central regions are unlikely to narrow significantly in the short term. The key to reducing such differentials is to give full rein to the resource potential of Western and Central China, and to support development in poverty-stricken areas. The state should encourage horizontal economic co-operation among different regions and use work-relief and other subsidies to encourage farmers in Central and Western regions to engage in water conservancy, tree and grass planting, etc. This will help enhance natural conditions for agriculture, limit rural population growth, alleviate environmental pressures, and promote agricultural growth and raise the overall level of development in Central and Western China.

Document 5.4

'Lessons from the four major reforms of the rural land system'

JIANG LI

Academic Research, 1994, No. 4

[In the first sections of this paper, the author analyses the rationale of the first three major reforms of China's land system undertaken by the government after 1949. These were: (a) the early land reform campaigns, which 'transformed a system of feudal land ownership to a new system based on private land ownership by the peasants'; (b) the creation of elementary agricultural producer cooperatives, which 'changed the system of private land ownership to one in which private ownership of land remained, but with centralised collective responsibility for management and utilisation'; and (c) the introduction of higher agricultural cooperatives and the move towards people's communes, which 'changed this system of private-cum-collective ownership combined with centralised land use and management to one in which even land ownership became collectivised and centralised'. (Ed.)]

... It is noteworthy that while this [collective] framework remained in effect, the state implemented a system of agricultural management based on a high degree of centralisation and central planning. Collective economic organisations were denied independence and autonomy in terms of production and the disposal of output. The scale of operations under communes and brigades was in a state of constant flux, and policies designed to guarantee mutual benefit at equivalent prices were not put fully into practice. The communist vogue towards 'egalitarianism and arbitrary transfer' merely exacerbated the negative effects of this land system.

The fourth reform transformed the land system based on collective ownership and centralised management to one based on the management and utilisation of collectively-owned land through the implementation of household contracts. In this way, plots of land were contracted out and worked by individual households in return for a guarantee that the households would provide an output quota to the collective and state. Anything in excess of this quota could be retained by the household.

With the introduction of this land system, the state also began to liberalise its policies towards agricultural production planning, farm product prices, and the marketing and supply system. Step by step, the farm economy underwent a transition from a centrally planned to a market system.

The main feature of the new land system lay in the distinction between collective rights and individual rights. That is, ownership rights belonged to the collective, while individual households enjoyed the rights of production and utilisation. Thus, the household became the basic managerial unit. This enhanced production incentives, since all household members were equally affected by profits or losses. Households were encouraged to make use of all available resources, raise their utilisation rate and maximise returns. The scale of land management was more appropriate to the forces of production than in the past and corresponded better to producers' operational and managerial expertise. Agricultural production and farm management improved, facilitating rises in yields well above their former levels. There was a much closer relationship between land use and material benefits for producers, and levels of income were more directly dependent on whether land was managed well or badly. This encouraged farmers to invest more, improve soil fertility and increase commodity output. Producers enjoyed quite a high degree of autonomy and could make production and marketing decisions with a view to economic benefits, taking into account market supply and demand, soil characteristics and other local and seasonal conditions.

All this raised the operational return from land, enabling the new land system to play a crucial role in increasing farm production and raising rural incomes. But even this system had its limitations, especially through constraints imposed by the 'leftist' ideology of traditional socialist theory. At the time, the rural forces of production were weak and the principal way in which the rural population could make a living was by working the land. There was, however, an inherent contradiction between a system based on households working small, identically-sized and fragmented plots of land, and the future modernisation of the rural economy. The blockading tactics, isolationism and petty nationalism that local communities used to protect their personal land and production rights were in direct contradiction to the development of commercial production and the creation of a socialist market economic system. What was needed was the intensification of the reforms and perfection of the rural collective land system.

From today's perspective, the four reforms of the land system have taught us several important lessons, which will help guide the future development and perfection of the rural collective land system:

The first lesson

The implementation of a new system of collective land property rights must accord with levels of development and of the rural forces of production. Methods of expropriation, with or without compensation, must not be used; and peasants' rights to land ownership and inheritance must not be suddenly revoked. When land that was formerly privately owned became part of the lower-level agricultural cooperatives, land use rights were transferred to the collective and production operations also became a collective responsibility. Peasants received a fixed rent for their land and had the right to recover their land if they left the cooperative. But after a while, the collectives began to use methods of expropriation without compensation and land rents were abolished. Peasants received no financial reward from their land, and confiscation became the basis of collective land ownership.

These actions were wholly opposed to the ideas and theories of Marx and Engels. Engels said: 'When we are in power, we must not use violent methods to deprive small peasants (no matter whether compensation is offered or not).' Marx said: 'In the course of bringing privately owned land into collective ownership . . . we cannot adopt measures that will offend the peasants. For example, we must not proclaim the abolition of inheritance rights and peasants' rights to land ownership. ... We must allow peasants to proceed down the economic road themselves in order to realise this process.'

Concrete evidence shows that there was widespread opposition to the haste with which lower-level cooperatives were introduced, and to the excessive scale of management that was completely divorced from the level of productive forces of the time. Although most peasants were willing to accept cooperatives as a system that embodied individual ownership combined with collective land use and production rights, there was wholesale opposition to a land system based on collective ownership, centralised management, planned labour, and uniform distribution based on work points. Peasants spontaneously adopted methods of passive resistance to the creation and implementation of this system. These included slaughtering cattle, felling trees, seizing collectively-owned land and other property, neglecting public assets, resisting participation in collective decision-making and management, running up long-term debts with the collective, and persisting with individual household production.

Moreover, this happened despite enormous political pressure to criticise 'leftist' and capitalist tendencies, and adopt the principles of class struggle and the struggle between the socialist and capitalist roads.

But after the Third Plenum of the Eleventh Central Committee and under the guidance of the Party's new ideology of 'seeking truth from facts', the peasants managed spontaneously to break the shackles imposed from above. The outcome was the implementation of a collective land household responsibility system. Although in its practical application this system acknowledged peasants' rights and interests over land, peasants still failed to recover their rights to ownership and inheritance. Nominally, collective land belonged to all commune members, but for a long period there was some confusion as to who owned what land and how much. Eventually, rights to land ownership and eligibility to share in collective income were determined unconditionally by whether or not a household was registered as part of the collective. If the number of household members and its associated labour power increased, they were unconditionally allowed to share in income distribution. If, however, the number decreased or if household registration was transferred elsewhere, the distribution share was forfeited. Rights to land ownership and share of income could not be inherited or transferred. In practice, this was still a system of land rights based on ownership by the entire people – one that encouraged short-termism in both production and income distribution, and placed limits on the optimum allocation and rational flow of rural economic resources (land, labour and capital). This set back the development process of farm modernisation and made it impossible to establish a genuinely effective system of collective management and administration.

Thus, historical experience has shown time and again that in moving from a system of private land ownership to one of collective ownership, it is essential – on the basis of highly developed production forces and a high economic level – to proceed step by step, taking into account the economic interests of both collective and individuals. Egalitarianism, the indiscriminate transfer of resources and the use of administrative sanctions must not be used to realise these goals. This theoretical framework is the basic guiding principle for the future reform and perfection of the collective land system.

The second lesson

The land ownership system comprises rights to ownership, management and utilisation (the 'three rights'). Rights to ownership can be further divided into rights of ownership, distribution, profits and disposal (the 'four rights'). All such rights must be distinguished rationally according to the development of specialised and socialised production. Experience shows that under conditions of basic self-sufficiency with petty commodity production, there is a high degree of integration between the 'three rights' and the 'four rights'. This promotes the effective development and use of resources such as land, and helps boost output growth. At the same time, its persistence may hinder longer-run and larger-scale commercialisation, specialisation and socialisation of production, thereby restricting the optimum allocation of agricultural resources. As commercialisation and socialisation proceed, it is increasingly necessary to liberate and develop the productive forces and agricultural resources in order to raise the effectiveness of resource use. This can only be achieved by making a clear distinction between rights of land ownership, management, and utilisation; making a clear separation of the rights of occupation, allocation, profits and disposal; and constantly emphasising the optimum allocation of resources. Under the impact of reform, the rural forces of production have shown significant development and production has, to a large degree, become specialised, socialised and commercialised.

Such success owes most to the implementation of the household responsibility system and the separation of rights to land ownership and management. Along with the increasing socialisation and commercialisation of labour, utilisation rights became separated from management rights and changes were made to the previous system with its high degree of integration between rights of ownership, utilisation and management. This has encouraged the optimum allocation and rational flow of the various factors that make up the forces of production. The main problems now stem from restrictions on collective rights to land ownership imposed by the 'leftist' excesses of traditional socialist theory, and the belief that a separation of the rights to land occupation, allocation, profit and disposal is tantamount to the privatisation of collective land. This has interfered with the proper handling of the relationship between the land and property rights of the collective and individuals. The failure to resolve the ambiguities surrounding collective rights to land ownership has held up the development of a socialist market economy for factors of production. We must rely on an intensification of the rural reforms in order to improve this situation.

The third lesson

A system of collective land management must accommodate the linkages between natural reproduction and economic reproduction that are so characteristic of agriculture. It must also provide ample incentives for both the collective and the individual, without favouring one or the other. Historical experience shows that a highly centralised system (with unified planning, management, administration, labour and profit allocation) can concentrate labour, material and financial resources, develop production, improve the basic production infrastructure, and increase returns from land use. This is only appropriate to a situation in which the forces of production are at a low level, land management is on a small scale and managerial personnel have corresponding capabilities. But such a system dampens individual enthusiasm, curbs individual creativity and does not exploit the full potential of available talent. In circumstances where land is worked on a large scale, production operations are varied and managerial expertise is lacking, this kind of system will not only dampen individual enthusiasm and creativity but will also generate chaotic production and management, inappropriate resource use and distribution, and major wastage of land, labour and capital. It is also likely to impede increases in productivity and output.

The implementation of the household responsibility system and other contract responsibility systems broke down the high degree of centralisation and concentration characteristic of previous systems of management and administration. A two-tier system of management was established, based on the principle of clearly separated rights and a combination of central and local responsibilities. In terms of land management, a clear separation was made between the rights of the collective and those of the contracting individual. In addition, reflecting local differences in the development of production forces and the economy, production operations became, as appropriate, the responsibility of households. At the same time, work requiring unified collective management that could not be effectively handled by households – for example, basic infrastructural construction, combating natural disasters, disaster relief, and unified land disposal and management – remained the collective's responsibility. This two-tier system of management was much more suited to the level of the rural forces of production and able to provide incentives for both collective and individual. It satisfied the requirements of agricultural reproduction, as well as of management and administration. Land resources could be rationally allocated and operational returns from land increased. Thus, the new system was full of vitality and able to accommodate development requirements at various levels of management and at various stages of production. Its versatility meant that it could regulate the jurisdiction of land management and the work of both collective and individual household according to the economic level of the local region.

For the two-tier system to work properly, however, the collective organisation needed a certain basis of economic strength. The poor and undeveloped nature of the collective economy meant that there were some collective tasks that neither the collective nor the individual household could perform. This affected the development of production – the poverty of the collective economy and the inability of ordinary peasants to raise needed funds sometimes even causing work to grind to a halt. Developing and strengthening the *collective* economy is therefore a prerequisite of improving the two-tier system of management and a necessary condition for enhancing the basic land infrastructure, raising land fertility and helping individual households to raise production. The development of the collective economy should not be viewed as a retrograde step that will increase regional economic isolation. Rather, the adoption of varied advanced economic methods and management forms – for example, contract management, joint stock systems, renting and leasing, etc. – can create an open collective economy without the 'iron rice bowl'.

The fourth lesson

The scale of land management must be at an appropriate level and conform to the needs of development and the level of the agricultural forces of production. The creation of a modernised farm sector depends in part on attaining a certain scale of high-level management. Without this, it will be impossible to move towards specialisation, the use of advanced equipment and technology, operational endeavours based on the concentration of technological and financial resources and the establishment of enterprises, the pursuit of large-scale production, and improvements in labour and land productivity. The scale of land management must, however, conform to the quality of the labour force and administrative personnel, the level of managerial and administrative expertise, the availability of funds, inputs and production facilities, and the level of application of science and technology. Practical experience shows that when these factors are scarce or remain under-developed, an excessively large scale of land management will not only prevent returns to scale, but will also lead to an irrational allocation of agricultural resources, a serious waste of resources, and poor economic benefits. By contrast, when the forces of production are fairly well developed, an excessively small scale of land management is likely seriously to inhibit agricultural modernisation.

Following the introduction of household responsibility systems, the establishment of the household as the basic managerial unit transformed the excessively large scale of management, liberated and developed the forces of production, and greatly improved farm production and the rural economy. China's agricultural economy now is fundamentally different from that of the period just after the introduction of the household responsibility system. We have seen exponential improvements in our basic modernised infrastructure, in the application of advanced science and technology, in the use of various kinds of advanced material and labour inputs, and in the level of rural incomes. Agriculture has passed through its stage as a primary industry and is developing into an integrated combination of primary, secondary and tertiary activities. The non-agricultural and non-arable sectors of the rural economy, and the proportion of labour inputs devoted to these sectors have now reached over half. The livelihoods of the rural population have become much less dependent on land cultivation.

Such developments have given rise to new problems stemming from the contradiction between the small-scale, scattered nature of the household responsibility system and the need to promote agricultural modernisation, as well as rural industrialisation and urbanisation. This contradiction is particularly severe in the more economically developed regions. It manifests itself specifically in the following ways: difficulties in improving the effectiveness of land use, because of the inability to develop unified and rational planning, distribution and land use strategies; constraints on developing large-scale distribution systems, because of the fragmented and small-scale production of goods that cannot be produced in bulk;

limitations on the effective use and promotion of advanced technology and scientific improvements in order to develop modernised, specialised and enterprise-based production; damaging effects on perceptions of the importance of agriculture and farm investment as a result of the failure to generate returns of scale, especially in the traditionally low-return sectors of grain and sugar cane production; difficulties in developing secondary and tertiary industries and promoting the growth of rural towns, due to the failure to transform the 'market-gardening' nature of farming and control the net outflow of labour and capital from agriculture. All these factors have introduced elements of instability in the scale of land management and the scale of production operations. The scale of management must accommodate the need to develop the forces of production and must be adjusted to the level of the forces of production and the level of economic development. Such adjustments cannot be forcibly implemented by administrative decree. They must be gradually introduced by economic methods, in line with the demands of the masses.

Document 5.5

'A brief overview of China's strategy for fixed capital investment in agriculture'

RESEARCH GROUP FOR FIXED CAPITAL INVESTMENT IN AGRICULTURE

Study Materials for Economic Research, 1993, No. 43

The importance of agricultural fixed capital investment for purposes of farm development

At the Eighth Plenum of the Thirteenth CCP Congress, it was pointed out that:

> Agriculture is the foundation of economic development, social stability and national strength. Problems arising among the rural population and in villages have always been fundamental issues for the Chinese revolution and China's construction.

History has repeatedly shown that when there is an abundant harvest, the economic state of the nation is healthy and society is stable. A poor harvest, however, has the opposite effect. Thus, the sustained, stable and coordinated development of the national economy can only be achieved on the basis of the sustained, stable and coordinated development of agriculture.

The history of agriculture in China and elsewhere shows that raising fixed agricultural capital investment is an essential condition for transforming farm production, raising the farm sector's production capacity, and promoting the sustained, stable and coordinated development of agriculture. It is also an essential means of ensuring that agricultural growth matches that of other sectors of the national economy.

The benefits of fixed asset investment in agriculture become apparent some time after the initial capital outlay. If there are large fluctuations in such investment or it is absent over long periods of time, there will be a delayed effect on farm production. The outcome may be to make agriculture a weak link in the national economy and a break on overall economic growth.

China's fundamental problem is that it must support a large population from a small arable area. Per capita land availability will continue to fall as China's population grows and the arable area further contracts. The situation is exacerbated by various other factors. These include the scarcity of natural resources, insufficient sources of water in many regions, low rates of forest cover, serious problems of soil erosion, a poor ecological farming environment, and the devastating impact of serious natural disasters. Over the last ten years, flooding and drought have, on average, damaged some 34.48 million hectares of land each year. In 1991, economic losses and expenditure on disaster relief resulting from flooding in the Huai River and the Tai Lake region totalled more than 70 billion *yuan*, or the equivalent of total state investment in water conservancy projects since 1949. Meanwhile, industrial output worth some 120 billion *yuan* has been lost as a result of water shortages in over 300 cities throughout China. Economic development, rising population and improvements in living standards also place rising demands, both quantitatively and qualitatively, on agricultural and subsidiary farm products.

Objective analysis of agricultural development conditions in China suggest that continued rises in unit output total hold the key to increasing total production. Yet the level of agricultural modernisation remains low, infrastructure is weak, the quality of farm labour is poor, and overall agricultural capacity can meet neither its own production needs nor the demands of national economic development. To remedy this requires an expansion of farm capital construction (especially the implementation of water conservancy projects), improvement of the agricultural infrastructure, and continued rises in fixed capital investment in farming. Such measures will help raise agricultural yields, promote the stable and coordinated development of the farm sector, and fulfil the goals for agricultural development laid down in the Ten Year Programme [1991–2000] and the Eighth Five Year Plan [1991–1995].

The central government has already formulated appropriate policies to meet such targets. The key question now is how relevant departments can effectively implement these policies. Associated with this is the need to address widespread concerns about the required scale of investment during the next decade, the calculation of expenditure outlays on the various components of agricultural investment, and the formulation of measures that will guarantee increases in fixed capital investment in the farm sector.

A brief review of fixed capital investment in agriculture since 1949

After 1949, great emphasis was placed on agricultural development. Production relations were gradually changed, and large-scale farm construction projects were simultaneously initiated, focusing on irrigation and water conservancy. These required huge inputs of labour, material and financial resources. Of the 381 billion *yuan* of fixed capital investment allocated to agriculture during 1953–1990, 66% was undertaken by rural collectives and individual farmers, the rest being carried by the state. Some 54.2% of this investment was made during 1953–1980, compared with 47.8% between 1981 and 1990.

During 1953–1990, state capital investment in agriculture totalled 119.5 billion *yuan* (6.6% of all state construction investment), of which 71.3 billion *yuan* were directed to water conservancy projects. State investment in upgrading and restoring existing facilities and associated expenditures (worth 9.91 billion *yuan* between 1980 and 1990), would raise this figure to 129.4 billion *yuan*. Since 1979, international financial institutions, such as the World Bank and Asia Development Bank, as well as preferential loans by foreign governments have made available funds of over US$5 billion for agricultural development.

During 1953–1990, fixed capital investment in agriculture undertaken by rural collectives totalled 92.6 billion *yuan* (39.2 billion *yuan* in 1981–1990). The corresponding figures for investment by individual farmers were 159 and 83.4 billion *yuan*.

The state has also raised funds for agricultural construction through a variety of other channels. Incomplete statistics suggest that under the Seventh Five Year Plan [1986–1990], such funds reached 50 billion *yuan* – more than twice the level of state capital investment in agriculture in the same period. Most of these funds were used for farm construction, although they are not officially recorded as agricultural fixed capital investment.

Between 1953 and 1990, the state allocated 43.4 billion *yuan* (2.4% of total state capital construction investment) to agricultural support industries, such as the production of fertilisers, pesticides and farm machinery. During 1981–1990, 3 billion *yuan* were invested in plastic sheeting, fodder, and livestock chemical manufacturing industries. Such funds serve farm production, although they are not officially recorded as fixed capital investment in the agricultural sector.

Since 1949, large-scale agricultural construction has raised the farm sector's production capacity and created the conditions for increasing output, especially in the livestock industry. The historical problem of feeding China's huge population has now basically been solved. Providing sufficient food for 22% of the world's population on a mere 7% of the global arable area is a remarkable achievement.

Yet China's agricultural development has followed tortuous path, the main lessons of which are as follows:

- **We have been too impatient for success.** During the Great Leap Forward, mass labour mobilisation for grain production and irrigation projects was excessive and inappropriate, given prevailing conditions. Many of the resultant problems remain unresolved to this day, such as sub-standard or unfinished engineering projects (especially defective reservoirs), poor coordination in project implementation, and lack of proper arrangements for the settlement of migrant workers.

- **We have displayed short-termism.** Absence of strategic long-term planning in agricultural construction has led to instability. Whenever farm production seems to be progressing well, we become reluctant to maintain investment at appropriate levels Since 1980, state capital investment in agriculture has fluctuated widely, and declined in both absolute and relative terms. Agriculture accounted for 11.1% of total state capital construction investment in 1979, but by 1990 it had fallen to 4%. The farm sector's share in investment by collective and individuals has also declined. These shortfalls have had a negative impact on agricultural development.

- **Poor design, defective management and functional duplication have undermined construction projects, causing considerable loss and waste and generating poor returns on investment.** Between the Sixth and Seventh Five Year Plans, the rate of fixed assets transferred for use in agriculture fell from 81.3% to 70.4%.

Fixed capital investment in agriculture: projections for the 1990s (1991–2000)

- **Guiding Principles.** We must shift agricultural fixed capital investment from the traditional remit of centralised planning towards that of the socialist market economy in order to improve output, quality and efficiency. This will also help raise agriculture's production capacity. To expand fixed capital investment in farming is to implement the Party line, which states that agriculture is the foundation of the national economy.

The level of farm investment should be dictated by prevailing conditions and national strength. It must be supported by the joint efforts of state, region, collective and individual in order to generate enthusiasm from all quarters in the interests of achieving practical results through systematic project planning. Efforts should be made not only to increase farm investment, but also to raise its economic efficiency. Special care should be given to the potential contribution of science and technology to agricultural production.

- **Suggested Plans for Investment.**

  [On the basis of differing criteria, four investment scenarios are introduced at this point. Depending on the assumptions used, they indicate investment requirements for agriculture, forestry, water conservancy and meteorology, totalling between 444 and 550 billion *yuan* during the Ten Year Programme [1991–2000], and between 175 and 214 billion *yuan* under the Eighth Five Year Plan [1991–1995] (Ed.)]

Agriculture's share of basic capital construction investment has grown from 3.4% in the Seventh Five Year Plan period to between 6.8% and 7.4%. But it has still not reattained its 1980 level of 10.6%. In order to fulfil the goals of the Ten Year Programme and promote the economic development of rural collectives and individual farmers, consumption and accumulation ratios should remain at the levels reached under the Seventh Plan, while collective and individual shares of total fixed capital investment should rise from 1990 levels of, respectively, 19% and 15% to around 20% (the level attained under the Sixth Five Year Plan). In this way, the goal of setting aside sufficient funds to allocate 450–500 billion *yuan* as national fixed capital investment to the farm sector is readily attainable.

  [At this point, the original text lists key investment projects, to be implemented during 1991–2000. They include large-scale projects to bring major rivers and lakes under control, as well as huge engineering projects designed to divert water from southern to northern China. Plans for reclamation, regional farm growth, and forestry and meteorological development are also included. Their implementation promises significant benefits, including an enhanced ability to combat flooding, extension of the irrigated area by 5.3 million hectares, transformation of 27 million hectares of medium and low-yielding land, and reclamation of 3.34 million hectares of wasteland. Grass-planting and pasture improvements will transform a further 10 million hectares of land, while 40 million hectares will be newly afforested (8 million hectares to be planted under fast-growing, high-yielding forest cover).2 (Ed.)]

Investment relationships and how to manage them properly

- **The relationship between agricultural fixed capital investment and overall national investment must be handled carefully in order to strengthen agriculture's fundamental position in the national economy.** Since 1949, improvements in farm performance and bumper harvests have been accompanied by reduced state investment in agriculture, while low production levels have generated increased investment. This has caused major long-term investment fluctuations. We must learn from the major reductions in farm investment by the state that have occurred under the Sixth and Seventh Five Year Plans. The CCP Central Committee and State Council have repeatedly called for continuing rises in farm investment and we propose that the National People's Congress should formulate an 'Agricultural Investment Law' (or a 'Basic Law for Agriculture') in order to institutionalise and legalise the guiding principles of the Party and government policy. National planning documents and budget forecasts should clearly state the share of capital investment that is to be allocated to agriculture and agro industry, the proportion of state financing to be earmarked for agricultural aid, and the level of foreign investment destined for agriculture.

- **Investment shares of state, collective and individual must be carefully regulated in order to promote a coordinated system of investment embracing all three parties.** Since 1949, 66% of agricultural fixed capital investment has come from collective and the individual sectors, and 34% from work units under ownership of the whole people. In our proposed plan for the next ten years, investment by the collective sector and individual farmers will rise to around 72%. Four further measures are necessary to strengthen agriculture's capacity for self-development:

  (i) In the interests of rural economic development, we must encourage and help farmers to increase grain production, using this as a base from which to diversify operations.
  (ii) We must raise both land and labour productivity. This will help rationalise relative industrial and agricultural prices, and resolve the twin problems of declining agricultural product prices and the comparatively low profitability of farm production (especially grain cultivation). It should also help to close the 'price scissors' differential between industrial and agricultural products.
  (iii) We must encourage and help farmers to manage their consumption and accumulation properly. Accumulation should be increased and the unfair burdens placed on farmers should be reduced. Farmers' accumulation and capacity for self-development must be reinforced.
  (iv) We must adopt various economic measures to encourage farmers voluntarily to increase investment, and devote more labour to farm construction.

Channels for investment must be expanded, so that funds can be raised by various means (including foreign investment, individual fund-raising, joint stock systems, enterprise groups, and bond issues). Our policies must respect the principle that investment should be the responsibility of its beneficiaries. Engineering projects such as irrigation works, water-transfer projects, afforestation for wood and paper production, and comprehensive farm development projects – all offer benefits to different parties. From now on, the burden of investment must be spread among beneficiaries according to the relative benefits that each party promises to gain from the relevant project.

• **We must carefully manage the relationship between shares of investment originating in agriculture and coming from the locality, so that we gradually develop a rational and effective investment structure.**

(i) Irrigation is the lifeblood of agriculture and fundamental to national economic and social development. Since 1980, alongside a marked decline in capital investment in agriculture there has been an even steeper reduction in irrigation investment. Between 1981 and 1990, state investment in agriculture fell from 10.6% to 3.9% of total basic capital construction investment. In the same period, capital investment in irrigation fell from 62.3% to 54.8% of farm investment (from 6.6% to 2.1% of total state capital investment). Such reductions run contrary to the needs of agriculture and the development of the national economy. In order to help remedy this situation, irrigation investment should be increased – and listed as a separate item.

(ii) We must increase investment in upgrading and renewing agricultural facilities, and fully exploit the potential of existing engineering projects. Since 1981, the share of such investment in agricultural fixed investment has been a mere 15.8% for farm activities under public ownership. If such investment is too low, many agricultural, forestry and irrigation engineering projects will become increasingly defective and ineffectual. Henceforth, work units under the ownership of the entire people should increase the proportion of fixed capital investment devoted to upgrading and renewal to around 20%. In order to facilitate fulfilment of this goal, a system of capital funding for large-scale upgrading and renewal in agriculture be established to provide a guaranteed source of funds.

(iii) In terms of regional investment distribution, relatively high returns on investment in central regions with a fairly low level of agricultural production should be further improved, and investment funds transferred to agriculture in western regions, where there is heavy reliance on grain production and where the population is relatively poor.

• **We must carefully control the relationships between speed and quality, and construction and management, in order to change the thrust of agricultural fixed capital in such a way as to make efficiency the prime of focus of investment activity.** This requires implementation of the following measures:

(i) Planning must be comprehensive and investment kept under tight control. It is recommended that in drawing up an 'Agricultural Investment Law', the State Council should make clear:

- the origin of investment funds
- the general remit for using each channel of investment
- the methods by which investment funds are to be planned, arranged, managed and inspected.

(ii) A system of rights and responsibilities for the use of agricultural capital should be established. Relevant departments should assume responsibility for the development of both agricultural investment and production. Some policies – for example, the construction of bases for producing commodity grain and the economic responsibility system for quota production – have already achieved remarkable results. We must build on these and establish strict audit systems and administrative mechanisms for the recovery of reimbursable investment.

(iii) We must proceed in accordance with a strict order of planning appropriate for capital investment. The principle of appraisal and discussion before coming to a decision must be upheld and we must be careful to select only those projects that offer clear benefits. Mechanisms must be established for monitoring important projects throughout their implementation.

(iv) We must set up management systems tailored to the relevant industry, including administrative mechanisms for the imposition of water charges, and for funding risk insurance, etc.

• **We must carefully regulate the relationship between raising agriculture's production capacity and raising the production capacity of individual industries related to agricultural production. We must also improve external conditions for agricultural construction and ensure a high degree of coordination within overall agricultural production capacity.** The Eighth Plenary Session of the Thirteenth Party Congress stressed the need to raise agriculture's overall production capacity. Accordingly, we must increase the output capacity of crop farming, forestry, livestock, fishing and subsidiaries. We must also expand the production and supply of capital goods for agriculture and extend capacity at every stage of the production process. This is a more complex process than merely strengthening agricultural construction and increasing fixed capital investment in farming. That is, we must also strengthen other industries and services that are related to agricultural production – including building facilities for agro industry, transportation, communications, energy resources, commerce, supply and marketing, education, technology, information, private and public finance, etc. All of this will help ensure that overall production capacity is both comprehensive and coordinated.

Document 5.6

'China throws itself into international competition: agriculture faces a new challenge'

FANG YAN

Economy and News, 1993, No. 2

China is preparing to participate and compete in the international market on a larger scale than ever before. Related problems faced by agriculture impinge not only on the farm sector itself, but also on industrial enterprises that use agricultural and sideline products as major raw materials.

China's status in world agriculture is improving

Under the impact of economic reform and liberalisation, China's increasing contact with the outside world has ended a long period of agricultural isolation. China now has reciprocal relationships based on agricultural support, exchange and cooperation with over a hundred countries and territories. The creation of this network has facilitated the exchange of resources and new product varieties, agricultural training and technological cooperation, and has attracted capital. All this has accelerated China's agricultural development and enabled China to take its rightful place in global agricultural development.

The 1980s saw large-scale increases in China's production of farm products, with the annual rate of output growth for major agricultural products exceeding the world average. Output of cotton, sugar-cane, tobacco, pork, beef and mutton increased annually at twice the world rate, and there were notable improvements in China's world output ranking. Except for sugar beet, China now ranks among the top four countries in the world in the production of major agricultural products.

The increase in farm output (especially cash crops) has boosted exports not only of agricultural goods, but also of textile and light industrial products that use agricultural raw materials. Associated with this has been a degree of structural adjustment. Between 1980 and 1990, the value of China's merchandise trade moved from deficit into surplus, with total export earnings rising by US$43.88 billion (of which agricultural exports totalled US$3.6 billion, imports meanwhile growing by US$400 million). Agricultural exports have gradually evolved from basic raw material products into 'new agricultural products', lying somewhere between pure agricultural and pure industrial goods (for example, canned and quick-frozen products). The higher degree of food processing embodied in these processes has increased the foreign exchange value of farm exports and widened China's international market. Between 1980 and 1990, the export value of light industrial food and textile products rose by US$8.5 billion,

Table 5.7 China's agricultural output and its world ranking

	Output (m.tons)		As % global output		Global ranking	
	1980	1990	1980	1990	1980	1990
Food Grains	183.9	407.8	18.1	20.8	–	11
Cotton	2.7	4.5	19.5	24.8	2	1
Peanuts	3.6	6.4	21.2	27.9	2	2
Rapeseed	2.4	7.0	22.4	28.7	2	1
Sugarcane	22.8	57.6	3.1	5.5	9	4
Sugar beet	6.3	14.5	2.4	4.7	12	5
Tobacco	0.7	2.6	13.6	37.8	2	1
Tea	0.3	0.5	16.3	21.4	2	1
Pork, mutton and beef	12.1	25.1	10.9	19.6	3	1
Fish	4.5	12.4	6.2	12.3	3	1

Note: Output figures in million tons.

Table 5.8 World output of agricultural products

	Global output (million tons)		Average growth p.a. (%)	
	1980	1990	World	China
Grain	1,565.0	1,955.0	2.2	3.6
Cotton	13.9	18.2	2.7	5.2
Peanuts	17.0	22.9	3.0	5.9
Rapeseed	10.6	24.2	8.6	11.3
Sugarcane	721.9	1,044.3	3.7	9.7
Sugar beet	264.0	305.3	1.5	8.7
Tobacco	5.3	7.0	2.8	13.9
Tea	1.9	2.5	3.1	5.9
Pork, mutton & beef	110.4	128.0	1.5	7.6
Aquatic products	72.1	100.3	3.3	10.6

showing the farm sector's ability to generate sufficient raw materials to expand textile and other light industrial exports.

The climate of international trade and the General Agreement on Tariffs and Trade (GATT) have had a major impact on China's agricultural imports and exports

Accelerated agricultural development in China coincided with great changes in global agricultural production. The extension of mechanisation, combined with the adoption of long-term agriculture-support subsidies in the US, Japan and the EEC in order to promote domestic production, led to a rapid rise in global farm output. There were large increases in world output of major agricultural products – especially staples, such as grain and cotton. EEC countries that had previously been net importers of grain became net exporters. Some developing countries, such as India and Pakistan, also used international funds in order to promote agricultural development, thereby raising grain self-sufficiency ratios and boosting exports of cash crops.

Higher output of major agricultural products dampened international prices. Meanwhile, developed countries' use of their economic strength to open up international competition posed a major threat to developing countries' export trade. Predictions suggest that the rate of increase in world demand for farm products will decline from an average of 1.8% p.a. in the 1980s to 0.8% by the year 2000. In the same period, output rises based on scientific and technological advances promise to generate excess supply of agricultural goods in international markets. Such changes in the international trade climate are likely to pose a new challenge to farm development in China.

Weakening agricultural prices in international markets and an increase in imports will threaten domestic production

Accession to GATT would give China the benefit of favourable customs tariff conditions. The elimination of administrative intervention would have advantages and disadvantages for the import and export of agricultural products. Competitive conditions for China's exports would be enhanced, but domestic production might be damaged by a flood of imports. In recent years, the annual world trade volume of grain has reached around 200 million tons (about 100 million tons of wheat, more than 80 million tons of coarse grains, and over 10 million tons of husked rice). The low level of China's annual grain exports – between 5.5 and 7.5 million tons (a mere 2.5% – 4% of the global trade volume) highlights China's competitive weakness.

The volume of China's grain imports is about 15 million tons. These are mainly shipments of wheat and account for some 14% of the global wheat trade. Currently the price of wheat on the international market – about US$ 130 per ton in hard currency – is weak. When additional expenses are included, this translates into RMB 0.45 *yuan* per *jin*,[52] or approximately the same as the domestic wheat price (though imported wheat is of higher quality than its domestic equivalent). The Chinese government's recent decision to raise the contract quota purchase price of wheat will push the domestic market price above the international market price. At present, grain imports into China are subject to central controls and exempt from

52 1 jin is approximately 0.5 kg. (Ed.)

customs duties. Once administrative intervention has been revoked, domestic production will be severely damaged by imports, with grain production in coastal regions bearing the brunt of the competition.

Three major factors affecting the competitiveness of Chinese agricultural products

The three factors mentioned here are: low domestic labour productivity; rising production costs; and weak international competitiveness of domestic products.

With limited resources and a vast population, per capita access to natural resources in China is severely constrained. Average per capita arable land availability is only 0.84 hectare – less than a third of the world average. The corresponding figure for water resources is 2700 cubic metres – a quarter of the world average – placing China 84th in the world ranking. Water resources per arable *mou*[53] are 1300 cubic metres, or half the world average. But China's rural population stands at 840 million people (35.8% of the global figure). The absorptive capacity of land and capital under traditional agricultural conditions has long since been surpassed. Between 1957 and 1975, agricultural productivity fell by about 30%. After 1978, the annual transfer of 5–7 million surplus rural labourers to non-agricultural rural industry helped to check the declining trend in labour productivity. Even so, the labour force was growing faster than the rate at which surplus labour could be absorbed by non-agricultural industry. Moreover, persistent rises in the prices of farm inputs led to diminishing capital returns.

In short, output of agricultural and sideline goods per unit of labour is relatively low. At present, every Chinese farmer supports 3.4 people – the same as in the 1950s. In the USA, the corresponding figure has risen from 58 to 75 people, and in West Germany, from 10 to 67 people. Grain production per unit of labour in China is only 56% of the world average. Meanwhile, reliance on large-scale price rises in order to sustain farm output has driven the prices of many goods to a level that is the same as or higher than in international markets, making it difficult for Chinese producers to compete. With 25% of global output, China is the world's largest producer of cotton – a position that should give it some advantage. But policy mistakes in recent years have caused cotton production to fall significantly and forced China to withdraw from the international market that it was just beginning to penetrate. Following two price hikes, the real price of cotton is now close to the international market price. Given the limitations of international market capacity, intensified competition is likely to exacerbate China's difficulties.

---

53 1 *mou* = 0.67 ha. (Ed.)

Incompatibility between the development of agro-industry and the demands of agricultural modernisation

China's chemical fertiliser production accounts for 11.26% of world output, but 17% of global consumption. Its main fertiliser products are nitrogenous and phosphate fertilisers (16% and 9% of global output). Of 105.52 million tons of fertiliser applied in China in 1990, 62% was nitrogenous, 26.8% was phosphate, and 3.1% was potash; only 8% comprised compound fertilisers. Its use of nitrogenous, phosphate and potash fertilisers accounted for 23%, 13.6% and 5.9% of global applications. The current global ratio of nitrogenous, phosphate and potash fertiliser is 1.00:0.48:0.35, compared with 1.00:0.43:0.08 in China – figures that highlight the low share of potash in total applications. China has abundant phosphate resources, but because the phosphate fertiliser industry has developed slowly and domestic supplies are scarce, reliance on imports continues. The use of organic manure to compensate for deficiencies in phosphate and potash fertiliser would help resolve such problems.

There is also a lack of farm machinery in China, where equipment tends to be old, worn-out and short of parts, and renovation and renewal of obsolete machinery takes a long time. China has 6.1 tractors for every 6,667 hectares of arable land – two thirds less than in the USA. Overall, the existing capacity for mechanised sowing and harvesting, as well as for irrigation and drought-resistance is quite inadequate.

Limitations on agricultural development caused by the low rate of scientific and technological improvements

Agricultural science and technology have advanced to fairly high levels in China, with some projects ranking among the best in the world and others at the cutting edge of global agro-technology. China leads the world in the development of hybrid rice, irradiated breeding and the '*Machuanpin*' LP Vaccine. It ranks among the world leaders in selective breeding technology for hybrid varieties of maize, wheat, rape and potatoes. Significant results have also been achieved in the development of various forms of rural energy from solar, wind, biological and geothermal sources. The results of such research in China have reached international standards. But only 30% of the fruits of agricultural research are translated into practical use, compared with 70–80% in developed countries. Matching developed countries' implementation rate would facilitate a qualitative leap in agricultural production.

The main reasons for the slow take-up rate are insufficient funds and staffing to disseminate improvements and the poor quality of the rural workforce. China employs 555,000 people in agricultural science and technology – a mere 5.7% of the global figure – each one of whom is responsible for 172 hectares of arable land and 1,615 farmers. The high rate of illiteracy among China's rural population – approximately 35%

(30 percentage points higher than in the USA and Japan) is another major obstacle to developing a rural commodity economy.

The future direction of agricultural development

Under the impact of technological modernisation and more scientific management, the 1990s herald great changes in the outward manifestation of China's agricultural production. Developments in transport and communications are facilitating the emergence of a global economy, and domestic problems can no longer be resolved behind closed doors. Active participation in international markets and international resource exchange to overcome domestic resource gaps offer shortcuts to accelerated economic development. Against the background of its distinctive problems – the scarcity of resources, large population and low labour productivity – China must formulate long-term policies that can use the international market to boost its agricultural development.

First, with the domestic economy as the foundation, we must actively participate in international markets. As economic development proceeds, China will seek to sell more and more products in such markets. But market expansion is a reciprocal process and if China wants to increase its exports, it must be prepared to open its own market in return. When farm products are in short supply, exporting such goods can be even more powerful than exporting oil products. Even when agricultural goods are in surplus, their export is a kind of weapon. From now on, with domestic production as the starting point, we must take advantage of current favourable conditions created by abundant international supplies of farm products and formulate long-term plans to stabilise our imports. We should use grain imports to strengthen our bargaining position in international trade and create the conditions in which an outward-looking economy can be developed.

Second, we must focus on the long-term, avoid short-termism, and develop the foreign-currency-earning potential of agriculture. We must make good use of our vast territory, producing a wide range of goods from both tropical and temperate regions. We also need to develop our characteristically 'high value, small variety' agricultural and subsidiary products according to international market demand, and raise the quality and value-added of Chinese products.

Third, we must promote the development of an efficient agriculture through more effective implementation of scientific and technological improvements. We must adopt advanced technology in order to exploit agriculture's full potential. We must promote the rational development of all agricultural, social and economic resources, protect the natural environment, create a comprehensive farm system, raise land productivity, realise the optimum allocation of all natural resources, reduce production costs and improve economic benefits.

China is a major agricultural country. There is a close relationship between China's agricultural development and world agriculture. China must find its own distinctive path of agricultural development within the wider global context and make its own distinctive contribution to world agricultural development.

Document 5.7

'Short-term policies and long-term strategies for solving China's grain supply problems'

FAN GANG

China Rural Survey, 1993, No. 2

Since last year, China's grain production and agricultural development have become topics of fierce debate. Why has grain output shown signs of instability during the past few years and why does grain production appear to be on a downward trend? Various reasons – for example, insufficient farm investment, excessively low prices of farm products – have been put forward and various remedies suggested. But the real issue is how to formulate a long-term agricultural development strategy in the wider context of domestic and international markets. The scope of enquiry must be broadened so that it is not a purely agricultural debate.

[In the first two sections of this article, the author briefly analyses investment trends and argues that low rates of return and associated low farm incomes have been the main reason for the inadequacy of agricultural investment in China. He goes on to suggest that underlying depressed levels of income reflect a basic contradiction between agriculture's diminishing share of GDP and the excessively high share of the labour force still employed in farming – this, in turn, resulting from China's high man-land ratio, capital shortages, low rate of capital utilization, and the necessity of industrialising from a very low industrial base. In the early 1990s, agriculture still absorbed over 50% of total employment, even though its share of GDP had fallen to around 20%. Having to share this limited income among a still huge agricultural population meant that per capita farm income remained depressed for a long period. Fan Gang suggests that for the time being, this situation is likely to persist and may worsen. (Ed.)]

We cannot keep relying on rises in the price of grain in order to generate agricultural development

'Irrational' prices are an important reason for the low level of rural income, leading many to conclude that farm product prices must be raised in order to promote agricultural development.

This is undoubtedly a serious problem. The last few years have witnessed the general liberalisation of prices of cash crops and livestock products, as well as industrial and processed goods. Only the prices of grain, cotton and other agricultural crops have remained artificially suppressed. It is true that for a certain period, grain prices rose somewhat. But such increases were accompanied by higher prices of capital goods, which largely offset any improvement in farmers' real income. In 1994, for example, there was a significant rise in both the market price and state purchase price of farm products. Meanwhile, however, the price of industrial products – especially capital goods for agriculture – also increased, so that the increase in farm incomes attributable to price changes was a mere 5%. This has been a common scenario in the past: since 1979 there has been a close connection between China's 'agricultural production cycle' and the 'price adjustment cycle' for farm products.

Over a period of one or two years, adjustments in grain prices and increases in farm income, combined with administrative measures and other government policies designed to address falling agricultural production, may succeed in stabilising agricultural growth to some extent. But this will only work in the short run. The real problem is what to do beyond the short run, when the effects of grain price adjustment policies have worn off.

In other words, is it possible to rely on rises in grain prices in order to maintain increases in grain production? It is significant that market prices in China for the most important varieties of grain are currently [1995] very close to international prices and if they continue to rise, they will soon reach parity. Under free economic conditions, the international market price sets an upper limit for the domestic market price. In the last couple of years, in addition to grain imports arranged by central government departments, rising domestic grain prices have generated big increases in the consumption of imported grain in developed coastal regions of the country. If we want to raise and keep prices of domestic farm products above international levels, the government must either restrict imports or implement strict protectionist policies for agriculture.

How far will grain prices have to rise in order to bring farm incomes to the same level as those enjoyed by non-agricultural workers? Suppose that non-agricultural activities grow at an annual rate of only 10% in the next few years. During the same period, agriculture will also grow. Assume too that the agricultural share of the total work force falls to 45% by the end of the century, and that there are no increases in industrial product prices. Even on these assumptions, equalising income levels between non-agricultural and agricultural workers would require an almost fivefold rise in the price of grain to a level even higher than that of Japan, where the grain price is currently 430% above the international market price. It may be argued that this is an extreme hypothesis – after all, it is not essential that agricultural and non-agricultural incomes should be exactly equal. But the analysis shows that given the existing economic structure, the price of grain would have to rise to a very high level in order to resolve the problem of low farm income. But although the problem of raising farm incomes might be resolved, that of farmers' reluctance to invest in agriculture would remain unresolved. In any case, simply relying on raising grain prices in order to bring the rate of increase of agricultural incomes in line with that of industrial workers is not enough. As long as there remains a wide gap between rates of return from industrial and agricultural investment, rises in farm income are unlikely to generate increases in farm investment, and agriculture will still be unable to achieve long-run and stable growth.

An even more pressing question is whether it is wise for a developing country like China to use protectionist methods in order to keep the domestic price of grain high, even when its international market price is low. A rise in the domestic grain price and higher labour costs are bound to have an effect on the pace of industrialisation and the development of non-agricultural rural industry. It will also influence inflows of foreign investment. Will this benefit the development of the economy as a whole? Comparative advantage has never resided with China's agriculture. As a developing country with a very high man-land ratio, we must look where our comparative advantage lies in order to maintain the impetus of long-run growth and accelerated capital formation. Obviously it does not lie in agriculture, nor for the time being does it seem to lie in high-tech industries. Our comparative advantage lies in processing industries based on low labour costs. But grain is a major determinant of labour costs and if the domestic price of grain continues to be kept above international market levels, the result will be a rapid decline and eventual loss of our key advantage, which will damage long-run growth prospects.

This is not to suggest that henceforth we should impose total control on prices, nor that we should prevent prices from rising in accordance with the forces of market demand and supply. Nor does it mean that we should extend *no* protection to the domestic market. But the analysis does indicate that trying to secure agricultural development on the basis of continuing rises in the price of grain will threaten overall economic growth.

It will be difficult to resolve the problem by relying on major increases in government agricultural investment or by offering farmers more subsidies

An increase in government investment in agriculture can be achieved by making available more funds or by subsidising agriculture. No matter which approach is used, the basic idea is the same: when farm incomes are low and farmers lack incentive to invest in agriculture themselves, the government should step in and 'use industry to subsidize agriculture' by redirecting funds in a targeted manner. Agriculture is the cornerstone of the national economy. Given its public ownership characteristics, it needs government involvement and the support of public expenditure. As a matter of urgency, we need to reform the system of public finances and to redirect more funds from non-farming activities to agriculture. But in the short term, do all levels of government have the capacity and motivation to increase real farm investment? In 1993, the total level of agricultural investment, narrowly defined (i.e. investment in basic construction, and renewal and renovation) was a mere 2.55 billion *yuan* – just 0.37% of the national total. Even including all the productive fixed capital formation undertaken by individual peasants and assuming that it was used for agriculture, the total would become 14.79 billion *yuan*, (1.18% of total social investment). On the broadest definition, investment in agriculture was a mere 1.9% of overall social fixed capital investment in 1994, or 0.3 percentage points lower than in 1993. At current prices, capital investment in agriculture plus investment in water conservancy and irrigation increased by only 13% between 1992 and 1993 – far below the corresponding national figure for aggregate capital investment of 58.5%. At constant prices, this would be translated into *negative* growth. If agriculture's share of national investment were to be brought in line with its share of national income, farm investment would have to rise to over 300 billion *yuan* (at 1994 prices), or ten times its current level. In the absence of any incentive for individual farmers to invest, reliance on government to make up the shortfall would necessitate having to spend 60% of its current budget on agriculture. This is wholly unrealistic. The farm sector's share of public expenditure – currently some 8% – has been in decline for some years. But public expenditure's share of GDP has also been falling – from 16.2% to 11.8% between 1993 and 1994 alone. Admittedly, local government has access to large amounts of non-standard, extra-budgetary income, but this is very rarely used for agricultural investment.

In short, under present circumstances, to rely on government to raise agricultural investment by even a single percentage point would be extremely difficult. ... Current government policy is to strengthen and increase agricultural investment in order to offset reductions in investment from other sources. We must, however, be fully aware of government limitations. If we were to rely entirely on government efforts to the detriment of other measures, we might have another agricultural and grain crisis on our hands.

From another perspective, given the current level of agricultural development, more and more investment is needed to increase grain production and it is becoming increasingly difficult to secure such rises in output. Although total grain output is quite low, unit area yields are fairly impressive (around 4.4 tons per hectare, compared with the world average of 2.8 tons). Yields in China are similar to those of the US (4.75 tons), but below those of Japan (5.35 tons) and some European countries. Without major scientific and technological breakthroughs, the potential to increase capital and labour productivity is very limited. The inference is that a rise in agricultural investment will not generate a significant increase in rural incomes, nor will it resolve the problem of insufficient incentives for farmers to grow crops and promote agricultural development. Furthermore, more and more investment would be needed to raise grain output by a given increment, and at a price that would get higher and higher.

No matter whether we raise the prices of farm products, increase government investment or provide more agricultural subsidies, the effect will be to redirect more economic resources towards agriculture. For the time being, this is necessary. But we must recognise that the allocation of more and more resources towards producing increasingly expensive grain is bound to threaten national income growth and overall economic development. Structural change and development have reached the stage at which rapid growth in market demand for non-agricultural products has led to high value-added and high rates of return on non-agricultural investment. As a result, those who have a vested interest in non-farm production have strong and persuasive grounds for opposing any increase in farm investment.

The long-run strategy lies in enhancing the use of farm science and technology and transferring large numbers of agricultural labourers to other professions

We have illustrated the problems presently facing agricultural production and suggested the limitations inherent in current policies, such as raising grain prices and increasing government investment, designed to promote agricultural development. Only through a sober and thorough examination of these problems will it be possible to identify a practical and feasible alternative strategy.

The key to restoring impetus to long-run agricultural development lies in raising farmers' – not 'rural' – per capita income. This can be achieved in two ways, one of which is to 'increase the value of the numerator', defined here as aggregate agricultural income. This is the goal that the various policy measures analysed above seek to fulfill. From a long-term perspective, however, the basic way of increasing the numerator is not to expand agricultural subsidies nor to raise the general level of farm investment. Rather, what is most important is to increase investment in agricultural science and technology in order to achieve a new breakthrough in these areas. Given the constraints on farm output growth, China cannot rely on continuing transfers of funds or the 'use of industry to subsidise agriculture' in order to 'expand the numerator'. Because of their small agricultural populations, developed countries can achieve an equitable long-run distribution of income by allocating 1%–2% of GDP to agricultural subsidies. But because of its much larger farm population and the existence of wide per capita income differentials, China cannot do the same. Even if the equivalent of 10%–20% of GDP were taken from non-farm industry and used for agricultural subsidies, income equality would not be achieved. In the long term, China simply cannot afford to rely on such subsidies.

The inability to rely on subsidies has led to increasing advocacy of another way of increasing farmers' incomes: namely, to 'reduce the denominator', or cut the number of agricultural income recipients. This is a critical condition of stable agricultural development in China.

Of course, reducing the farm population cannot be achieved by agriculture alone. It may be possible to cut farm employment (for example, by expanding the scale of operations), but an associated precondition is that other sectors of the economy should provide more work opportunities. Otherwise, those who lose their jobs in farming will merely become unemployed members of the farm population and still be dependent on agricultural income. The basic way in which to reduce the agricultural population is therefore to increase the rate of growth of the non-agricultural sector of the economy. The development of non-agricultural rural industry has already provided major employment opportunities and has absorbed many surplus farm workers. Once this large-scale transfer of labour has been completed, available farm income will be shared among a smaller number of remaining agricultural workers. The result will be a major increase in per capita income, which will, in turn, guarantee farmers' willingness to engage in production. By the same token, farmers will have the necessary motivation and capacity to increase agricultural investment – including scientific and technological improvements – thereby promoting the long-term, stable development of agriculture and increases in grain supplies. Thus, it is clear that agricultural development is not a matter for agriculture alone. We must transcend the farm sector and see the problem from the perspective of the whole economy.

The short-run strategy is to make full use of international resources in the international market, to increase grain supplies, and to accelerate the transfer of labour from agricultural to non-agricultural activities

The current problem is that in the short-term, grain production is unlikely to increase rapidly. This reflects the impact of various factors limiting agricultural development, such as the tension between the traditional economic structure and the process of economic modernisation, and the natural constraints imposed by a high man-land ratio. This raises the question of how domestic demand for grain can be satisfied without simultaneously raising prices and farm subsidies to such high levels that they damage economic growth and slow down the transfer of labour from agricultural to non-agricultural production.

Provided that China can maintain sufficient growth momentum to generate adequate purchasing power and can keep its low-cost competitiveness as a developing country in international markets for industrial goods, there is one way in which both objectives can be satisfied. That is, as domestic grain prices gradually reach international market levels, we should use imports of relatively cheap grain to fill short-term gaps in domestic supply resulting from our inability to increase agricultural investment. In this way, we can make huge resource savings in order to develop non-agricultural rural industry and accelerate the transfer of farm labour.

From this perspective, we should not place undue emphasis on grain 'self-sufficiency'. To ignore cheap grain that is available in the international market and insist on undertaking large-scale investment in order to produce small amounts of high-cost domestic grain would be unwise. There are some in the West who say that as development proceeds, China will be unable to support itself and who argue that by the 2030, 'China will have a grain shortfall of 370 million tons'. Some of this analysis reflects the sincere hope by honest and well-meaning academics that China can obviate a future agricultural crisis. We must, however, also guard against the 'Sinophobia' expressed by representatives of political, media and business circles in developed countries to the effect that the rapid expansion of Asian economies, including China's development, will adversely affect their real income levels by generating increased competition in industrial markets, robbing them of employment opportunities and raising the world prices of grain, oil, and other raw materials.

Such concern has nothing to do with preventing famine in a developing country. But if we use high prices to maintain grain self-sufficiency, undertake large-scale agricultural investment and slow down the growth of the non-agricultural sector, we will be doing exactly what these Western commentators want us to do. They will continue to benefit from low grain prices; they will avoid increased competition in the market for industrial goods; and they will be able to maintain their hegemony in the world economy.

It is high time that China began to use international markets in order to boost its own economic modernisation. It is time for us to start influencing world prices and to consume more of the resources enjoyed by mankind as a whole. We must not allow ourselves to fall into the 'grain self-sufficiency' trap that has been set for us by others. Buying a little more grain from the international market is not the end of the world. We must simply make sure that the bulk of our grain is produced domestically and that the grain we buy comes from many different sources, rather than a single country. In this way, we can benefit from international market competition.

As for specific measures, apart from increasing grain imports through different channels, we could also consider the establishment of our own grain bases in countries, such as Russia or Brazil, where the man-land ratio is low. The associated costs would be considerably less than those involved in trying to increase output on our own land. Economic liberalisation in China is under way and our economic strength and market development require that we consider problems of resource allocation from a broad international perspective. Of course it is possible for Chinese people to 'support themselves'. But this does not necessarily mean that we must grow our own grain. We can use our own money to buy the grain that we need. Nor does it mean that we have to use our limited arable land base to grow our own grain. Just as Western countries have set up enterprises throughout the world in order to support themselves, so China's grain can be grown in various different parts of the world.

6

Population and Labour

POPULATION

China's population remains a dramatic and controversial arena of policy concern.[1] Within China, policy makers continue to grapple with the food, employment and general developmental consequences of population growth. Outside interest in China's population is also high. One reason for this is that since China accounts for more than one fifth of the world's total population its population trends have a global as well as domestic and regional impact. Global impact in the sense that world population and environmental objectives depend on China's population performance. Regional impact in the sense that failure to manage the size and movement of China's population could result in unwanted migrations and environmental damage for China's immediate neighbours. These would be of particular concern for small economies, including Hong Kong.

Another reason for international interest in China's population is the controversial character of Chinese population policies. Over the past fifty years these have focused on campaigns to limit fertility by employing powerful incentive and coercive techniques. Most recently there has been world wide concern with the demographic, social, and human rights implications of the unique 'One Child Family' policy. All these concerns may be summarised in the question: should developing countries take China's population policies as models to emulate, or should they avoid them?

Because population trends shift relatively slowly and because the population policies of the reform period were very deeply rooted in the preceding history of population experience, we start with an over-view of population developments in the period from 1949 to the announcement of the One Child Family policy in 1980.

1 The general sources used for this section are national and regional population journals. I have also referred to annual issues of the *Almanac of China's Population* and other major official publications.

POPULATION PROBLEMS AND CHINESE POLICIES, 1949–1980

Population policies in developing countries are primarily concerned with fertility. This is because mortality tends to decline automatically as modern infrastructures appear, and this downturn is likely to be particularly strong where health administration is good and where international agencies support programmes to eliminate life threatening diseases.

The crucial issue for policy makers, therefore, is how long is the gap in time between the downturn in mortality and that of fertility, and how rapid the decline in fertility will be once under way. With *no active policy*, a number of factors associated with urbanisation and social modernisation will tend to reduce fertility automatically. For example, the costs of child nurturing and education will rise; openings for children to participate in the labour market will decline as the labour market becomes more formal and regulated; and opportunities for women to work and participate in life outside the household will rise.

This 'natural' tendency for fertility to decline may be *assisted* by population related policies. Particularly important are those to educate women and support the medical infrastructure, especially in rural areas. Such an approach represents the second broad option for population policy. (The first consists of waiting passively for the downturn). The third option arises when the 'natural' rate of fertility decline is judged to be altogether too slow, or not yet to be in operation at all. In these circumstances, governments may decide on *active*, direct policies to induce a rapid fertility decline.

Over the long run since 1949, Chinese population policy has moved increasingly in the direction of the third alternative. This advance, however, has not been steady. It has been limited by inadequate understanding of demographic analysis, lack of reliable data, and by inexperience in implementing radical fertility reduction measures. The trajectory of population policies was also disturbed by political and ideological movements and in particular by swings in Mao's willingness to accept any type of population restraint.

Population policy in the early 1950s was driven by two considerations. One was Mao's ideological rejection of theories that implied any form of 'population pessimism' for China. Mao insisted that socialist transformation was the solution to China's population 'problem'. China's post-war economic recovery (1949–1952) gave superficial support to this view. The other element of population policy was the Soviet tradition of anti-abortion legislation and an ideology favouring population expansion.[2] This was ingrained in the Soviet Ministry of Health and transferred to the Chinese

---

2 According to the Soviet *Handbook* of *Political Economy*, high population growth was a mark of the superiority of socialism. However this dogma was developed in Russia where the population to land ratio was very favourable, while population trends in the advanced capitalist countries at that time were downward and giving rise to concern about their negative economic consequences.

health bureaucracy. Soviet style regulations strictly limiting abortion were introduced in China in 1950 and 1952.

Major doubts about these pro-natalist policies surfaced between 1954 and 1957. One source of doubt was the result of China's first national population census in 1953. This indicated that population was then nearly 600 million and growing by about 10 millions a year – 100 millions per decade. In the context of poor economic performance in 1954 and 1955, radical re-thinking based on this new evidence began. This was led by Liu Shaoqi and supported by Zhou Enlai and Deng Xiaoping. New measures included more permissive regulations on abortion and measures to facilitate and encourage a family planning programme.[3]

In September 1956 Zhou Enlai made a crucial ideological shift. In his *Second Five Year Plan for the Development of the National Economy, 1958–1962*, he detached population from health policy and attached it to the issue of economic development. In early 1957 Mao was also reported as supporting a ten year programme for trials, dissemination and full implementation of population control. However, in Autumn of the same year Mao attacked population experts in the Anti-Rightist Campaign that followed the Hundred Flowers movement. The most notable casualty of this was Professor Ma Yinchu of Beijing University. During the Great Leap Forward of 1958 short term increases in food production and rising employment in backyard steel campaigns reinforced Mao's old orthodoxy that, given socialist institutions and education, China did not need population control at all.

The events of 1957 to 1958 were of profound importance. Because although population policies were re-introduced in the 1960s and 1970s, the professional study of demography (and statistics) became a virtually forbidden area until the economic reforms began in 1978. Thus while administrative experience developed, demographic understanding hardly advanced at all between 1957 and 1978.

The impact of the post Leap economic depression on China's population is still debated. The highest estimates of population loss are in the range of 50 to 60 millions.[4] The lowest (Chinese) estimates argue for figures as low as 18–20 millions. Whatever the exact figures, the population rebound as

3 Present day articles emphasise the role of Deng in population policy since the early 1950s and his unique contribution to theory. It is clear that Deng did join forces in favour of population policies at the very outset. However, the evidence is overwhelming that the power and master mind in this field was Zhou Enlai, who was effectively in charge of economic affairs from the mid-1950s until his death in 1976. It was Zhou who joined population to economic policy. In the reform era, Deng refined Zhou's approach to link population to living standards. In the 1950s and 1960s Liu Shaoqi was also important, although he is now rarely mentioned.

4 'Loss' is defined as the difference between actual population totals and the hypothetical population that would have obtained had not extraordinary factors influenced vital rates during 1960–1961. An authoritative view on this subject from China is that by Li Chengrui, 'Fluctuations in population induced by the "Great Leap Forward",' *Population Research*, 1958, No. 1. Li's views are particularly interesting because he was formerly Director of the State Statistical Bureau.

health and economic conditions improved triggered a renewal of population policies. Population accelerated in 1962 and in 1963 there were more
than 30 million births with a the fertility rate of over 40 per thousand. The
1964 Census confirmed a total population in excess of 700 millions. The
Party reacted quickly.

In the 1950s population policy had been inconsistent and focused mainly
on easing controls on abortion and on first steps in disseminating birth
control techniques. No proper infrastructure was in place to support these
policies at any level

In the 1960s the Government set firm, progressive targets to reduce
overall population growth. For example one target was to reduce urban
population increase to only 1% per annum growth by 1975. Total
population was to be limited to 800 millions in 1970 and this implied that
the population growth rate be reduced from 2.7% in 1964 to 1.7% by
1970.

To achieve these goals the Party began to encourage late marriage which
was normally 23 for rural women and 25 years of age for others. They also
put forward a new slogan: 'To have one [child] is not too few. To have two
is excellent. To have three is too many.' These policies were supported by
various organisational initiatives, including the rural barefoot doctor
programme.

But once again politics destroyed Zhou Enlai's efforts. During the first
chaotic phase of the Cultural Revolution (1966–1970) more than 100
million births occurred and the Crude Birth Rate, instead of falling below
25 per thousand as planned, rose to 33 per thousand.[5]

In 1970 Premier Zhou began his third campaign to develop a working
population control policy and for the first time he appeared, crucially, to
have gained Mao's consistent support.[6] Still fighting the health bureaucrats,
in June 1970 Zhou affirmed that: 'Birth planning is a matter of national
planning. It is not a health problem but a planning problem'. The new long
term target was again reduction to 1.5% per annum growth and this was to
be achieved by a combination of late marriage, spaced births, and small
completed families. The slogan of the 1960s was amended in the 1970s to
run in the stricter form of: 'Best is one [child]; the maximum is two; three is
forbidden.'

Leadership of these campaigns was vested in 1973 in a new State Council
Small Group and strong economic and political pressures were used to
achieve local targets. At about this time, however, political pressure on

5 The Crude Birth Rate is the number of births per thousand of the population in any
  year. It is 'crude' and unsatisfactory for trend measurement because it takes no
  account of shifts in the population age structure. Thus the rate may rise simply
  because the number of females of child bearing age is rising.

6 Mao's commitment in the form of a document, *Chairman Mao's Directive on Planned
  Births*, still does not appear to be available. But it was published internally in a State
  Council Small Group publication in 1976. Presumably the Small Group used the
  document with Mao's name to ward off leftist attacks by underlining the orthodoxy
  of their policies.

targets became so great that falsification of local statistics was endemic. Overall, however, there is no doubt that population policy in the 1970s was pursued with a new determination. Goals were again specific, administration of policy strengthened, and in spite of a nominally 'voluntary' policy of family limitation, compliance enforced with strong measures.

Even allowing for statistical problems, results were remarkable and China recorded one of the sharpest falls in fertility in human history during that decade. It is estimated that the Total Fertility Rate fell from 5.812 in 1970 to 2.238 in 1980[7] and the Crude Birth Rate from 28 per thousand to 11.9. Annual additions to the population almost halved to about 12 millions per annum.

Nonetheless, in spite of these favourable trends and the historically unprecedented success of policy, acute anxiety about population issues remained in the late 1970s as Zhou and Mao died and as China approached its age of economic reform. In 1978 the State Council Small Group issued a report describing population control as Chairman Mao's 'Great work of many years', but reporting nonetheless that population programmes were 'anarchic' in many areas, with birth rates on the rise again. The Group proposed a new target of reducing the growth rate to below 1% by 1981 with the intention of keeping total population within 1.2 billion by the year 2000. Perhaps the leadership did not trust any of the figures available at the time or were in any case so alarmed at the weak performance of the economy that they felt another extreme push was necessary.

In February 1980 Finance Minister Li Xiannian pointed to one particular source of anxiety when he revealed that while population had grown by 49% between 1957 and 1977, grain output had grown by only 45%. Thus finally, in September of 1980 the Central Committee published an 'Open Letter' (*gong kai xin*) announcing the One Child Family (ICF) policy.

POPULATION POLICIES 1980–1991

In this document the Party opened its case by emphasising the long term perspective. It pointed out that whereas in the 109 years between 1840 and 1949 population had grown by only 130 millions, in the thirty year history of the People's Republic it had grown by 430 millions. Otherwise, the particular emphasis of the document was on the food problem and the difficulties inherent in raising grain supplies to keep pace with 12 million new mouths every year. (Estimated to be an additional 5 million tons of grain per annum). Essentially the new policy can be seen as the latest of a long line of attempts to keep China on track with old population growth targets by adopting a yet more extreme rule for permitted fertility. Actually,

---

7 The TFR is a measure of the number of children expected to be born to a woman on completion of her cycle of child-bearing years. No account is taken of the sex of the children or their expected mortality. The indicator is of great value because it eliminates the influence of age structure on measurement of fertility. A TFR of a little over 2 suggests that a population is replacing itself.

the most extreme rule (one child) that could be imagined as a public statement. The only general exclusion from the policy at this stage were to be the areas of minority (mainly Muslim) population which were normally also quite sparsely populated regions. Interestingly, the new policy was more extreme than its predecessors in another sense. The one child principle had been proposed earlier but at that stage the policy's 'proposal' (*tichang*) implied a desired rather than required pattern of conduct for couples. Although the new proposal used the same terminology, authoritative commentary stated that this time the term implied that no freedom of choice was permitted for those outside the official 'exceptions'.

During its early years the ICF policy was not successful. One problem was that the policy had been devised with little expert demographic input.[8] It therefore took no account of likely trends in nuptuality and fertility based on age structure, regional and historical factors. In addition, the targets were too simplistic with the question of 'exceptions' not worked out in the detail necessary for successful implementation in the field. In some areas, it was reported that reaching population targets would actually have required compulsory abortions of *first* pregnancies.

Even more fundamental was the failure to appreciate that the reform of the economy, particularly in rural areas, made it extremely difficult to secure compliance by means of incentives and control of resources. In the 1970s, local cadres controlled food, work allocations, access to welfare and education as well as having the support in population planning of the general climate of political coercion created by the Cultural Revolution. As the economy was decentralised and market forces introduced these levers of power were weakened. Indeed, the establishment of the household rather than the collective as the key to rural reform made the incentives to child bearing quite different from the household viewpoint. Rural reform not only strengthened the desire for more children, but also for male rather than female children.

By 1984 matters were in a crisis. Cadres complained that lack of detail made the policy unworkable and hostility in rural areas was intense. As one analyst summed it up: 'In the countryside we were in a dilemma with the One Child Policy. We couldn't continue with it, but we couldn't delay it either'.

Between 1984 and 1991 the Party continued to struggle with these difficulties, gradually acknowledging that policies had to take account of realities both in the overall demographic situation and in the aspirations of individual households. The problems, however, were indicated by the reception to the Central Committee's 'Document No.7' (April 1984). This

8 In 1973/1974 Zhou had encouraged a Beijing group to begin population research again to provide advice to the State Council. However, scholars were generally far too nervous to make a major effort on this work, bearing in mind the fate of their predecessors in 1957. After 1978, the United Nations made a major contribution to the training of a new generation of Chinese demographers. The nervousness of demographers even in the late 1970s is described in an article by Wu Zhongguan, 'Reflections on my work as a demographic researcher', *Population Research*, 1998, No. 4.

had much to say about the importance of birth planning and the roles of education and persuasion. But cadres complained that the directive's essence was: 'Targets made of steel; methods made of soybeans'.

Construction of new policies was made even more difficult by the fact that reliable data were hard to get. At the higher bureaucratic and academic levels the arrangements for data collection and analysis were improving, but in the field the crucial surveys (especially the 1% sample census) needed to estimate fertility were becoming difficult to complete. These depended on accurate information on births being given to investigators, but hostility to officials in the countryside was making this impossible. Such information as there was, however, suggested that during 1986–1988 the policy stalemate was leading to yet another upturn in the underlying fertility rate.

The 1990 national census confirmed that unreported births were occurring at a rate of at least one million a year and the data implied that the target of restricting population to 1.2 billion in 2000 would have to be abandoned. A further intense re-examination of the issues was therefore inevitable.

ACHIEVEMENTS, ISSUES IN THE 1990S, FUTURE PROSPECTS

In 1991 the Party made one more attempt to formulate a workable population policy. This policy took a more realistic view of growth prospects, acknowledging that growth would continue at about 1.25% for at least a decade. Nonetheless, with the annual population addition being estimated as at least 14 millions, the urgency of the problems was still emphasised. Five new elements were injected into population policy at this time, and these indicate how much understanding of the complexities of population and their implications had grown since 1980. These elements were: new emphasis on the importance of stability as well as realism in policy; emphasis on the need for respecting legality in population administration; emphasis on the supremacy of local responsibility for policy implementation; analysis of the environmental dimension to population issues; and finally, the linking of local population policies to local poverty alleviation programmes.

The 1990 Census was the last fully published to date and using official data we may sum up China's trends in population as follows. Since, as argued above, policy in the reform era grafts directly onto policy initiated in 1970/1971, data are shown for the whole period.

The data suggest striking results but major issues remain.[9]

First, all historical experience since 1949 shows that there is a danger of an inbuilt tendency to optimism in official population data. At present,

9 In terms of Crude Birth Rate decline, using UN data for 1965/70 and 1990/95, China's annual rate of reduction was .16. Of 33 other developing countries, only South Korea exceeded this rate (.19) and Taiwan and Thailand equalled it. The worst performer, Yemen, achieved no reduction at all.

Table 6.1 Population trends, 1970–1998

	Birth rate	Death rate	Natural increase	TFR	% of women married by 20 years old	% of woman having 3 or more children
1970	33.34	7.6	25.83	5.8	43.05	62.21
1979	17.82	6.2	11.61	2.8	–	–
1993	18.09	6.6	11.45	2.0	12.9*	9.6*
1998	16.03	6.5	9.53	1.8	–	–

*1992 official data.
Note: Birth, Death and Natural Increase rates are per thousand of the population.

there are at least two major problems with these that may affect forecasts. One is the difficulty of estimating present and future Total Fertility Rates. All observers agree on this and the consensus is for stability in the early years of the next millennium at about 1.7. Second is the problem that approximately 100 million Chinese are now members of the 'floating population' which is not properly recorded or understood in demographic terms. One Chinese expert recently described this as 'the great black hole' of Chinese population statistics.

Second, the fertility, nuptiality and other behaviour of the children born under the One Child Family system is very difficult to forecast. For example, current surveys find evidence that the single children reveal a preference for high fertility. This means that population trends may reverse themselves in geographical terms. This is because the ICF and population reduction have been most successful in advanced areas, which may in future grow relatively rapidly because of this factor.

Third, the speed of the recent reduction (1990s) has somewhat outstripped expectation and the implications for both the age structure and the sex balance are turning out to be more serious than had been envisaged.[10] Some of these problems were foreseen in 1980, but their implications seemed too far away for concern. Chinese demographers now argue that this is this is no longer the case and that the data and analytical capabilities available make new research urgent.

Third, geographical variations in population policy and the problems of the minority [Muslim] population give rise to many issues. Until very recently the minority areas were simply treated as exceptions. Now they are subject to policy but treated carefully. It is unclear whether this approach will be successful.

10 Between 1982 and 1990, the sex imbalance rose from 108 (boys):100 (girls) to 111:100. The current (1999) rate is believed to be still more unbalanced with a figure of 116:100 being quoted. An example of current anxieties among demographers is Qiao Xiaochun's article, 'Reflections on research for China's birth policies at the approach of the 21st Century', *Population Research*, 1999, No. 2.

EMPLOYMENT AND INCOMES

The two main economic implications of population trends are employment and food. The food issue is dealt with in Chapter 4. The employment question will be summarised here.

In 1997, total employment in China was 696 millions. Of this 70% was in rural areas (including small rural townships) and 30% was in cities.

The structure of employment has undergone rapid transformation since the reform and this is shown in Table 6.2.

A remarkable feature of China's labour force is the very high participation rate of women. Nearly half the labour force are women and currently it is estimated that 90% of women aged 20 to 40 are economically active.

The fundamental issue for China is whether its economy can absorb this huge army of workers. This is partly a matter of the economic growth rate that can be maintained and partly a matter of labour organisation and other policy issues.

The past variations in fertility and population growth outlined earlier all have implications for the changing supply of labour, since population surges are echoed in the labour supply as they enter the 16 year old age bracket. Slumps and downturns in births have the reverse effect. During the reform period there have been two helpful demographic features. One is that as fertility declined, the numbers of dependent children have shrunk. The number under 14, for example, has shrunk from 40% in 1975 to 27% in 1995. The former figure reflects loss of population control during the Cultural Revolution. The other feature is that the proportion of population of working age and overall labour participation have been gently rising. Under conditions of high demand for labour, this has been helpful to economic growth.[11]

According to the official projection the future scenario is as shown in Table 6.3.

Table 6.2 Employment structure, 1978–1997

Sector	1978	1997	% change in share
Primary (agriculture, fisheries etc.)	70.5	49.9	−29.2
Secondary (industry etc.)	17.3	23.7	+36.9
Tertiary (services)	12.2	26.4	+116.4

11 I have used age structure data supplied by Judith Banister in, 'Population Growth in China and its Economic Implications', First Annual Conference of the EU-China Academic Network, January, 1998. Elsewhere I have relied on the authoritative data and estimates in Wang Dongyan et.al., *A Forecast of the Development of China's Labour Activity, 1996–2010*, Beijing, 1995.

Table 6.3 Population, labour and unemployment, 1995–2010

	1995	2000	2010
Population (billions)	12.167	12.837	13.822
Of which: Urban (millions)	364	412	496
Rural (millions) (including rural townships)	853	872	886
Population aged 16+ (millions)	868	923	1040
Population of working age (millions)	740	778	849
Estimated official urban unemployment rate	3.6%	6.4%	6.6%

Source: Wang Dongyan, op.cit.

However, many contemporary analyses see these data as misleading and too optimistic. They fail to take into account three groups of people, these are: unemployed/underemployed workers in the rural areas who might choose to migrate to the cities; workers in State Owned Enterprises (SOEs) who have been subject to the procedure of *xia gang* (formal layoff) and other employees of all kinds who represent concealed unemployment. In 1997, 55% of all urban employees were in SOEs – amounting to 100 million workers. Continued reform of this sector as promised by Premier Zhu Rongji therefore represents a major employment problem.

In 1993, *xia gang* layoffs amounted to 3 million people. In 1997 and 1998, this number rose to 12 millions. local surveys suggest that of these, 70% were aged 25–44 and about the same percentage only had junior or at best middle school education.

A three year unemployment perspective for 1997–2000 has been calculated to suggest that at the end of the year 2000, a 'true' unemployment estimate might be made up as follows:

Official urban unemployment	16 millions
Unemployment from *xia gang*	30 millions
Rural unemployment	137 millions
Total	183 millions.

The latter figure would represent 24% of the population of working age and represents a fairly optimistic view.[12]

Clearly an unemployed pool of this size represents a formidable economic and social challenge. In what is now described as the 'first peak' of unemployment (early 1980s), 70% of all crimes were committed by 14–25 year olds, many unemployed. This crime wave was met with the 'Strike Hard' campaign in which thousands were executed.

12 Optimistic both in approach and also in the assumption common in 1997 and 1998, that China's growth rate could be maintained at 8% per annum. A figure not sustained.

Contemporary commentators believe that this 'Strike Hard' was not a successful campaign and that the Party must address the root problem – lack of jobs and income.

Several measures are suggested for this. These include reform of the labour market and of social security and housing systems that at present make it difficult to diminish the 'iron rice' bowl mentality and increase labour mobility and much more emphasis on employment in services and the non-state sectors. Also emphasised are measures to increase demand and keep economic growth at 7% or higher, and measures to increase labour productivity and employability through training and education.

The latter is certainly a key to both population and labour issues. If population and labour supply growth are to be sharply reduced, economic development calls for a rising skill level that will offset (and more than offset) the loss of raw labour power. This was precisely Deng Xiaoping's point. Rising incomes in China should also have enabled the economy to afford this training and put the economy into a spiral of upward development. The problem is that the education system in China has insufficient elements of the market in it to enable it to play its role. Until very recently, student numbers have been planned and employment allocated on graduation.

In international perspective China's educational level appears in a poor light. In the 1990 Census 180 million people were found to be illiterate or semi-literate and the proportion of graduates or recipients of any form of higher training was very low by developing country standards. (Less than 2% of the relevant age cohort have degrees.) State spending on education is also low and has been falling as a percentage of total public expenditure in the 1990s. At the same time, the Chinese have accumulated huge savings which they seem reluctant to spend. Unless China's household private resources are brought into play in the educational system, China will be in danger of having the worst of both worlds: a smaller population but still unskilled by world standards.

There is no doubt that economic reforms in China have raised average real incomes in all sectors. Income distribution, however, has clearly worsened. Our translations refer to statistical data showing worsening distribution along almost every dimension: i.e. between rural and urban areas; within rural and within urban areas; between different branches of the economy;and between the skilled and unskilled.

Under the planned economy incomes could be controlled by administrative means. In the modern urban sector, workers and staff were graded in complex systems based on Soviet practice. Outside in the collective sector, incomes were still kept low by various means. During the twenty year period 1957 to 1977, incomes were largely frozen and household living standards only maintained at near their 1957 levels by a huge increase in the proportion of the population that were economically active.

Under reform, controls have been lost. In the planned sector, enterprise freedoms have been used to provide income in kind and 'bonuses', many of which were not 'earned' in the sense that they reflected productivity gains. Also, in the collective and the newly growing private sectors, incomes grew rapidly and unevenly. In the longer run the authorities hope that incomes will reflect 'market' values and that macro-economic controls will ensure that aggregate wages remain in line with the requirements of anti-inflation policy. However our documents show clearly that the transition from planning to market is producing major irrationalities, which means that the remuneration system is failing to ensure proper allocation of labour and effort, and leaving millions in unacceptable poverty traps. The combination of labour and wage problems could therefore become as much a social and political danger as a purely economic one.

Document 6.1

'Population problems under market economic conditions and scientific research into population'

TIAN XUEYUAN (POPULATION RESEARCH INSTITUTE, CHINESE ACADEMY OF SOCIAL SCIENCES)

Chinese Demography, 1994, No. 1

The recovery and development of demography in China over the last twenty years or so has led to a number of remarkable achievements and in some respects, the discipline already stands at the forefront of the science. So what should be our next step forward? I believe we must firmly adhere to the establishment and completion of a socialist market economic system and explore the new population problems that arise as a result of this enterprise. The key is to raise our research to a higher level by using a combination of theory and practice.

Since China started down the path of reform in the second half of the 1970s, our objective of transforming the economic system from 'a combination of a planned and market-regulated system' into 'a socialist commodity economy' and then into 'a socialist market economy' has finally been determined. Without doubt, this will not only have a direct effect on the development of the national economy, but will also have a profound impact on the material, spiritual and cultural life of society as a whole. Is this likely to have an effect on population growth, and if so, to what extent? What kind of relationship exists between the socialist market economy and population control in China? The answers to these questions fall into three main schools of thought:

The first school holds that a socialist market economy does not fall within the same sphere of reference as population growth and family planning. The latter are not subject to the law of the market and market activities and the two should not therefore be forcibly drawn together. The main reasons for this way of thinking are, first, that the establishment of a market economy does not completely exclude the possibility of a certain degree of planning with regard to economic development. Even developed countries with a high reliance on the market still use planned government intervention to direct the economy. Similarly, and perhaps even more significantly, market economics does not preclude planning with regard to population growth. Second, China's future population control should continue to use administrative means as the main tool and market and administration do not fall within the same sphere.

The second school is based on the belief that we should bring population, especially population control, into line with the market economic system. The market should be promoted with regard to population management in the same way that it is promoted with regard to the economy. It is advocated that 'guidance plans' should be introduced for administering population targets and family planning. The family should be made the centre for child-bearing decisions and Western-style programmes of 'family planning' should be introduced.

The third school believes that although population reproduction and family planning do not belong within the realm of the market, the effects of the market and restrictions imposed by the market economy should not be underestimated. We must pursue the cause of reform and begin to establish population control mechanisms that are appropriate for a market economy.

I am inclined to agree with the third point of view and this view has been formed and developed over a number of years. In the second half of the 1970s, a serious attempt was made to bring order out of the chaos that population theory had fallen into. A major force behind this venture was Mr. Ma Yinchu and the rehabilitation of his book New Population Theory.[13]

In the 1980s there was a move towards exploring different strategies for population development and this resulted in an emphasis on population control and strategic thinking which combined quantitative controls with improvements in population quality and structural adjustment. The first half of the eighties was mainly preoccupied with research into ways of controlling population from a quantitative point of view, while in the latter half we stressed research into China's demographic structure and issues raised by an ageing population.

At the end of the 1980s, there was a switch to an exploration of population studies at the micro-economic level. In this we fused proven achievements in demography from overseas with the realities of China under reform and opening. This culminated in the elaboration of a child cost-benefit theory and its practical application to China, and research into

---

13 See Kenneth Walker, "Ideology and economic discussion in China: Ma Yin-chu on development strategy and his critics", *Economic Development and Cultural Change*, Vol. XI, no. 2, January 1963; and valuable material in, *Population Research*, 1982, No. 4. (Ed.)

new methods of solving population problems under conditions imposed by a socialist commodity economy and a market economy. The following basic conclusions were reached:

1. China has been achieving remarkable results with regard to controlling population growth ever since the 1970s, and this has been thanks in large part to the implementation of family planning policies. These form a basic national strategy that has been carefully formulated in line with China's population, level of resources, economic development and social structure. In this sense, therefore, the situation in China is quite unlike the situation in developed Western countries where economic and cultural development has been accompanied by an automatic fall in the birth rate. China's strategy also has little in common with the types of 'family planning' practiced in a number of other developing countries. There have been several specific 'adjustments' of policy over the last 20 years in order to ensure the successful implementation of our fundamental strategy. Officials at all levels of leadership have consistently adhered to the policy and taken overall responsibility for methods of implementation. In keeping with the spirit of keeping population under control, they have met this basic requirement by focusing on education and the dissemination of information. Thus, by placing population control at the very heart of population management, it is clear that in general, our methods do not belong in the realm of the market economy, but in the realm of administrative control. Under the present market economic conditions, we need to maintain this kind of administrative control. It is not a feasible proposition to blindly 'introduce the market' into the sphere of population reproduction.

2. Emphasising the role that policy factors should play in bringing down the birth rate is not to say that we should ignore the impact of economic factors on the birth rate. In 1992 the CASS Population Research Institute joined together with other relevant organisations to carry out a sample survey of household economy and child-rearing in ten provinces and municipalities. The survey showed that there was an inverse correlation between a household's average monthly income and the number of children in the family. Those with a monthly income of less than 25 *yuan* per capita had an average number of 2.64 children, while those earning a monthly sum of between 26–100 *yuan* per capita had 2.37 children. Those with a per capita income of 101–300 *yuan* per month had 1.93 children. There have been large-scale increases in both urban and rural incomes following the economic development of the last 20 years, particularly since the introduction of the reforms. If we compare 1991 to 1978, then net per capita income for rural households has grown from 134 *yuan* to 709 *yuan*, and net per capita income for urban residents has risen from 316 *yuan* to 1544 *yuan*.[14] We should not ignore the contribution that this has made towards bringing down the birth rate.

14 *China Statistical Year book 1992*, Beijing: China Statistical Publishing House, 1992.

However, there are a number of other factors that have played an even more important role in bringing about changes in the birth rate. These include: changes in the function of the household economy within a reformed economic system, intensified competition in the marketplace and among qualified workers, the gradual urbanisation of the population, the swelling migrant population, and people's changing attitudes towards child-rearing. The latter part of this essay will concern itself with an elaboration and analysis of these factors. While it is true, therefore, that the reproduction of the population belongs within the non-market realm, it is important not to underestimate the influence of economic development and the establishment of a market economic system. Otherwise we are liable to be thrown into a state of inaction and passivity.

3. It would appear from observation of current trends that although economic development and the establishment of a market economic system is likely to be a long drawn-out process, our initial progress along that road has already helped curb population growth and limit population reproduction. Reflecting these changes we find that in household choices relating to births, the influence of 'profit' [i.e. material welfare] considerations has strengthened at the expense of the regulatory function of administration. This trend gives rise to serious issues, and we must now devise appropriate methods of adjustment and find a suitable path for reform, which is based on a comprehensive analysis of the positive and negative effects of the market economy on population control and population reproduction as a whole.

II

If we consider the intrinsic qualities and long-term nature of our strategy for economic development, we are likely to see a growing number of positive benefits stemming from the decision to allow the establishment of a market economic system in helping to solve our population problems. The main ones are as follows:

1. The establishment and completion of a market economic system will necessarily give rise to the emancipation and further development of our productive forces. This will provide a new material base for solving our population problems. It is common knowledge that China's economic reforms began with the introduction of the Household Responsibility System in the countryside and that this led to the phenomenon of 'encircling the cities from rural areas'. This was followed by the implementation and diffusion of a growing number of urban reforms: from the decision to give greater autonomy to enterprises to the introduction of a variety of different contract systems and from the development of single ventures, joint ventures and foreign ventures to a general system of company shares- these the reforms have led step by

step to the development of a market economy. Finally this all culminated at the Fourteenth Party Congress which made it a clear objective to establish a new socialist market economic system in China. Experience tells us that in order to establish a market economy with producer autonomy, market-orientated economic operations, an intermediate role for macro-adjustment, and standardised methods of management, we must escape from the highly centralised planned economy of the past and from the out-dated notion that 'centralisation leads to death and liberalisation leads to chaos'. We must conceive of a more rational and beneficial distribution of human, financial and material resources which will unleash the national economy and facilitate the further development of our social and productive forces. Between 1979, when the reforms were initiated, and 1991, GDP was growing at an annual rate of 8.6%, National Income was increasing by 8.4% per year and the level of household consumption was rising by 6.5% China was the only country to flourish during that period of world recession. Needless to say, population problems, particularly the problem of surplus labour putting pressure on the productive forces, are essentially a question of economics, a question of the level of development of our social forces of production. The socialist market economic system has given new impetus and life to the development of the national economy. It has also provided a new material base for finding solutions to all of our population problems, especially that of curbing population growth, and will play an increasingly important role in this respect.

2. The formation and perfection of a labour market and the increased competition for qualified workers will, from the point of view of development, encourage families to shift away from investment in children in terms of quantity towards investment in terms of quality. Because of current discrepancies between the level of economic development and the reach of the market, there has been a growing trend in some areas for elementary and middle school students to play truant or give up studying altogether. In other areas, particularly those which have a high level of economic development and a highly developed market economy, people's child-rearing preferences have already switched from a pursuit of numbers to a pursuit of quality. The money they used to spend on large numbers of children has now been redirected towards improving the quality of life for smaller numbers of children, particularly with regard to education. The 1992 survey of ten Chinese provinces and municipalities investigated the relationship between household finances and child-rearing. It asked households to state the level of education up to which they were willing to support their children. The results for the whole country were as follows: elementary school – 3.6%, junior high school – 18.8%, senior high school – 16.8%, junior college – 9.6%, senior college – 6.5%, university – 29.2%, post-graduate level – 3.1%, and 'no preference' – 12.3%. Thus the

largest proportion of respondents were willing to support their offspring until graduation from university, with junior high school in second place, and senior high school in third. This shows that a considerable number of people already realise that, under market economic conditions, competition basically means competition for highly qualified workers. They are therefore willing to invest in education and their aspirations for their children are naturally linked to the market economy. The labour market is a constituent part of the market economy. Competition for qualified workers is likely to heat up along with the consolidation and perfection of the market economic system. Increased expenditure on the quality of the population will at some stage lead to a great rise in quality and this will encourage people to turn away from having large numbers of children towards having fewer children and providing them with a high-quality upbringing and education.

3. The development of the commodity and a market economy will lead to a fall in the benefits of having children as an insurance policy for old-age. There are three main aspects to this.

   (a) The establishment of a market economic system, rapid economic growth, increases in labour productivity, and a rise in social accumulation will all help lay the foundations for the growth of social insurance establishments run by the state, business or by other social organizations. In other words there is a growing trend towards socialised systems of support for the elderly. Old-age insurance establishments have been established in most regions, especially in those rural regions that have begun to grow in prosperity. This has eroded the status and function of children as a provider for their parents in old-age.

   (b) The growth in the wealth of those who are not eligible for old-age pensions according to the rules laid down in the current retirement policy (workers in individual and collective enterprises and the vast number of rural labourers) has enabled them to save up their own money for their retirement or take out retirement pensions. Statistics show that in 1991 expenditure on old-age pensions rose to 3,313,780,000 *yuan*, 18.8 times higher than in 1985. This is a remarkable rate of growth. The future support of tens of thousands of retired workers will no longer be based on traditional methods of support provided by their children. Thus, there has been a relative decline in the benefits of children as an insurance policy for old-age.

   (c) Traditional ideas of 'raising children to care for old age' have weakened. The development of a commodity and market economy is exerting a subtle, corrosive influence on traditional ways of thinking and people's values are gradually beginning to change. This has helped to reduce the emotional connotations of certain conventional attitudes and the traditional idea that it is the duty of children to support their parents has begun to fade in many people's minds.

There are a growing number of cases where people are refusing to support their elderly parents and this has led to lower parental expectations.

4. In order to win in the face of acute market competition, people must be prepared to exert greater energy and devote increasing amounts of spare time to their working life. The consequent reduction in leisure time clearly means that parents will have less time to play with their children. At the same time, the tense, ever-changing and multifaceted nature of the market economy is having a psychological effect on people. While small farmers used to rely on children as their main means of enjoyment and stress-relief after a hard day's work, they are now beginning to look towards more modern, scientific and stimulating means of relaxation. People are now less inclined to believe that children are the essence of 'family happiness' and this rising trend is becoming increasingly evident as the market economy develops.

5. The market economy is encouraging people to devote more of their personal assets to market competition and improve their own skills at competing in the market. They are much less willing therefore to spend large amounts of money on child-rearing. There is a special theory within population studies known as the 'capillary theory'. This states that under fixed financial conditions, the less money that parents spend on themselves, in terms of daily living expenses and leisure pursuits, the more that is spent on child-rearing. This relationship can be pictured as a U-shaped connecting pipe – as one side goes down, the other side goes up. Conditions [of under-development] therefore lead to the birth of a large number of children. On the other hand, an increase in the amount of money needed by the parents [for consumption] will mean a reduction in the sum that can be devoted to child-rearing. This will necessarily lead to a reduction in the number of children born. The establishment of a market economic system has helped to reinforce [the positive aspect of] this 'capillary effect' and has begun to erode the traditional idea that 'the more children in a family, the richer it becomes'. This will help to curb population growth.

6. A market economy benefits population control and other population issues because it promotes a rationalised industrial structure and accelerates the urbanisation of the population. In fact, there has always been a natural connection between the city and the market. In Chinese, the word 'city' is made up of two characters: *cheng* and *shi*. *Cheng* originally referred to the four walls around an urban centre that were erected as a means of defence. It later became used in a general sense to refer to the urban centre itself. The character *shi* referred to a centre for business transactions and trading. The ancient book *Book of Changes* states: 'the market [*shi*] begins when the sun is high in the sky'. When the market was over, people would automatically disperse. Originally, therefore, the market did not continue round the clock on a systematic

daily basis. The process of urban development cannot be separated from the degree of development of the commercial economy and the market. The establishment of a socialist market economy will promote the diversification of agriculture and a shift from self-sufficiency and semi-self-sufficiency to a commodity-based economy. This will increase farmers' direct involvement in the market and urban life so that they will effectively become urbanised either on the basis of 'leave the land but not leave the village' or of 'leave land and village'.

The brisk industrial and commercial activity in the cities, the expansion of urban/rural communications and of tertiary industry, have all encouraged the large-scale urban migration of surplus rural labour and the development of a new force in the countryside: township and rural enterprises. The urbanisation of the population is proceeding at an unprecedented rate. And the birth rate among the urban population is much lower than in rural areas. This will eventually take us up to a new level in our search for effective ways to keep population under control and for solutions to other population problems.

It is worth pointing out that several aspects of the effect of the market economy on population – i.e. the material foundations necessary for population reproduction, marginal costs and benefits of having children, the growth of the urban population etc – are all closely interrelated and mutually enhancing. As the market economy develops it will gain an improved capacity for promoting the development of the social forces of production and the transformation of the material foundations for population reproduction. Increased market development will also help to bring down the marginal benefits of having children and raise the qualitative costs. The further the market economy develops, the more effective its impact will be on accelerating the process of urban growth.

Although progress in only one particular area is to be welcomed, it is not likely to achieve very much. Only when progress is made in all of the areas mentioned above will it be possible to unleash the real potential of the market economy to solve our problems of population growth. We must therefore approach the opportunities that the market economy offers with regard to population control from a developmental and historical perspective. Everything must be viewed in terms of the long-term course of development – we cannot expect immediate or instant results. Generally speaking, it is unlikely that we will see many positive effects arising from the areas detailed above during the initial period of market economic development. In fact, negative and unhelpful effects are likely to be more apparent during the initial period and will therefore attract greater attention.

III

The negative effects on population that we are currently experiencing as a result of the establishment of a market economic system are as follows:

1. There have been a number of deleterious effects on the cost-benefits of child rearing due to the advance of the market. Notably:

   (a) There has been a rise in the marginal economic benefits to be gained from child labour. The initiation of reform, promotion of a market economy, and establishment of the Household Responsibility System have all enabled households to recover their age-old function as a base for production. The successful rise of individual and collective enterprises in rural areas has also allowed many households to engage in a variety of production and production-related activities. In those households which are now actively involved in these activities, there has been a new and urgent demand for labour, particularly male labour. The consequent rise in the economic value of child labour is an important factor behind above-quota childbirth in these types of household. Even though there is an inevitable wait for a number of years before children are old enough to become part of the workforce and 'far off waters cannot relieve a nearby drought', small producers are much happier if they can rely on members of their own family to join their workforce as and when necessary, as an alternative to employing extra workers from the official labour market. Small producers believe that this is the most reliable, cost-effective and convenient way of operating, particularly among those households that have a shortage of male workers.

   (b) There has been a reversal in the trend of having children as an insurance policy against the problems of old-age. It was previously argued that the introduction of a market economy would basically lead to a fall in the benefits to be gained from having children to forestall the problems of old-age. This is conditional upon the growth and spread of alternative methods of social insurance for the elderly and an increased capacity for elderly people to support themselves and for working people to set aside savings for their retirement. These conditions have already been met in coastal regions and other inland regions that enjoy a relatively high level of development and a relatively advanced market economy. In these areas, there has been a clear fall in the benefits of having children in order to forestall the problems of old-age. However, in the vast regions of the country that still have a relatively low level of development and limited market economic activity, traditional concepts of child-bearing still hold sway. In these areas, raising children continues to be the main way to provide for oneself in one's old-age. During the era of the People's Communes there was an unprecedented development of welfare facilities for the elderly (Retirement Centres, Elderly People's Homes etc.) in rural areas. This was especially true of areas with a low level of economic development. These facilities helped to support the relatively large number of people who did not have children to look after them.

While admittedly some model, well-run welfare establishments still exist in certain areas, the initiation of reform and the promotion of a market economy has dealt a crippling blow to the majority of these establishments. Thus, people in rural areas still feel instinctively that the most reliable way to ensure support for themselves in their old-age is to have children.

(c) For households that operate in the individual economy in urban and rural areas that have grown in prosperity, there has been a clear rise in the benefits to be gained from children inheriting the family property. It is common knowledge that our new socialist market economic system is being developed against the backdrop of thousands of years of feudalism which had an extremely imperfect, commodity-based economy. This was followed by a long period when both the commercial economy and the market were branded as 'capitalist'. This makes it easy for the new private business people that have emerged with the development of the market to lump business assets and household property together, package them up into a feudal or semi-feudal parcel, and pass them down to the next generation. Some are willing to pay any price to ensure that there is someone to inherit and pass on their property and, following the birth of many daughters, will try again and again to give birth to a son. This pattern of thinking is a great force to be reckoned with.

(d) With regard to the costs of child-raising, as previously stated, from a strategic and developmental point of view the market economy creates conditions for raising the costs of improving the quality of children (particularly with regard to education). It thus plays a key role in persuading parents to invest in a higher quality upbringing for fewer children rather than spreading their investment thinly among large numbers of children. However, there is one pre-condition for this to occur: the amount of money invested in the quality of a child's upbringing must pay off in terms of benefits. While this condition may be met in regions that have a highly developed market economy, for the vast majority of the country this is not the case. And in those areas that are influenced by the incoming incursions of the market but do not have a sufficiently developed economy, small producers' first priority is to create an effective role for their children in the marketplace. Thus, children are propelled out into the market to make money. A number of surveys suggest that this phenomenon of 'students selling eggs' is particularly common among elementary school children, and is a major factor behind truancy at this level of education.

2. Ideas and behaviour with regard to child-rearing have a tendency to be influenced by the market. In other words there is a growing trend for marriage and child-rearing decisions to be balanced according to financial considerations.

The founding of the People's Republic of China effectively brought to an end a number of despicable practices, including mercenary marriage, prostitution, and the abduction and selling of women, that were vestiges of the old feudal society. However, in recent years, the spread of reform and the development of the market economy has led to a worrying rise of a kind of 'money fetishism' among some people. This mindset has even been introduced into marriage and other family relationships. This has led to a modern-day resurgence of these ugly features of the old society and a number of new problems have emerged. These include a rise in the divorce rate and a growing trend towards extramarital affairs and the birth of children outside wedlock. These old and new social phenomena have become enmeshed together, exhibiting the features of both 'tradition' and 'modernity', and it is therefore going to be extremely difficult to find an effective solution.

It has been reported that while studying different methods of product specialisation, a farmer living deep in the Taihang Mountain region came up with the idea of setting his household up as a 'child production line'. He invited men who 'wanted to buy a son at a negotiated price' to come and stay for a while in his house and have a son with his wife or his daughters (a discount was given in the case of the birth of a daughter). After a few years, this poor and impoverished household became a booming business. This may be an extreme example, but the population problems caused by unconventional patterns of childbirth (through the abduction and selling of women, extramarital affairs, having more children even after divorce etc.) have become increasingly evident over recent years and such patterns have become commonplace in certain regions.

3. Management and administration cannot keep up with the changing circumstances of the market economy and the population.

The difficulties involved in making accurate numerical predictions with regard to the restraining effect that the market is likely to have on fertility has created contradictions in the sense that administrative controls cannot keep up with objective changes. The main problems are as follows:

(a) Government administration cannot keep up with the sudden rise in the migrant population.

There have been huge increases in the migrant population following the initiation of reform and the development of the market economy. Current estimates of numbers range from 50–80 million migrants nationwide, and the daily population flow to China's major cities such as Beijing, Shanghai and Guangzhou, is estimated to be in excess of 1 million people. This represents a great floating population on an unprecedented scale, giving rise to a series of new population control problems. The government departments responsible have already introduced a certain number of administrative measures to deal with this problem and these have achieved significant results.

However, controls have always been extremely difficult to enforce because of the nature of the migration and the sheer scale of the numbers involved.

In cases of highly concentrated areas of migration, such as the 'Wenzhou villages' created by the flow of the migrant population from Wenzhou in Zhejiang Province towards Beijing, and of Guangxi and Yunnan (areas with a falling population) the home region can send administrators to those cities. In some cases they have even set up special family planning organisations and associations. This has met with some degree of success. However, it is extremely costly to send officials over such long distances and besides, there are very few places where this kind of concentrated emigration and immigration exists. In the majority of regions, this kind of scheme is totally impracticable, and the only course of action is to rely on the area of final destination to implement administrative controls. However, there are also a number of problems with leaving it up to the area of final destination to deal with the migrants. The increasing material, financial and human resources that are required for this make it an unusually heavy burden. If we look at the whole picture, then the main problems are that both areas of net emigration and net immigration are attempting to control migration, but neither is having much success, and the returns are not high enough to justify the inputs.

(b) There is a conflict between the objective desire to strengthen administration and the tendency for administration itself to be weakened with the intensification of reform. In order to deal with population problems under market economic conditions, it is necessary to strengthen population management, especially through family planning. However, the development of a market economy results in weaker administration and management and leading officials at all levels are likely to devote increasing time and energy to the economy and the market and are likely to be less concerned with population reproduction. New circumstances and new problems are likely to arise with regard to human resources as a result of structural reform and the new market influences on workers. Increasingly, financial and material resources will flow towards the market. This will hopefully lead to a multiplication of their value but it will also influence unevenly the modernisation of the 'hardware' of management and weaken management's instruments and strength.

(c) A number of new questions and contradictions have emerged. For example, it is not possible to prevent parents from having tests to predict the sex of an unborn, above-quota child. An important reason for this is that the system of financial penalties is not working: those that undergo this procedure take the compulsory payment of a fine for granted and this has led to the introduction of the market into the technical process of sex-determination and child-birth. Another example is the rapid development of luxury apartments inhabited by professional business people who spend huge amounts of money on hiring bodyguards to protect their property and privacy. These represent serious obstacles to the spread and consolidation of birth control programmes. Problems such as this are closely related to changes in social attitudes that have accompanied the development of a market economy. They are likely to grow in number and present new issues for population control and population science research.

The creation of a socialist market economy is an unprecedented enterprise. It has both positive and negative effects on population control and other population-related issues. These advantages and disadvantages are tightly enmeshed and intertwined, and this makes scientific research into population all the more difficult. In the face of this challenge, we need to make our observations and undertake our research in a scientific way by laying stress on the theoretical methods and viewpoints of Marxism. We must focus on learning from the scientific results already gained from research in western countries and place a special emphasis on the synthesis of theory and practice. It is also important to remain rooted in reality, conduct investigative surveys, emancipate our minds and seek truth from facts. This is the key to whether or not we will succeed in accurately exploring the laws of population change under market economic conditions, and thereby raise the scientific study of the population to a new level.

Document 6.2

The emergence of DINKS households in China and a simple analysis of the reasons behind their development

XIE LEIGUANG AND CHENG GANG (POPULATION INSTITUTE, ZHEJIANG PROVINCE MEDICAL UNIVERSITY)

Population and Family Planning, 1995, No. 4

1. The meaning of DINKS households and the general situation in other countries[15]

The rapid course of industrialisation and urbanisation in the developed countries of the West and the advent of the so-called 'third wave' has been

---

15 The term used throughout the Chinese text is the western DINKS, i.e. 'Double income no kids'. (Ed.)

accompanied by a rapid emergence of non-traditional households (i.e. households consisting of arrangements other than a husband and wife with two or more children). These arrangements represent a strong challenge to the dominant position held by traditional family patterns.

2. The gradual emergence of DINKS households in China

In modern-day China, where people are no longer free to hold to traditional concepts that link increased personal happiness to the birth of children, a phenomenon has emerged that cannot be ignored – a growing number of DINKS households. According to statistics from relevant departments in China, during the ten years between 1978 and 1988, the number of voluntarily childless couples in China exceeded 300,000. And according to data supplied by the Shanghai Population Information Centre, DINKS households comprise around 2%–3% of China's total number of urban households. Other statistics suggest that in Hainan Province, 8.2% of women of child-bearing age have no intention of having children.

Although the number of DINKS households nationwide is still very small, the trend is rising rather than falling. Statistics from China's first and second Childbirth Surveys reveal that there is a rapidly growing proportion of women who do not want children. There are two possible explanations for this:

1. There has been a relatively rapid increase in the proportion of childless, married women for whom the ideal is a family with no children. The first Childbirth Survey revealed that there were great regional differences in the proportion of the total number of childless, married women who had no intention of having children. The highest proportion was in Shanghai, and the total for the two provinces of Shanxi and Hebei together with the municipality of Shanghai reached 5.3%. This means that out of every 1000 married women without children, approximately 5.3 women do not wish to give birth.

Statistics from the second Childbirth Survey, carried out two years later, showed that there had been a fairly large-scale increase in the proportion of childless, married women for whom the ideal was a family with no children, and there continued to be huge regional differences. Beijing municipality came top of the league with 35.4%, and even in Liaoning which registered the smallest proportion, the rate reached 7.9%. In the four provinces surrounding and including the municipality of Beijing, the proportion measured 16.4%, roughly three times the level of two years before. (See Table 6.4).

The proportion of the total number of women surveyed who were married, childless and who had no wish for children, (i.e. the total rate of women for whom the ideal was a family with no children) measured 0.9% during the second Survey, up from 0.3% during the first Survey. These statistics also show a three-fold increase. (See Table 6.5).

Table 6.4 The proportion of childless married women for whom the ideal is a family with no children. Units: %

Region	1st Childbirth Survey	Region	2nd Childbirth Survey
Shanxi Province	3.9	Beijing Municipality	35.4
Hebei Province	3.6	Liaoning Province	7.9
Shanghai Municipality	9.2	Shandong Province	17.3
		Guizhou Province	8.5
		Gansu Province	10.4
Total	5.3	Total*	16.4

Source: Compiled from 'Statistics from China's First Childbirth Survey' and 'A Preliminary Report on China's Second Childbirth Survey' in *Chinese Population Statistics Handbook* (1986).
* Statistics on Guangdong are not included, due to data error.

Table 6.5 The proportion of all women surveyed who were married, childless and for whom the ideal was a family with no children. Units: %

Region	1st Childbirth Survey	Region	2nd Childbirth Survey
Shanxi Province	0.2	Beijing Municipality	1.9
Hebei Province	0.2	Liaoning Province	0.3
Shanghai Municipality	0.5	Shandong Province	0.8
		Guizhou Province	0.5
		Gansu Province	0.9
Total	0.3	Total	0.9

Source: (as Table 6.4).

2. There has also been a relatively large-scale increase in the proportion of married women with children, who regret having had children in the first place. During the second Survey, the proportion of women with one child or more who regret having had children measured 1.2%. This rate of occurrence is almost 1½ times the rate registered during the first Survey. (See Table 6.6). This illustrates that a small number of women regret having had children because they 'cannot put up with the 'burdens' connected with bringing up children. As far as those who are unwilling to give birth to a first child are concerned, the heartfelt words of these women who have actually 'been through the experience' undoubtedly lends great support to the case for not having children at all.

The relatively rapid increase in the proportion of married women with children, but who regret having had children in the first place, is consistent

Table 6.6 The proportion of all women surveyed who were married with children, but who regretted having had children Units: %

Region	1st Childbirth Survey	Region	2nd Childbirth Survey
Shanxi Province	0.5	Beijing Municiplaity	2.3
Hebei Province	0.4	Liaoning Province	0.6
Shanghai Municiplaity	0.5	Shandong Province	0.2
		Guizhou Province	1.6
		Gansu Province	1.1
Total	0.5	Total	1.2

Source: (See Table 6.4).

with the increase in the proportion of women without children and who have no intention of having children. Behind the growth and development of these two trends lie a variety of socio-economic and cultural factors.

3. Types of DINKS household in China and a simple analysis of the factors behind their development

Types of DINKS household in China

The development of DINKS households in China is still in its early stages, and there is a consequent lack of full, accurate and representative data. Moreover, the subjective and objective factors that lead to the development of such households are rather complicated and it is therefore quite difficult to divide them into distinct categories. Nevertheless, in general, it is possible to distinguish two main types of DINKS household:

Type 1: The voluntarily childless household (i.e. where there is a subjective and voluntary desire not to have children):

In these households, husband and wife believe that having children would be highly detrimental to the development of their careers, lifestyles or leisure pursuits. They are not prepared to spend their whole life wasting precious time on domestic chores, and expect to have time for their own leisure interests outside the stressful environment of either work or study. They are keen to develop their full potential, both mentally and physically, and hope to achieve something worthwhile during the limited span of their own lifetime. This kind of outlook on life is already common among young urbanites with a high level of education. The relative weight given to these different reasons for not having children may differ from household to household. Careers may be more important for some, while others may place greater emphasis on leisure interests. And, of course, for a large number of households it may be a combination of the two.

Type 2: The household which remains childless because of social pressures:

Some couples may make a temporary decision not to have children because of objective criteria, such as their domestic financial situation, tension in their relationship, a fear of divorce etc. It is likely that couples in this category will join the ranks of those who do wish to have children as soon as the source of external pressure disappears.

Thus, the term 'DINKS household' should really be used in relation to those couples who remain voluntarily childless, and it is this category of household that constitutes the main target of our research.

A simple analysis of the factors behind the development of DINKS households

We believe that it is no mere accident that DINKS households have successfully managed to overcome obstacles and pressure from all sides to take root in China's ancient soil:

1. The rise in the social status of women in contemporary China, particularly in the cities, and the remarkable rise in women's economic status and position within the family, have provided the basic conditions for the emergence of DINKS households in China, especially in urban areas. This is because of the following factors:

   (a) The growth of employment opportunities for women as well as the clear rise in their economic and social status has given women the essential means to escape from their traditional dependence upon men, and made women's emancipation a real possibility. The growth in the number of women in work and women's financial independence provide the main guarantees for raising their status within society as a whole and achieving equality between the sexes.

   (b) The rise in the number of women in education, particularly in higher education, has awakened dormant desires for emancipation, and raised awareness among women as a whole. Women have begun to make a reappraisal of their own self-worth: 'Admittedly, giving birth is a way of perpetuating your own life, but it is unlikely to be a way of perpetuating your own self-worth'. This is a major factor behind the proliferation of DINKS households among the cultured urban classes.

Research from other countries also reveals that educational levels have a strong influence on whether or not people want to have children. [An Americam analysis has shown] that of those women who wish to remain childless, only 6.9% have not received a post-15 education, 10% have been educated to the age of 18, 11.9% have completed three years of higher education, 16.5% have completed four years of higher education, and 19.5% have completed five or more years of higher education. Therefore, the proportion of women who wish to remain childless increases in line with levels of education.

The relatively high social and economic status of women, especially in urban areas, lies at the root of women's economic independence and their relatively high levels of accomplishment. It is also a significant contributing factor to the elevated status of women in the household. Thus, the rise in the status of women, growing equality between the sexes, and the development of matrimonial relationships based on love (signifying that women are no longer regarded as child-bearing machines) have all provided the fundamental conditions for the emergence of DINKS households in China.

2. The value of children to parents has continued to fall. Child-rearing costs have a tendency to rise in line with economic development. However, the financial benefits of having children (how much children are worth to their parents) are likely to fall not only in relative terms, but also in absolute terms. The main manifestations of this are as follows:
   (a) There have been huge increases in the costs associated with having children (both direct and indirect costs). Along with economic, scientific and technological development, there have been large-scale increases in expenditure on children (investment), particularly with regard to educational and medical expenses. This represents a huge rise in the direct cost of child-rearing. In addition, since the work involved with raising children is extremely time-consuming, in today's world where time is becoming more and more precious to people, devoting great energy to childcare and domestic duties is likely to generate greater financial costs. In other words, there has also been a considerable increase in the indirect costs of child-rearing.
   (b) There have been huge reductions in the benefits associated with having children. Along with increases in per capita income and an ever-growing choice of cultural and leisure activities, the benefits that come with having children have fallen to differing extents. [In the study by the American scholar], Eichnerman, the case is advanced one stage further since he argues that any need previously met by having children can now be satisfied in other ways. In modern-day China, the diminishing benefits associated with child-rearing are mainly manifested in the following two ways:

On the one hand, there is now less of a need to rear children in order to forestall the problems of old age. For many people, the most direct reason for having children is to provide security for themselves in their old age. And yet, to what extent can raising children really guarantee this security? An analysis of the major sources of income for elderly people suggests that no matter whether in the countryside or in the city, elderly people rely mainly on retirement pensions and income gained from their own work – the proportion of those who depend mainly on their children is very low. (See Table 6.7). Another analysis of the conditions of mutual financial support between elderly people and their grown-up children reveals that

Table 6.7 Major sources of income for elderly people in urban and rural areas (percentage shares)

Urban/ Rural	Income from own work	Retirement pension	Provided by children	Other	Total
Urban	10.4	58.9	15.7	15.0	100.0
Rural	29.8	37.2	27.5	5.4	100.0

Source: Compiled using data from the 'Survey report on the ageing population' in '*Chinese Population Statistics Handbook*' (1989).

almost 50% of elderly people help their offspring out financially. This far exceeds the proportion of sons and daughters who set aside money for their elderly parents.

This shows that in the China of today, where the phenomena of 'reverse support' and 'living off the elderly' are equally prevalent, the function and role of children as a provider of support (particularly financial support) is not quite as important or indispensable as is generally imagined. Furthermore, children are no longer the sole link for holding together a family, improving one's enjoyment of life, or providing an emotional bond between husband and wife. Outmoded concepts of marriage as a partnership entered into reluctantly for the sake of having children have long since been overtaken by the times and replaced with new ideals: Marriage should be based on love – to cement a marriage together with children is both unfortunate and immoral. Some people even believe that not only are children ineffective in holding together or strengthening a marriage, they can even ignite the fuse that leads to a deterioration in the relationship between husband and wife, culminating in an irretrievable breakdown of mutual affection.

A number of academics overseas have conducted extensive research into the connection between the degree to which a couple are satisfied with their marriage and the life-cycle of the household. They have come to the conclusion that a woman derives the maximum satisfaction from her marriage during the initial period of matrimony. Her satisfaction falls after the birth of a child, and is at its lowest ebb when the child is of school-age. Her satisfaction rises again rapidly after the child has left home (the situation with the husband is similar to the wife, only with less marked variations). In other words, the stage in the cycle of the household when husband and wife have negative feelings towards their marriage correlates with the stage when dependent children form part of the equation.

3. The existence of population policies has a strong influence on whether or not married women want to have children. Statistics from China's second Childbirth Survey reveal that the proportion of childless married women who took the present population policy into account when they made the decision not to have children is markedly higher than the

Table 6.8 The proportion of childless, married women who do not want to have children under the conditions imposed by a 'population policy' (%)

Region	2nd Childbirth Survey
Beijing Municipality	20
Liaoning Province	14
Shandong Province	9
Guangdong Province	6
Guizhou Province	5
Gansu Province	7
Total	11

Source: Compiled using data from the 'National Report on China's Second Childbirth Survey'.

proportion who did not take the policy into account when making the same decision. (See Table 6.8). This is a clear indication of the role that population policy has played in bringing down the birth-rate in China.

To sum up, therefore, further improvements to the socialist market economy and the social security system, the continued development of cultural and educational facilities, and increased public awareness of China's population problems are all likely to be accompanied by a continued growth of DINKS households in China. DINKS households should neither be promoted nor disparaged – there is a certain inevitability with regard to their emergence and development. Running counter to conventional patterns of child-rearing, DINKS households may represent a powerful assault on the traditional belief that: 'Of the three unfilial acts, to lack an heir is the greatest'. They may also provide us with new angles of approach in our investigation into the socio-economic and cultural influences on family planning work in the countryside. Finally, DINKS households have provided us with an important insight into whether or not it is appropriate to make comprehensive changes to our current population policy.

Document 6.3

'Population in the Northwest over forty years'

ZHU JINTANG (NINGXIA PROVINCE STATISTICAL BUREAU)

Journal of Northwest Population, 1991, No. 1

The five provinces and autonomous regions of the Northwest, namely Shanxi, Gansu, Qinghai, Ningxia, and Xinjiang, cover an area of 3.02

million square kilometres, or around one third of China's total land area. Historically, the region has always been sparsely populated with a poorly developed economy and low cultural levels. Until China's liberation in 1949, population density measured only 2.7 people per square kilometre in the Xinjiang Uighur Autonomous Region, and 2.1 people per square kilometre in Qinghai Province.

After liberation, the population of the Northwest began to develop and underwent a number of changes. Its own particular regional characteristics gradually began to emerge.

The current situation and the history of population evolution in the Northwest over the last 40 years

Due to war, famine, poverty, a lack of medical care etc, the pre-1949 population of the Northwest basically conformed to the 'high birth rate – high death rate – low rate of growth' pattern of vital rates.

Under the leadership of the Party and the People's Government, the vigorous development of the economy in the Northwest over the forty years since liberation led to great improvements in the standard of living and environmental conditions of the region. This resulted in higher rates of population growth than during the initial period after liberation. By the end of 1988, the population of the Northwest had risen to 75.99 million people, an increase of 46.12 million people, or 154.4%, compared with 1949. This was equivalent to an annual growth rate of 2.36%. This compared with a national population growth rate of just 102.4% and a national annual growth rate of 1.82% over the same period. (See Table 6.9).

The 1980s saw great improvements in health and welfare provisions and the implementation of family planning work. Consequently the Northwest entered a phase characterised by a relatively low birth rate, a low death rate and a low rate of population growth. However, persistently high birth rates in certain areas ensured that the Northwest still conformed to the pattern of relatively high population growth, compared with the rest of the country.

The stages of population development in the Northwest

Nationally, the period 1949–1957 was a phase of comparatively high population growth. The Between 1958 and 1961 the birth rate fell and mortality rose. The birth rate fell even further between 1962 and 1973 – a period of anarchy as far as births were concerned – and this decline continued after 1974.[16] However, in the Northwest there was a basic underlying trend for population to rise throughout the whole period since 1949. Although population growth occurred at different stages in different provinces and regions, the stages of development for the Northwestern region as a whole did not coincide with the stages of growth for the rest of the nation.

16 This account is something of a simplification, see the introduction to this Chapter. (Ed.)

Table 6.9 Population development of Northwest China and its Provinces/
Autonomous Regions since 1949 (Millions)

Year	Accumulated total for the Northwest	Shanxi	Gansu	Qinghai	Ningxia	Xinjiang
1949	29.871	13.173	9.684	1.483	1.198	4.333
1952	35.416	15.279	10.647	1.614	1.240	4.652
1957	40.000	18.029	12.551	2.046	1.794	5.58
1962	43.506	20.078	12.400	2.050	1.988	6.99
1965	47.361	21.143	13.454	2.305	2.268	7.891
1970	53.704	24.279	15.877	2.829	2.773	7.966
1975	63.160	26.921	18.040	3.375	3.279	1.1545
1978	66.031	27.795	18.701	3.649	3.556	1.233
1980	67.836	28.314	19.184	3.769	3.737	1.2832
1985	72.263	30.017	20.413	4.074	4.146	1.3611
1986	73.427	30.426	20.711	4.211	4.243	1.3836
1987	74.610	30.882	21.034	4.279	4.352	1.4063
1988	75.988	31.400	21.357	4.342	4.445	1.4264
1949–1988 annual growth rate %	2.362	2.195	1.996	2.120	3.332	3.002
1978–1988 annual growth rate %	1.414	1.226	1.336	1.754	2.257	1.468
1949–1978 annual growth rate %	2.679	2.520	2.218	3.046	3.693	3.547

In addition, the frequent and systematic transfer of large numbers of people to the Northwest and the migration of people in connection with the construction of the 'Third Front' meant that, over the whole forty-year period since 1949, the population of the Northwest only registered negative growth in one year – 1961. Population fell from 43.36 million in 1960 to 43.04 million in 1961, but then rose rapidly again to reach 43.51 million people in 1962 – the dip was therefore only a small fluctuation.[17]

17 The 'Third Front' refers to Mao's ambitious plans to relocate Chinese industry away from strategically vulnerable areas. In economic terms this proved a costly exercise and it was reversed in the reform period. In addition millions of 'surplus' urban population were sent to Xinjiang during the 1960s, especially from Shanghai and Jiangsu Province. Finally, to this day Xinjiang has a large population in penal Labour Camps. These rarely return and are hence a permanent addition to the population of the Province. (Ed.)

The characteristics of population development in the Northwest

If we look back at the development of population in the Northwest over the forty years since 1949, the following features emerge:

1. Population has developed fairly rapidly

Population growth in the Northwest since liberation has provided abundant labour resources for exploiting the natural resources of the region and developing the regional economy. However, there is no denying that the rate of population development in the Northwest over the last forty years has been relatively high. (See Table 6.10).

This table shows that population growth in the Northwest has been higher during all periods than the average rate of growth for the country as a whole. During the thirty years before 1978 total population growth for the region was 43.34% higher than the national average. The difference in the annual growth rates was 0.77% higher in the Northwest. Over the last ten years, restrictions have been put in place to curb blind increases in the population and yet the population growth rate in the Northwest is still 0.11% higher than the national average.

In researching the rate of population growth in the Northwest it is important to bear the following facts in mind:

a) The population base is becoming larger and larger. In 1949, a 1% increase in population represented an absolute growth of only 299,000 people. However, by 1988 an increase of 1% meant a growth in population of 759,900 people. This means we should be even more conscious of the need to reduce the rate of population growth.

b) Migration increases have made a significant contribution. Population growth in the Northwest is closely related to 'mechanical' increases that were the result of the influx of production brigades to cultivate the land in the 1950s and 1960s, the transfer of companies to the region for the construction of the 'Third Front', and the state's systematic promotion of migration to the region. For example, during the 1950's and early 1960's, the average annual influx of people into Ningxia Province was

Table 6.10 The rates of population growth for the Northwest and compared with the national average. Various period 1949–1988 (% growth rates)

	National population growth over the whole period	Northwest Region	Difference
1988 compared with 1949 (%)	102.36	154.38	52.02
1978 compared with 1949 (%)	77.71	121.05	43.34
1988 compared with 1978 (%)	13.87	15.08	1.21

higher than the birth rate. This became particularly evident between 1958 and 1961, when the ratio of births to immigrants was 1 : 3.3, 1 : 4.5, 1 : 5.9, and 1 : 2.5 for each year respectively. This pattern was even more pronounced in Xinjiang.

c) There are still serious problems with incorrect population statistics. This is particularly the case in the Northwest with its high mountains, deep valleys and vast plains. In Ningxia, for example, there is a clear contrast between the sample survey carried out by the Autonomous Region Statistical Office and the population statistics forms collected for the whole area. (See Table 6.11).

If such serious discrepancies can occur in Ningxia, which covers an area of only 51,800 km², then the problems in vast regions such as Xinjiang, Qinghai, Gansu and Shanxi must be even worse. Some people are resigned to this and say: 'Perhaps the data from the Statistical Office does not reflect the true situation. In the economically deprived villages of Shanxi, people cannot afford to pay fines for having above-quota children and therefore often do not declare their 'black [i.e. illegitimate] children'. Even the household registration authorities and health departments admit that this may amount to a significant number of children, but it is impossible to know for sure exactly how many.'

2. The quality of the population is comparatively low

It is generally accepted that population quality should include physical health, mental capacity, and cultural and scientific levels. I would like to limit this definition now to the latter: i.e. cultural and scientific levels. Since

Table 6.11 The contrast between sample survey based estimates and population statistics forms in Ningxia.[18]

	1986 population statistics	1986 sample survey estimates	1987 population statistics	1987 sample survey estimates	1988 population statistics	1988 sample survey estimates
Births	174,396	86,161	89,495	108,038	83,428	109,070
Deaths	15,857	20,470	16,213	21,659	17,004	23,048
Net increase	58,539	65,187	73,282	86,379	66,424	85,989
Natural growth rate % per annum	1.396	1.554	1.706	2.01	1.51	1.955

18 The 'population statistics' quoted here must refer to the registered population as cumulatively recorded. Registration data are therefore one of three kinds of regularly collected data, the other two being the ten year Census and the 1% sample survey data. (Ed.)

Table 6.12 The number of students at different levels of schooling in the Northwest in 1949 and 1988. (Numbers per 10,000 of the total population)

Year	Ordinary Higher Middle School	Middle School	Junior School
1949	1.5	14.6	490.1
1988	23.2	233.0	1185.7

Note: Middle Schools include all kinds of technical secondary schools as well as ordinary secondary schools.

1949, there have been great improvements to the cultural and scientific quality of the population in the Northwest. (See Table 6.12.)

The figures above suggest that there have been great improvements in the cultural and scientific levels of the population of the Northwest, but in fact levels are still on the low side by comparison with the rest of the country. According to a 1% national sample in 1987, the proportion of illiterate and semi-illiterate people over the age of 12 was higher than the national average in every single province and autonomous region of the Northwest except Xinjiang. The [illiteracy] proportion for Xinjiang was 21.20%, compared to the national average of 26.77%. The illiteracy rates for Shanxi, Gansu, Qinghai, and Ningxia, however, were 28.96%, 43.92%, 51.61%, and 35.49% respectively.

The proportions of women who were either illiterate or semi-illiterate were even higher: 66.71% in Qinghai, 59.36% in Gansu, 47.62% in Ningxia, and 39.19% in Shanxi. This represents a decline in cultural and scientific levels, which has had a direct negative impact on the dissemination and adoption of new concepts and new practices and inevitably affects the quality of people's thinking.

Lack of economic development and shortfalls in material conditions also have a negative influence on the physical quality of the local population. However, the issue of education has always been neglected and people have not given the problem proper consideration. In Northern Shanxi, a large number of teachers and students still have to put up with poor school buildings and a lack of essential equipment. Indeed because there is no money to buy chalk and paper, teachers frequently have to force their students to go outside when it is raining to collect mud to use as chalk. Even on the Central Shanxi Plain, which enjoys relatively good conditions, there was a school that could not afford to pay the teachers' salaries. The teachers were therefore forced to chop down trees in and around the school grounds to sell for firewood to earn some kind of remuneration.

3. It is relatively difficult to carry out family planning work

Because natural conditions are so bad, poverty in the Northwest is tremendous and the region has a national reputation for having the three great 'western' regions of impoverishment. Traditional small peasant mentality has led the local population to place their hopes for economic transformation on increases in population, particularly male population. There is the story of the 41-year-old woman in Jingning County, Gansu Province, who had the 'misfortune' to give birth to ten girls, and of 'Old Man Wang' who was approaching sixty and who 'created 25 healthy young lives on a piece of poor standard land'.

According to statistics from the regions of Dingxi and Guyuan, in less than forty years after 1949, population grew by 150%. Scientific deductions from the International Conference on Desertification in 1978 suggest that the critical norm for population in arid and semi-arid areas such as Dingxi and Guyuan is 20 people per square kilometre of land. However the present population of this region is far in excess of this figure.

Continuing problems with population development in the Northwest

1. *The comparative mismatch between population development and economic development*

The population of the Northwest has grown rapidly with the result that it accounts for an increasingly large proportion of the population for the country as a whole. During the initial period just after 1949, the population of the Northwest accounted for only 5.52% of the national population, but by 1988 this had risen to 6.93%. This has placed increasingly heavy pressures on economic development.

Firstly, the problem of producing sufficient quantities of food has always been an important question for the local economy. Over the last 40 years, gross output of grain has been raised from 6.84 million tons to 25.43 million tons. However, in per capita terms grain output has only been raised by 46.1% from 458 *jin* per head to 669 *jin* per head.[19] This is far below lower the national average. Consequently, the 'three western' region and some areas in the north of Shanxi have still not managed to reach subsistence levels and life is still hard for a significant proportion of the local population. Except for Xinjiang, which is self-sufficient in grain production, the four other provinces and autonomous regions of the Northwest have to import grain from other areas every year. This has become one of the factors restricting economic development in the Northwest.

Secondly, if we measure economic strength in terms of local financial resources, regional financial income for the Northwest grew by a factor of 19.96 from 402.90 million *yuan* in 1952 to 8.45 billion *yuan* in 1988. However, regional financial income per capita only grew by a factor of 8.8 over the same period. In an attempt to counter economic and cultural under-development, the State has had no choice but to devote large

19 A *jin* is approximately half a kilo. (Ed.)

quantities of finance every year to support the rapid growth of population in the Northwest. According to regional statistics from Qinghai and Ningxia, the accumulated total of local financial resources for the two provinces reached 4.70 billion *yuan* between 1980 and 1988. However, the total sum of money given to the two provinces in the form of direct subsidies from central government amounted to 12.31 billion *yuan* over the same period. Thus the amount of money raised locally only represented 38.2% of the amount of money provided by central government subsidies. Given these financial circumstances, the continued heavy burden of population growth will have an inevitable impact on the development of the local economy.

Finally, let us measure the performance of the local economy against the economic indicator of Gross Social Product. The Gross Social Product of the Northwest reached 3.27 billion *yuan* in 1949 (at current prices – same hereinafter). This represented 5.87% of the National product. By 1988, Gross Social Product in the Northwest had grown to 147.29 billion *yuan*, a 44-fold increase compared with the initial period after liberation. However, over the same period, the Northwest's share of Gross National Social Product fell to 4.93%. In fact, this proportion has been on the decline since the beginning of the 1970s.

Over the last 40 years, the indicators of population and Gross Social Product have been moving in opposite directions when measured as a proportion of the national total. It is easy to appreciate, therefore, the gravity of the situation.

2. Population growth has exacerbated the destruction of the environment

The human population and the natural environment form an inseparable whole, and when population grows to the extent that it can no longer be supported by the natural environment, the inevitable result must be environmental degradation. The environmental conditions in the Northwest are extremely fragile because in most of the region, the water evaporation rate is higher than the rate of rainfall. Population growth makes the problem even worse. In the Dingxi region of Gansu Province and the Guyuan region of Ningxia Province, the local inhabitants use turf as a 'traditional' form of fuel. According to 1982 statistics from Dingxi County, the average household uses an area of 25.3 *mou*[20] of turf for this purpose every year. Vast amounts of turf have been cut from the mountainsides by the inhabitants of the county and the state must spend huge sums of money on transporting water to supply the farmers in some areas. Thus the environment has been plunged into a vicious circle. Statistics reveal that in Shanxi Province, soil erosion has spread to a total area of 13,479 square kilometres since 1949. Roughly 80% of the province's cultivable land suffers from soil erosion and this affects around 70% of the province's

20 The *mou* is 0.0667 hectares.

population. The admirable results of soil erosion control programmes have only had an impact on two thirds of the total area suffering from the problem. Around 60% of the total area of farmland in the province has a soil fertility rating of less than 1%; 60% of land has a nitrogen content of less than 0.075%; 70% of land has a quick-acting nitrogen content of less than 60PPM; and 80% of land has a quick-acting phosphate content of less than 20PPM. While land-bearing capacity is on the decline, the population burden continues to rise. It is the growth in population that is largely responsible for this environmental degradation, not to mention the pollution problems caused by light and heavy industry.

This is only a fraction of the large range of problems caused by population growth. Our historical glance at population development in the Northwest over the last 40 years suggests that we must continue to consolidate family planning work in the future. We also need to increase investment in education, science and technology and improve the quality of the population. Even more important, however, is the government's prompt adoption of preferential policies for the Northwest to accelerate the economic development of the region and promote social well-being through economic prosperity. Social forces must be used to curb population growth and raise the quality of the population. A new, prosperous and developed Northwestern region will help to enhance the glory and splendour of the nation as a whole.

Document 6.4

'The population requirements of the social and economic development of the Kunshan region until the year 2000, and strategies to accommodate them'

LI QUANLIN, (PARTY SECRETARY, KUNSHAN CITY, JIANGSU PROVINCE)

Population and Family Planning, 1995 No. 1

Situated between Shanghai and Jiangsu, the Kunshan region benefits from an advantageous geographical position and convenient sea, river and land communications. Covering a total area of 921 square kilometres, it is the administrative region for 20 towns and 466 villages with a combined population of 575,500 people. It contains 46,690 hectares of farmland and a total water surface area of 20,010 hectares.

Since 1980, Kunshan has fully recognised the need to link population control with economic development, and has managed to coordinate socio-economic development and population growth in a relatively harmonious way. In the ten years between 1981 and 1991, the value of Kunshan's GNP grew at an annual rate of 24%, 15% higher than in the previous ten years.

The average natural rate of population growth measured .624% per year, 0.18 percentage points higher than during the previous ten years. In 1993, the Gross Product of the city reached 6.04 billion *yuan*, or over 10,000 *yuan* per capita. Kunshan therefore ranks among the top producers of the 2000 plus counties (and municipalities) that make up the country as a whole.[21]

If we measure this against the criteria for 'moderate prosperity' promulgated by the State Statistical Bureau in 1990, then the Kunshan region matches or surpasses the criteria as defined by eleven separate economic indicators. These include, for example: per capita output, relative size of the tertiary sector, annual per capita income, housing area per capita, the Engels coefficient, rates of elementary and intermediate schooling, and average life expectancy.[22]

In our overall plans for the social and economic development of Kunshan, we are attempting to transform Kunshan into a medium-sized city with a full range of facilities and a preliminary level of modernisation. We are aiming for a thriving economy that is open to outside influences and advanced in terms of science and technology. We will maintain social stability and encourage the development of an attractive living environment for a community that is both wealthy and at ease with itself.

To build a medium-sized city with a preliminary level of modernisation is a highly complex project of engineering, and population problems in particular become a pivotal, key factor. The rapid process of modernisation inevitably leads to large numbers of the rural population becoming non-rural. The migration towards the city of large numbers of people as well as the urban settlement of those who have abandoned agriculture, means that we must make a full appraisal of the future trends in the development of the urban population. We need to be scientific in our forecasting and thorough in our research, so that we can plan accordingly and promote an even higher degree of coordination and unification between population growth and socio-economic development. This will help to ensure the successful attainment of the levels of modernisation that we envisage.

We must have a correct understanding of the principles of Marxist population theory and use them to guide our future practice. We must firmly support and implement the policies and programmes on family planning that have been formulated by the Party Central Committee and the State Council. All areas of work that are initiated in Kunshan must be linked together in a realistic and creative way and we must always adhere to the principle of harmonising social and economic development with population growth. In order to achieve this, our general requirements are: control of total population, a raising of population quality, adjustment of the urban/rural structure, and the maintenance of a dynamic equilibrium.

21 Kunshan is indeed a rich city. Its per capita output reported here was higher than that of Shanghai and nearly double that of Beijing at this time. (Ed.)
22 Moderate prosperity (*xiao kang*) is to be the first landmark on China's progress to economic modernisation in the reform era. It was a target set by Deng but defined in a complex way with many indicators. (Ed.)

1. We must recognise the need to develop a harmonious relationship between population and socio-economic development

The essential meaning behind the 'two kinds of production' concept in Marxist theory is that there must be mutual compatibility and harmony between the reproduction of population and the reproduction of material goods. If this is not the case, then a series of problems and contradictions are likely to emerge in both social and economic development. Notably, excessive increases in population will lead to the consumption of vast quantities of material wealth which will influence and restrict the accelerated development of the economy and society. Only an appropriate relationship between the two can ensure sustained economic growth and sustainable economic development; and only an appropriate relationship between the two can satisfy the growing material and spiritual needs of the population and maintain and develop a superior environment for the next generation.

We are very familiar with these principles in Kunshan. From the initial period after 1949 until the end of the 1970s, Kunshan enjoyed great quantitative increases in terms of economic growth, but this did not translate into a commensurate rise in the standard of living for the people as a whole. This was because of excessive population growth. In other words we ignored the proportionate relationship between population reproduction and the reproduction of material goods.

Since the 1980s we have taken pains to take full consideration of the relationship between the two kinds of production and have ensured the implementation of each and every policy on family planning. On the one hand we have actively promoted economic development and economic expansion, and on the other we have achieved a total urban family planning rate of around 99.8%. This has promoted coordination between population growth and socio-economic development. However, a coordinated relationship between population growth and socio-economic development should not be seen as an immutable, quantitative relationship. There are likely to be dynamic changes in this relationship in line with economic development and social progress

Our goal is to transform Kunshan into a medium-sized city with a preliminary level of modernisation by the end of the century. This means that we will be required to develop and establish new proportionate relationships according to the demands of modernisation. Kunshan is currently in the transitional stage between the preliminary and intermediate phases of industrialisation. The economy will maintain a relatively high but stable rate of growth over the next few years. If we address the problem in a simplistic way and insist on equal rates of growth for the economy and the population, then the result will be an expansion in gross economic output without a corresponding rise in levels per capita. If this were the case, then achieving modernisation would be little more than an empty pipe dream. Therefore, keeping strict control over population growth is still one of the cornerstones of modernisation. So what exactly should be regarded as 'an appropriate and harmonious proportionate relationship between population growth and socio-economic development' for Kunshan until the year 2000.

We believe that the total population of Kunshan should be kept at around 620,000 people. This means we need to place tight controls on natural population growth and ensure that there is an average annual increase of no more than 0.5%. At the same time we should attract people into the city as appropriate, ensuring that the annual growth rate for migration is kept at around 0.4%. In this way, there will be a net increase in the total urban population to the tune of around 50,000 people over 7 years. This will guarantee that all our per capita targets will meet the criteria for preliminary modernisation at the appropriate time. And this in turn will facilitate the realisation of a new, coordinated relationship at an even higher level in line with standards of modernisation.

2. We need to make adjustments to our industrial structure to encourage the rational flow and distribution of the working population

According to our overall projections, by the end of the century, the working population of Kunshan will have risen to approximately 420,000 people out of a total urban population of 620,000 people. However, in terms of the demands of economic development and the absorbtive capacity of Kunshan city as a whole, the total urban labour force will need to stand at around 500,000 people.

We anticipate that the following three measures will help to encourage the rational flow of labour towards the urban areas and the optimum allocation of labour resources:

First, we must actively make adjustments to the industrial structure and adjust the distribution of labour among the three branches of industry:

Currently, the industrial employment structure of our urban labour force is as follows:

Primary industry	29.1%
Secondary industry	49.3%
Tertiary industry	21.6%

Over the next few years, one of our main objectives should be to raise rapidly the level of agricultural mechanisation and promote increases in the scale of agricultural operations. We should transfer 50,000 agricultural workers out of agriculture and into urban employment. By the turn of the century, the primary, secondary and tertiary structure of industrial employment should have changed to 15%, 45% and 40% respectively.[23]

23 Kunshan City includes agrarian suburbs and it is the agricultural workers in these that are referred to here. Indeed, Kunshan City was itself a mainly agricultural area before its accelerated development in the 1980s, which required that much agricultural land be converted to industrial use. Local planners in Kunshan informed me in 1988 that the peasants were persuaded to relinquish all this land in return for improved educational facilities and promises of industrial jobs for their children. (Ed.)

Second, we must devote our energy to raising total labour productivity and controlling any overheating in the demand for labour. From now on, we must accelerate the renovation and renewal of technical equipment, introduce large quantities of advanced technology from overseas and make a serious attempt to set up capital- and technology-intensive enterprises. Since 1993, we have attracted large amounts of foreign capital and established a large number of large-scale, high-technology foreign business and investment companies. These include the Japanese companies: Toyota, Makita and Shimano; the Taiwanese companies: Juda, Tongyi, Zhengxin, and Nanzi; French and American companies and the Swiss company Ciba-Geigy. Companies such as these have been eager to invest, and it is estimated that gross investment by the companies mentioned above stands at around US$800 million. This outstrips the current value of total urban industry fixed capital investment, and yet these companies require a labour force of only 6,500 people after commencing production.

Third, we must strive to raise labour specialisation and cooperation and avoid excessive labour intensive production.

3. We need to appropriately absorb and attract labour from elsewhere and maintain a dynamic equilibrium in total population

The further development of open-door policies towards outside influences and the gradual establishment of a market economic system will both help break down the detached and isolated nature of different regions. This in turn will promote the migratory flow of large amounts of labour and the trend is likely to grow in terms of both numbers and range distances migrants travel.

Essentially, we need to consider the fundamental national characteristics of China when managing and controlling population flow, and use a combination of market adjustments and planned control to achieve our aims. In particular, we must begin to address the key issue of the household registration system and carry forward and perfect reforms in line with the demands of new circumstances. The following measures are necessary:

1. The upper echelons must gradually relinquish their tight grip on power and break through the ossified patterns of household registration planning according to quota. For many years, those in authority have kept tight control over the targets issued for the transfer of labour from agricultural to non-agricultural production and for urban migration. These strict restrictions have effectively kept numbers down. This is inappropriate in relation to current and future trends of accelerated development.

2. We must implement a new 'green card' system of administration as a pilot project. Under this system, those with secure employment who are willing to settle in Kunshan will, on proof of their identity and position, be issued with an alien residence permit which must be validated once a year. They will then become liable to pay an appropriate contribution

into urban development funds each fiscal year. These people will enjoy the same benefits as native residents of Kunshan in terms of medical care, housing, employment, schooling, border-crossing permits etc.

3. We must consolidate our control over Kunshan's transient population. A large number of those who have come to work in Kunshan are engaged in jobs and business activities of a seasonal or temporary nature. This group is made up of a complicated mixture of people with a great tendency to drift from place to place. In an attempt to deal with this issue, we initiated a number of research projects and surveys in 1992 which resulted in the institution of almost 300 special work teams over the whole urban area during the following year. These teams have been set up to provide a tier of government and administration for those who have migrated to the city from elsewhere and consist of representatives from the Municipal Party Committee, the Municipal Government, the Politics and Law Committee and the Family Planning Committee together with members of other relevant departments. These teams employ over 800 people as administrative assistants for household registration and they have established a whole raft of measures to deal with transient population registration, including the issue of certificates, the signing of public order bonds, the collection of funds for the maintenance of public order and improved management of privately rented accommodation. Documents issued by the Municipal Government clearly stipulate the following:

In connection with family planning work among the migrant population, it has been ruled that a married woman may only register for temporary residence once she has registered her child-bearing capacity with her local family planning department (above village/county level). Additionally, in keeping with the principle that 'those who are responsible must bear responsibility', employers of migrant workers, landlords who let to migrant workers and individual women of child-bearing age must all personally sign 'family planning guarantees' or 'agreements' with the government. This will all help to strengthen administrative measures and thereby facilitate our macro-control over the numbers of migrants into Kunshan. It will also promote adjustments in the micro-economy and help to bring about a dynamic equilibrium.

4. We must place emphasis on investment in human capital and raise the quality of the population.

The development of a medium-sized city with preliminary levels of modernisation not only requires abundant labour resources, it also necessitates improvements in the quality of the labour force as a whole. Admittedly, a certain amount of economic growth can be achieved by increasing conventional capital, but the rate of growth will be extremely limited. It is completely impossible to achieve modernisation without taking full stock of our vast quantities of human resources. We must therefore adhere to the internal rules of economic development and shift our strategic emphasis away from the development of material resources towards the development of human resources, in line with the demands of modernisation. We must raise the quality of the working population as a whole and thereby promote the sustained, stable and coordinated development of the economy and society.

Our primary task is to improve the physical capabilities of the population. This is a long-term, systematic and fundamental project to change the traditional customs that relate to partnership and marriage. We should use the current trends of migration and population flow to encourage the gradual expansion of the geographical boundaries within which people look for a potential husband or wife. This will lead to beneficial results in terms of strong marital partnerships and eugenics. At the same time, we must encourage people to improve their diets and patterns of daily living, so that they are consistent with scientific reasoning and provide benefits for health. An even more important task is to establish strong, socialised systems of healthcare to provide people with excellent guarantees for medical treatment and recovery.

Our second task is to raise the mental capabilities of the population. We must increase investment in education to strengthen mental development and place educational facilities in a prominent, leading position. We need to consolidate the basic nine years of compulsory education and implement a trial two-track system for education at the Higher Middle level. There must be an expansion in the provision of vocational education in Senior Middle Schools with an emphasis on developing a reserve force of workers with the professional skills necessary for carrying forward the industrial development of Kunshan.

By 1997, the graduation rate for Lower Middle School students will surpass 75% for the urban area as a whole [including rural suburbs] and 90% for the core city. By 1998, will basically have achieved universal Higher Middle education. By the year 2000, we plan to have sent 7000 new qualified students to intermediate vocational colleges and institutes of higher education, and to have trained 32,000 people to become qualified workers to help build up the local economy. We aim to ensure that 250–300 people out of every ten thousand will be qualified at university/polytechnic level or higher. We also need to devote time and energy to promoting life-long education and improving on-the-job training.

Our third task is to raise the ideological quality of the population. We need to develop an effective network of inspirational and educational institutions across the city with the general aim of fostering and nurturing a new socialist generation; we must forge ahead with the liberation of people's minds so that they are able to adapt successfully to new situations and circumstances; we must strengthen people's cultural awareness so that they can absorb new knowledge and new concepts; we must help people adapt to a new pace and rhythm of life that will facilitate the development of a medium-sized modern city. We must strive also to foster a pioneering spirit of enterprise among the people so that they will always retain their motivation for self-improvement and advancement and become even more determined to transform Kunshan into a medium-sized city with preliminary levels of modernisation by the turn of the century.

Document 6.5

'Some tentative ideas on the reform of China's labour system'

LIU YONGREN

The Journal of the Shanxi Institute of Finance and Economics, 1985, No. 5

The labour system comprises a number of different systems including the labour employment system, the vocational and technical training system, the labour hiring system, and the social labour force management system. Under China's socialist system, the labour system should be used to facilitate the rational distribution and use of labour power, promote a greater integration of labour power and capital goods, and stimulate the enthusiasm, initiative and creativity of workers. In this way, the labour system can act as an important means of realising China's socialist modernisation through the search for ever higher economic efficiency.

However, the labour system currently operating in China is a long way from meeting the demands listed above. For a long time, there have been a number of problems with our labour employment, hiring, training, and management systems that are incompatible with the development of a socialist market economy. For example, labour management is over-concentrated and excessively centralised. Labour and personnel departments are still in charge of a number of areas which they are incapable of managing properly. Thus individual businesses have little autonomy in hiring staff, increasing salaries etc. and this is a major cause of the current lack of vitality within businesses. These problems have become a serious obstruction to our economic development.

According to the spirit of the 'Decisions' of the CCP Central Committee and with the pre-requisite of overall government planning, enterprises now have the right to select, hire, and dismiss their own workers according to the regulations.[24] They have the right to decide their own methods of employment as well as the salaries and bonuses that will be paid to their employees. The reform of the personnel and wage systems must be carried out along these lines. I shall use the rest of this essay to discuss some of the problems with the reforms to the labour system in China.

24 This refers to the regulations on enlarging enterprises powers of self management, published on 10 May 1984. (Ed.)

1. The labour employment system

For a long period in the past, China operated a unified control and allocation labour system. It was the government's responsibility to find positions for all those eligible for employment. The adoption of methods which limited the development of a collective and individual economy engendered a hierarchical conception of economic activity in people's minds: 'national – collective – individual'. Over time, an acute conflict developed between the narrow channels of employment and the growth of the working population. This gradually began to affect social and economic stability.

After the Third Plenary Session of the Thirteenth Party Congress, we started to make changes to the structure of industry and the system of ownership. This enabled large numbers of young people to find employment not only in heavy industry, but also in light industry, textiles, manual work, food processing etc. They were able to undertake individual economic activities as well as find work in state-owned or collective organisations. According to incomplete statistics, townships and cities nationwide placed a total of over 39 million people in employment between 1979 and 1983. This is an average of almost 8 million people per year. By the end of 1983, the proportion of young people awaiting employment in towns and cities had fallen to 2.3%. In 1984, employment was found for an extra 3.53 million people leading to a further fall in the unemployment rate of this group to 1.9%. This clearly indicates that our reforms are appropriate for the current situation, otherwise these remarkable results could not have been achieved. However, there is no cause for complacency and [for the following reasons] our employment tasks should continue to be an important area of focus for some time to come.

1. Almost 6 million new workers migrate to towns and cities in search of employment every year.
2. Since the reforms, enterprises have had to cope with the problem of over 10 million surplus employees.
3. The development of the rural economy will have encouraged an estimated 90 million farmers to look for other forms of employment by 1990.
4. The inherent instability of the collective and individual economies are likely to give rise to re-employment problems, and these will probably become fairly widespread.
5. People's work expectations will rise with the growing choice of employment opportunities.

The above factors suggest that in the coming years we must persist with reforms and improvements to the labour system. We need to exploit China's rich labour resources in order to create stable social conditions for the reform of the economic system. This is likely, however, to be a very difficult task. In facing up to this reality, we should look for solutions to

337

China's employment situation by implementing the following three major measures;

1. We must conscientiously put into practice the relevant policy decisions that have been promulgated since the Third Plenary Session of the Eleventh Party Congress. We must adhere to the philosophy of 'liberalisation' and 'revitalisation' and open new doors to employment. This must all be integrated with China's specific situation to establish a healthy and effective labour management system with Chinese characteristics in order to bring about rapid economic growth.
2. We must continue to make changes to the industrial structure and devote major efforts to developing tertiary industry. This is an important part of the solution to our future urban employment problems. In some developed countries, tertiary industry accounts for the employment of 60%–70% of the total working population. In China, however, the proportion is only 15%. It is easy to see, therefore, the great potential employment opportunities in tertiary industry. Moreover, rapid results can be achieved with relatively small amounts of investment and tertiary industry can be adapted to a variety of different systems of ownership. It could be of particular use in developing the collective and individual economies.
3. In order to make changes to the structure of the system of ownership and develop the collective and individual economies, it is necessary to formulate realistic policies and regulations to ensure that losses are not incurred in the process.

2. The hiring system

Since the founding of the People's Republic, the hiring in China has been based on permanent employment system. This type of system provides job security for workers and has played an active role in maintaining social and political stability. It also helped production make a rapid recovery from the scars of war. However, the deficiencies of this system have become apparent along with the rise in the level of China's forces of production and its negative aspects have become increasingly difficult to overlook. This form of hiring, which essentially guarantees 'lifelong employment', encourages laziness and inertia, and makes it very difficult for enterprises to deal with problems of unwanted workers. The right of everyone to eat from the same 'iron rice bowl' fosters a mentality of complacency and idleness. Under these conditions it is not easy for workers to change jobs, even if the job they were assigned in the first place is completely inappropriate. This has a negative impact on worker motivation, initiative and creativity. People are unable to exploit their talents to the full to increase the vitality of the enterprise and raise economic efficiency.

So how should we change this irrational system? An effective way would be to change the permanent hiring system to a labour contract system. The introduction of a labour contract system retains some of the advantages of the former system and also compensates for many of its shortcomings. According to statistics, by the end of September 1984 approximately 780,000 workers in enterprises under the ownership of the whole people were already employed under a labour contract system.

The results of this reform are clear: the rate of attendance for workers on fixed contracts is high; they engage actively in work and production; and they are sufficiently motivated to gain new vocational and technical skills. This is clear evidence of the great latent potential of the labour contract system. However, some people do not have a clear understanding of the nature of the labour contract system and some employees are confused and muddled in their thinking. Imperfections in various types of parallel and complementary systems have given rise to problems with labour insurance for contract work, systems of welfare etc. This suggests that the two main problems we now need to address are as follows:

1. We must address the problem of people's misconceptions, clarify the implications of the labour contract system and ensure that people understand its true nature. The labour contract system is based on the principle of fixing the relationships between the state, the collective and the individual. It is a means of determining the labour relationships between the three parties through consultation on the basis of equality, and clearly lays down the responsibilities, rights, and interests of the two parties concerned in the hiring system.

Under this kind of system, enterprises can select their own personnel as necessary, and people can choose their own jobs. This freedom and lack of coercion benefits both parties. Moreover, any choices that are made are not automatically fixed forever. There may be a variety of different patterns of hiring and employment according to differences in people, business affairs, or locality. Contracts may be long-term, short-term, seasonal, temporary, rotational etc. They can be tailored to suit different types of work in order to promote the rational mobility of labour. The contract system has helped us to overcome the stagnation that had developed in the area of labour administration. The implementation of the labour contract system has helped to affirm the dominant position of the worker since all contract workers are the owners of their enterprise with no distinction according to status. This has helped to counteract the unhealthy tendencies of the past where 'permanent workers look on, while contract workers and temporary workers do the work'. The realisation that if they do not perform satisfactorily they are likely to be sacked has given workers a new sense of urgency. Some people believe that signing labour contracts is tantamount to creating a 'hired hand' relationship between socialist enterprises and workers. This view does not stand up to scrutiny, since what we are changing is merely the form of employment, not the socialist system of public ownership as a whole. Many socialist countries in Eastern Europe have already introduced labour contract systems, and their experience proves that this is a system of employment which is appropriate to socialist relations of production and the development of the socialist forces of production. It is a means of invigorating the labour system and promoting better integration between the labour force and capital goods. In this way, it facilitates the operation of the socialist principle of distribution: 'from each according to his ability, to each according to his work', and helps to revitalise business activities and raise the efficiency of enterprises.

2. We must effectively carry out parallel and complimentary reforms and establish a series of related systems that are compatible with the labour contract system.

   a) The wage system. The wages of workers employed under the contract system must conform to the principle of distribution according to work. The ideal situation would one in which workers receive the highest remuneration when they are at their optimum age and achieving optimum results. The previous wage system, which paid low wages to competent, high-achievers and high wages to incompetent, low-achievers is incompatible with a system of contract employment, and it must be reformed and adjusted appropriately. The main method of adjustment is to fix remuneration according to the size of a worker's individual contribution. In view of the present co-existence of permanent and contract systems of employment, it is important to consider the extent to which contract workers are mobile and how much higher their wages and welfare provisions should be than those of permanent workers. Contract workers and permanent workers should be treated equally and without discrimination in terms of housing, child-care, health provision etc. The state should gradually begin to find answers to these questions through the socialisation of welfare service facilities.

   (b) We need to set up and perfect systems of social insurance. In particular we need to provide social insurance for aged, sick, and infirm workers and benefits for those out of work. We must set up funds for unemployment insurance in order to provide workers with a certain sense of security, just like those that have been adopted by many Western countries. Current systems of insurance are also in need of reform: standards of treatment do not necessarily have to be unified; insurance expenditure must be treated as pre-tax payments; and the individual should be able to pay a small amount.

3. Systems of vocational and technical training

The present structure of education in China is irrational. The main reason for this is that we have constantly stressed the promotion of general education at the expense of technical and vocational education. This has meant that graduates from Lower and Higher Middle Schools lack proficiency in technical skills, and have to undergo initial training when they enter the workplace. It could be said therefore that 'first employment, then training' is a kind of sickness within the sphere of technical and vocational training in China. This has created a low-quality work force which cannot properly adapt to the requirements of production and construction. In general, the current scientific and cultural level of rank and file workers in China as well as their technical abilities are completely incompatible with China's need for modernisation and construction, and the work force is of very poor overall quality. There are only around 7 million natural scientists and technicians in China – 67 for every 10,000 people. Of China's 40 million workers with technical skills, around 70% are on grade three or below and only 2.3% are on high grades.[25] Therefore, strengthening vocational and technical training has become an extremely urgent task. Our major courses of action are as follows:

1. We must make changes to the irrational structure of education by increasing the proportionate amount of vocational education and setting up a standardised system of vocational training.
2. We must pool the wisdom and efforts of everyone and promote the socialised operation of educational institutions. We need to establish at various different levels, a variety of forms of vocational and technical training. In view of China's present circumstances it would appear that it is not enough to simply rely on current educational departments to improve vocational and technical training. In addition, we should encourage various departments, businesses, enterprises, social organisations and individuals to use their own strengths and expertise to set up their own training courses and institutions. We should also promote the use of foreign investment etc. All of this will provide good foundations for the improvement of vocational and technical training.
3. We must reform the irrationalities of the hiring system. This includes gradually putting an end to the irrational practice of 'inherited jobs' where the sons and daughters of workers are automatically allowed to take their place.[26]
4. We must end the single-minded pursuit of educational qualifications without a corresponding emphasis on practical competence. One of China's main aims at present is to train people to an intermediate level of technical competence. Not all of those trained can go on to take doctorates or master's degrees. Students attending polytechnics are of more use to society than those studying at China's most popular universities. The notion that research students are of less practical value than university students is not completely unfounded, and we should focus our attention on this issue.

25 This refers to the eight grade wage system for permanent industrial employees that the Chinese adopted from the Russians in the 1950s. After 1957, staff were frozen on existing grades, thus as older workers retired, this both lowered the average wage and depressed incentives. (Ed.)
26 This system is commonplace. In order to encourage retirements, enterprises have allowed the system of 'job inheritance'. (Ed.)

4. The social labour force management system

Over the next few years, labour service companies should develop with the aim of regulating the whole of the labour force so that, gradually, they can help not only those that have lost jobs through rationalisation and those waiting for employment, but can create systems for supplying enterprises with qualified staff at appropriate times.

They must develop their expertise in the organisation, management, training and allocation of the labour force to become powerful tools in all these respects of labour management.

Document 6.6

'Integrating family planning and poverty relief'

YANG KUIFU

Population and Family Planning, 1996, No. 4

The initiation of reform in China ushered in a period of unprecedented social and economic development accompanied by a rapid fall in the number of people living in poverty. The number of impoverished people with insufficient food to eat fell from 250 million in 1978 to 80 million in 1993. In a further attempt to tackle poverty, the government officially promulgated the 'National Plan to Combat Poverty' in March 1994.[27] This clearly stated that by the turn of the century (i.e. within around seven years) a basic solution would be found to the nutritional problems of the 80 million people still living below the poverty line. (By the end of 1995, the number of people with insufficient food to eat had been reduced to 65 million). The implementation of this Plan is part of the strategy for China's social and economic development and represents a major attempt to change the face of rural poverty. It is a concrete manifestation of the superiority of China's socialist system.

Poverty is the result of a variety of different factors and its elimination therefore requires the application of a range of different measures that can work together to bring about a real improvement. But there is one thing that must always be borne in mind: the reality of impoverished regions has shown that poverty is likely to lead to the birth of large numbers of children, and yet excessive population growth exacerbates poverty. Our efforts to combat poverty over a number of years have revealed that the

27 In February/March 1994, the State Council held an anti-poverty conference which produced a plan to eliminate by the year 2000, the poverty of the 80 millions then estimated to be in that state. (Ed.)

elimination of poverty demands a two-pronged approach – the promotion of economic development and the strict implementation of population controls. We must always be aware of the connections between these 'two spheres of production' and integrate our strategy for family planning with our strategy to alleviate poverty. This is the only way to cast off poverty and increase prosperity.

1. The population has grown too fast in impoverished regions

In 1990, the results of China's 4th Census revealed that 18 provinces in China had higher rates of population growth than the national average (14.7%), and that these tended to be the provinces with the highest levels of poverty. Population growth in these regions was growing at a much higher rate than in ordinary regions. The population density of a large number of poor counties is far higher than that of non-impoverished regions. A sample survey carried out by the State Family Planning Committee in 1989 revealed that those provinces where more than 20% of households had more than one child tended to be the provinces which suffered the lowest levels of economic development. Of the 16 provinces with a higher birth rate than the national average, no less than 15 had a comparatively high concentration of impoverished areas.

2. The declining quality of the population in impoverished regions

Due to historical reasons and current limiting factors, the physical quality of the population in impoverished areas is, generally speaking, lower than in ordinary regions. The proportion of deformed people and spread of debilitating disease are both higher in these regions than in non-impoverished regions. According to projections made on the basis of a sample survey of people with deformity in 1987, the proportion of the population of impoverished areas that are deformed is 2.75 percentage points higher than the proportion for the country as a whole. The relative frequency of early marriage, marriage between close family members, and marital exchange has led to the relatively frequent birth of dull-witted and retarded children in impoverished regions. Furthermore, insanitary conditions and poor health facilities have encouraged the spread of local diseases (of the 109 counties nationwide with serious local disease problems, 94 are impoverished). This is having a direct impact on the physical quality of the population.

For a variety of reasons, educational facilities in impoverished regions are under-developed and population growth is creating even more problems for the development of educational, health and other social institutions. School buildings and equipment in impoverished regions are of poor quality, the quality of teaching and student attendance rates are low, consolidation is poor and education in general is not up to standard. Illiteracy rates are far higher in impoverished regions than in affluent areas.

While the national illiteracy rate stands at 25%, the rate for impoverished regions exceeds 50%. All of this means that the overall educational level and cultural quality of the population of impoverished regions is low.

3. It is more difficult to control population growth in impoverished regions

The majority of impoverished regions in China at present are those regions with a comparatively poor geographical environment. They tend to be remote, with poor travel connections and communications, and low levels of development of secondary and tertiary industry. Their populations generally rely on farming to eke out a living. The traditional and out-moded methods of labour and production that have persisted in these regions over a long period of time have resulted in a fall in labour productivity and a rising demand for agricultural labour (particularly male labour). This means that in the vast majority of impoverished regions there exists a powerful hidden force encouraging people to have large numbers of children. This force has been strengthened even more by the introduction of household-based production.

4. Shrinking land area per capita has resulted in environmental destruction

At the current stage of development, the amount of land area per head of population is a crucial factor in solving problems of hunger and starvation in impoverished areas. Excessive population growth in impoverished areas over recent years has led to a rapid decline in per capita cultivable land area. In a desperate attempt to make a living, farmers have stopped at nothing to maximise their total land area. Forests have been destroyed to make way for cultivation and, in response, nature has wreaked its own revenge in the form of soil erosion, ecological degradation, and increasingly serious natural disasters. This vicious circle has become so extreme in some areas that it has not only affected current profits, it has also damaged long-term prospects for sustainable development. People must be made fully aware of the 'perils of population growth' in impoverished regions.

5. Economic development has been limited by the decline in the cultural quality of the population

The mismatch between the population of impoverished regions and socio-economic development is not only manifested in excessive population increases, but also in the decline in the cultural quality of the population. This qualitative decline in the population and the labour force has had an adverse effect on the dissemination and application of science and technology, and on the effort to counter traditional concepts of fatalism and isolationism. This has limited the potential for a rise in the level of the forces of production and held back economic development. The current shortage of scientists, technicians and other qualified personnel is a serious problem in impoverished regions and has become a major factor limiting the spread of science and technology to these areas. We must make a great effort to change this situation.

In conclusion, excessive population growth is a major cause of chronic poverty in impoverished regions. It has placed great pressures on economic and social development. We need to focus on solving the population problems of impoverished areas and make this an important part of our overall strategy. On the one hand, we must find effective ways to bring excessive population growth under control and on the other, we must improve the quality and structure of the population. This is both a crucial condition for eradicating poverty and an important pre-requisite for achieving the anti-poverty Plan. It is, moreover, a major strategy for realizing the long-term sustainable development of impoverished regions.

7

China's Foreign Economic Relations

With WTO membership a reality, China is poised to be fully integrated into the global system of free trade and investment flows. This will effectively complete the twenty year search for a viable economic relationship with the outside world. Looking back, the policy search that first emerged from the collapse of the familiar Maoist policy doctrines of 'self-reliance' and autarchic nation-building were, in the first instance, basically a strategy to achieve the Four Modernisations through rapid technology transfer from the West and Japan. However, what was initially manifested as hugely enhanced demand for technology imports, transformed itself into a process that has resulted in the opening up of China to the world in a far reaching way. The subsequent sequence of events is familiar, but the logic underlying this is worth further exploration, and as we shall see, what has happened is broadly consistent with the Dengist philosophy of incremental reform and a gradual transition from the planned system. Let us look at the main changes that have occurred.

LIBERALISING TRADE AND FDI FLOWS

The early phase of change was epitomised in the mammoth Baoshan Steel Complex project of 1978/1979. This type of huge capital goods import had to be paid for by rapid expansion of exports. To achieve this the highly centralised trade system was by the early 1980s drastically decentralised, with trading authority being increasingly allocated to local governments, industrial ministries, and selected state-owned producer enterprises. The rationale for this was simple: compared with the dozen or so national foreign trade corporations (FTCs) based in Beijing, local authorities and producer enterprises were in a much better position to organise the highly heterogeneous Chinese export trade in ways that could tailor it to varying overseas market niches. Thus, centralised export planning collapsed rapidly[1], with the number of FTCs increasing from around 12 in 1978 to some 9,400 in 1994 and more than 30,000 by year 2000. These numbers take no account of the 160,000 foreign-invested enterprises (FIEs) and the newly acquired 'trading rights' now also being extended to privately funded firms as well.[2]

Similarly, when the entirely new policy of courting foreign direct investment (FDI) was first introduced with implementation of the Sino-foreign Joint Venture Law in 1979, this was also motivated in large part by the prospect of attracting large multinational corporations (MNCs) to bring in advanced technology through investments in target industries. However, as it turned out, with a few significant exceptions, FDI inflows through the 1980s have been virtually all from investors in Hong Kong and Taiwan. Nonetheless, the hundreds of thousands of small-scale, labour-intensive factories so funded have proved to be valuable sources of foreign exchange earnings for China, by virtue of their successes in the consumer goods markets of the United States and Western Europe.[3] This has helped release the country's foreign exchange constraint for boosting technology imports. This export orientation also explains why, over the years, the Chinese government has become increasingly liberal towards FIEs in terms of ownership restrictions in particular.[4] Indeed, it is worth noting that most of the FIEs of Hong Kong and Taiwan origin established after Deng's celebrated 'South China inspection tour' in 1992, fall into the category of 'wholly-foreign-owned enterprises'.

IN SEARCH OF A WORKABLE EXCHANGE RATE REGIME

To implement the decentralisation of the trading authority successfully it was also clear that the artificially fixed and highly overvalued renminbi had to be readjusted as well. Thus, as a first step, an 'internal settlement rate' (ISR) of 2.8 *yuan*, as against the official rate of 1.5 *yuan* to the US dollar, was adopted in 1981. This enhanced the profitability of many export industries.[5] Even more important, it made the many newly emerging FTCs

1 The number of export commodities subject to central balancing stood at around 3000 by broad categories in 1978, but virtually all were abolished by the early 1990s.
2 See *Impartial Daily* (Hong Kong), 10 July 2000, p. C3.
3 Investors from Hong Kong and Taiwan are certainly keen to develop the huge domestic market, but the established Chinese policy has been to restrict their sales to local customers to not more than 30% of total output. In general, all such FIEs are required to 'balance their own foreign exchange requirements' through export earnings. Import-substitution FDI is rarely permitted, except for selected investments from Taiwan, which promote 'compatriotism'.
4 The FIEs' importance extends, of course, to employment generation as well (some 16 million jobs created by the mid 1990s); this is in addition to the much needed but less visible, managerial knowhow.
5 The higher ISR enabled the exporting enterprises to convert their foreign exchange earnings into a much larger renminbi revenue. Without the ISR, many producer enterprises might lack the incentive to engage in export sales. The ISR was gradually raised to 3.2 yuan to the US dollar by late 1985, when the first wave of renminbi devaluation simply made the ISR the new official exchange rate, thus ending the dual exchange rate system that existed between 1981 and 1985.

capable of becoming self-sustaining economic entities, entirely detached from the state budget with respect both to subsidies and to mandatory profit delivery.[6] The renminbi was subsequently subject to several further devaluations, namely in late 1985 (to 3.2 *yuan* to the US dollar), summer 1987 (3.7 *yuan*), December 1989 (4.7274 *yuan*), November 1990 (5.2221 *yuan*), and most significantly, in January 1994 (8.72 *yuan*). In the last case, the then officially fixed exchange rate (5.76 *yuan*) was realigned with the market-driven rate prevailing at the familiar 'swap centres',[7] to become a unified exchange rate under the new 'managed float' regime.

The long-term economic significance of the 1994 unification of the two different exchange rates can hardly be overstated. It is important to note that this took place at a time when domestic price liberalisation was virtually complete (see Chapter 3) and that it was part of a process in which the link between domestic and world market prices was firmly established for tradable goods – a process that included the introduction of the 'trade agency' system in the mid 1980s.[8] Under these circumstances, the realignment with the higher, market-based exchange rate effectively spelled an end to the controversial Chinese practice of 'subsidising exports' and imposing 'import (regulatory) taxes' on top of normal custom levies.[9] More

6 Note that this paralleled reforms in the domestic sector that required all SOEs to be fully accountable for their own profits and losses.

7 The swap centres were first established in 1985 to enable approved SOEs and FIEs to exchange, among themselves, excess foreign exchange holdings for renminbi. These funds were needed respectively by firms short of renminbi to buy inputs from the domestic markets and those requiring hard currencies to import machinery and equipment from overseas. This represents the first step towards foreign exchange decontrol; see next section.

8 See Joseph C.H. Chai, *China: Transition to a Market Economy*, Oxford, 1997, p. 144. Under the system, FCTs acted as import/export agents for domestic enterprises for a commission, and domestic end-users were charged at and export producers received the foreign price equivalent. By the early 1990s, 90% of imports and 80% of export commodities already had their prices determined this way.

9 The practice had been a constant source of trade disputes between China and western trading partners, the United States, in particular. In the past, Chinese domestic prices were completely divorced from world market prices, due to years of official price-fixing and the non-conventional practice of price formation (ignoring such cost elements as land rentals and interest charges). Under the circumstances, export quotations therefore could not be obtained by simply applying the artificially fixed renminbi exchange rate to convert domestic procurement prices into foreign prices. Rather, they were generally made according to the prevailing world market prices for comparable commodities. The upshot, with renminbi being grossly overvalued, was that for a wide range of industrial exportables, the proceeds converted from foreign currency earnings were not sufficient to cover the export procurement costs in renminbi reckoning. Conversely, for many imported goods, the import costs in renminbi, as converted from world prices, might be well below the prevailing domestic prices. This did not pose any serious problems for China in the past, as under the familiar *Preisausgleich* scheme, the resultant losses and profits could be balanced out within the Ministry of Foreign Trade working as an accounting entity to which the FTCs were all subject. But after the trading rights were decentralised, and before the said price distortions could be fully corrected, the necessary 'export subsidies' provided and 'import taxes' levied one way or the other, had increasingly appeared to be 'unfair' trade practice in the eyes of China's major trading partners.

important, both export and import trade now relates to explicit scarcity price signals rather than being 'conducted in the dark' – as was characteristic of all former Soviet-type economies. The linkage to world market prices enables Chinese enterprises and consumers to respond to unified market prices and to identify and exploit China's natural comparative advantage in the world system.

IMPORT DEREGULATION AND FOREIGN EXCHANGE DECONTROL

The pace of import deregulation in China has, however, lagged far behind that of export decentralisation during the past two decades. The same is true for foreign exchange decontrol. This all reflects the economic strategy inherited from the past of a forced-draft modernisation drive. Under this kind of strategy, all imports have to be strictly controlled and priority concentrated on machinery and equipment with embodied new technology. Also, foreign currencies earned have to be strictly subject to centralised allocation to forestall leaks that might finance non-priority imports. The only major difference from the past in this respect, has been the hugely expanded scale of technology imports. Thus, constrained by this inherited basic policy orientation, the initial stage of import relaxation in the early 1980s was merely designed to allow major domestic end-users, notably in the metallurgy and machine-building industries, to have direct contact with foreign suppliers to familiarise themselves with the technical complexities and suitability of the products concerned. Import plans remained centrally controlled and the necessary foreign exchange allocated by the state treasury directly to the national FTCs, rather than to the end-users.

The real breakthrough in import deregulation did not come until the introduction of new provisions that allowed eligible FTCs to *retain* part of their foreign exchange earnings. Specifically, the scheme introduced in the early 1980s as a stimulus to exports, gradually contributed to the establishment of a growing pool of foreign exchange, outside of the official holdings by the state treasury. However, as an incentive to good use, the holdings of enterprises had to be disposed of, either by way of expenditure on direct imports, or by sale for renminbi supplied by other foreign exchange short enterprises through the swap centres established in 1985.[10]

By 1993/1994, turnover at the various swap centres accounted for 80% of the country's total foreign currency transactions, all being cleared at the

10 See supra note 7; and Nicholas Lardy, *Foreign Trade and Economic Reform in China 1978–1990*, Cambridge, 1992, pp. 57–66, for the origin and development of the swap centres through the late 1980s. Note that initially the foreign exchange share accruable to the exporting enterprises was given as 'retention quota' (*erdu liucheng*) which could only be redeemed with renminbi at the official exchange rate, subject to approval by the authority for the intended import uses. At times, total retention quotas accumulated but not redeemed, had exceeded the country's total foreign exchange reserves. Beginning in 1993, quota retention was changed to 'cash retention (*xianhui liucheng*)' to further enhance export incentives.

swap rate, of course.[11] The other side of the story has been the growing number of domestic enterprises given autonomous import rights[12], and more decisively perhaps, the accelerating import tariff reductions and the abolition of import quotas, licenses, and other non-tariff barriers, all made by the Chinese government (Table 7.1) as part of its bid for WTO membership.

This has all led to the winding up of the foreign exchange retention scheme and the merging of the official exchange rate with the market-driven rate of the swap centres in January 1994. What is now emerging is new provision which resembles the western banking system for settling, selling and buying of foreign exchange, for all domestic export and import enterprises allowed to deal with designated banks.[13] More significantly, in April 1994, a nationally unified foreign exchange market was established with the debut of the China Foreign Exchange Trading Centre in Shanghai, which serves as a national network for interbank exchange and clearing, thus effectively phasing out the swap centres. This clearly all helped to pave the way for the renminbi to be made fully convertible for current account transactions, beginning December 1996.[14]

THE EMERGING PATTERN OF TRADE AND CAPITAL FLOWS

There are two dimensions to the impact of trade and FDI liberalisation in China. The first is the changing scale of the country's participation in the world economy, as it relates to enhanced technology imports and the corresponding export drive. The second concerns changes in the pattern of investment flows and trade structure that have taken place in response to the realignment of domestic prices with world market prices and China's closer integration with the global economy.

From 1978 to 1999, the volume of China's exports and imports taken together, has grown by an annual average of 15%, outstripping by a

11 Compare with Yin-ping Ho, 'China reforming itself into a trading nation', in *China Review 1998*, Hong Kong, 1999, p. 419.
12 As a matter of fact, by 1992, the number of import commodities subject to central planning and control was reduced to 11 categories, accounting for not more than 20% of total imports; see Joseph C.H. Chai, *China: Transition to a Market Economy*, op.cit, p. 142. However, the figures still appeared 'unfavourably' relative to export deregulation; see note 1 above.
13 These include the four major state-owned specialist banks, namely, the Bank of China, Industrial and Commercial Bank, Bank of Agriculture, and Bank of Construction, and most of the newly established commercial banks. Prior to July 1996, FIEs were exempt from the foreign exchange settlement requirements. They were allowed to keep all their foreign earnings in a separate account. Domestic export enterprises may, after the settlement with the designated banks, still retain foreign exchange in cash up to 15% of their annual value of trade. The limit is raised to 30% in July 2000, presumably in accord with the government's intention to widen the yuan's trading range in preparation for the country's entry into WTO; see *South China Morning Post* (Business section), 14 July 2000, p. 6.
14 Save some restrictions of a procedural nature, and on non-trade exchanges, notably tourism.

Table 7.1 Reducing import tariffs and non-tariff trade barriers (NTBs) in China, 1992–2005.

	Reduction of Import Tariffs			Reduction of NTBs (Import licenses and quotas)
Year	Unweighted Average (%)	Weighted Average (%)	No. of commodities affected	No. of commodities affected
1991	46.4	–	–	–
1992	39.1	31.2	3596	16
1993	35.6	–	2898	283
1994	–	–	–	195
1995	35.6	28.1	–	176
1996	23.4	19.8	5000	–
1997	17.0	–	4874	–
2000	15.0	–	–	–
2005	17.5	(10.0) 16.2	–	–

Sources and notes: The World Bank,*China Engaged: Integration with the Global Economy*, Washington, D.C., 1997, p. 37; and other scattered sources. The 2005 bracketed figure of 10% was commitment made for industrial products by President Jiang Zemin at the APEC Summit held in Vancouver, November 1997. Weighted tariff averages are lower than the unweighted ones, due to exemptions and concessions made for imports by FIEs for export-processing. Note, however, that in the Sino-USA Accord of 15 November 1999, China agreed to have the overall average tariff rate reduced to 9.4% upon WTO accession.

considerable measure GDP growth of 9.5%.[15] As a result, the relative openness of the country as measured by the trade (exports plus imports) to GDP ratio, has increased remarkably over the past two decades, from some 10% in 1978 to 36% by 1999.[16] This compares favourably with such large

15 The two figures are not directly comparable, as the trade figure is based on a current US dollar measure of imports and exports. Nonetheless, even if the US inflation is adjusted for, the discrepancy would still remain substantial.

16 The two figures are obtained by simply relating the official Chinese total trade and GDP estimates, both given in current yuan prices. They appear to be roughly in line with the World Bank's estimates of 10% for 1975–1979 and 36% for 1990–1994; but it should nevertheless be noted that the World Bank variables are based on constant 1987 prices; see World Bank, *China 2020: Development Challenges in the New Century*, Washington, D.C., 1997, pp. 84 and 95; and *China Engaged: Integration with the Global Economy* (in the same China 2020 series), pp. 2 and 6. All these estimates should at best be treated as rough guide, subject to biases associated with (a) fluctuations in exchange rate which was used for converting the trade volume usually measured in US dollar, into renminbi value; (note renminbi was depreciated by 83% against the US dollar between 1980 and 1994); and (b) the under valuation of non-traded goods which are included in China's GDP estimates; among other things. An alternative World Bank estimate for 1995, adjusted by the 'purchasing-power-parity method, e.g., brings down the Chinese trade to GDP ratio to just about 10%, suggesting an economy more open than India (6%), but about the same as Brazil (10.5%); ibid.

developing countries as India and Brazil. China now ranks as the seventh largest exporter country in the world, a most impressive rise from the position of 32nd in 1978. China now accounts for around 4% of total world trade, up from a share of less than 1% just twenty years ago. At the end of June 2000, the country held total foreign exchange reserves of US$158.6 billion, the second largest after Japan.

Similarly, the massive effort made by China since 1979 to attract foreign capital has helped advance the country to the status of the second largest FDI recipient since 1992, after the United States.[17] Between 1979 and May 2000, the country amassed a cumulative FDI stock of US$320.6 billion, under the auspices of some 350,000 registered FIEs.[18]

In 1999, the industrial output (in terms of value-added) produced by the existing 160,000 FIEs accounted for 21% of the national total. Their share in state tax revenue was 16%, and in national total exports, 48.38%. These enterprises employed a startling total of 20 million workers, who constituted about 10% of the entire urban workforce.[19] Again, in 1999 alone, total new FDI in terms of effective inflow, rather than amount pledged, was equal to a hefty 12% of total fixed asset investment in the country as a whole.

Changes in China's trade structure, as well as in the pattern of FDI diversification over the past two decades, appear equally remarkable. On the eve of economic reform and opening up in 1978, 'industrial products' as a broad category of exports, as opposed to 'primary commodities', did already account for 46.5% of the country's total exports, suggesting that the forced-draft industralisation strategy had begun to pay dividends. However, as a result of increased trade liberalisation, that share has increased even more rapidly over the past twenty years, reaching 50% by 1985, 74% in 1990, and 84% in 1999. This seems to suggest that with the domestic price system being rationalised, the country has indeed been able to find its international comparative advantages for promoting exports.

Within industrial exports, the swiftly rising share of machinery and electronic (ME) products appears to be the most remarkable phenomenon. By 1999, the share had already risen to some 40%, consistently surpassing in recent years that of the textile and clothing industries, who used to be the single most important foreign exchange earner for China (see Table 7.2).[20]

Nonetheless, two important points of qualifications need to be made in this context. First, compared with the state-of-the-art advanced technology in the United States and Japan, Chinese ME exports represent little more than 'intermediate' technology products tailored to industrially less

17 China's position dropped to the third, next to the United Kingdom, in 1999, as a result of reduced FDI intake amidst the impact of the Asian financial crisis.
18 Ma Xiuhong (Assistant Minister of foreign Trade and Economic Cooperation), 'Progress in FDI intake and new policy', in *Impartial Daily*, 5 July 2000, p. D4.
19 Ibid.
20 The strong rebound in 1999 of ME exports from the cutback suffered in 1998 amidst the escalating Asian financial crisis, is especially noteworthy. Perhaps it testifies to where the competitive edge of the country now lies.

Table 7.2 China's exports (X) and imports (M) of machinery and electronic products, 1999

	US$ 10 million	Growth over 1998 (%)	Share in total X/M (%)	Remarks
Exports total of which:	7696	14.7	39.5	Rate of growth by 8.6% points higher than that of overall exports; net increase of US$9.87 billion accounting for 88% of overall increases in exports and hence 5.7% points of overall export growth of 6.2%; being single largest export commodity category consecutively for five years now; high and new technology products accounting for more than 80% of national total of high-tech commodity exports; continuous shift to technology-intensive and comparatively high value-added lines of exports.
– electromechanical products and equipment	6934	15.7	90.1	
– data processing equipment and components, integrated circuit, microelectronic components, mobile communication equipment, aircraft/vehicles/motorcars and accessories, video recorders and players, and vessels	3080	17.3	40.0	
– whole plant exports	610	23.7	7.9	
– general trade	1719	9.7	22.3	
– import processing trade	4289	12.3	55.7	
– share of SOEs	2828	14.9		
– share of FIEs	4642			
Imports total of which:	7760	21.2	46.8	A net increase of US$13.6 billion over 1998; rate of growth higher by 3% points than that of overall imports; most remarkable import growth (50%) within general trade, namely by 28.8% points higher than the 21.2% increases in the overall imports of machinery and electronic products; raising thus its share from 27.8% in 1998 to 37.1% in 1999, as given.
– electrical and electronic products	3523	33.9	45.4	
– IC and microelectronic components	792	66.0	10.2	
– automatic data processing equipment and components	325	80.0	4.2	
– automatic data processing equipment accessories	371	7.0	4.8	
– colour TV sets and TV tubes	260	81.0	3.4	
– automatic control equipment and tools for measuring, testing and analysing	224	17.0	2.9	
– processing machine tools		81.0		
– vehicle accessories		34.0		
– general trade	2879	50.0	37.1	
– share of SOEs	2957	28.3	38.1	
– share of FIEs	4639	16.4	59.8	

Source and note: Bureau of Imports and Exports of Machinery and Electronic Products, Ministry of Foreign Trade and Economic Cooperation, China, in Impartial Daily, 27 April 2000. National total of exports and imports for 1999 are US$194.93 billion and US$165.72 billion respectively.

developed, third country markets. Second, and perhaps more important, Chinese ME exports, particularly in the sphere of electronics, have been dominated by FIEs using imported rather than home-grown technology.[21] Note that 'processing trade' accounted for 56% of ME exports in 1999, and ME imports were also largely sponsored by FIEs, rather than the SOEs.

In regard to Chinese imports, however, ME, including aircraft and other transport equipment (making up 46.8% of total imports in 1999), together with such conventional producer goods imports as rolled steel, iron ore, crude oil, and petroleum products, (but excluding chemicals and chemical fibres), made up 70% of total industrial imports or 60% of all imports. This suggests that the import structure of the country has remained stable over the years, consistent with the old strategy of maximising industrialisation and technology transfer and the relative strictness of the import control system. The most notable departure from the past has probably been increased import-substitution investment and production by FIEs, especially in the sphere of the electronics and passenger car industries.

It is important indeed to notice that since the early 1990s, FDI has increasingly been diversified from essentially export-oriented undertakings to import-substitution investments, reflecting the vigorous efforts made by the Chinese government 'to exchange (the huge domestic) market for technology transfer'. It is against this background that the share of the annual flow of FDI from small investors based in Hong Kong and Taiwan has steadily declined from 78% in 1992 to only than 47% by 1998, with increasing flows from large MNCs who are targeting the domestic market potential.[22] At present, most of the 500 world's largest corporations are now involved in various investment projects in China.

WTO ENTRY AND WHAT IS AT STAKE

A good point of departure for this discussion is to think of China as a 'country of two economies'. That is, on the one hand there is a wide open, export-oriented sector catering for foreign investment and export drives;

---

21 Virtually all technologies used in China for the electronics industry are controlled by joint venture partners and supplied from outside. Thus, the Chinese-side contributions to the production of VCD and micro-computer, e.g., are essentially limited to processing and assembling; see Institute of Industrial Economics, CASS, *China Industrial Development Report 1999*, op.cit., p. 187. As the Chairman of the State Development and Planning Commission, Zheng Peiyan puts in, 'China lags behind [advanced international standards] by 10 to 20 years in electronic and microelectronic technology, as well as in precision processing in the area of traditional techniques. It is also a late starter in new technology in such areas as communications, biotechnology, and software manufacturing'; see his *China's National Economic and Social Development Report 1999* (ed.) Beijing, 1999, p. 208.
22 The reduced FDI share of Hong Kong and Taiwan is partly a matter of investors relocating their office registrations to the British Virgins Islands in the Caribbean sea and such free havens as Samoa in the remote South Pacific around and after the handover of Hong Kong to China. See Y.Y. Kueh, *The Greater China Growth Triangle in the Asian Financial Crisis*, World Bank, forthcoming.

and on the other, a highly protected, import-substitution industrial system thought of as the vehicle for the country's ambitious pursuit of modernisation. As long as the 'two-economy' dichotomy is maintained, this not only implies a denial of a strategy of full integration of China with outside economies, but, by extension, it also precludes capital account convertibility (as indeed is the case) so as not to deprive the protected priority-industry sector of necessary investment funds. The only major linkage between the two economies exists in the mission given to the open, export-oriented sector to generate sufficient foreign exchange earnings to finance investment in the protected one.

What is portrayed above is of course a highly stylised image of the Chinese economy. As a matter of fact, since the South China tour of Deng Xiaoping in 1992, the high wall of industrial protection has already developed serious cracks as a result of selective and welcome 'intrusion' by major foreign investors. Viewed in this way, the main implications of China's imminent WTO accession may be summarised as follows:

First, with increased deregulation of FDI along the lines of the WTO's TRIMs accord[23], large numbers of existing, export-oriented FIEs are likely re-target their output to the domestic market as well, thus breaking the 'two-economy' dichotomy.

Second, with the dismantling of import tariff and non-tariff barriers, a number of highly protected infant industries including automobiles, chemicals, and electronics, are likely to undergo substantial restructuring. Specifically, direct exports by large MNCs to China may increasingly substitute for tariff-jumping, import-substituting FDI. As a result, there will be either increased withdrawal of existing investors or, enhanced capital injection to achieve scale and other efficiencies to head off import competition, depending on the circumstances in each sector or product[24]

Third, it is virtually certain that with foreign ownership restriction being phased out in the years to come, the four newly emerging Chinese industries to be opened for foreign investment, namely, telecommunications, banking, insurance, and professional services and commercial distributions, (to which market access has been vigorously fought for by both the United States and the European Union), will be rapidly flooded with FDI by major MNCs.

Fourth, after China's accession to WTO, FDI inflow will be dominated more by large MNCs than by the small investors from Hong Kong and

23 This refers to the 1993 Uruguay Round agreement on 'trade-related investment measures' which prohibits discriminating against foreign investors by limiting sales of output to the domestic market, requires investors to balance their own foreign exchange expenditure, imposes technology transfer requirements, and stipulates localisation rate or local content.

24 As it presently stands, the situation still appears mixed, as revealed by extensive press interviews conducted with various major foreign car-makers in China, subsequent to the Sino-US WTO accord of November 1999. Some seem quite confident about their relative competitive edge; some clearly fear an influx of cheaper, new foreign car models. As a matters of fact, as a result of increased 'localisation rate', the highly hailed Santana made by Volkswagen in Shanghai is reported to be far less sophisticated in technology than the comparable model produced in Germany.

Taiwan. Indeed, out of a cumulative total of (realised) FDI inflow of US$273 billion between 1979 and June 1999, 87% arrived in China after 1993, following the promulgation of the country's policy of explicitly promoting 'exchanging (domestic) market for (foreign) technology'. Most of this investment was targeted at the highly protected automobile, chemical, and electronics industries.[25]

Taking all this into account, along with the terms of the country's accord with the United States (November 1999) and European Union (May 2000), we may expect that by 2005, China will probably be as open as many newly industrialised economies, or any of the western industrial powers. And with increased capital inflow, there will surely come mounting pressures to complete reform of the external sector by making the capital account convertible.

Document 7.1

'A strategy for upgrading exports structure'

SUN GUANGXIANG

Intertrade, 1997, No. 184

The structure of commodities that needs to be adjusted

The readjustment of the commodity structure of exports is an important aspect of the two changes to be effected in the area of foreign trade and economic cooperation. It is also a component part in the readjustment of China's overall economic structure. China's export targets set in the Ninth Five Year Plan and the long term perspective plan for 2010 are: total exports to reach US$200 billion by year 2000 and US$400 billion by 2010. Being a developing country, with a relative shortage of [natural] resources in per capita terms, China will find it difficult to realize these grand goals by relying on exports of resource-intensive primary products and labour-intensive light industry and textiles over a long period of time. We must therefore make great efforts to readjust the structure of export commodities in two ways: first we must raise their technological content and added value, and second, China must also as quickly as possible shift from exporting rough-finished, light industry and low added value products, to exporting intensively and finely processed products.

In the next 5–15 years, the scale of international trade will grow steadily. Total world commodity trade is expected to exceed US$5,600 billion in

---

25 See Song Hong and Chai Yu, 'More than promised: the impact of WTO accession on China's intake of foreign capital', in *International Trade*, No. 3, 2000, p. 12.

1997 and to approach the figure of US$7,000 billion by 2000. The general trend of changes in the commodity mix on the international market will be as follows: the market for resource-intensive primary products will be basically in a state of stagnation; trade in labour-intensive light industry and textiles will grow amidst turbulence and increasingly intense competition; technology-intensive products, especially complete sets of equipment of high added value and high-technology (hi-tech) products will both become pillar products, exhibiting faster export growth, the biggest expansion of trade, and the most promising development prospects. International trade will not only grow considerably in volume, but will also witness a big improvement in quality. The commodity mix will become more and more refined.

The general development trend of China's export commodity makeup since its founding in 1949 is that it is being gradually refined along with the development of the country's science and technology and progress in industrialisation. As a result of continued development over the years, at the end of the 1980s China's export commodity structure had changed from one mainly exporting primary products to exporting mainly industrial products. At the beginning of the 1990s [the structure] started another transformation. In 1994, China's total exports amounted to US$121.04 billion and in 1995, US$148.77 billion. The makeup of export commodities was as follows: primary products dropped from 16.3% in 1994 to 14.4% in 1995, while industrial products rose from 83.7% in 1994 to 85.6% in 1995. In 1996, total exports were US$151.072 billion and the ratio between primary products and industrial products was basically the same as that in 1995. This indicates that the second change in the export commodity makeup was undergoing a turn for the better. However, in general, China's export commodity structure is at present still backward, whether in terms the overall or partial perspective, and this is especially so if we as compare China with the ten best traders in the world. The expansion in the scale of [our] exports has been mainly supported by large quantities of low added value goods. The proportion of intensively and finely processed products of high added value is still very small. With the continued expansion in trade, there will not be much room for the further development of the resource-intensive primary products and labour-intensive light industry and textiles which have bolstered China's export trade for a long time. Now that China's exports have exceeded US$150 billion, it will be extremely difficult to push them further up to US$200 billion by relying on increasing the volume of low added value commodities alone. Even if they somehow reached this level, they cannot possibly move up further to US$300 billion or US$400 billion. Viewed from international experience, the Western trading powers with exports in excess of US$400 billion rely generally on intensively and finely processed products, especially hi-tech, high value-added products. In this context, therefore, insufficient refinement of the export commodity structure is a critical issue in the development of China's external trade. To extricate itself from this situation, China must enhance its competitiveness and gather greater momentum for the export trade. It must earnestly implement the strategy of invigorating trade by means of science and technology and rely on science and technology to raise the quality, grade, and sophistication of export products. It must increase the proportions of finished products of higher technological content and greater added value in its exports. In particular, it must support, on a priority basis, the development of technology-intensive mechanical and electrical products, especially complete sets of equipment and hi-tech products. This is the basic way to refine the export commodity structure and upgrade China's export commodities. This is where hope for a sustained and steady growth in the export trade lies.

Vigorously expand exports of complete sets of equipment and hi-tech products

The exports of complete sets of equipment and hi-tech products are exports which are technology intensive, high added value, and which earn good economic returns. We have held seminars in China [dealing with trade in] complete sets of equipment, electronic apparatus, computer parts and components, automobiles and their parts and components, communications equipment, aircraft and ships, and we have invited experts to advise in this field. Studies conducted by the Simulation Research Institute reached the conclusion that the technological intensity of complete sets of equipment is as high as 74% and that their rate of their added value is as high as 73%, both being the highest among the seven classes of intensively-processed export products. In recent years, China has exported a number of complete plants of large and medium sizes, the unit export price of which range from tens of million to hundreds of millions of dollars. For example, the contract value of a 300,000-kilowatt nuclear power station exported to Pakistan was US$560 million, of which some US$20 million was technical cost. It can be seen from this example that the economic benefits and foreign exchange earnings derived from exports of complete sets of equipment are difficult for other products to match. Therefore, the readjustment of the export commodity structure should be geared chiefly to increasing the proportions in the export trade of mechanical and electrical products of high technological content, high added value and high exchange-earning capability, especially complete sets of equipment and hi-tech products. Thus at the same time as continued efforts are made to expand the exports of traditionally favoured products and to accelerate their upgrading, great stress must be given to developing the exports of mechanical and electrical products, complete sets of equipment and hi-tech products, thus gradually making them principal items of the export trade, in order to create a new [type of comparative] advantage for China in international competition.

As seen from international practice, countries among the front ranks of the world's trading partners, such as the United States, Germany and Japan, have all gone through a similar process of refinement of their export commodity makeup, switching their emphasis first from light industry and textile products to steel and heavy chemical products and then to complete sets of equipment and hi-tech products of high technological content and high added value. In particular, Japan has attached great importance to the export of complete sets of equipment, regarding it as the 'hope for upgrading the export structure'. Its exports of complete sets of equipment grew at the annual average rate of 40%. Back in 1979, its exports of complete sets of equipment has already reached US$12.911 billion. By 1990, such exports accounted for 70.6% of its total exports of high-tech products, thus achieving the aim of upgrading its export commodity structure.

In China's specific conditions, to vigorously expand its exports of complete sets of equipment and hi-tech products in the course of implementing the strategy of readjusting its export commodity structure is not only an objective requirement but is also feasible. Objectively speaking, at the present stage [of our development] China's exports of labour-intensive light industry and textile products make up about 50% of total annual exports. But it is unlikely that we can maintain our low price competitiveness on the international market by relying on our cheap labour cost advantage in light industry and textile products. The reasons are threefold. First, China is now facing increasingly fierce competition from exports of labour-intensive products by a number of Asian, African and Latin American countries, which are developing such products with great efforts. Second, China's low-cost exports to the international market are now increasingly threatened by trade protectionism; in particular, its textile exports are subject to import quota control by many countries and regions. Third, China's exports of labour-intensive light industry and textiles are now increasingly circumscribed by the smallness of the international market; this situation is especially pronounced in the markets of developed countries. For example, China exported 700 million pairs of shoes to the United States in 1994, averaging nearly three pairs for each American. Toy exports, on the other hand, now take up about 50% of the American toy market. Such roughly processed products are taking up too large a proportion in the export trade as a whole, yet their ability to earn foreign exchange is low. Take, for example, the makeup of China's commodity exports in 1994. Exports of agricultural and sideline products, petroleum, coal and charcoal, nonferrous metal ores, industrial chemicals and other resource-type products totaled US$19.69 billion, representing 16.3% of total exports. The resources used in some of these low added value products are not replaceable and therefore they cannot be regarded as a permanent source of export commodities. Even among exports of industrial products, primary, raw material-type light industry and textile products accounted for 9.3% of total exports, while raw material-type mechanical and electrical products, such as metal products of different kinds, took up 6.6%. Added together, these three classes of commodities made up 32.2% of China's total export trade. Even in 1996, exports of agricultural and sideline products, petroleum, coal and charcoal, steel and iron, nonferrous metals and industrial chemicals still accounted for 14.7% of China's total exports. This situation indicates that year on year, China has to use large quantities of primary products in low added value and roughly processed industrial products to exchange for finely processed products of high added value from the developed and near developed countries. Such a pattern of exports is not only low in foreign exchange earning power, but also gives China poor terms of trade. Moreover, for a long time China's exports of technology-intensive mechanical and electrical products have made up less than 30% of its total exports, showing a considerable shortfall in comparison with the average of 35.5% for such exports in the world's total volume of trade. In 1991, for example, Japan's mechanical and electrical exports made up 76.3% of its total exports; Germany's 55.3%; United States' 51.3%; and those of Britain, Italy and France around 40%. It is thus clear that readjusting China's export commodity structure brooks no delay, and that it is imperative to expand exports of full sets of equipment and hi-tech products.

As a large developing country, China has over the past fifty years formed a comprehensive industrial and agricultural production system and a scientific research system of considerable standing. This process has accelerated in the 19 years of reform and opening up to the outside world. We have mastered numerous industrial technologies, many of which are up to advanced international levels. Complete sets of equipment and hi-tech products produced in China are supported by a strong capacity to provide what is needed for the construction and operation of a project, and their prices are quite competitive. Since the implementation of the policy of reform and opening up, China has started to export complete sets of equipment, and such exports have developed rapidly. From 1980 to 1996, China exported a total of 10,251 complete sets of equipment and technology worth US$31.09 billion, with complete sets of equipment accounting for over 90% of this figure. These were exported to 79 countries and regions, including developing countries as well as many developed countries. Industries producing these complete plants and hi-tech equipment included machine-building, shipbuilding, construction materials, electronics, industrial chemicals, textiles, light industry and, metallurgical, energy, communications and medical and pharmaceutical. For many years the proportion of exports of complete sets of equipment and hi-tech products in the overall export trade has been rather small, not because China lacks the actual capacity to develop technology-intensive products for export, but rather because it has failed to give full play to its existing economic and technical superiority and other essential advantages. From now on, the relevant departments should strengthen their coordination and cooperation and form enterprise conglomerates and groups to expand the scale of and capacity for exports of complete plants and hi-tech products and gradually realize a strategic upgrading of the export commodity structure.

Document 7.2

'Promoting exports of whole plant'

XU WENHAI AND ZHANG PEIJI

Intertrade, 1997, No. 184

Characteristics of whole plant trade

According to statistics, exports of complete plants by various provinces and municipalities generally make up only 8%–10% of China's total exports of mechanical and electrical products. Shanghai, as the best performer, exported US$171 million worth of complete plants in 1994, making up 8.8% of its total exports of mechanical and electrical products for that year; US$280 million in 1995, equal to 10.5%; and about US$500 million USD (estimated) in 1996, equal to 15%. The rate of increase is quite large, but its proportion in total exports of mechanical and electrical goods is still relatively small.

What is the cause of this? The crux of the matter is that the measures taken have not been properly oriented and the industry has not been given adequate support.

China's exports of complete plants and major mechanical and electrical products have four special characteristics, with four associated problems needing to be addressed.

First, complete plants and major mechanical and electrical products require long production cycles and large investments, while their export risks are higher than ordinary mechanical and electrical products. The production of a large and medium-size complete plant often requires 3–5 or even 7–8 years. When it is ready for delivery, the circumstances are often quite different from those when the contract was first signed. Large projects require large capital outlays. It will be more difficult to raise the money and still harder to find guarantors for the funding. Some export enterprises are obsessed by 'short-term behaviour'; they think that exports of large projects are a 'thankless task'. The leader in charge who signs the contract may have left his post when the time comes for foreign exchange settlement. [The management] therefore beat a retreat in the face of difficulties and are not enthusiastic about it. The support policy currently in force is not adapted to this characteristic.

Second, complete plants and major mechanical and electrical products involve technical complexities and a broad sphere of activities. On average, a large complete power plant involves some 200 supplying units. Apart from the three major units (boiler, steam turbine and generator), [the plant] also requires large quantities of ancillary equipment and auxiliary products. Moreover, the technical requirements for large projects are quite different and their auxiliary equipment cannot be produced in large batches but have to be manufactured individually in small batches. A complete set is often made up of a multitude of customised equipment and not ordinary run-of-the-mill goods. There are many things to take care of in organising the production and export of a complete plant. Any mishandling is liable to put one in a double squeeze, and [managers] may even be thrown out of their jobs. The existing mechanism for organising exports of mechanical and electrical products is not yet adapted to this characteristic.

Third, the export of large and medium-size complete plants and mechanical and electrical products is often in the nature of a government act. Competition is especially fierce. Exports of large projects are generally targeted at developing countries, while competitors are often the industrialised countries. Weak export partners and strong competitors is yet another characteristic of the [market situation for Chinese enterprises] engaged in the export of complete plants and mechanical and electrical products. Western governments are often involved in the export of large complete plants. On occasion even their Prime Ministers, Ministers and other high officials support such exports projects in person. China finds it difficult to compete with this. This is yet another point to which we need to adapt.

Fourth, the trend of development is such that because the developing countries are having difficulty in financing the exports of complete plants and major mechanical and electrical equipment, competitiveness in such exports tends to move towards the issue of the competitiveness of the provision of financial arrangements. There is growing demand for handling projects on BOT and BOO terms. This requires organising exports in the form of a turnkey project, extending all the way from research and designing to production and export of the complete plant and then to maintenance services. In this context, China is not quite adapted to making overall arrangements for funding and other support.

Main problems

Current problems affecting exports are mainly superficial, such as delay in tax refunds, financial strains, the 'three rates' being on the high side, and soaring raw material prices.[26] Enterprises handling exports of complete plants and major mechanical and electrical products are also affected by these problems, possibly to a graver extend than those exporting ordinary goods. It will be more difficult for them to resolve these problems. However, deeper problems are those arising from the export characteristics noted above. Those are the crux of difficulties.

1. The support policy does not meet all the needs. We need strong and stable policy geared towards the needs [of these markets]. Since complete plants and major mechanical and electrical products involve a long production cycle, it is often the case that policy preferences at the time an

26 The three rates are interest rates, exchange rates and tax rates. (Ed.)

order is accepted are different from those prevailing at the time when the order is executed.

Ten years ago the State Council adopted a series of preferential policies for the export of mechanical and electrical products, which benefited the enterprises greatly. However, along with changes in the situation, many of the measures are no longer suited to the times. It is necessary to formulate a special policy to encourage and support the export of hi-tech products, major mechanical and electrical products and complete plants and equipment.

2. It is difficult to arrange finance in big amounts. Many projects failed to obtain the funds originally promised to them, and had great difficulties in getting secured mortgage loans. Buyers of complete plans and major mechanical and electrical products often require prior bank under-takings, and would not sign the contract until they have the necessary assurances. On the other hand, the banks demand to see the contract first, and will release loans only according to the contract amount. This causes uncertainty in financing and buyers are forced to back out from signing the contract.

Many problems pertaining to security and mortgages for large and medium-size projects have also come to light. The bigger the project, the more difficult it is to arrange security and the longer it takes to go through the process. It is therefore necessary to change the current practice of demanding the same security for all mortgages regardless of the size of the project.

3. Because of the complicated technology involved in making complete plants and major mechanical and electrical products and also their high quality requirements, two prominent contradictions exist at present. The first is that those having the capacity to undertake such export tasks are generally the large and medium-size State Owned Enterprises, whose equipment, technology and personnel are generally old. They are in need of timely technical transformation and their personnel need to update their knowledge. They are also generally suffering from a brain drain.[27] Second, large projects involve subcontracting to up to a hundred factories. Some of the subcontracted factories may not pay much attention to coordination, and troubles occurring on auxiliary products are liable to affect the overall situation, which may lead to failure to secure follow-up projects. Therefore, proceeding from the need to augment our export capacity for large projects, systematic support should be given to technical transformation, equipment renewal, introduction of advanced technology and enhancing quality control, in order to achieve product upgrading and stronger competitiveness.

4. According to international practice, some degree of government intervention in the export of major projects is necessary. Export

---

27 The drain will be mainly to the private or foreign sector enterprises. (Ed.)

enterprises bidding for large projects are urgently in need of government backing. In time of need, the government should come out and say something to strengthen the position of the exporting units engaged in negotiations. This will raise their chances of winning the bid.

5. The work of forming export conglomerates has made only slow progress. It is far from meeting the requirement for 'macro economics and trade' and 'macro conglomeration'. The three main problems are. First, there is considerable ideological resistance. Second, great efforts are still required to form trans-industrial and trans-regional conglomerates. And third, conglomerates incorporating scientific research, industry and trade are notably not in evidence. This is unfavourable to undertaking large projects which involve scientific research and designing to get under way.

On the other hand, the agency system is an important link in organising exports of complete plants and major mechanical and electrical products. At present, disorderly competition is quite serious. Enterprises engaged in external trade and industry and trade complain that many production enterprises act on their own once they are authorised to deal in exports, as if they were 'off the hook'. Moreover, they have taken away their old clients. There are very few cooperative projects.

6. The expansion of exports of complete plants and major mechanical and electrical products relies greatly on communication channels. At present, the flow of information is still not smooth. Enterprises are often late in getting information about international tender invitations. It is therefore necessary to improve information work, and set up information libraries to solve the problem of information inaccessibility.

Document 7.3

'The import demand for developing the machine building industry'

ZHENG GUOWEI

Study Materials for Economic Research, 1997, No. 1098

I The general situation and characteristics

According to customs statistics, China's imports and exports of mechanical and electrical products in 1996 totaled US$109.56 billion, up by 6.3% as against US$103.04 billion in 1995. Within this, exports valued at US$48.21 billion showed an increase of 9.9% and accounted for 31.9% of the country's total exports valued at US$151.07 billion. Mechanical and electrical products thus continued to occupy the first position among China's export commodities. Imports in 1996 amounted to US$61.35 billion, up 3.7% and comprising 44.2% of the country's total imports valued of US$ 138.84 billion. The overall trade balance in this sector showed an adverse balance of US$13.15 billion, down US$2.16 billion from US$15.3 billion in 1995. Among the imported goods, mechanical products accounted for US$30.08 billion or 49% of the total; electrical appliances and electronic products US$18.94 billion or 30.9%; means of transportation US$5.34 billion or 8.7%; instruments and meters US$3.54 billion or 5.8%; other products US$1.52 billion or 2.5%; and metal products US$1.91 billion or 3.1%. Four prominent characteristics were noted in 1996 imports.

1. The product mix of imports has continued to improve, with imports of new and high technology products and key components and parts urgently needed for China's construction increasing markedly. As shown in Table 7.3, imports which experienced substantial increases in 1996 include integrated circuit and microelectronic parts and components of computer, semi-conductor, automobile, internal combustion engine, aviation equipment, and steam turbine. Imports which were substantially reduced, however, included automobile and chasis, (especially small passenger cars), ships, video recorders and parts, colour television set and tubes, photocopiers, metal pressing machine and parts, and building and mining machinery.

This important development is attributable to the guidance of China's industrial policy, the strengthening of state macro-control, and the readjustment of the tariff policy, all of which have prompted a change in the structure of import demands. It is also directly related to the higher technological level attained by China's manufacturing industry.

2. A major change has taken place in the structural pattern of the import trade. The volume of conventional imports fell drastically, from the first position in 1995 to the third position. The volume of imports by foreign-owned enterprises and by the processing trade took the second position. In 1996, imports by the conventional trade were valued at US$15.68 billion, down US$5.36 billion or 25.4% compared with US$21.04 billion in 1995. Equipment imported by foreign-owned enterprises as part of their investments were valued at US$22.34 billion, a sharp increase of 31.6% by the same comparison. Imports by the trade processing materials and assembling parts supplied by clients rose 10.8% to US$18.76 billion. Additionally, imports by bonded warehouses amounted to US$1.35 billion, up 86.3%; and by the leasing trade US$1.21 billion, up 41.8%. However, imports through barter trade dropped to US$67.5 million, down 62.4% mainly due to a change in the tax remission and reduction policy. This change in the pattern of the import trade is mainly attributed to state control of the scale of fixed

Table 7.3 Changes in composition of imports of machinery and electrical products, 1995/1996 (in US$100 million for 1996 and% changes between 1996 and 1995)

Commodities	Import value	Growth %	Commodities	Import value	Decline %
1 Integrated circuit and micro-electronic parts	26.0	18.7	1 Automobile and chassis	8.3	−45.7
			1−1 Small cars	3.7	−52.5
2 Computer parts	19.1	41.4	2 Ships	3.9	−41.6
3 Semi-conductor components	6.8	47.6	3 Video recorders and parts	0.594	−69.4
4 Cable communication accessories	10.2	9.8	4 Colour television sets	2.4	−26.8
5 Automobile parts	10.7	26.0	5 Colour TV tubes	4.5	−15.0
6 Internal-combustion engine parts	4.3	18.6	6 Photocopiers	0.102	−46.8
7 Aviation equipment and parts	4.9	109.4	7 Metal pressing machine and parts	3.5	−32.2
8 Switches and electrical circuit protection devices	14.3	11.7	8 Building and mining machinery	6.3	−23.1
9 Passenger lifts	5.6	19.6			
10 Steam turbine parts	1.1	32.7			

asset investments and the implementation of an appropriately tight finance policy, and to scant effective demand from domestic enterprises, which resulted in a big drop in imports by the conventional trade. On the other hand, as China took further steps to improve the investment environment for foreign merchants, the amount of foreign investments actually utilised in 1996 rose to US$42.35 billion, up 12.9% compared with that in 1995. The more than a dozen American, Japanese, French and Korean international corporations in the Pudong Zone in Shanghai increased their investments by US$500 million, representing 102% of their original investments. Moreover, the policy of reducing and remitting duties on equipment brought in by foreign investors led to a big increase in equipment imports.

3. Among the trading partners engaged in imports of mechanical and electrical products, Japan, the United States of America, the Taiwan

region, Germany and the Hong Kong Special Administrative Region took the first five positions. Imports from Japan greatly surpassed those from other trading partners, amounting to US$17.94 billion and accounting for 29.2% of the total imports. Big increases in imports were recorded from the following countries: the Republic of Korea, up 34%; Sweden, up 32.5%; Russia, up 119.4%; Malaysia, up 64%; and Thailand, up 130%. On other hand, imports from the following countries dropped heavily: Canada, by 23.6%; Belgium, by 24.9%; Spain, by 52.1%; and Australia, by 26.3%. As far as imports and exports of mechanical and electrical goods are concerned, among the top five importers, China enjoys a favourable trade balance with the United States of America and the Hong Kong Special Administrative Region, but a greatly unfavourable balance with Japan, Taiwan Province and Germany. The China mainland imported US$6.66 billion worth of mechanical and electrical products from Taiwan, yet mainland exports amounted to only US$1 billion in 1996, due to restrictions imposed on imports from the former by the latter. The trade imbalance across the Taiwan Strait is very serious, with the China mainland suffering an adverse balance as high as US$5.66 billion.

4. Among enterprises importing mechanical and electrical products, solely foreign-funded enterprises, Chinese-foreign joint ventures and cooperative enterprises were the biggest importers, taking up the main portion of such imports. Their imports amounted to US$40.56 billion, showing an increase of US$8.48 billion or 26.5% compared with the 1995 figure, and taking up two-thirds of the total amount of such imports. Among them, Chinese-foreign joint ventures imported US$23 billion worth of such goods, up 26%; and solely foreign-funded enterprises US$13.63 billion USD, up 38.8%. On the other hand, imports by State Owned Enterprises were valued at US$19.19, a decrease of 25.8% and making up 31.3% of the total amount of imports; imports by collectively-owned enterprises were US$400 million, down 10.5%; and by private a mere US$6.43 million, though the amount was more than double that of 1995. Imports by other enterprises amounted to US$1.18 billion, up 62.2%.

II Imports of four major product categories: conditions and characteristics

Among China's imports of mechanical products, machine tools, power generating equipment, engineering machinery and automobiles constitute four major categories which are prominent because of their relatively large volumes and their influence on the domestic industries.

1. Metal fabrication machines. Imports amounted to a total of US$2.52 billion in 1996, i.e. an increase of 14.6% over 1995. This robust growth climaxed a continuous upsurge experienced in the past three years. In

broad categories, imports of metal cutting machines reached US$1.56 billion and that of forging press machines US$0.95 billion in 1996, representing an increase of 14.9% and 14.1% respectively, as shown in Table 7.4. Two major points are noteworthy.

First is the large-scale growth of imports of numerically controlled metal cutting machines, totalling US$0.6 billion in 1996, or an increase of 26.8% over 1995. Both numerically controlled lathes and grinders carried the greatest weight within this category of imports (see Table 7.4); and both are indeed very much in demand by domestic industries.

Second is the point that imports of conventional (non-numerically controlled) fabrication machines are still very substantial, taking up nearly half of the import amount of US$2.52 billion for fabrication machines taken as a whole (see Table 7.4). The most popular items include grinders, lathes, forging presses, bending, sheering, and punching machines.

2. Electricity generating equipment. Among the four major categories, imports of both steam turbine and hydraulic turbine increased, but that of boiler (including auxiliaries) and generators declined as is also revealed in Table 7.4. Several points may be made.

First is the point that around three quarters of the imports in 1996 were for steam turbine parts. Nonetheless, imports of steam turbines of a capacity larger than 0.35 million kilowatts increased most drastically (by 8 fold), reflecting the changing demand of our country power stations. Most importantly, a total of US$28.229 million was spent on imports of steam turbines smaller than 0.35 million kilowatts – a kind that can basically be produced domestically. Serious attention must be drawn to this.

Second is the remarkable increases in boiler imports, up by 50.5% from 1995 to 1996. These comprised boilers with a steam capacity larger than 900 tonnes/hour worth US$0.128 billion for 20 units, (an increase of 69.7%), and those with a smaller capacity down to 45 tonnes/hour worth US$14.25 million for 148 units (an increase of 34.7%). However, imports of both auxiliary boilers and parts declined very substantially.

Third, is the decline of imports of alternating current generators, by 15.9% in 1996 (Table 7.4), which is essentially accountable for by reduced imports (by 66.4%) of parts for generators with a capacity larger than 0.35 million kilowatts. As a matter of fact, imports of generator with a capacity smaller than 0.35 million kilowatts (worth US$61.599 million) increased by 9.5% in 1996, and that with a capacity larger than 0.35 million kilowatts increased even much more remarkably.

3. Engineering machinery. Among the 14 different categories, virtually all saw their imports reduced, quite substantially indeed. The notable exceptions were electric fork lift and portal gantry travelling loading cranes, both recording significant import increases.

Table 7.4 Trends in the imports of four major categories of machinery, 1995/1996 (US$100 million and year on %)

	Import value 1996	1995/96 % change
1. Metal fabrication machine	25.2	14.6
1–1 Numerically controlled metal cutting machines	6.0	26.8
1–1–1 Numerically controlled lathes	2.0	73.1
1–1–2 Numerically controlled grinders	1.8	23.4
1–1–3 Numerically controlled boring machines	0.1642	82.1
1–2 Numerically controlled forging press machines	n.a.	n.a.
1–2–1 Bending machines	0.6614	6.6
1–2–2 Shearing machines	0.6042	23.3
1–2–3 Punching machines	0.4781	26.9
1–2–4 Forging and pressing machines	1.3	−15.0
1–3 Special fabrication machines	n.a.	n.a.
1–3–1 Electrical fabrication machines	0.5452	43.3
1–3 2 Laser and photonic fabrication machines	0.1959	45.9
1–3–3 Single unit combine fabrication machines	0.11756	51.5
1–4 Conventional fabrication machines	11.7	18.1
1–4–1 Grinder	1.4	34.5
2. Electricity generating equipment	6.1	0.0
2–1 Steam turbines	1.56	20.4
2–1–1 Above 0.35 million kilowatts	0.0923	800.0
2–1–2 Below 0.35 million kilowatts	0.2823	n.a.
2–1–3 Steam turbine parts	1.18	32.7
2–2 Boiler and auxiliaries	3.4	−8.1
2–2–1 Boilers	2.38	50.8
2–2–2 Auxiliary boilers	0.4968	−47.7
2–2–3 Boiler parts	0.5565	−53.8
2–3 Alternating current generators	0.8674	−15.9
2–3–1 Above 0.35 million kilowatts (3 units)	0.0815	2200.0
2–3–2 Below 0.35 million kilowatts	0.6160	9.5
2–3–3 Parts for generators larger than 0.35 million kilowatts	0.1699	−66.4
2–4 Hydraulic turbines and water wheels	0.252	65.5
3. Engineering machinery	5.2	−16.6
3–1 Fork lifts	1.6	35.0
3–1–1 Electric fork lifts	0.3287	52.7
3–1–2 Portal gantry travelling loading cranes	0.3913	250.0
3–2 Civil engineering machinery	n.a.	n.a.
3–2–1 Loading machines	0.2021	−35.4
3–2–2 Bulldozers	0.1885	−53.8
3–2–3 Road levelers	0.141	−72.1
3–3 Mobile cranes	n.a.	n.a.
3–3–1 Truck cranes	0.2606	−45.2
3–3–2 Wheeled cranes	0.0544	−59.7
3–3–3 Tower cranes	0.1122	−42.6

	Import value 1996	1995/96 % change
4. Motor vehicles and motorcycles	20.1	−19.7
4–1 Cars, light off-road vehicles, and motorcycles	n.a.	n.a.
4–1–1 Cars	37000 (units)	−52.5
4–1–2 Light off-road vehicles	0.0867	−76.0
4–1–3 Special vehicles	2.4	−35.4
4–1–4 Motorcycles	0.0151	−93.2
4–2 Off-road dumper trucks	0.5687	32.8
4–3 Buses with 30 or more seats	0.2354	more than 100.00
4–4 Auto parts	n.a.	n.a.
4–4–1 Car parts	10.7	26.0
4–4–2 Motorcycle parts	1.0	6.3

4. Motor vehicles and motorcycles. Imports of whole vehicles declined across the board quite significantly, in favour of automobile parts, in particular. The notable exceptions were buses (especially with 30 or more seats) and off-road dumper trucks. Imports of both increased remarkably, because of limitation in domestic manufacturing capacity and technology.

III The need to speed up the development of products of higher technological content of the kind now being imported in great volume and to raise the technological level and competitiveness of China's machine building industry

The import situation and characteristics discussed above form an important basis for assessing China's domestic market demand, as well as for the research and development of new products and for drawing up development plans for the industry and the enterprises. They are also an important source of information for China's utilisation of foreign capital and for the development of Chinese-foreign joint ventures and cooperative projects. In the light of the import conditions of mechanical and electrical products in 1996, and also in consideration of the development of relevant industries in China, we need to study the development of the following products all of high technological content, which are being imported in great volumes or are rapidly growing.

1. The machine tool industry. Among numerically controlled machine tools, imports of machining centres, numerically controlled lathes, numerically controlled grinders and numerically controlled forging and pressing machines were biggest in volume. Imports in 1996 totalled 11,000 units valued at US$930 million, representing 81.3% of the total imports of numerically controlled machine tools which were valued at US$1.15 billion. Among them, imports of lathes and grinders grew very

fast, respectively by 73.1% and 23.4%. With regard to machining centres, it is necessary to attach importance to the development of vertical tri-axial tandem machining centres of medium and small sizes, and to improve the reliability and lower the price of existing products. With regard to numerically controlled grinders, emphasis should be on the development of cylindrical grinders (256 units were imported in 1996, valued at US$51.84 million, accounting for 28% of total imports of numerically controlled grinders valued at US$186 million), and of various special grinding machines (such as those for use by the automobile industry). As for numerically controlled forging and pressing machines, great efforts should be devoted to developing the bending, shearing and punching varieties (2,145 units imported, valued at US$170 million, accounting for 56% of total imports of numerically controlled forging and pressing machines) to meet the requirements of different users. Emphasis should also be given to expanding the variety of multi-station, modular machine tools and numerically controlled electro-processing machines and to raising their quality level. As for non-numerically controlled machine tools, it is especially necessary to enhance the reliability of various grinding and pressing machines and see to it that their prices are competitive.

2. The power-generating equipment industry. Imports of boilers made up 56% of total power-generating equipment imports. Boilers with an evaporation capacity of 900 tons per hour or higher took up a major portion of such imports. It is therefore necessary to increase the domestic manufacturing capacity of these boilers. Regarding steam turbines and steam turbo-generators, continued efforts have to be made to optimize imported models of 300,000 and 600,000 kilowatt KW capacities to improve their performances and efficiency. It is necessary to speed up the process of developing a capacity to make steam turbine components and parts domestically, and on this basis to develop and manufacture bigger capacity units. As regards hydropower equipment, it is necessary to develop large-capacity generating units as quickly as possible, including pumped-storage generating units of 200,000 KW or bigger capacity, and through-flow units of 35,000 KW or bigger capacity. It is also necessary to improve the reliability of full sets of generating units.

3. The engineering machinery industry. Topping the import list of this industry were fork lifts, including container fork lifts and power-operated fork lifts, and hydraulic excavators. Imports of these two types of products amounted to US$330 million, making up 64.6% of the total imports of 16 types of engineering machinery valued at US$520 million. Domestic enterprises must focus their utmost efforts on raising the quality and reliability and increasing the variety of their products, and on developing economies of scale. In recent years, the rapid development of [domestic production of] bulldozers and loading machines has resulted in a big reduction in imports, but there is still an urgent need

to develop heavier-duty varieties, such as bulldozers of 320 or bigger horsepower and loading machines of 5.4 cubic meter and bigger capacity, and to expand the scale of production. The development of engineering vehicles should give priority to the production of key components, parts and accessories, and to raising product quality and reliability and economies of scale should be aimed at.

4. The automobile industry. Automobile imports dropped heavily in the last two years. Imports in 1995 were valued at US$1.54 billion, down 55% from the 1994 figure, and dropped a further 45.7% in 1996. This is attributed first, to China's tightened currency policy and, secondly, to the increased production of small cars by Chinese-foreign joint ventures, which have taken up a bigger share of the domestic market. It is also attributable to the availability on the domestic market of automobiles assembled with parts smuggled in from abroad. Currently, there is an urgent need to develop economy cars suited to the consumption level of a considerable portion of the people, which should be manufactured in bigger batches and sold at lower prices. Imports of dumpers for off-highway use and buses of 30-seat or bigger capacity have risen rapidly. And electrical cement mixer trucks continue to be imported on a large scale (1,476 units worth US$90.43 million), hence it is necessary to accelerate their development. Continued efforts should be made to expedite the development and increase the domestic production of automobile and motorcycle spare parts and accessories, all of which are being imported in great quantities.

5. The research and development of several other kinds of products needs to be stepped up as they are being imported in very large quantities.

Because of the rapid growth in imports, the instrument and meter industry needs to accelerate the development of distributed industrial process control systems (imports amounted to US$94.71 million, up 39.9%); duplicating machines and parts and accessories thereof (imports amounted to US$320 million, up 25%); and gas or smoke analysers, vehicle speedometers, profile projectors and some measuring and testing instruments and automatic regulating apparatus.

Additionally, measures should be taken to expand the variety, improve the quality and develop according to priority the following: dairy products processing machinery; pastry and noodles processing machinery; web-fed offset presses, flat paper offset printers; metal molds; plastic molds; plastic injection machines; blow molding machines; fully automatic arc welding machines; large-capacity diesel generating units; wind-driven generating units; and air-conditioners of 4,000 kilocalorie or bigger capacities.

The above items reflect [the needs of] the market. It is suggested that they be incorporated into the three major campaigns now being carried out in depth by the machine-building industry for the purposes of improving product quality, optimising the organisational structure and raising development capacity, in order to achieve solid and substantive results.

IV To strengthen macro-control on imports and adopt appropriate measures to optimise the structure of products imported in line with international practice

Along with the development of China's economy and the strengthening of its economic and technical cooperation with other countries and regions, China's utilisation of foreign capital will become even more rational and efficient. The scale of imports will be expanded correspondingly and the proportion of mechanical and electrical imports in the country's total imports will also increase. Therefore, it is necessary on the one hand to actively support the importation by enterprises of advanced technology and equipment and urgently-needed goods for the domestic market, in order to promote our technological advancement, raise the technological level of our enterprises, and hence enable us to make full use of international resources to achieve an optimal disposition of China's industrial resources. This will have important significance for promoting a change of China's economic growth pattern from an extensive to an intensive [type of development]. On the other hand, it is necessary to attach great importance to controlling imports of ordinary products, of the kind which can be produced in good quality domestically. Measures should be adopted to halt excessive imports to protect the domestic industry, and to optimise the structure of such imports.

1. To strengthen macro-control and perfect the import monitoring system

The still voluminous imports have seriously affected the development of relevant industries in China. Consequently, the market share of State Owned Enterprises has been declining. With part of their production capacity being laid idle, they are experiencing great difficulties in operation. In the case of machine tools, conventional fabrication machines (not numerically controlled), which can be domestically produced, were still being imported in great quantities. Imports in 1996 amounted to US$1.17 billion, up 18.1% from the 1995 figure, which included 8,862 conventional fabrication machines valued at US$70.21 million; 6,414 conventional milling machines valued at US$55.67 million; 739 planing machines and shaping machines valued at US$3.688 million; and 2,985 hydraulic presses valued at US$64.87 million. Because of these heavy imports, the output of China's machine tool industry has been falling steadily for three consecutive years. Domestically-made machine tools now take up only about 30% of the domestic market. Many enterprises are not operating to their capacity, and, with declining economic returns, they are confronted with serious [financial] difficulties.

In the case of power-generating equipment, due to voluminous imports over the years, domestic enterprises are operating under capacity. In 1996, a production capacity of 5 million KW was left idle; the idle capacity in 1997 is expected to be even greater. 40% of the generating equipment required for the Ninth Five-Year Plan has been ordered from abroad. Foreign manufacturers have grabbed a bigger share of the domestic market. Domestic enterprises have experienced a worrying decline in economic returns.

Excessive imports have also been an important cause for the continued decline in the output of the engineering machinery industry for three consecutive years. In particular, bulldozers of 320 or lower HP, which are already manufactured in batches in China and are competitive on the export market, are still being imported in large quantities. In the case of truck cranes, the industry has acquired a considerable competitive strength as a result of product development and technology imports over a number of years. However, in 1996 alone 116 truck cranes with a lifting capacity of 100 tons or below were imported at a cost of US$16.57 million. As a result, six major domestic manufacturers were seriously short of orders and their profits dropped accordingly. Another important factor affecting the domestic market is the blind import of used equipment. A few departments approved such imports against regulations (for example, a certain South China city approved the import of 106 used excavators against regulations).

The State has stipulated that imports of certain important products such as numerically controlled horizontal lathes, loading machines, excavators and metal and plastic molds must go through a public tender process. In reality, however, some companies treat this as a mere formality, and agreed to import such products without going through the bidding process. Some individual import control departments violated the rules and approved such imports beyond their vested authority. This is yet another cause for excesses in imports.

In light of the above situation, there is an urgent need to strengthen macro-control and perfect the import monitoring system. It is necessary to employ such means as tariffs, quality and technical standards, anti-dumping measures and quota permits to prevent blind imports and control excessive imports. It is necessary to amend and improve the *Methods of Import Control on Mechanical and Electrical Products*, which have been in force for three years, to suit the new situation. It is necessary to readjust the control list, simplify the procedures and raise efficiency in accordance with the requirements for domestic economic development and for opening wider to the outside world, giving full consideration to the development of relevant industries and to the impact of excessive imports on the domestic industry. It is necessary to strengthen the supervision over bidding work and seriously investigate and deal with discipline violations by units which have approved imports beyond their vested authority. Under the premise of maintaining continuity of the import policy, China needs to constantly improve its import control system in line with prevailing international practices.

2. To institute controls on imports of equipment by foreign-owned enterprises as part of their investments

At present, unlike the controls on imports by domestically-owned enterprises, imports of equipment by foreign-owned enterprises as part of their investments do not fall within the sphere of the state's centralised control. Instead, they are subject to a foreign exchange quota for imported equipment fixed at the time when the project is approved by the department in charge. Within this quota, the enterprises can decide by themselves the list of equipment to be brought in. Moreover, this imported equipment is exempt from import duties and value-added taxes. Although the state has abolished the preferential import tax policy on newly-approved projects as from 1 April, 1996, projects approved before that will nevertheless continue to enjoy such preference in the next one to two years. This provides much room for freedom of action not bound by the regulations, causing a loss of macro-control. According to customs statistics, in 1996 foreign investors imported equipment worth US$22.34 billion, up 31.6% from 1995 and accounting for 36.4% of total imports of mechanical and electrical products. Among these, metal fabrication machines accounted for US$1.9 billion, making up 75.3% of total machine tool imports; fork lifts and lift trucks amounted to US$95.33 million; construction machinery such as bulldozers, loading machines and excavators US$160 million; vehicles other than small cars US$69.24 million; welding machines US$130 million; measuring and testing instruments US$440 million; and printing machines US$580 million. It is quite obvious that these imports, or a considerable part thereof, brought in under the preferential policy, have dealt a direct impact on the production of domestically-owned enterprises. It is therefore necessary to regulate the equipment imports by foreign-owned enterprises as quickly as possible. They should be treated in the same way as the domestic enterprises and placed under unified control by competent state authorities. This will enhance the state's macro-control capability and create an environment for fair competition.

3. To adopt a sound tariff policy, adjust duty rates and strengthen customs control

China reformed its tariff policy in 1995. A number of provisions for tax reduction and remission were abolished, but another number of preferential provisions were retained. The tax remission policy retained for materials imported by enterprises in the Special Economic Zones for their own use has resulted in large quantities of imported duty-free materials being resold to the interior. This has put products of interior enterprises in an unfavourable position price-wise and dealt a blow on the interior market. It is therefore necessary to further sort out and adjust the tax reduction and remission regulations and enforce them strictly, in order to create conditions for fair competition.

It is necessary to study the feasibility of implementing a tariff quota system on some mechanical and electrical products such as power-generating equipment; machine tools; fork lifts, excavators and other engineering machinery; duplicating machines; and metal and plastic molds. (Many countries now practice such a system. For example, the United States of America has imposed such a system on imports of Chinese textile products, while China has also implemented such a system on wheat and other grains sine 1996). We should implement two tariff schedules, one for imports within the quota, which will be taxed according to current rates, and the other for imports in excess of the quota, which will be taxed at double the current rates. The yearly import quotas will be fixed by competent state authorities in collaboration with the Ministry of the Machine-Building Industry and other departments concerned.

China has indicated that it will endeavour to have the general tariff level lowered from the current 23% to about 15% before 2000. The current general tariff level for mechanical products is 15.8%, which is close to that of the developing countries. Currently, priority should be given to resolving the following issues: (1) rationalisation of the tariff structure. It is necessary to change the phenomenon presently existing in the tax rates for certain mechanical products, which are lower than the rates for raw materials. For example, a 6% import duty is imposed on steam turbines of 350 megawatt or higher capacity, whereas the duty on alloy steel plates for the production thereof is 8%–10% and that on cold-rolled stainless steel plates 22%. Such an upside-down phenomenon is unfavourable to the development of the domestic manufacturing industry, and needs to be changed. (2) the import duties on key components and parts for mechanical and electrical products and for products needed to be imported to meet domestic requirements should be lowered to reduce costs. (3) the duties on products whose excessive imports are producing an impact on the domestic industry must not be lowered. (4) it is necessary to study the feasibility of lowering the duties on small cars, currently fixed at 100%–120%.

It is necessary to further strengthen customs supervision. First, the customs should strengthen its control over materials imported by the processing trade for eventual export after processing, which are placed in bond. Secondly, the customs should prevent untaxed commodities in bonded areas from being shipped to interior markets for sale. Thirdly, the customs should prevent tax evasion by means of making customs declarations at depressed prices. It must pay special attention to checking the prices of goods sold to the interior by the processing trade, and goods imported by enterprises in the Special Economic Zones for their own use.

Document 7.4

'Whither the Special Economic Zones?'

XIA XIAOLIN AND SUN ANQIN

Management World, 1995, Vol. 1, No. 58

I Development of the Special Economic Zones over the past 15 years

China's Special Economic Zones (SEZs) have gone through two stages of development since they were established in the early 1980s. Radical changes in political and economic conditions, resulting from Deng Xiaoping's 'Southern Tour' and the Fourteenth Congress of the Chinese Communist Party in 1992, have put a new perspective on the role of the SEZs, and mark a new phase in their development.[28] At about the same time, the goal was set for China to strive towards becoming a socialist market economy. The international political and economic scene also changed drastically in the late 1980s and early 1990s as a result of the termination of the 'Cold War'.

Prior to 1992, the 'Open Door' policy implemented by the Chinese government was subject to various constraints: (1) it was restricted to the coastal region only, with greatest attention to the southeast coastal provinces, especially the [original four] SEZs, (2) foreigners had limited access to the Chinese domestic market, and faced strict export ratio [requirements], and (3) the range of industries in which foreign firms could invest was also restricted.

During this period, China was still at a low level of development in terms of industrial structure, and large-scale multinational corporations did not become major foreign investors in China. China's membership status in the General Agreement for Tariffs and Trade (GATT) was still in abeyance, and the country's laws and procedures pertaining to foreign trade and investment remained yet to be standardised. For example, the SEZs were supported and protected by special preferential policies and administrative measures, all of which were largely inconsistent with the rules of the GATT. Abiding by the rules of the GATT would have negatively affected the open coastal areas, especially the SEZs. The opening of the Chinese economy after 1980 was experimental, and necessarily limited. Their functioning was far from being consistent with the rules and requirements set by the GATT.

Since 1992, and especially after the opening of the Fourteenth Congress of the Chinese Communist Party, the economic opening of China to the rest of the world has entered a new stage with wider regional coverage, more diversified industrial scope and [supported by] large-scale infra-structural projects. The main features of this period are as follows: all regions have

28 The Zones referred to here are Shenzhen, Zhuhai, Shantou, Xiamen and Hainan province i.e. the original zones. (Ed.)

been opened to foreign investments; the pace of opening of various industries has accelerated; the Chinese domestic market has been further opened to foreign investment and trade; [new] fundamental rules and operational mechanisms have been gradually formulated and implemented and these conform to the general rules applied internationally; finally, the direction of foreign direct investment [policy] has been shifted from a regional to an industry based orientation.

In the run-up to China's resumption of her membership in the GATT, the Chinese government has accelerated reform and the establishment of rules for foreign trade and external economic relations.[29] The withdrawal of the regional-oriented preferential policy was necessary to conform with the non-discrimination principle, i.e. foreign trade and investment could now take place in all regions of the country.

The structure of the Chinese economy has changed from emphasising growth in light manufacturing to growth in heavy and chemical industries. Market forces have played an important role in accelerating economic growth and structural change. Prior to 1991, national economic growth was largely led by rapid growth in consumption goods industries. This was essentially a correction to balance out the almost exclusive focus on heavy industries in the past. However, the rapid growth of consumption goods industries tended to result in an identical, small-scale industrial structure everywhere, and heavy industrial production fell behind.

Domestic industries were slow and responded less to technological progress, and increasing demand [for heavy industry output] raised by downstream industries could not be met, reflecting structural rigidities. Thus surplus production capacity in the middle and downstream industries coexisted with shortages of energy and basic materials in the up-stream industries, which were in turn further reinforced by high growth in the former. This structural contradiction hindered economic growth in the medium and long term.

In the second half of 1991, higher growth in the heavy and chemical industries began to emerge. Patterns of light manufacturing industries, capital allocation, and [resource] flows started to change. Some provinces and enterprises which had previously had industrial cooperation and linkages with Guangdong and Fujian provinces, started to shift their investments to more northern regions, especially Shanghai. Consequently, capital flowed out of the SEZs. Foreign investment from the West, Hong Kong and Taiwan, also headed north. Inter-regional economic competition become more intense, as the relative status of each region in the national economy changed.

Under these circumstances, regions with a solid foundation in the heavy and chemical industries have considerable advantages compared with other regions, and competition among regions whose economic structure is based

---

29 The remarks related to GATT accession now relate in almost the same way to WTO accession. (Ed.)

on light manufacturing industries is becoming tougher. For instance, consumption goods produced for both domestic and overseas markets by Jiangsu and Zhejiang provinces have to a large extent replaced those produced by Guangdong. As a result, the import-substitution industrial system established in Guangdong province in the 1980s is facing serious difficulties, with market demand declining.

In addition, international conditions have changed considerably since the end of the 'Cold War' in 1990. Globally, international relations have become more business-oriented, with a trend towards economic regionalisation among groups of countries, and towards trade protectionism. As new technologies are adopted, labour-intensive industries are declining in importance. China now faces tougher competition from other developing countries as well as from Eastern Europe.

However, large multinational corporations from industrialised countries have shown a strong interest in entering the Chinese market, with investments increasingly being oriented to the northern parts of China, especially Shanghai, Jiangsu, Zhejiang and the region surrounding the Bohai Sea.[30] It is true that many of the investment projects with multinational corporations are experiments. The total investment made by large American corporations in China over the past 13 years was less than 1% of their total global investment in 1992. The same is true of the multinational corporations from other countries. If China resumes her GATT membership status in the 1990s, there will probably be much higher investment.

II In the 1990s the SEZs enter a new period of transformation

The conditions and circumstances surrounding the initial establishment of China's SEZs have changed radically since the early 1990s, with more challenges emerging.

1. Shifts in the domestic and international economies have altered the traditional advantageous status of the SEZs, forcing them to adapt

A. The rapid progress in transforming the national economy into a 'socialist market economic system' has reduced the SEZs' status as 'the experimental zones' of a market economy. Their initial remarkably positive effects are diminishing under the new conditions. In the first decade of economic reforms, they possessed the 'early starter' advantage in institutional transformation and policy reforms. However, as market-oriented reforms rapidly spread over the entire country, other regions are beginning to overtake the SEZs.

---

30 The Bohai Sea Zone of China relates particularly closely to Japanese cities and regions facing it. (Ed.)

An important characteristic of the economic growth in the SEZs is the expansion of low technology and labor intensive industries in which small and medium-sized enterprises, especially foreign-invested and 'processing trade' enterprises, play a major part. The focus is on the absorption of the foreign investment and on ensuring optimal production performance. Institutional innovation, of the kind needed for needed for the restructuring of productive capacity between industries, is not emphasised.

In fact, a major problem impeding the economic development of China is the inefficient reallocation of economic resources among industries. The demand for institutional innovation and policy adjustment to facilitate industrial restructuring is much stronger in the non-SEZ regions, where there has been faster progress in the development of enterprise groups, enterprise acquisitions and property trading over the past 10 years. In the process of institutional innovation required for medium-and long-term economic growth, provinces whose industries were largely based on a comprehensive range manufacturing and heavy industries have tended to be at an advantage. This suggests that the demonstration and 'tutoring' effects of the SEZs for other regions in terms of institutional innovation and reforms, have been constrained by their economic structure and development pattern. In contrast, the development of Shanghai Pudong Zone and the resultant economic growth and changes in the Yangzi Delta, have provided a highly effective model for national development.

B. The decline in the 'window' role played by the SEZs in opening up to the outside world has occurred for the following reasons: the 'Open Door' policy now applies to the entire country; some institutional changes and policy adjustments have been made by the Chinese government in order to try to resume the GATT membership; industry-oriented development policy has become more important than region-oriented policy; and the Shanghai Pudong New Area and Changjiang Delta are rising as the new focus for economic development.

C. The shift from region- to industry-oriented policy in the 1990s has reinforced the difficulty for the SEZs to maintain or change the light-industry-dominated growth pattern. Economic resources [now] tend to flow, either as a result of central government allocations or of market forces, to heavy and chemical industries, and they are also guided by foreign investment flows. This intensifies competition between the SEZs and other regions of similar industrial structure. The SEZs are in a disadvantaged position due to their high labor costs and land prices, and some enterprises in Shenzhen, Xiamen and Hainan have started to move to other regions. In fact, the ability of the SEZs to choose and change their industrial structure is becoming more difficult in the 1990s. Shifting toward heavy and chemical industries is difficult and, with an unclear future. If low technology and labor-intensive industries are maintained as 'pillar industries', there is no sound potential for further development. Furthermore, rises in production costs in the SEZs force the relocation of some manufacturing industries into adjacent regions. Consequently, the initial stimulating effects generated by the export-processing zones are also fading away.

D. Foreign investment in the SEZs has come mainly from Hong Kong, Taiwan and Macao. This adds uncertainty to the SEZs' future development in the 1990s. Several factors are involved:

(1) In the 1990s, investment from Hong Kong, Taiwan and Macao has not been region-specific, it is going to all areas of the country.

(2) As Hong Kong and Macao reunite with China, their relations with neighboring countries such as the ASEAN (Association of Southeast Asian Nations) economies will become more competitive. Hong Kong may even be replaced as a regional financial center.

(3) For political reasons, the Taiwanese authority's attitude towards bilateral economic relations with the mainland is still quite conservative. The present situation puts the mainland at a disadvantage, [and this is why] China has an excessive trade deficit with Taiwan. This impedes sustainable growth in economic relations. In the American and Japanese markets especially, the export competition between the mainland and Taiwan for a large number of products has become intense due to the similar structure and composition of their exports. This is expected to hinder the development of healthy bilateral relations.

(4) The economies of Hong Kong, Taiwan and Macao are also undergoing structural change, which is a slow process with unclear prospects, especially for Hong Kong whose manufacturing industries have already largely relocated to other regions or countries. All these external factors contribute to uncertainty about the capital supply conditions for the SEZs in the 1990s.

The reunification of Hong Kong with China has given rise to some particular difficulties and uncertainties for the SEZs. Firstly, it has made the Shenzhen SEZ become an experimental zone for the 'one country two systems' policy because of the difficulties, in both theory and practice, in the early stages of development to integrate Hong Kong, a free capitalist economy, with Shenzhen, an immature market economy. Secondly, Hong Kong's and China's interface with other countries is closely related. Hong Kong's economic performance in 1997 and thereafter will be affected by a number of uncertain political and economic factors. This uncertainty will affect the Shenzhen SEZ, and could in turn influence economic development in the Pearl River Delta and Southern China. The other SEZs including Zhuhai, Shantou, Xiamen and Hainan province may also be influenced to some extent.

In addition, there is at present a strong investment trend towards north China, where multinational corporations from industrialised countries are becoming involved in manufacturing, and the heavy and chemical industries. This trend is supported by the industrial policy of the Chinese government which has tried to encourage foreign capital to flow into resource development and comprehensive manufacturing industries. While this has been going on, regional organisations in Asia and their member countries such as the ASEAN, and even India and Vietnam, have become quite attractive to foreign investors. For example, Japanese firms established more than 400 enterprises in Thailand in the 1980s, employing nearly ninety thousand workers. This is larger than the Japanese investment in China's SEZs over the same period.

In order to resume membership in the GATT and join the World Trade Organization (WTO) in the 1990s, China needs to practice the prevailing rules governing international economic activities. The government must implement a uniform policy for all regions and reduce or remove the special preferential policies applied to the SEZs. The financial subsidies provided to loss-making enterprises located in the SEZs, and favourable tax treatments for export-oriented enterprises must also be eliminated.

The newly developed high technology industries such as sensitization materials, magnetic recording materials, electronics and chemicals are facing tougher competition from overseas producers. Although the SEZs still possess competitive advantage in some labour-intensive products, they produce negligible marginal revenue. In the medium and long term, the survival and development of the labour-intensive industries will face ever more challenges.

2. *The previous development pattern and characteristics of the SEZs are hindering further growth in the 1990s, and need to be changed*

A. Rapid growth in labour-intensive manufacturing is difficult to sustain in the SEZs, and prevents progress towards the middle stage of industrialisation.

Firstly, the existing industrial structure dominated by small-scale, low technology and labour-intensive manufacturing indicates that industrial development in the SEZs is still at a very low level. Within such an industrial structure, economic growth relies largely on the expansion of inputs rather than improvements in efficiency. Shenzhen is a typical example. According to an estimate by the Economic Development Bureau of Shenzhen, the relative contributions of the [different] factors of production to the industrial growth are respectively: labour 53%, capital 31%, and technology 16%. In other words, economic growth in the Shenzhen SEZ relies mainly on expansion of labor and capital inputs, while technology plays an insignificant role.

In 1992 high and new technology products accounted only for 30% of the value-added of Shenzhen's industrial sector. This was lower than the national average of 35%. In Shenzhen and Shantou, output value produced by high and new technology enterprises accounted for less than 10% of the total industrial output value. In other SEZs, this proportion was even lower. Obviously, based on such an industrial structure, the SEZs will find it difficult to face both international and domestic inter-regional competition in the 1990s.

Secondly, increases in labour costs and land prices have increased production costs in the SEZs, and made them less attractive to domestic and foreign investors hoping to establish labour-intensive industries. Manufacturing industries have actually started to relocate from the SEZs to other regions, as predicted by the 'export processing zone life cycle theory'. Some enterprises with internal links with other domestic enterprises in other regions (termed internally-linked enterprises, *neilian qiye*) have withdrawn or cancelled investments in the Shenzhen SEZ in recent years. In the 1990s, capital outflows from Shenzhen have exceeded capital inflows. Investments from Hong Kong and Taiwan have also shifted to adjacent areas and even inland areas.

In the Xiamen SEZ, the average salary was 1,099 *yuan* in 1987, which was 542 *yuan* higher than in Quanzhou, and 641 *yuan* higher than in Zhangzhou. By 1991, the average salary in Xiamen increased to 3,694 *yuan*, widening the salary gap with Quanzhou (1,275 *yuan*), and with Zhangzhou (1,083 *yuan*). The rise in labour costs occurred simultaneously with a sharp increases in land prices. For example, one square metre of land in the metropolitan area was priced at more than 500 *yuan* in 1989, but 2,000–3,000 *yuan* by 1991. It further rose to 8,000 *yuan* in 1992, much higher than in Quanzhou and Zhangzhou. Production cost increases result in a decline in the profitability of enterprises. Between 1981 and 1992, the average profit rate of industrial enterprises in Xiamen declined from 18% to 6%.

The increase in production costs has caused Xiamen to lose its advantage in attracting foreign investment and its relative economic prominence is declining. In 1985, 61% of the total foreign investment in Fujian Province flowed into Xiamen, but this share decreased to 25% by 1990, and fell further to 21% in 1991. In contrast, Quanzhou, Zhangzhou and surrounding areas have made significant progress in the development of labor-intensive industries using foreign investment and have become strong competitors for Xiamen. Thus it can be argued that the economic structure dominated by labour-intensive industries has become an important factor impeding economic growth in Xiamen. In 1992, the total output value of the industrial and agricultural sectors, the foreign-invested enterprises, and newly approved foreign investment contracts in Xiamen grew at lower rates than those in Fuzhou, Zhangzhou, Quanzhou and Futian. It is clear that if the current trend continues, the role played by the SEZs as 'export-processing zones' will deteriorate, with the manufacturing industries declining in importance. In response to the structural difficulty, some SEZs have started to shift their development focus to the tertiary industry and have even tried to relocate their manufacturing industries out of the SEZs.

Thirdly, labor-intensive manufactured goods are subject to declining demand and face increasing competition in both the domestic and foreign markets. All five of the SEZs are similar in industrial structure, as well as market structure in both domestic and overseas markets. As such structural characteristics are shared by other open coastal areas in China, the SEZs face difficult market competition. In addition, other Asian countries such as those making up ASEAN and Vietnam, are of similar industrial and market structure, and are also in a competing position with the SEZs. Moreover, due to some preferential trade treatments that are not always offered to China, these countries benefit from stable overseas markets and are able to increase exports easily. All of these factors tend to worsen the terms of trade for China's SEZs and impede their growth momentum.

Fourthly, on the basis of the existing industrial structure dominated by small-sized labour intensive manufacturing with a large amount of capital stock, it is very difficult for the SEZs to create large-scale, modern industries. This is because labour-intensive manufacturing industries are characterised by simple production processes, low technological content, use of simple and crude equipment, limited capital, lack of linkages with other industries, poorly trained employees and inefficient management. To upgrade the industrial structure and develop new industries would require large investments. If such a structural transformation were to occur, many traditional enterprises would perish in the competition, and/or lose their traditional conditions for survival.

However, whether this sort of structural transformation is suitable for all the SEZs remains an open question. A series of issues need further study. For instance, are the funds required for such structural transformation available? and would this transformation intensify competition with comprehensive manufacturing industries, thereby reinforcing inter-provincial competition in heavy and chemical industries?

B. The current industrial structure of the SEZs impedes development of large-scale manufacturing. with the small-scale enterprises dominating

A small-scale enterprise is a suitable organisation for low technology and labor-intensive industrial activity. In the SEZs, small and medium-scale enterprises have been the major form of industrial organisation. This is a result of relocation of labour-intensive industries from other countries and regions in the past. The economic growth of the SEZs has been dominated by small and medium-scale enterprises, of which foreign-invested enterprises and trade-processing enterprises have been the major players, and have also been the principal contributors to exports from the SEZs. However, as labour costs and land prices rise, and market competition becomes tougher, small- and medium-scale labour-intensive enterprises are losing their competitive advantage. In addition, due to their intrinsic production nature and industrial characteristics, it is difficult for them to grow into large-scale enterprises using advanced production methods.

C. Internal funds are insufficient to finance large-scale infrastructure construction and support the development of capital and technology-intensive industries.

The growth of the SEZs in the 1980s and the first half of the 1990s relied mainly on self-accumulation and domestic savings, with small amounts of foreign direct investment as an additional source of finance. In the

Shenzhen, Xiamen and Hainan SEZs, the financial sources of basic capital construction investment in the 1980s were as follows: 30% to 40% from self-raised funds; 20% to 30% from domestic loans; and 10% to 20% from foreign capital. Since the 1990s, the growth pattern of the domestic economy has shifted from 'demand-pull' to 'investment-push' and domestic funds have been in short supply. The situation has been much more severe for the SEZs because of the industry-oriented development policy and the increased development interest in the northern parts of China. It will be very difficult for the SEZs to rely on their internal funds and domestic savings to finance the expansion of production to raise the technology level of their industries and to carry out large scale, infrastructural construction. Furthermore, the small amount of foreign direct investment is sufficient only to facilitate the growth of small and medium-scale labour-intensive enterprises. Foreign investment in some individual, large projects cannot radically change the tight financial situation faced by the SEZs as a whole.

3. Choosing the correct development strategy for the SEZs in the 1990s is the pre-condition for an improved development pattern and transformed industrial structure

Given the changed circumstances of the 1990s, three points must be considered:

First, it is unrealistic for the SEZs to remain 'leaders' in terms of economic reform, opening and development in the 1990s through the use of traditional policies applied since the early 1980s.

Second, if the SEZs can maintain their leading position in economic reforms, and create a sound investment environment, they may successfully upgrade their industrial structure. For example, the Hainan SEZ is undergoing a transformation from a traditional agricultural society to a modern economy. However, this may have limited implications for the other SEZs whose economies are largely integrated with other regions.

Third, the SEZs should not only take the 'early start' advantage, maintain a leading position in institutional reforms and innovation, and achieve industrial upgrading, but they should also play an active role in economic integration with Hong Kong, Macao and Taiwan, utilising their special inter-regional relations to develop the economy. This can be the basis for formulating a development strategy for the three SEZs in Guangdong and in the Xiamen SEZ in Fujian province over the next 10 years.

In short, the two radical conditions which supported the development of the SEZs in the 1980s, special management system and preferential policies, cannot continue in the 1990s. They also cannot help to solve problems accumulated over many years. Each SEZ needs to take advantage of its 'early start' in economic reforms, openness and locational advantage (i.e., proximity to Hong Kong, Macao and Taiwan). Further studies must be carried out to choose appropriate bases for development in each case, and from this they can formulate a development strategy for the 1990s and next century.

4. Issues for further study

To understand the developmental direction of the SEZs in the 1990s up to the early 21st century, and to formulate an appropriate development strategy, it is necessary to study the following issues:

A. In recent years, while large amounts of funds were required to upgrade the industrial structure of the SEZs, some enterprises relocated to, or invested in, other regions of China. The new direction of domestic capital flows followed those from Hong Kong, Taiwan and Macao to the other regions of the mainland. Therefore, the pace, scale, causes, trends and impacts of the outward shift of industries and factors of production from the SEZs to other regions, as well as inward flows of capital from overseas and the inland regions, should be carefully studied.

B. If the de-industrialisation trend continues in the SEZs of Guangdong and Fujian, how will this affect Hong Kong's economic growth? How will Hong Kong, which is losing its backyard for manufacturing, in return react to new relations with the SEZs?

C. One popular opinion maintains that the second stage of economic growth in the SEZs will achieve a structural shift from labor-intensive to technology intensive industries. At present, the SEZs' major investors, namely, Hong Kong, Taiwan and Macao, have not completed such an industrial transformation. It is unlikely that Hong Kong and Macao ever will achieve this transformation. Taiwan is expected to play only a small role in helping the mainland to realize such an industrial transformation because the Taiwanese government is reluctant to support structural upgrading on the mainland. As the SEZs' development in the past has been based on low technology, labour-intensive industries, it will not be easy to upgrade into technologically intensive industries. Issues needing particular study and [framing of] appropriate polices include: testing the feasibility of achieving industrial transformation by using domestic high technology resources. Finding out who will make the large investments and incur the risks associated with industrial restructuring – domestic investors or multinational corporations from industrialised countries? And finding out whether it is possible to use international loans to facilitate industrial structural upgrading?

D. The pattern of industrial upgrading is the same in each of the five SEZs. It is also similar to that in other open coastal cities and areas, and in some inland regions. How will the similarity in the industrial structure of different regions affect nation-wide economic development, and to what extent will the industrial upgrading process based on similar industrial structures be affected by resuming China's membership of the GATT? What is the best way to incorporate the development orientation of the SEZs and overall economic development strategy into China's membership bid?

E. Will the service industries in the SEZs and other open coastal regions tend to be similar in structure, causes and outcomes?

F. The SEZs have built some free trade or tariff-free zones. Can these solve the development problems faced by the SEZs? Following the SEZs, many coastal cities are rushing to create free trade or tariff-free zones. How many are needed in China?

G. To what extent is the Shenzhen SEZ prepared for economic integration with Hong Kong, and what policies are available to deal with all possible outcomes?

H. Can the Xiamen SEZ make significant progress in development by utilisation of its own resources or is it just waiting for large investments from Taiwan? Alternatively, can Taiwan develop its economic relations with the mainland without Xiamen?

I. Can Hainan, the least-developed SEZ, use its special locational characteristics to shape a unique development pattern and create new opportunities which are different from those in the other SEZs?

J. For a large developing country like China, the economic opening at its mature stage should be based on an appropriately developed industrial structure, with an 'Open Door' policy being broadly applied in all regions rather than implemented only in some coastal regions. Under these new circumstances, the role of the SEZs in China's economic development, and their opening in the second half of the 1990s and first decade of the 21st century, need to be properly assessed.

Obviously, clear answers to the above listed questions are needed to formulate a development strategy and set the orientation of future growth for the SEZs. It is unwise to continue debate about whether 'special' policies should be applied in SEZs, as before. Otherwise, we may lose development opportunities in the future. A key issue in the economic development of the SEZs in the late 1990s and after is to choose a rational development strategy and orientation, and to formulate appropriate policies for upgrading industrial structure.

Document 7.5

Integrating FDI within the domestic economy

LI HAIJIAN

China Industrial Development Report 1997

1. New modes of FDI Entry and their Impact

Since the early 1990s, the intake of foreign direct investment (FDI) in China has displayed some major changes.

First, acquisitions and mergers with existing local firms have become an increasingly popular as a way for foreign firms to invest in China. This stands in sharp contrast to the past practice of directly contributing capital and equipment for setting up equity joint ventures (EJV) and contractual joint ventures (CJV), and this [mode of entry] tends to focus on large-scale State Owned Enterprises (SOEs), especially those which are highly profitable. Moreover, a more focused approach has also emerged, in that foreign investors purposefully purchase and merge all SOEs in a particular locality or, [they concentrate on] the pillar (dragonhead) enterprises of a particular industry dispersed in different areas.

Second, is the attempt to establish a controlling stake in joint ventures with a view to monopolising the domestic market. This involves increasingly large-scale multinational corporations, which have invested heavily in China since the early 1990s. A majority share is normally obtained by continually injecting additional investments to crowd out the Chinese partners who very often lack the necessary matching capital for balancing the equity share. It can also take place by way of acquisition of existing enterprises, or simply putting up enough capital to be the majority shareholder in a new EJV. By 1995, foreign-invested enterprises (FIEs) already held sizable market shares in a wide range of consumer goods such as: detergents and laundry powder 35%, cosmetics 36%, soap 40%, beer 20%, electronics 30%, and beverages 19% (with carbonated beverages alone holding 37%). This is of course very different from the situation in the 1980s, when FIEs were generally required to export a fixed proportion of their output to overseas markets.

Third, whereas in the 1980s foreign firms generally entered the Chinese investment market with cash or capital equipment, they now essentially come with the brand names of their own products. Chinese brands are either directly replaced by foreign brands, or first purchased by foreign investors, to be subsequently abrogated. Some SOEs surrender their brand names to the joint ventures at bargain prices as an equity contribution, but after a certain period, are all driven out of the market and replaced by foreign brands.

The new modes of FDI entry into China not only threaten to reduce the market share of China's own industries, but also the very existence of many SOEs. There are two aspects to this. The first is that State Owned Enterprises are already very much disadvantaged in terms of the various policy and institutional privileges exclusively accorded to foreign-funded firms. Second is that SOEs are heavily burdened with a wide range of social responsibilities unknown to their foreign counterparts. The result is increased exodus of critical managerial talent from SOEs to foreign-funded enterprises. Worse still, foreign firms now usually choose only high-performing SOEs or just take the most promising parts thereof for acquisition and merger, leaving the Chinese enterprises to struggle with the debts, retirement benefits, and resettlement fees for redundant workers. Thus, when a new joint venture is established, this often dooms an SOE to collapse.

Foreign-funded ventures have also seriously eroded the export market share of domestic firms. Under the country of origin principle, their exports inevitably count as Chinese exports. Especially where import quotas are imposed by foreign countries, the odds go increasingly against the domestic exporters, as they normally lack the necessary international trade expertise and worldwide marketing network to compete against the foreign-funded enterprises.

Some Chinese domestic firms are also motivated to join forces with foreign firms to compete against or defeat domestic rivals in the same industry. For example, when the television set producer, Chang Hong, reduced its prices, a number of smaller TV manufacturers in China attempted to establish joint ventures with foreign firms in order to strengthen their market position.

A malpractice observed among SOEs in the process of forming joint ventures with foreign firms, is that managers or factory directors intentionally under-value state-owned assets in return for maintaining their original positions in the new joint ventures or obtaining a higher salary. In some cases, if state-owned assets are undervalued by one percentage point, their salaries can be expected to increase correspondingly. Obviously, the state asset management department has become the target of rent-seeking.

Currently, the losses to the domestic sectors brought about by foreign capital have become increasingly visible and worrisome.

1. The ability of foreign firms to control production and marketing is strengthening. Initially foreign firms established joint ventures, but lately, they have formed head offices or mother companies to control and coordinate the production and marketing activities of all their sub-affiliates in China.
2. Foreign firms have used Chinese enterprises to increase their power. Their primary motivation in forming joint ventures with local firms is to use the latter's existing market share in the domestic market. Foreign firms literally buy market share from local firms. In addition, a large proportion of joint venture profits are spent on market promotion aimed at raising the reputation of their product brand, which serves the strategic goal of holding a sizable share in the Chinese market in future.
3. The value-added ratio of processing for trade in FIEs is low. Chinese statistics show that over 70% of foreign-invested enterprises engage in processing for trade, with a very low ratio of value-added. The value-added ratio in FIEs was 1: 1.09 in 1994, and 1:1.13 in 1995, compared to 1:1.36 and 1:1.49 respectively in State Owned Enterprises. As a result of a lower value-added ratio in FIEs compared to state-owned enterprising, a series of losses arise on the Chinese side.[31]

31 What this implies is that much of the value of final output is made up of imported components and that the factor rewards for Chinese local contributions of labour or capital are correspondingly small. Branded toys are a glaring example of this problem. (Ed.)

2. Fraudulent practices of Sino-foreign joint ventures

Four types of fraud exist in Sino-foreign joint ventures, including phoney equity joint ventures, fraudulent operating losses reported by FIEs, phoney exports, and phoney bankruptcy. These frauds result in huge financial losses for China. The Chinese government and industry management must watch for these and take steps to ensure that the development of joint ventures occurs in line with Chinese laws and regulations, and is of benefit to all parties concerned.

A. *Phoney equity joint ventures*

These refer to enterprises solely owned by Chinese nationals and which have no real foreign capital participation, but are registered as FIEs. This type of joint venture can be formed by converting an existing domestic enterprise, or by establishing a new foreign-invested enterprise. The principal forms of phoney joint ventures are: (1) foreign firms provide only documents indicating their capital participation in the joint ventures but do not actually make any investment. In return they charge the Chinese side for the service, or are offered some units of the company shares. (2) Chinese domestic companies transfer their funds overseas and then invest them back to China under the name of a foreign company including the foreign branches of state-owned companies, and (3) Chinese domestic enterprises and/or foreign firms use false asset evaluation reports and bank deposit certificates to acquire a registration certificate indicating foreign involvement. Investigations shows that this type of phoney joint venture, called 'empty shells', account for a sizable proportion of all FIEs.

The main reason why domestic firms create phoney joint ventures is to gain the preferential policies and treatment granted by the Chinese government to FIEs, including income tax concessions, favourable tariffs for imports and exports, and more autonomy in import, export, foreign exchange, income distribution, labour employment, and wages.

Foreign firms, when establishing joint ventures in China, sometimes move their outmoded machinery and equipment from their home countries to China, selling them at high prices to Chinese companies, or use them as an investment share at an overvalued price. The Chinese domestic firms, often SOEs, thereafter bear three burdens: redundant personnel, business debt, and social responsibilities. These make it almost impossible to improve the performance of the enterprises. Often the less profitable portions of the SOEs that are left out of the joint venture agreements are run by less qualified managers, and the result is bankruptcy because they are legally exempted from business debt.

B. *Fraudulent operating losses*

According to an official investigation, during the Eighth Five Year Plan period (1990–1995), 40% to 50% of FIEs reported operating losses. In some regions and particular years, this proportion was even higher. However, nationally, FIEs did not reduce their scale of production or withdraw capital from existing enterprises, but continued to expand production and increase investments, actually increasing the number of loss-making FIEs. Obviously, not all loss-reporting FIEs undergo true losses. Only a small proportion experience losses, with the majority of them making profits or phoney losses.

The phoney losses in FIEs have two distinguishing features. First, they occur only in China. Beyond the national boundary they represent profit. In FIEs, international marketing channels are usually controlled by foreign firms. The foreign investors underprice FIE exports to their overseas subsidiaries who resell the goods at much higher prices in overseas markets, making huge profits using the 'transfer prices'. According to Customs data, the reselling prices of some FIE exports in overseas markets are usually about 60% higher than the prices of SOE exports. This indicates that foreign firms often shift enormous profits to their overseas affiliates by using transfer prices. This is particularly the case for FIEs engaging in export processing activities. According to official statistics, over 80% of total imports and exports by FIEs are processed and assembled with imported materials.

Second, the losses occur only for the Chinese side, whereas the FIEs make profits. In general, foreign firms can take revenue from four stages of FIE operation. Upon the establishment of the FIEs they can overcharge for the equipment and machinery they provide, then, after the FIEs start running, they over-invoice imports from their overseas subsidiaries. They also underprice exports from FIEs to their overseas subsidiaries using transfer pricing, and enjoy profit distribution from the FIEs. Clearly, foreign investing firms not only gain back all their investment outlays in the first two stages, but also make considerable profits with the third and fourth stages being less important.

In addition, FIEs sometimes artificially create accounting losses by tampering fraudulently with accounting records and changing investments into loans. As far as fraud account items are concerned, under the current income tax law, FIEs with an operation period of ten years or longer are eligible for a two-year tax holiday from the profit-making year, and a 50% tax concession for the following three years. To prolong their eligibility for these tax benefits and defer tax payment, some FIEs adjust account items, reporting more expense items than revenue items so as to make accounting losses.

As for transferring investments into business loans, note that income distribution for investments are made after tax, whereas interest payments to loans are treated as business costs and are paid before tax, meaning that foreign investors have a financial incentive to make such transfers. A transfer from foreign investment to foreign loans will largely reduce the registered capital in an FIE, and change a large portion of enterprise profit into interest payments to foreign investors. This reduces an FIE's normal profit, and may even result in losses for some FIEs. In fact, the victim of fraud losses is the Chinese side. Not only is there no profit distributed to the Chinese enterprises, but there is also no tax income accruing to the Chinese government.

It is estimated that the rate of return on investment is normally about 10%–15% world wide, while return to investment in China is as high as 50%, and even higher in particular industries. Therefore, under normal conditions with proper management, it is unlikely for a large number of FIEs to have operating losses.

C. *Phoney exports from Foreign-Invested Enterprises*

The direct motivation for FIEs to undertake phoney exports is to gain tax drawback on exports. China ended the export subsidy policy in 1990, and since then has applied the tax drawback policy on exports. Between 1990 and 1993, the average tax drawback on exports was 11.2%. As of January 1994 the government adopted a new tax system, in which the tax drawback rates were set at 13% and 17%, equivalent to a 14.2% concession of tax based on product prices on average. As exports increase, more tax drawbacks are offered by the government. These represent a considerable drain on the central government, with a large amount of tax revenue to be returned to exporting enterprises.

For this reason, the tax drawback rates for exports have been lowered into three grades since July 1995, i.e., 14%, 10% and 3%, with the average being 8.29%. According to official statistics, the package of tax drawback on exports in the government budget amounted to 55 billion *yuan* in 1995. With the general commodity trade of US$80 billion, the tax drawback should be 90 billion *yuan*. Although general commodity trade as a share of total trade by foreign-invested enterprises was only about 20%, FIEs' share of China's total foreign trade has grown rapidly. It was 16.8% in 1991, 20.5% in 1992, 27.5% in 1993 and 28.7% in 1994. Therefore, it is clear that in the huge amount of tax drawback on exports, foreign-invested enterprises gain a sizable share.

The principal methods used by FIEs to conduct phoney exports are as follows:

1. Use of forged documents – FIEs achieve exports through forged approval documents, falsified receipts of transactions and counterfeit official seals. Although fraud-prevention techniques used by the Chinese Customs have been continuously updated and improved, the skills of the perpetrators are even more developed. According to survey statistics, in 1995 the Guangdong Customs Authority examined more than ten thousand transaction records and documents stamped with seals, and found that over four thousand involved a value of 450 million *yuan*. This was only a limited investigation. What is the true proportion of transaction documents, receipts and seals that are forged?

2. Use of counterfeit goods – In order to grab more tax drawback on exports, some foreign investors report commodities with lower tax drawback rates as commodities with higher ones. They also sometimes claim a quantity of low quality goods or wastes as high priced goods, and then dump them into the sea after obtaining export certificates for tax drawback.
3. Cheating in both importing and exporting – FIEs are largely engaged in trade processing with imported materials and equipment, which is free of tariffs, i.e., the import of materials for export processing and re-export of the processed goods are tariff-free. If the processed products made from imported materials are not exported, but are sold in Chinese domestic markets, FIEs are required to pay back import tariffs. In practice, however, in export processing with imported materials, some domestically made materials and parts are also needed for producing final products. In exporting practice, FIEs artificially raise the proportion of domestically made materials and parts used in producing final products in order to gain more tax drawback on exports. In addition, to keep the overall value in balance, these enterprises lower the proportion of imported materials in the value of final products, and sell the rest in the domestic market so as to avoid paying import duties.

More importantly, as tax drawbacks for exports are paid by the central government, some FIEs cooperate with government officials to create phoney exports. The two sides share some gain as government officials acquire bribes from firms. This sort of fraudulent activity is inspired by local protectionism.

D. Phoney bankruptcy

Since the mid-1980s, China has practised bankruptcy law in some enterprises, and imposed certain restrictions on the bankruptcy of SOEs. However, some foreign investors have been found to exploit the loopholes existing in the low-developed market economy, and to employ phoney bankruptcy' tricks and intrigues. There are several factors at work:

1. Selling poor quality equipment and machinery to China – Under a government policy in effect before 1 April 1996, FIEs were allowed to import cars for their own use free of tariffs and other duties. They could also similarly import materials and equipment. To take advantage of the preferential policy, some foreign investors registered multiple joint ventures and imported cars, equipment and materials free of tariffs, then closed them by claiming bankruptcy. Some time later they registered new enterprises again. They enjoyed benefits from each registration of a new FIE, using China as a huge market in which to dump their poor quality machinery and equipment at overcharged prices. After 1 April 1996 the Chinese government resumed imposing import duties on machinery and equipment.

2. Extending the period of preferential tax treatments – Some foreign investors have been found to withdraw capital from exiting joint ventures before the expiration of their two-year tax holiday and three-year tax concession period and claim bankruptcies. Afterwards, they register new enterprises and once again become eligible for the preferential tax treatments. Through such multiple rounds of establishment and bankruptcy of FIEs, some foreign investors have continuously enjoyed preferential tax policies.

3. Dodging legally from enterprise debts – As pointed out earlier, some foreign investors create phoney losses, resulting in a large debt. They then claim enterprise bankruptcy, legally dodging from their enterprise debt. Obviously, a major reason why foreign investors claim FIEs bankruptcy is to escape enterprise debt.

4. Avoiding social security responsibilities assumed by enterprises – An investigation shows that most Chinese employees in FIEs are aged between 18 to 45, with young employees aged 18 to 25 accounting for 51%, the 25–35 age group for 29%, the 35–45 age group for 12%, and those aged over 45 for 8%. If FIEs are operated for 20 years, employees aged 35 or over will retire by then, and this represents a huge financial burden for enterprises. In order to avoid this huge expense, some joint ventures, especially those in labour-intensive and trade processing activities go into false bankruptcy before the joint venture contracts expire, so as legally to evade their responsibilities for the social security of retired employees. After skirting around the financial load of retirement allowances, the FIEs re-register as new enterprises and hire new workers who are young and technically qualified. Worse, when the enterprises no longer exist, and the social insurance fund or other broad social security programme they initially bought is not sufficient to cover social security payments, the social security responsibilities for the retired employees from FIEs eventually have to be assumed by the Chinese government. This problem deserves special attention. It is especially important in those situations where foreign investors hold a majority of shares.

3. Effective and rational utilisation of foreign capital: a strategic view

It is apparent that foreign investment has had a tremendous impact on the development of the Chinese domestic economy, both positive and negative. On the positive side, it has provided SOEs with challenges and opportunities for further development, which have facilitated the elimination of the traditional centrally-planned economic system, and the formation of a new economic regime. In competition with foreign-invested enterprises, domestic enterprises can be propelled towards further growth and development. Government departments and agencies are forced to accelerate the pace of self-reform under the pressure created by further opening up to the outside world, and to shift their work focus to the provision of services for enterprises, stimulating the process of transformation to a market economy. Though all of this may be true, the foreign involvement must be sufficiently strong and extensive to cause changes in value judgement, remove the old system, and educate people about the workings of a market economy. Such intangible positive impacts are much more important than the quantifiable ones.

On the negative side, the possibility that foreign firms can control the Chinese economic lifeline through investment acquisitions cannot be completely ignored. At present, foreign firms already hold considerable economic power in some individual regions and industries, though they are still far from full control over the entire national economy. To prevent further shocks to domestic industries brought about by foreign investment, some effective and strong policy measures must be taken which are in accordance with international practice.

A. Practicing the principle of National Treatment

Some of the policy measures now taken by the government to deal with foreign investment violate the National Treatment principle. On the one hand, excessive preferential policy treatment is offered to foreign investment, representing 'upper-class' treatment. On the other, some restrictions are imposed on foreign investment, resulting in inferior treatment. The inferior treatment needs to be removed. However, the main problem at present is the special treatment for foreign investments, which takes various forms: (1) excessive preferential policies provided by the central government plus additional favorable treatment offered by local governments, (2) there is no restriction on the maximum share held by foreign firms, or on export requirements for output from foreign-majority joint ventures, leaving the domestic market free for foreign firms to enter, (3) FIEs do not, or rarely assume their social security responsibilities, enabling them to reduce the costs of production, and pay higher wages to employees. This gives them a competitive edge over State Owned Enterprises, and (4) FIEs are allowed to enter into economic sectors in which domestic non-state-owned firms are prohibited. The excessive preferential treatment enjoyed by FIEs has resulted in a deteriorating competitive position for SOEs. This is an important reason for the ineffectiveness of SOEs in resisting foreign firms. The implementation of the National Treatment principle to all FIEs gives SOEs equal status which is a very basic condition for vigorous enterprise growth and a strong domestic economy.

B. Formulation of anti-monopoly laws

Although market-oriented policies in some countries are applied to firm mergers and acquisitions, there are still anti-monopoly laws and regulations which set clear restrictions, with detailed technical roles and categories. In this area, China has a gap to fill. One possibility is for supervision and inspection at both the industry and the national levels to be carried out using three indicators: total asset value, total output value and market share. At the industry level in particular, where the largest foreign-invested enterprise accounts for 10% of the total asset value, output value and market share of the industry, or if all FIEs nation wide account for 30% of the total asset value, total output value and market share in a particular industry, the government should take effective steps to curb the market power of FIEs. The quantitative boundary for imposing restrictions depends on the actual situation and impact.

C. Further support for famous SOE brand names

The policies applied to foreign-invested enterprises should also be applied to SOEs. For those with strong management, technical efficiency and sound profitability, but suffering from a shortage of capital or heavy debt burden, the government should provide strong support. Otherwise, they will be taken over by foreign firms through acquisition or holding majority share, resulting in the outflow of huge profits and yet more foreign control in the national economy. The government should ensure that the Chinese side holds the majority share in joint ventures. If the share held by the Chinese side declines as a result of increases in foreign investment, special development funds should be established to support advantageous domestic enterprises and famous brands. These funds should be managed and coordinated by governmental departments in collaboration with particular industrial sectors.

D. Implementation of a multilateral cooperation strategy for the utilisation of foreign investment

In operating joint ventures with foreign firms which possess capital and technological expertise, special strategies should be adopted to ensure that the majority share is held by the Chinese side. Multilateral cooperation is one such strategy and refers to a share structure whereby several foreign firms invest with the Chinese company, with each foreign investor holding a small share. Although the sum of the foreign investment in absolute value exceeds that of the Chinese company, the Chinese company still holds a relatively larger share as compared to any individual foreign investor. Thus, the Chinese company can control the joint venture with a small investment. The Shuang-Hui Company Group based in Luohe City, Henan Province, is a good example. Thanks to application of a multilateral cooperation strategy and the attraction of several foreign firms, the Chinese company controls the largest individual share in the joint venture although foreign investors collectively hold 69% of the total share.

An alternative strategy is for a number of small and middle-sized domestic companies to join together on the basis of their economic, technical, or geographic links, to form a strong group (of enterprises), and then develop a joint venture relationship with foreign firms. Such an arrangement can produce two benefits. First, it avoids the situation in which an individual domestic company has to compete with foreign firms. Second, multilateral cooperation and combination by domestic firms can create new competitive advantages and productive capacity. It can also effectively prevent internal conflicts from occurring when competing for foreign investment and potential profits.

E. Effective utilisation of the industrial linkage effects of Foreign-Invested Enterprises

In planning and establishing joint ventures with foreign firms flexible methods can be made. For instance, domestic companies can make agreements with foreign firms to allocate some funds from the joint venture for superannuation funds to be given to aged employees or create re-employment allowances for employees who lose their jobs. Some domestic enterprises, while establishing equity joint ventures with foreign firms, can also form contractual joint ventures using the remaining buildings, facilities, equipment and human resources, providing the equity joint ventures with production services, parts and associated manufacturing. This arrangement not only properly utilises surplus employees and idle machinery and other assets, but also strengthens the capacity of enterprises for vigorous development.

In this respect, the experience of Tianjin City is particularly valuable. When a joint venture is developed, a competitive product emerges, leading the growth of the whole industry and assisting a number of enterprises to survive. Since 1994, many domestic enterprises in Tianjin have produced parts, components and fittings, or have provided other production services for foreign-invested enterprises. Over 80 are involved in the production network of FIEs and produce more than 100 associated products for famous products, including Motorola mobile communication equipment, OTIS elevators, Yamaha electronic musical instruments, digital exchange communicators, Samsung video cameras and recorders, Honda motorbikes and Master Kung noodles. Thanks to the stimulus provided by FIEs through their industrial linkages, these domestic companies have developed rapidly.

Conceptually, the utilisation of foreign capital and development of the domestic economy can be mutually beneficial. Foreign investment accelerates the development of the domestic economy, which in turn further attracts more foreign investment and also strengthens the dominating role of domestic firms in the economy.

In the domestic market, competition occurs not only between foreign-invested enterprises and domestic firms, but also increasingly among foreign-invested enterprises. The competition in the latter is even tougher and at higher technical levels. Facing tougher competition in the Chinese domestic market, many foreign firms have become cautious about investing in China. As the domestic market is shared among existing firms, foreign-invested enterprises have to export some portions of their products. Lowering import tariffs forces FIEs to improve the quality of their products. As the policy measures gradually become complete and improved, infrastructure will become a new focus for foreign investment. The initial preponderance of financial capital in foreign investment is currently being replaced by industrial capital which involves advanced technologies and modern management expertise, with view to long term development. In this process, huge profits can be made through re-structuring and listing enterprises in the share market, and from the increase in market value of enterprises. All of this shows that FIEs in China, operating under market forces, are growing in a healthy direction.

Bibliography

CHINESE AND JAPANESE BOOKS AND ARTICLES

'Avoid the trap of agricultural reform', *Gaige neican* (Inside Information on Economic Reform), 1999, No. 2.

Bai Gang, 'Correctly handle the relations between development and stability', *Renmin ribao neibu canyue* (*The People's Daily* Internal Reading Materials), 1999, No. 68.

Bo Yibo, *Wen xuan* (The Selected Works of Bo Yibo), Beijing, 1992.

Chen Qian, 'Deng Xiaoping's theory of opening [the economy] and the road to a common prosperity', *Nankai daxue xuebao* (Nankai University Journal) (Tianjin), 1998, No. 6.

Chen Yongjie and Zhang Tai, 'An analysis and some proposals concerning preserving stable growth in the industrial economy', *Jingji yanjiu cankao* (Study Materials for Economic Research), 1998, No. 68.

Chinese Academy of Agricultural Sciences and Ministry of Agriculture (Eds), *Deng Xiaoping nongye sixiang yanjiu* (An Investigation of Deng Xiaoping's Thinking on Agriculture), Beijing, 1998.

Chinese Academy of Social Science Population Research Institute, *Zhongguo renkou nianjian* (Almanac of China's Population), Beijing, annual.

Contemporary China Economic Management Editorial Office, *Zhonghua renmin gongheguo jingji guanli dashiji* (A Big Chronology of Economic Management in the People's Republic of China), Beijing, 1986.

Contemporary Planning Work Office, *Zhonghua renmin gongheguo guomin jingji he shehui fazhan jihua dashi jiyao, 1949–1985* (A Chronology of the Chinese People's Republic's National Economic and Social Plans, 1949–1985), Beijing, 1987.

Duan Yipo, 'The question of assets and property rights in the transformation of State Owned Enterprises', *Jingjixue dongtai* (Development in Economics), Vol. 4, 1997.

Economic Department of the Party School, *Deng Xiaoping shichang jingji de gouxiang yu shijian* (Deng Xiaoping's Concept and Practice of the Market Economy), Beijing, 1994.

'Emancipate the mind for an overall balance in economic development', *Renmin ribao* (The People's Daily), 24 February 1979.

Fan Gang, 'Short term policies and long term strategies for solving China's grain supply problems', *Zhongguo nongcun guancha* (China Rural Survey), 1995, No. 5.

Fang Hengshan, *Jingji tizhi gaige cidian* (A Dictionary of the Reform of the Economic System), Beijing, 1988.

Fang Yan, 'China throws itself into international trade competition: agriculture faces a new challenge', *Jingji yu xinxi* (Economy and News), 1993, No. 2.

Gu Longsheng, *Zhongguo gongchandang jingji sixiang fazhanshi* (A History of the Development of the Economic Thought of the Chinese Communist Party), Taiyuan, 1996.

'Grasp the favourable opportunity; accelerate the progress of reform', *Jingji yanjiu* (Economic Research), 1992, No. 5.

He Qinglian, *Zhongguo de xianjing* (China's Pitfall. The Primary Capital Accumulation in Contemporary China), Hong Kong, 1997.

Hu Angang, 'The impact of inundation disasters and our country's strategy to lessen them', *Renmin ribao neibu canyue* (*The People's Daily* Internal Reading Materials), 1998, No. 37.

Jiang Li, 'Lessons from the four major reforms of the rural land system', *Xueshu yanjiu* (Academic Research), 1994, No. 4.

Jiang Luan, 'Reinforcing the key role of the State Owned Enterprises in the industrialisation of science and technology', *Zhanlüe guanli* (Strategic Management), 1995, No. 3.

Jin Lin, 'Some problems in the development of our country's iron and steel industry', *Jingji yanjiu cankao* (Study Materials for Economic Research), 1998, No. 74.

Li Changming, 'China's textile industry; from size to strength', *Zhongguo gongye fazhan baogao* (China Industrial Development Report), Chap. 11, 1997.

Li Chengrui and Zhang Fuyuan, 'Concerning some problems of implementing socialist modernisation at high speed', *Jingji yanjiu* (Economic Research), 1979, No. 2.

Li Chengrui, 'Fluctuations in population induced by the Great Leap Forward', *Renkou yanjiu* (Population Research), 1998, No. 1.

Li Qiang. 'The widening gap between rich and poor: one fifth of households earn half total income', *Gaige neican* (Inside Information on Economic Reform), 1995, No. 16.

Li Quanlin, 'The population requirements of the social and economic development of the Kunshan region until the year 2000 and strategies to accommodate them', *Renkou yu jihua shengyu* (Population and Family Planning), 1995, No. 1.

Ling Zhijun, *Chen fu. Zhongguo jingji gaige beiwanglu* (Ups and Downs. A Memobook of the Chinese Economic Reform, 1989–1997), Shanghai, 1998.

Liu Guoguang, 'Some issues relating to the theory of the Socialist Market Economy', *Jingji yanjiu* (Economic Research), 1992, No. 10.

Liu Guoguang, 'The important issues involved with China's strategy for economic development', *Zhongguo shehui kexue* (Chinese Social Science), 1983, No. 6.

Liu Suinian and Liu Qungan, *'Wenhua da geming' shiqi de guomin jingji (1966–1976)* (The National Economy during the 'Great Cultural Revolution' 1966–1976), Heilongjiang, 1986.

Liu Yongren, 'Some tentative ideas on the reform of China's labour system', *Shanxi caizheng xueyuan xuebao* (Shanxi Institute of Finance and Economics Journal), 1985, No. 5.

Marukawa Tomoo, *Shijo hassei no dynamics. Ikkoki no Chugoku keizai* (The Dynamics of Market Emergence. The Transition of the Chinese Economy), Tokyo, 1999. (In Japanese.)

Meng Qingse, 'A comparison of Chinese society's development from [the thought of] Mao Zedong and Deng Xiaoping', *Liaoning daxue xuebao* (Liaoning University Journal) (Shenyang), 1998, No. 6.

Ministry of Agriculture, Planning Department, *Zhongguo noncun jingji tongji daquan, 1949–1986* (Compendium of Statistics on China's Rural Economy, 1949–1986), Beijing, 1989.

Ministry of Agriculture, *Zhongguo nongye fazhan baogao, 1998* (Agricultural Development Report), Beijing, 1998.

Ministry of Metallurgy, Development Planning Department, 'Tentative suggestions for structural re-adjustments in the steel industry', *Yejin jingji yanjiu*, (Metallurgy Economics Research) 1998, Nos. 1–2.

Ministry of Metallurgy, Development Planning Department, 'Tentative suggestions for structural re-adjustments in the steel industry', *Yejin jingji yanjiu*, 1998, Nos. 1–2.

Nakagane Katsuji, 'A reconsideration of China's transition policy of gradualism from the perspective of comparison with the old socialist economies', *Keizai kenkyu* (Economic Research), October, 1999. (In Japanese.)

Ni-Chu keikyo journal (The Journal of Japan-China Economic Co-operation), Tokyo, monthly. (In Japanese).

'Our country's income differentials continue to grow', *Gaige neican* (Inside Information on Economic Reform), 1999, No. 16.

Qiao Xiaochun, 'Reflections on research for China's birth policies at the approach of the 21st Century', *Renkou yanjiu* (Population Research), 1999, No. 2.

Research Group for Fixed Capital Investment in Agriculture, 'A brief overview of China's strategy for fixed capital investment in agriculture', *Jingji yanjiu cankao* (Study Materials for Economic Research), 16 March 1993.

Shan Shanhua, Guan Kezhen, Wang Xiaoming, 'The iron and steel industry. Some issues to be considered in changing the pattern of growth in the Ninth Five Year Plan', *Yejin jingji yanjiu* (Metallurgy Economics Research), 1996, No. 18.

She Jianming, 'The role of the State in the Socialist Market Economy', *Xiandai qiye daokan* (Modern Enterprise Herald), Vol. 5, 1997, No. 155.

State Statistical Bureau, *Zhongguo guiding zichan touzi nianjian, 1950–1995* (China Statistical Yearbook on Investment in Fixed Assets, 1950–1995), Beijing, 1997.

State Statistical Bureau, *Zhongguo nongcun tongji nianjian, 1999* (Rural Statistical Yearbook of China, 1999), Bejing, annual.

State Statistical Bureau, *Zhongguo tongji nianjian* (Chinese Statistical Yearbook), Beijing, annual.

State Statistical Bureau, *Zhongguo tongji zhaiyao* (Chinese Statistical Abstract), Beijing, annual.

Su Changchuen et al. (Eds), *Zhongguo shinian gaige gaikuang* (A Survey of China's Ten Years of Economic Reform), Beijing, 1989.

Sun Xiangyi, 'The emerging new price system and price control', *Jiage lilun yu shijian* (Price Theory and Practice), Vol. 8, 1997.

Sun Zhonghua and Li Shaohua, 'Learning from Comrade Deng Xiaoping's exposition of agricultural problems', *Zhongguo nongcun jingji* (China's Rural Economy), 1997, No. 3.

Tao Yongli and Wu Qijie, 'A comparison of "modernisation" in the thought of Mao Zedong and Deng Xiaoping', *Beifang luncong* (Northern Essays) (Harbin), 17–20 January 1999.

Tian, Songnian, 'A summary of the Fourth Five Year Plan', *Dang de wenxian* (Party Documents), 2000, No. 2. (This issue also contains the Plan document and a very short speech by Zhou Enlai dated 11 February 1971).

Tian Xueyuan, 'Population problems under market conditions and scientific research into population', *Zhongguo renkou kexue* (Chinese Demography), 1994, No. 1.

'The role of the Law of Value in cotton production', *Guangming ribao* (Enlightenment Daily), 9 December 1978.

Wang Dong, 'The four new creative [elements] in Deng Xiaoping's theory and the reform of China's economic system', *Zhongguo dangzheng ganbu luntan* (The China Government and Party Cadres Forum) (Beijing), 1988, No. 10.

Bibliography

Wang Dongyuan et al. *Zhongguo laodong shiye fazhan yuce 1996–2010* (A Forecast of the Development of China's Labour Activity, 1996–2010), Beijing, 1995.

Wang Yifu, *Xin Zhongguo tongji shigao* (An Outline History of Statistics in New China), Beijing, 1986.

Wei Zhong (Ed.), *Zhonghua renmin gongheguo jingji da shiji, 1949–1980* (A Big Economic Chronology of the Chinese People's Republic, 1949–1980), Beijing, 1984.

Wen Guifang, 'Problems with the intensification of grain price reform', *Jingji yanjiu cankao* (Study Materials for Economic Research), 25 November 1993.

Wu Xiang, 'Why did China's reforms start in the countryside?' *Zhongguo renli ziyuan kaifa* (China's Human Resource Development), 1995, No. 1.

Wu Zhongguan, 'Reflections on my work as a demographic researcher', *Renkou yanjiu* (Population Research), 1998, No. 4.

Xie Leiguang and Cheng Gang, 'The emergence of the DINKS households in China and a simple analysis of the reasons behind their development', *Renkou yu jihua shengyu* (Population and Family Planning), 1995, No. 4.

Xie Xiaohua, 'The burgeoning electronics industry', *Zhongguo gongye fazhan baogao* (China Industrial Development Report), Chap. 1, 1997.

Xu Chongwen, 'The spirit of the age reflected in Deng Xiaoping's theory on the essence of socialism', *Zhongguo shehui kexue* (Chinese Social Science), 1995, No. 2.

Yan Qinghua, 'The three creative milestones in Chinese economic theory in the past hundred years', *Jingji pinglun* (Economic Review), 1998, No. 3.

Yang Kuifu, 'Integrating family planning and poverty relief', *Renkou yu jihua shengyu* (Population and Family Planning), 1996, No. 4.

Yang Peixin, 'Applying the theory of the 'three balances' [in our policy for] checking inflation', *Gaige neican* (Inside Information on Economic Reform), 1995, No. 1.

Yang Yiyong and Li Jianwei, 'An estimate of our country's labour demand and supply situation during the next three years', *Renmin ribao neibu canyue* (The People's Daily Internal Reading Materials), 1999, No. 8.

Yueh Shan, 'Deng Liqun criticises Deng Xiaoping, praises Jiang Zemin', *Cheng Ming* (Hong Kong), 1 August 1999.

Zhang Keyun, 'A study of the regional development and distribution of Chinese agriculture', *Jingji yanjiu cankao* (Study Materials for Economic Research), 1 July 1955.

Zhang Yunting, 'Why must we stick to the socialist road?', *Renmin ribao canyue* (The People's Daily Internal Reading Materials), 1999, No. 36.

Zhang Zhufan, 'A discussion of the special characteristics of Deng Xiaoping's theory of the world economy', *Shehui kexue zhanxian* (Social Science Battlefront) (Changchun), 1988, No. 6.

Zhao Ying, 'The automobile industry. On the threshold of a brilliant turn', *Zhongguo gongye fazhan baogao* (China Industrial Development Report), Chap. 10, 1997.

Zheng Bijian, 'A speech at the twenty year anniversary conference on theoretical research', *Zhonggong zhongyang dangxiao baogao xuan* (Select Reports from the Chinese Communist Party Central Committee School), 1998, No. 5.

Zhou Shulian, 'A twenty year review and forward look at China's enterprise reforms', *Jingji gongzuozhe xuexi cailiao* (Materials for Economic Workers), 1998, No. 52.

Zhu Jintang, 'Population in the Northwest over forty years', *Shibei renkou* (Journal of Northwest Population), 1991, No. 1.

Bibliography

WESTERN LANGUAGE BOOKS AND ARTICLES

Ash, Robert F. and Richard Louis Edmonds, 'China's land resources, environment and agricultural production' in Richard Louis Edmonds (Ed.) *Managing the Chinese Environment,* Oxford, 2000.

Ash, Robert F. 'Grain self-sufficiency in mainland China: a continuing imperative', in R.F. Ash, Richard Louis Edmonds and Yu-ming Shaw (Eds), *Perspectives on Contemporary China in Transition,* Taipei, 1997.

Ash, Robert F. 'The grain issue in China: domestic and international perspectives' in M. Brosseau, Kuan Hsin-chi and Y.Y. Kueh (Eds), *China Review 1997,* Hong Kong, 1997.

Ash, Robert F. 'The performance of China's grain sector: a regional perspective', in OECD, *China in the Global Economy: Agricultural Policies in China,* Paris, 1997.

Ash, Robert F. 'Agricultural Policy and the impact of reform', in Y.Y. Kueh and R.F. Ash (Eds), *Economic Trends in Chinese Agriculture: The Impact of Post-Mao Reforms.* Oxford, 1993.

Baechler, Jean, *Le Capitalisme* (two vols.), Paris, 1995.

Bank for International Settlements, *68th Annual Report,* Basle, 1998.

Baum, Rick, *Burying Mao: Chinese Politics in the Age of Deng Xiaoping,* Princeton, 1994.

Brown, Lester, *Who Will Feed China? Wake-Up Call for a Small Planet,* New York and London, 1995.

Chai, Joseph C.H. *China. Transition to a Market Economy,* Oxford, 1997.

Facts about Liu Chien-hsün's Crimes, Honan, 12 March 1967. (English translation.)

Feinstein, Charles and Christopher Howe (Eds), *Technology Transfer in China in the 1980s,* Cheltenham, 1996.

Fu, Jun, *Institutions and Investments. Foreign Direct Investment in China during an Era of Reforms,* Ann Arbor, 2000.

Gerschenkron, Alexander, *Continuity in History and Other Essays,* Cambridge Mass. 1956.

Harding, Harry, *China's Second Revolution,* Washington, 1987.

Howe, Christopher, *Japan and China's Changing Economic Environment: with particular reference to Foreign Investment and Industrial Restructuring,* Centre for Financial and Management Studies, London, 1999.

Howe, Christopher, *Wage Patterns and Wage policy in Modern China, 1919–1972,* Cambridge, 1973.

Kelliher, Daniel, *Peasant Power in China: The Era of Rural Reform, 1979–1989,* New Haven and London, 1992.

Kornai, Janos, *Overcentralization in Economic Administration. A Critical Analysis based on Experience in Hungarian Light Industry,* translated by John Knapp, Oxford, 1959.

Kueh, Y.Y. Joseph C.H. Chai and Gang Fan (Eds), *Industrial Reform and Macroeconomic Instablity in China,* Oxford, 1999.

Lardy, Nicholas R., 'The role of foreign trade and investment in China's economic transformation' in Andrew G. Walder, *China's Transitional Economy,* Oxford, 1996.

Lee, Clara, 'Battle to keep the Red Flag flying', *South China Morning Post,* 2 July 2000.

Lin, Cyril Chiren, 'The reinstatement of economics in China today', *The China Quarterly,* No. 85, March 1981.

Lin, Justin Yifu, Fang Cai and Zhou Li, *The China Miracle. Development Strategy and Economic Reform,* Hong Kong, 1996.

Naughton, Barry, *Growing out of the Plan. Chinese Economic Reform 1978–1993,* Cambridge, 1996.

Bibliography

Nolan, Peter, *China and the Global Economy: National Champions, Industrial Policy and the Big Business Revolution*, New York, 2001.

Oi, Jean, 'Two decades of rural reform in China: an overview and assessment', *The China Quarterly*, No. 159, September 1999.

Oi, Jean, *Rural China Takes Off*, Berkeley, 1999.

Oi, Jean, *State and Peasant in Contemporary China: The Political Economy of Village Government*, Berkeley, 1989.

Rawski, Thomas, 'Implications of China's Reform experience' in Andrew G. Walder, *China's Transitional Economy*, Oxford, 1996.

'Review of 30 years of electronics development', Beijing Radio, *Foreign Broadcast Information Service*, 25 January 1980.

Sachs, Jeffrey D. and Wing Thye Woo, *Understanding China's Economic Performance*, Harvard Institute for International Development, Cambridge, Mass. 1998.

Sicular, Terry, 'Redefining state, plan and market: China's reforms in agricultural commerce' in Andrew G. Walder (Ed.) *China's Transitional Economy*, Oxford, 1996.

Stiglitz, Joseph E., *Whither Socialism?*, Cambridge Mass. 1996.

'State-owned firms "using units as ATMs"', *The South China Morning Post*, 16 March 2001.

Sun, Laixiang, *Emergence of Unorthodox Ownership and Governance Structures in East Asia. An Alternative Transition Path*, Helsinki, 1997.

Walder, Andrew G. (Ed.) *China's Transitional Economy*, Oxford, 1996.

Whiting, Susan H., *Power and Wealth in Rural China. The Political Economy of Institutional Change*, Cambridge, 2000.

Wintrobe, Ronald, *The Political Economy of Dictatorship*, Cambridge, 1998.

Winiecki, Jan, 'Impediments to institutional change in the former Soviet system', in Lee J. Alston, Thrainn Eggertsson and Douglass C. North, *Empirical Studies in Institutional Change*, Cambridge, 1996.

Winckler, Edwin A. *Transition from Communism: Institutional and Comparative Analyses*, Boulder, 1999.

Woo, Wing Thye, 'Why China grew' in Peter Boone, Stanislav Gomulka and Richard Layard (Eds), *Emerging from Communism. Lessons from Russia, China and Eastern Europe*, Cambridge Mass. 1998.

Xue Muqiao, 'Economic work must grasp the laws of economic development', *Report to the State Economic Commission Research Conference on Enterprise Management* (Mimeo), 14 March 1979.

Yabuki, Susumu, *China's New Political Economy, the Giant Awakes*, Boulder, 1995.

Yang, Dali, 'Economic crisis and market transition' in Edwin A. Winckler, *Transition from Communism: Institutional and Comparative Analyses*, Boulder, 1999.

'Zhao Ziyang attends Sichuan forum on economic problems', *Foreign Broadcast Information Service*, 12 March 1979.

Zhu Rongji, 'Government Work Report', *Beijing Review*, 5–11 April 1999.

Zweig, David, 'Distortions in the Opening. 'Segmented Deregulation' and weak property rights as explanations for China's 'Zone Fever' of 1992–1993', Hong Kong Institute of Asia-Pacific Studies, Hong Kong, 1999.